175 Easy-to-Do
HALLOWEEN CRAFTS

Edited by
Sharon Dunn Umnik

CREATIVE USES · FOR RECYCLABLES ·

175 Easy-to-Do
HALLOWEEN
CRAFTS

Edited by Sharon Dunn Umnik

BOYDS MILLS PRESS

Inside this book...

you'll find a fabulous assortment of crafts made from recyclable items and inexpensive things found in or around your house. Have pencils, crayons, scissors, tape, paintbrushes, and other supplies for craft making close by.

When you're trick-or-treating, practice Halloween safety: Always trick-or-treat with an adult or a group of friends. As you go to friends' homes, take off your mask, or slide it to the top of your head so you can see clearly.– *the Editor*

Copyright © 1995 by Boyds Mills Press
All rights reserved

Published by Bell Books
Boyds Mills Press, Inc.
A Highlights Company
815 Church Street
Honesdale, Pennsylvania 18431
Printed in China

Publisher Cataloging-in-Publication Data
175 easy-to-do Halloween crafts : creative uses for recyclables /
edited by Sharon Dunn Umnik.—1st ed.
[64]p. : col. ill. ;   cm.
Summary : Includes step-by-step directions to make
Halloween masks, decorations, cards, and more. Also includes
instructions for decorating pumpkins.
ISBN 1-56397-372-3
1. Handicraft—Juvenile literature. 2. Halloween decorations—
Juvenile literature. 3. Recycling (Waste)—Juvenile literature.
[1. Handicraft. 2. Halloween. 3. Recycling (Waste).]
I. Umnik, Sharon Dunn. II. Title.
745.5—dc20   1995   CIP
Library of Congress Catalog Card Number 94-79157

First edition, 1995
Book designed by Charlie Cary
The text of this book is set in 11-point New Century Schoolbook.

10 9 8 7

Craft Contributors: Caroline Arnold, Barbara Baker, Katherine Corliss Bartow, B. J. Benish, Bea Blasing, Linda Bloomgren, Doris D. Breiholz, Mindy Cherez, Kathleen Conrad, Liby Croce, Sandra E. Csippan, Patti DeLotell, Ruth Dougherty, Paige Matthews Eckard, Kathy Everett, Deanna Fendler, Tanya Turner Fry, Julie Fultz, Roberta Glatz, Alice Gilbreath, Connie Giunta, Mavis Grant, Evelyn Green, Janet Grottodden, Jean Hale, Edna Harrington, Barbara Albers Hill, Velma Flower Holt, Loretta Holz, Carmen Horn, Tama Kain, Shirley Kallus, Garnett C. Kooker, Sylvia Kreng, Virginia L. Kroll, Ella L. Langenberg, Lee Lindeman, Jean Lyon, Agnes Maddy, Jo Ann Markway, Betty Merritt, Evelyn Minshull, June Rose Mobly, Mary Lou Murphy, James W. Perrin Jr., Deanna Peters, Jean Reynolds, Terry A. Ricioli, Jean F. Roath, Kathy Ross, Vivian Smallowitz, Andrew J. Smith, Beth Tobler, Sharon Dunn Umnik, Bernice Walz, Bonnie Wedge, Margaret Joque Williams, Agnes Choate Wonson, Jinx Woolson.

Balloon Goblins

These Halloween decorations may be used either as large party favors set on top of a paper cup or as party decorations. They can be hung from the ceiling or doorway. (Remember that balloons are fragile. Even with care one may pop as you work on it and give you a Halloween scare! Be sure to clean up any broken pieces of balloon and throw them away immediately.)

PUMPKIN
(balloon, poster board, construction paper)

1. Cut a base for the pumpkin from a piece of poster board.

2. Blow up a balloon and knot the end. Roll a piece of tape, secure it to the balloon, and attach the balloon to the base.

3. Cut features from black construction paper, and tape in place with small strips of rolled transparent tape. Cut a stem from green construction paper, and tape to the top of the balloon.

CAT
(balloon, plastic-foam cup, construction paper, permanent marker)

1. Blow up a balloon and knot the end.

2. Attach a piece of tape to the inside of a plastic-foam cup, leaving half of it bent like a tab over the opening of the cup. Do the same on the opposite edge of the cup.

3. Place the balloon with the knotted end inside the cup. The tabs of tape should hold it in place. Tape the cup to the work surface to hold the balloon upright.

4. Cut ears, eyes, nose, mouth, and bow tie from construction paper, and attach with pieces of rolled transparent tape. Add whiskers and eyelashes with a permanent marker.

OWL
(balloon, construction paper, permanent marker, string)

1. Blow up a balloon and knot the end.

2. Cut a large V shape from black construction paper. Cut eyes from pieces of black and white paper and the beak from orange paper. Attach to the balloon with pieces of rolled transparent tape.

3. Draw feathers on the balloon with a permanent marker.

4. Tie a string around the knotted end of the balloon, and hang the owl where it can swing in the breeze.

Real Pumpkin Heads

These pumpkins are fun because they are created with many different materials. Use plastic rings cut from food containers to make necks for some of the pumpkins.

SWEET SUE
(pumpkin, two copper scouring pads, toothpick halves, felt, pompons, lace)

1. For the hair, stretch two copper scouring pads over the top of a pumpkin. Hold in place with toothpick halves.

2. Cut eyes, a nose, a mouth, cheeks, and ears from felt. Roll pieces of tape and attach to the back of the features. Press the features in place. Glue a pompon on each ear lobe for an earring.

3. Add a felt-and-lace bow to the hair. Hold in place with a toothpick half. Wrap a strip of lace around the neck.

PAINTED PAT
(pumpkin, poster paint)

1. On a piece of paper, sketch a face for your pumpkin. Then lightly draw it on the pumpkin itself.

2. Paint the features with poster paint and let dry. You may want to go over the features a second time.

3. Display the pumpkin inside a window where it is dry.

VEGGIE VERN
(pumpkin, table knife, two apples, cucumber, toothpick halves, marshmallows, paper, celery)

1. Have an adult help you when using a knife. Cut two apples and a cucumber in half. On the pumpkin surface, trace around one top-half section of the apple for the mouth, two bottom-half sections of the apples for the cheeks, and one half of the cucumber for the nose. Cut around the tracings with a table knife, cutting through the pumpkin wall, and push the apple halves and cucumber inside the pumpkin.

2. Insert two whole toothpicks where the eyes should be, and place a marshmallow on each one. Add a pupil to each eye made from paper. For the eyebrows, cut small sections from the leftover cucumber and attach them with toothpick halves.

3. Cut the leafy sections from a bunch of celery. Attach them with toothpick halves to the top of the pumpkin to make hair.

WENDY WITCH
(pumpkin, construction paper, fabric)

1. On construction paper, draw a large circle with a smaller one inside to make the hat brim. Cut out the small circle, cutting tabs along the inside edge of the doughnut shape. To make the hat top, draw a circle on another piece of paper. Cut off about half of the circle and save for features. Roll the other section into a cone shape, fitting it over the tabs of the brim and taping in place.

2. Cut strips of paper and tape inside the hat for hair. Place the hat on top of the pumpkin. Cut out facial features, and attach with rolled pieces of tape.

3. Add a piece of fabric around the witch's neck.

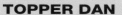

TOPPER DAN
(pumpkin, cotton balls, plastic lids and tops, teaspoon, paper, poster board, chenille sticks, fabric)

1. For hair, brush glue around the top of the pumpkin and press cotton balls into it.

2. On the pumpkin surface, trace around two plastic lids for eyes, a plastic top for the nose, and a plastic lid for the mouth with a pencil. Using a teaspoon, dig out shallow holes within the traced circles. Twist the lids or tops into the holes.

3. Cut out pupils from paper, and glue them on the eyes. Cut out a mustache shape from a piece of poster board, and cover it with cotton. Trim around the edges with scissors if needed. Glue the mustache between the nose and mouth.

4. Twist two chenille sticks together to make eyeglasses, and place the earpieces snugly in the hair. Cut two ears from large plastic lids. Have an adult help you cut a slot on each side of the head, and insert the ears. Use a strip of fabric for a bow tie.

CARVED CAROLINE
(pumpkin, table knife, spoons)

1. With the help of an adult, use a table knife to cut around the stem of the pumpkin and remove the top. With a large spoon, scoop out the seeds and inner membranes of the pumpkin. (Save the seeds and roast them later.)

2. On a piece of paper, sketch a face for your pumpkin. Then lightly draw it on the pumpkin itself.

3. With an adult's help cut out entire sections of the pumpkin. Or cut just below the skin surface and scoop out with a small spoon.

4. Place a small light in the center of the pumpkin to make it shine at night.

PUMPKIN CHAIN
(construction paper, permanent marker, ribbon)

1. Stack four or more pieces of orange paper. (The more pieces of paper, the more pumpkin shapes, and the longer the chain.) Place a pumpkin shape on top of the stack, and cut around it.

2. Using a permanent black marker, draw only eyes and mouths on the pumpkins. Leave room in the middle, where the nose will be, to cut two vertical slits in each pumpkin.

3. Make a pumpkin chain by weaving a long piece of ribbon through the slits in each pumpkin.

SPOOKY MOON MOBILE
(heavy cardboard plates, poster paint, facial tissue, string, construction paper)

1. Cut two crescent moon shapes from heavy cardboard plates. Paint them yellow inside and out and let dry.

2. Place the moon shapes together, with the plate bottoms toward the outside, and staple them along the curved edges.

3. To make a ghost, tightly crumple a white tissue into a ball. Place it in the middle of a second tissue, and pull the tissue smoothly around the ball. Tie it at the neck with string. Glue on paper eyes.

4. Make pumpkins the same way as the ghost, but cut off the tissue to make a stem. Paint the pumpkins orange and the stems green. Add a paper face.

5. Cut bats from paper. Punch two holes in the centers, and tie a long string through them.

6. Punch holes along the inner curve of the moon. Tie the strings from the ghosts, pumpkins, and bats to the holes. Punch another hole in the top of the moon and attach a string for a hanger.

CAT HAND PUPPET
(sock, thread, felt)

1. Gather material on each side of the toe portion of a sock for the ears. Tie the ears with thread.

2. Cut out eyes and whiskers from felt, and glue them in place on the foot of the sock.

3. Place your hand inside the sock to make your cat perform.

GHOST PIN
(white felt, permanent marker, safety pin)

1. Cut two matching ghost shapes from white felt. Glue them together and let them dry.

2. With a permanent marker, draw on the ghost's face and outline the body.

3. Glue a safety pin to the back of the ghost. Then glue a small strip of felt across the opened pin and let it dry.

HALLOWEEN TABLE DECORATION
(cereal box, two toothpaste boxes, construction paper, yarn)

1. Cover a cereal box and two toothpaste boxes with construction paper.

2. Cut off two corners of each toothpaste box at an angle, and glue the boxes to the bottom of the cereal box for feet.

3. Cut features from paper, and glue on yarn for hair.

PAPER-PLATE SPIDER
(black paper, two small paper plates, poster paint, string)

1. Cut eight long strips of black paper for the spider's legs and a circle for the spider's head.

2. Glue the two small paper plates together, plate bottoms facing out, with the legs and head placed between the edges.

3. Paint the body black. Glue a long piece of string to the middle of the back so the spider can dangle from the ceiling of your room.

CORNCOB WITCH

(corncob with husk, paint, dried beans, paper, lightweight cardboard)

1. Remove the kernels from a dried corncob and trim the ends. Paint the body black except for the head. Glue on dried beans for eyes, a nose, and a mouth. Trim the cornhusks for the hair.

2. To make the hat, cut two circles from black paper. Cut the center out of one circle. Cut a slit to the center of the other circle and roll it into the shape of a cone. Glue the cone shape onto the flat circle, covering the hole. Glue the hat to the cornhusk hair.

3. Attach a cardboard base of black feet so that the witch can stand.

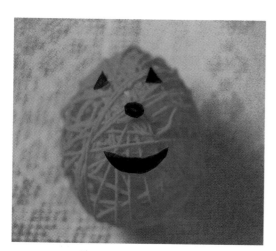

YARN JACK-O'-LANTERN

(plastic food container, glue, water, balloon, orange yarn)

1. In a plastic food container, make a mixture of equal amounts of white glue and water.

2. Blow up a balloon and knot the end. Tie a piece of string around the knot.

3. Dip orange yarn into the glue-and-water mixture. Wrap the yarn around the balloon. Hang the balloon until the yarn has dried.

4. Pop the balloon and carefully pull it through the strands of yarn. Cut and glue paper features to the yarn pumpkin.

HAUNTED-HOUSE CARD

(construction paper)

1. Fold a piece of construction paper in half. Draw a house with windows and doors on the front of the card. Cut around three sides of each window and the door so they will open and close.

2. Open the card and glue a piece of white paper inside, then glue the card shut.

3. Open all the windows and the door and write messages behind them or draw scary pictures. Close them up and send your card to a friend.

HALLOWEEN HANG-UP
(round cardboard container, poster paint, construction paper, yarn)

1. Cut off the bottom of a round cardboard container. Trim the container to form a cat shape, as shown. Cover it with poster paint and let dry.

2. Cut features from construction paper and glue in place.

3. Punch a hole on opposite sides of the cat shape, and tie a piece of yarn for a hanger.

GOBLIN POP-UP
(poster board, yarn, tongue depressor, plastic-foam cup, paper)

1. Cut a goblin head from poster board. Add yarn hair and other features from paper. Glue the head to one end of a tongue depressor.

2. Push the other end of the tongue depressor through the bottom of a plastic-foam cup so the goblin is hiding inside the cup. Add paper decorations to the outside of the cup.

3. Hold the stick with one hand and the cup with the other. Make the goblin pop in and out of the cup.

BAT HAT
(two 9-inch paper plates, small brown paper bag, scrap newspaper, black paper, yarn)

1. Cut the center out of one paper plate without cutting through the rim. Cut another paper plate from the edge to the center.

2. Pull the cut edges together to form a cone shape and tape. Glue the cone to the rim. Poke a hole on each side and add yarn for ties.

3. Stuff a small paper bag with scrap newspaper. Fold down and staple the top of the bag. Cut a round hole in the bottom of the bag. Add glue to the rest of the bag bottom, and press the bag onto the cone so the point of the cone is in the hole.

4. Cut wings, feet, eyes, and a mouth from black paper and glue in place.

FABRIC PUMPKIN CENTERPIECE
(fabric, pizza pan, needle and thread)

1. Place a pizza pan on a piece of orange fabric. Trace around it with a pencil and cut out the circle.

2. Sew around the edge of the circle using long stitches. When you get all the way around, pull the thread ends to gather the fabric, leaving a small hole in the center.

3. Stuff old fabric scraps into the hole, forming the pumpkin shape. Roll green fabric into a stem and push it into the hole.

4. Pull the thread very tightly and secure with a few stitches. Glue on pieces of fabric to make a face.

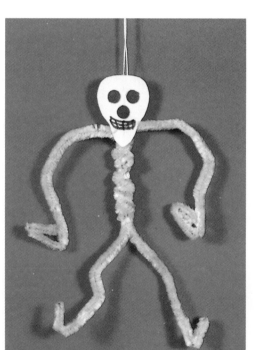

SCARY SKELETON
(chenille sticks, paper, thread)

1. Bend a long chenille stick in half. Below the bend, twist a second chenille stick around for the arms.

2. Just below the arms, wrap a third chenille stick around the first for the body, leaving two lengths for the legs.

3. Cut out a paper head and glue it to the body. Bend back the ends of the arms and legs to make the hands and feet.

4. Add a thread loop to the head, and jiggle it to make the skeleton dance.

TREAT BOX
(milk carton, construction paper, yarn)

1. Cut the top from a milk carton, leaving an open box. Cover the sides with glue and construction paper.

2. Decorate the box with cutouts from construction paper and yarn to make funny and scary faces.

3. Punch a hole on opposite sides at the top of the box. To make a handle, thread two pieces of yarn through the holes and knot the ends.

BREAD-DOUGH WITCH NECKLACE
(slices of bread, table knife, bowl, tablespoon, white glue, mixing spoon, waxed paper, paper, poster paint, toothpick, yarn)

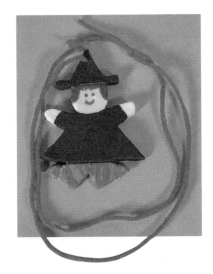

1. Remove the crusts from a couple of slices of bread. Tear the bread into small pieces and put them in a bowl, add a tablespoon of white glue, and mix together with a spoon. Work the dough into a ball with your hands until it is smooth and elastic.

2. Press the dough out on waxed paper. Draw and cut out a witch paper pattern. Place the pattern on the dough and cut around the witch with a table knife. Make a hole with a toothpick and let the witch dry.

3. Paint details on the witch. When dry, thread a piece of yarn through the hole for a necklace.

MILK CARTON CAT
(one-pint milk carton, poster paint, cardboard)

1. Use a one-pint milk carton for the cat, with the opened peaks forming the ears. Draw the eyes and mouth on the side of the carton and cut them out. Paint the carton and let dry. (Add a little dishwashing detergent to the paint to help make it stick to the carton, if needed.)

2. Cut a slit in the bottom of the carton below the cat's face. Cut a strip of cardboard as wide as the carton and as long as needed to reach the carton top. Place the strip in the slit and trace the eyes and mouth on it.

3. Paint the eyes on the cardboard strip. Draw a long tongue on another piece of cardboard that will fit inside the cat's mouth. Cut it out and paint it. Glue one end of the tongue to the strip of cardboard so the other end of the tongue can slide in and out of the mouth.

4. Hold the carton with one hand and the cardboard strip with the other. Make the cat's tongue and eyes move up and down.

HOOTY OWL
(paper plate, markers, construction paper)

1. Cut along the inside of the fluted edge, except for two inches on the top and bottom, as shown.

2. Fold the two cut edges inward so that they overlap, and glue them down.

3. Color the owl with markers. Cut eyes, ears, feet, and a beak from construction paper and glue them in place.

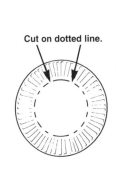

Cut on dotted line.

CAT PICTURE
(construction paper)

1. Cut construction paper into long, thin strips. Tape the strips to make a large circle for the cat's body and a smaller one for its head. Make a pumpkin the same way.

2. Add a tail, ears, and eyes to the cat.

3. Glue the circles to a spooky-looking background.

EGG-CARTON BAT BRANCH
(plastic-foam egg carton, construction paper, thread, tree branch, yarn)

1. For each bat, cut two cups from a plastic-foam egg carton. Make wings from black paper and glue them between the cups.

2. Cut pointed ears from paper and glue in place. Add paper-punch dot eyes and a mouth cut from paper.

3. Glue a thread to each bat and tie each one to a fallen tree branch. Tie pieces of yarn to the branch to hang it as a mobile.

SCRAP-HAPPY WITCH
(cardboard, fabric, yarn, felt, buttons, construction paper)

1. Draw and cut out a witch from a piece of cardboard. Glue on fabric for the face and trim around the edges. To make hair, glue loops of yarn around the witch's face.

2. Draw and cut out a hat from a piece of felt. Glue it on top of the hair. Glue on two button eyes and other facial features from fabric.

3. Decorate the hat with felt cutouts. Add a felt collar under the witch's chin. Glue a loop of yarn to the back of the witch for a hanger.

PUMPKIN NAPKIN HOLDER
(bathroom tissue tube, poster paint, permanent marker)

1. Measure about 1 1/2 inches in from each end of a bathroom tissue tube, and draw a pencil line around the tube.

2. At one end, draw a pumpkin from the edge of the tube to the pencil line. Draw another pumpkin at the opposite end. Then draw two more identical pumpkins on the other side of the tube.

3. Carefully cut around the pumpkin shapes and the pencil line with scissors.

4. Paint the tube and let dry. Draw features on the pumpkins, and place a rolled napkin through the middle of the tube.

HALLOWEEN BERRY BASKET
(plastic berry basket, ribbon, poster board)

1. Start at a corner and weave lengths of ribbon in and out through the sections of a plastic berry basket. Tie each ribbon into a bow at the end.

2. From a piece of poster board, cut out the head of a cat with a long neck. Decorate it with other pieces of poster board and markers.

3. Cut small slits in the neck section and weave them into the berry basket sections at the corner above the bows. Fill the basket with treats.

BAG OWL
(small brown paper bag, old newspaper, construction paper, self-adhesive reinforcement rings)

1. Loosely stuff a small brown paper bag half full of old crumpled newspaper.

2. Bring the top of the bag together, fold the two outside edges in toward the center, and glue to form a point.

3. Fold the point down over the other half of the bag and glue in place.

4. From construction paper, make a paper beak and glue to the point. Make feet and glue to the bottom of the bag. Add two self-adhesive reinforcement rings for eyes.

SPOOKY SEE-THROUGH
(glue, food coloring, plastic food wrap, construction paper)

1. Mix a few drops of food coloring into white glue to make paint. Paint a picture on a piece of plastic food wrap. While it is still wet, cover your painting with another sheet of plastic food wrap. Press the plastic together.

2. Cut strips of construction paper, and glue them around the edges for a frame.

3. Add a loop of yarn to the back for a hanger. Hang the picture in a window where the light will filter through it.

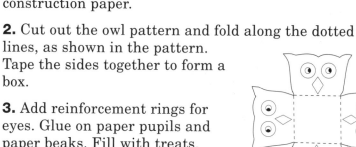

OWL CANDY BOX
(construction paper, self-adhesive reinforcement rings, cardboard egg carton)

1. Draw the owl pattern, as shown, on a square piece of construction paper.

2. Cut out the owl pattern and fold along the dotted lines, as shown in the pattern. Tape the sides together to form a box.

3. Add reinforcement rings for eyes. Glue on paper pupils and paper beaks. Fill with treats.

Fold on dotted lines.

EGG-CARTON PUMPKINS
(cardboard egg carton, poster paint, construction paper)

1. Cut six cups from a cardboard egg carton. Glue them together in pairs to make three pumpkins. Paint them orange.

2. Cut a section of three peaks from the egg carton for the base. Trim two peaks for different heights. Paint the base black.

3. Glue the pumpkins to the base. Attach cut-paper features to the pumpkins.

JACK-O'-LANTERN FAVOR
(plastic margarine tub, construction paper, chenille stick)

1. Wash and dry a plastic margarine tub and lid.

2. Cut out a paper circle to fit the top of the lid. Cut out eyes, a nose, and a mouth from the paper circle, and glue it to the lid. Color the pupils in the eyes and add a stem from paper.

3. Punch two holes, about 1/4 inch apart, near the top rim of the tub; then punch a second pair of holes 2 inches away from the first set.

4. Push each end of a chenille stick through the pairs of holes and twist together, making a handle.

BOTTLE WITCH
(1-liter plastic beverage bottle, 2 1/2-inch plastic-foam ball, poster board, lightweight cotton cloth, ribbon, sequins, black paper, self-adhesive stars)

1. Remove the top of a 1-liter plastic beverage bottle, and spread glue around the inside and outside of the spout. Twist and press a 2 1/2-inch plastic-foam ball into the spout for the head.

2. Draw and cut shoes from a piece of poster board, and glue them to the bottom of the bottle.

3. Cut a 24-inch round piece of lightweight cotton cloth. Cut a slit to the middle. Spread glue around the neck of the bottle and wrap the cloth around it, adding more glue if needed. Tie a piece of ribbon around the neck.

4. To make hair, cut and glue strips of cloth to the ball. For the face, cut features from cloth and glue in place. Add sequins for eyes.

5. To make the hat, cut two circles from black paper. Cut the center out of one circle. Cut a slit to the center of the other circle, and roll it into the shape of a cone. Glue the cone shape onto the flat circle, covering the hole. Then glue the hat to the head.

6. Add self-adhesive stars to the hat and cloth.

MOUSE HAT
(construction paper, chenille stick)

1. Cut out a 9-inch square of construction paper for the hat. Fold it into a triangle.

2. To make the band, cut a strip of paper 11 1/2 inches long and 1 1/2 inches wide. Staple the band to each of the corners opposite the fold.

3. Glue on features made from circles of cut paper. For the tail, staple a curled chenille stick to the top corner.

Hand Masks

Here are simple hand masks to create and carry with you while trick-or-treating.

PIGGY
(heavy cardboard, thread spool, wooden tongue depressor, poster paint)

1. Draw and cut out two 9-inch circles, one from heavy cardboard and one from pink construction paper. Cut two ears from pink paper, and glue them to the cardboard circle. Glue the pink circle to the front of the cardboard circle.

2. Draw two circles for the pig's eyes, and cut them out. Glue on a thread spool for the snout. Use a marker to draw on a mouth and add other details.

3. Paint a wooden tongue depressor and let it dry. Glue the tongue depressor to one side of the pig's head to use as a holder.

CAT
(platter, poster board, paper, paint stir-stick)

1. Cut out a platter shape from a piece of black poster board. Cut a slit to the center, as shown. Pull one edge of the slit over the top of the other to raise the center slightly. Glue to hold it in place.

2. To make the eyes, cut shapes from paper. Glue one on top of the other, and then glue in place on the mask. Cut holes in the center of each paper eye. Add ears, whiskers, and a mouth made from paper. Add a paper bow tie.

3. Glue a paint stir-stick to the inside of the mask for a handle.

Cut

TROPICAL BIRD
(corrugated cardboard, tempera paint, paper, two tongue depressors, yarn)

1. Ask an adult to help you cut out the mask shape and holes for eyes, as shown in the diagram, from corrugated cardboard. Paint one side of the mask, making a beak with a different color.

2. Cut feather-shaped pieces of paper, and glue them around the mask. Roll strips of paper, and glue them around the eyes.

3. Glue two tongue depressors together, overlapping two ends, and let dry. Glue one end to the back of the mask for a handle. Criss-cross yarn from one end of the handle to the other and glue in place, leaving the ends hanging down.

PANDA
(heavy paper plate, construction paper, lightweight cardboard, poster paint, paper towel tube)

1. Draw a panda face on the bottom of a heavy white paper plate. Cut out holes for eyes and a small mouth. Glue a red tongue cut from construction paper near the mouth.

2. Cut ears from lightweight cardboard and paint them black. Staple them to the plate with the smooth section of the staple inside.

3. Cover a paper towel tube with black construction paper and fasten with tape. Staple the tube to one side of the panda face for a handle.

CATERPILLAR
(heavy paper plates, poster paint, poster board, yarn)

1. Paint the bottoms of heavy paper plates with poster paint and let dry.

2. Make a face on one plate with pieces of poster board and glue. Cut out holes for the eyes, draw eyelashes, and staple on antennae.

3. Cut legs from poster board and staple them opposite each other on the plates. Add dots cut from poster board.

4. To connect the body, punch two holes, about 1 inch apart, at the edge of the plate where the neck would be. Punch two holes in another plate so the holes will line up. Place the holes over each other and tie with a piece of yarn. Do the same with the rest of the plates.

5. Cut a 1 1/2-inch section from the center of a plate. Cut in half, overlap, and staple together. Attach the handle over the neck area on the underside.

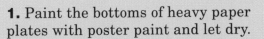

ELEPHANT
(four rectangular facial tissue boxes, masking tape, plastic gloves, white and black shoe polish, cloth, paper, paint stir-stick)

1. Measure 1 inch up from the bottom of three rectangular facial tissue boxes and draw a line. Cut on the line. Discard the tops.

2. Glue two boxes at right angles to one box to form the head. Cut and glue a trunk from the remaining box in place.

3. Cut the side boxes in the shape of ears. Cover the head and the ears with pieces of torn masking tape.

4. Cover your work space and wear plastic gloves. Mix black and white shoe polish together to make a gray color. Wipe the polish on the tape with a cloth.

5. Glue on large paper eyes. Cut out eyeholes. Glue on a paint stir-stick.

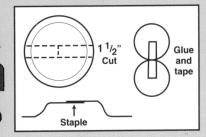

ROCKY PUMPKIN
(rock, yarn, felt)

1. Find the best sitting position for the rock you have chosen.

2. Starting at the bottom, squeeze glue on the rock and wrap yarn around it. Add more glue and yarn until the entire rock is covered. Let dry.

3. Cut the eyes, nose, and mouth from felt and glue them to the rock to make the jack-o'-lantern's face. Add a stem to the top.

HALLOWEEN STICK PUPPET
(construction paper, wooden tongue depressor)

1. To make the body of the witch, cut pieces of construction paper, and glue them to a wooden tongue depressor. Add hands, feet, hair, and facial features cut from paper.

2. Hold the tongue depressor in your hand and soar your witch through the air.

PLASTIC-FOAM NECKLACE
(plastic-foam tray, permanent marker,
self-adhesive reinforcement rings, yarn)

1. Draw and cut out ghosts from a white plastic-foam tray. Add facial features with a marker.

2. Place a self-adhesive reinforcement ring at the top, on the front and back of each ghost, so the holes are lined up.

3. Thread a long piece of yarn through each hole and tie a knot. Do this for each ghost.

4. Tie the ends into a bow.

TRICK-OR-TREAT REFLECTIVE BAG
(brown paper bag, aluminum foil, yarn)

1. Fold over the top of a paper bag several times to make a cuff. Decorate the bag with jack-o'-lanterns cut from foil.

2. To make the braided handle, cut three pieces of yarn the same length. Line up the pieces, and tie them together into a knot about 1 inch from one end. Braid by folding A over B and then C over A. Continue until the yarn is braided. Tie the ends into a knot again about 1 inch from the end.

3. Staple the handle ends to the sides of the bag.

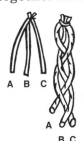

SPOOKY PICTURE
(construction paper, yarn)

1. Draw the outline of a spooky picture on a piece of construction paper.

2. Spread glue over one area of the picture at a time. Press strands of different-colored yarn into the glue.

RUB-A-DESIGN
(poster board, colored chalk, construction paper, paper towel, hair spray)

1. Draw and cut out a Halloween shape from a piece of poster board. On one side of the shape rub some colored chalk.

2. Place the shape with the chalk side faceup on the top of a folded sheet of construction paper.

3. With a small piece of paper towel, rub from the center of the chalky shape onto the paper. Lift the shape and see the design on the paper.

4. To keep the picture from smudging, spray it lightly with hair spray. Use the design to decorate a Halloween card.

JINGLE GHOSTS
(one-gallon plastic milk jug, thread, bells)

1. Wash and dry an empty one-gallon plastic milk jug. Cut ghost shapes from the sides of the jug.

2. Using a paper punch, make eye holes in each ghost. With a pen, punch a hole in the top of each ghost, and tie a thread loop for a hanger.

3. Poke a small hole with a pen at the bottom of each ghost. Place a small bell on a piece of thread, and tie it to the bottom of each ghost.

4. Hang the ghosts where the wind will make them flutter and the bells jingle.

HALLOWEEN PUZZLE
(plastic-foam tray, construction paper)

1. Cut a large square from the flat part of a plastic-foam tray.

2. Draw a picture on a piece of paper the same size as the plastic square. Glue the picture to the square.

3. When the picture is dry, cut through both the picture and the tray to make the puzzle pieces.

YARN-COVERED WITCH
(small box, orange yarn, black construction paper)

1. Cover the outside of the box with glue, except the bottom.

2. Press orange yarn into the glue to completely cover the top and sides of the box. Leave some yarn hanging down in loops at the bottom before starting back up the box, as shown.

3. For the hat brim, cut a circle of black construction paper. Cut another circle twice as big as the first one, and cut it in half.

4. Roll one of the halves into a cone shape, tape the ends together, and glue it to the brim.

5. Cut and glue on paper eyes and a mouth.

PAPIER-MÂCHÉ PUMPKIN

(flour and water, white paper towels, round balloon, poster paint, heavy cardboard, construction paper)

1. To make papier-mâché, mix flour and water together until it is the consistency of ketchup. Tear small strips of white paper towel and dip them into the flour mixture. Place a layer of strips on an inflated round balloon and let dry. Add another layer and let dry.

2. To make the pumpkin, cut a section from the bottom of the round papier-mâché shape so it will sit level and not roll away. Cover with poster paint and let dry.

3. To make the base, cut a rectangular piece of heavy cardboard. Cut various leaf shapes and glue on top. Glue the pumpkin to the center.

4. Add a paper stem, leaves, and vines to the pumpkin decoration.

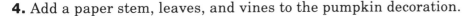

CORNY PLACE CARD

(white poster board)

1. On a piece of white poster board, draw and cut out the shape shown in the diagram.

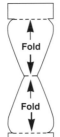

2. Color the cutout to look like a giant piece of candy corn. Add a guest's name with a marker.

3. Fold as shown in the picture and glue together. Make one for each of your guests.

SCARY BLACK CAT

(poster board, cardboard egg carton, yarn, paper, brass fasteners)

1. Cut a large cat's head, body, and a tail from black poster board.

2. Cut three cup sections from a cardboard egg carton. Glue two in place for the eyes and one for the nose-mouth area. Add paper whiskers and a nose. Draw pupils on the eyes.

3. Attach a brass fastener at the neck and tail. Change the cat's position anytime you like.

SITTING WITCH
(cereal box, construction paper)

1. Cut a large corner from a cereal box. Cover it with black construction paper.

2. To make the hat brim, cut a circle from black paper. Cut a square hole in the center, and glue it over the point of the box corner.

3. Decorate with facial features, hands, legs, shoes, and a broom made from paper. Glue the legs to the inside edge at the front of the witch.

4. Set the witch on a shelf or on the edge of a desk.

TRICK-OR-TREAT BUCKET
(round plastic jug, brass fasteners, construction paper)

1. Soak the plastic jug in warm water to help soften it. Then cut away the top portion.

2. From the top portion, cut off a long strip about 1/2 inch wide for the handle.

3. Attach the handle to each side with a brass fastener.

4. Cut Halloween decorations from construction paper, and glue them around the bucket.

GHOSTLY GOGGLES
(construction paper)

1. Draw two ghost shapes, as shown, about the size of your hand. Cut out two circles in the body large enough to see through. Draw on faces with a marker.

2. Cut a 2-inch-wide headband long enough to go around your head.

3. Glue the ghosts' heads to the headband with the body hanging below so you can see through the holes. Tape the ends of the headband together.

ROCK CRAWLER
(small rock, poster paint, construction paper, cotton, chenille stick)

1. Cover a small rock with poster paint and let dry. Cut and glue pieces of construction paper for eyes.

2. Place a piece of cotton soaked in glue in the middle of the rock. (This keeps the legs from falling off when they are dry.)

3. Cut pieces of a chenille stick, and glue them across the cotton to make three legs on each side of the body. Let dry thoroughly.

4. Turn the stone over and slightly bend the chenille sticks at the ends so the "rocky crawler" can stand more easily.

WITCH FINGER-PUPPET
(construction paper, felt, yarn, self-adhesive stars)

1. Roll and glue together a wide piece of construction paper so your middle finger will fit inside it.

2. Decorate one side of the paper roll with pieces of felt and yarn.

3. Place self-adhesive stars on the witch's dress and hat.

ON-OFF PUMPKIN
(construction paper)

1. Fold a 1-foot strip of orange construction paper into three even sections. Trim the sides of the paper to form a pumpkin, but do not cut the folds.

2. Unfold the paper and cut out eyes, nose, and a mouth in the center section, making a pumpkin face.

3. Cover the top section with yellow construction paper and the bottom section with black.

4. Fold again, with the pumpkin facing you. Glue on a paper stem. Add lines with a marker or crayon to outline the pumpkin.

5. Fold so that the yellow paper shows through the pumpkin face when it is "on" and the black shows through when it is "off."

WITCH MOBILE
(brown paper bag, newspaper, paint, black crepe paper, yarn)

1. Paint a witch's face on the front of a paper bag. Stuff the bag with crumpled newspaper. Fold over the top and glue it shut.

2. For hair, glue strips of black crepe paper on the top of the bag. Attach a long piece of black yarn to the head with staples. Tie a knot in the yarn about 2 inches above the head.

3. Cut a circle of black paper for the brim of the hat. Make a hole in the center, and pull the yarn through, letting the brim rest on the knot.

4. To make the top of the hat, roll a piece of black paper in a cone shape. Thread the yarn through the top of the hat and tape the cone shape to the brim.

5. Glue yarn on the hat for a hatband.

CLOTHESPIN CRITTER
(two spring-type clothespins, construction paper, white paint)

1. From construction paper, cut four leg shapes long enough to cover a spring-type clothespin. Glue the legs on each side of two clothespins, with the feet at the open end.

2. On a piece of paper, draw shapes for the cat's body, tail, and head. Cut out the shapes, and glue them together. Add features with white paint.

3. Clip the clothespin legs to the cat's body. Position the legs so the cat will stand.

NOISY GOBLIN
(one-pint milk carton, dried beans, construction paper, yarn, ice-cream stick)

1. Place some dried beans inside a one-pint milk carton, then staple the top closed.

2. Spread glue on the carton, and cover it with construction paper.

3. Draw a scary face on one side. Staple on yarn at the top for hair.

4. Poke a small hole in the bottom of the carton, and glue an ice-cream stick in the hole for the handle.

PAPER OWL
(construction paper)

1. Fold a 3-inch-by-6-inch piece of construction paper in half lengthwise.

2. Starting on the fold, cut 1-inch slits—about 1/2 inch apart—the entire length of the paper. Open and glue the ends together to form the body.

3. Cut eyes, ears, and a beak from paper. Glue them in place.

4. Cut a strip of paper for a handle, and glue the ends to opposite sides of the owl body. Hang the owl on a branch or use it to decorate a table.

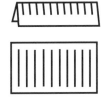

PUMPKIN PUPPET
(construction paper)

1. Cut two pieces of orange construction paper about 8 inches square. Staple them together on three sides with a stem at the top, as shown. Leave one side open.

2. To make the face, cut out and glue on eyes, a nose, and a mouth from paper.

3. Place your hand into the opened end to work the puppet. Make up spooky stories.

GLITTERY BRACELETS
(plastic or cardboard food containers, ribbon, aluminum foil, buttons, glitter, sequins)

1. From plastic or cardboard food containers, cut rings that will fit around your wrist as bracelets.

2. Decorate the rings with ribbon, aluminum foil, buttons, glitter, and sequins.

GHOST WIND SOCK
(sock, newspaper, ice-cream stick, black permanent marker)

1. Cut several slits in the leg section of an old white sock.

2. Wad up a sheet of newspaper, and stuff it into the foot of the sock. Place an ice-cream stick crosswise in the sock. Then stuff more newspaper in the sock to hold the ice-cream stick in place. Continue to stuff in more newspaper until you have filled the entire foot of the sock.

3. Make a face with a black permanent marker. With a pencil, poke two holes at the top of the ghost's head and pull a piece of yarn through them. Tie the ends together, and hang the ghost in a breezy place.

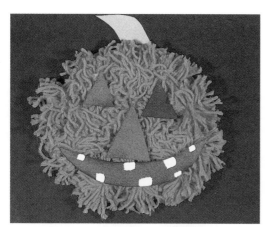

Wrap yarn **Tie around center** **Cut loops**

POMPON PUMPKIN
(lightweight cardboard, construction paper, orange yarn, poster board)

1. Cut out a pumpkin shape from a piece of lightweight cardboard, and cover it with orange construction paper.

2. To make pompons, wrap orange yarn around a piece of cardboard 4 inches square. (The more yarn you use, the fluffier the pompon will be.) Slip the yarn from the cardboard, and tie a piece of yarn tightly around the center, as shown. Cut through all the loops, and fluff up the yarn.

3. Glue the pompons on the pumpkin. Attach eyes, a nose, and a mouth made from black paper.

4. Attach the pompon pumpkin to a square piece of black poster board. Add a green paper stem. Glue a piece of yarn to the back for a hanger.

CAT NAPKIN HOLDER
(small cardboard tube, construction paper, napkin)

1. Cut a 1-inch section from a small cardboard tube. Cover it with black paper.

2. Draw a head, paws, and tail, as shown, on a piece of black construction paper and cut them out.

3. Decorate the head with features cut from paper. Glue the head, paws, and tail to the tube. Place a rolled napkin through the center.

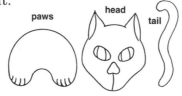

paws   head   tail

THE SPIDER AND THE WEB

(quart-size milk carton, yarn, construction paper, rickrack, cotton ball, paper cup, poster paint)

1. Measure 2 inches from the bottom of a quart-size milk carton, and draw a line around the outside of the carton. Cut along the line to make a small square box.

2. To create the web, poke eight holes around the sides of the box—one in each corner and one in the middle of each side. Tie a knot at one end of a long piece of yarn, and wrap a piece of tape around the other. Thread the taped end through the holes, as shown in the diagram, tying a knot in the yarn at the last hole. Take another piece of yarn, and loop it under and over the piece woven through the holes. Glue paper to the outside of the box and add rickrack.

3. For the body of the spider, dip a cotton ball into a small paper cup of water and poster paint. Squeeze the water out of the cotton ball and let dry. Separate a small piece of yarn into eight small strands. Glue the strands of yarn to the back of the cotton ball, letting the yarn hang down for legs. Add paper eyes and a mouth.

4. Glue the spider to the center of the web and wrap a few legs around the web.

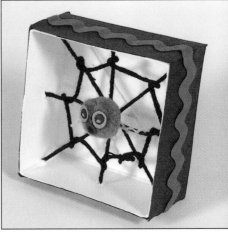

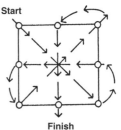

Start

Finish

HALLOWEEN POP-OUT CARD

(construction paper, plastic-foam tray)

1. For the card, fold a piece of construction paper in half. Fold it over in half again the other way.

2. Decorate the front of the card with cut pieces of paper. Write a greeting on another piece of paper, and glue it to the inside of the card.

3. Cut out a ghost from a plastic-foam tray and add paper eyes.

4. Cut two strips of paper and fold them over each other in the direction shown to form a paper spring. Glue the spring to the card and the back of the ghost.

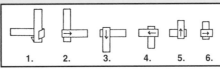

1. 2. 3. 4. 5. 6.

BOO TREAT BAG

(white paper, white paper bag)

1. Cut out two arms from white paper. Glue them to the sides of a white paper bag.

2. Draw a face on the front of the bag.

3. Fold down the top of the bag about an inch and trim the corners with scissors. Fill the bag with treats.

HANGING BATS
(construction paper, yarn)

1. Draw and cut out three pairs of bat designs from black construction paper. Divide into two sets. Set aside one of each bat design to use later.

2. Vertically lay the three bats of the first set on a table about 2 inches apart.

3. Cut a long piece of yarn, and lay it down the center of the bats. Glue the yarn to the bats.

4. Spread glue around the edges of the bats, and place the matching bat from the other set on top of its mate.

5. Tie a loop in the yarn above the first bat to make a hanger.

PUMPKIN CARD
(construction paper)

1. Cut a sheet of orange construction paper in half the long way. Fold in half again, as shown. Round off the corners into a pumpkin shape, being careful not to cut off the fold.

2. On the front, cut out the features. Cut a piece of black paper a little smaller than the folded card. Paste it behind the front of the card.

3. Write a message inside. Use the card as an invitation or greeting card.

GLITTERING WAND
(16-inch wooden dowel, poster paint, construction paper, felt, cotton balls, glitter)

1. For the handle, paint a wooden dowel and let it dry. Cut small stars from white construction paper, and glue them on the handle.

2. Cut two large identical stars from white felt. Spread glue on the edges of the stars.

3. Place a few cotton balls in the center of one star. Lay one end of the handle on top. Place the second star on top of the handle and the first star. Press the stars together at the edges.

4. Spread a thin layer of glue on one side of the star, and sprinkle with glitter. When it has dried, do the same to the other side.

PEBBLE PUMPKINS
(pebbles, paint, stick of wood)

1. To make pumpkins, wash and dry small round, flat pebbles. Paint them orange and create faces.

2. Use long, flat pebbles for the ghosts. Paint them white and create faces.

3. Glue the pumpkins and ghosts to a small stick of wood.

BEWITCHING EYES
(construction paper, brass fastener)

1. Glue together pieces of construction paper to create the witch's face, hair, and hat.

2. Cut two holes in the face for the eyes. Cut a small strip of paper and fold in the middle for the nose.

3. Draw and cut out a circle of white paper, no wider than the witch's face.

4. With the nose on top of the face and the circle behind the face, poke a brass fastener through the layers of paper to hold together.

5. Draw a pair of eyes on the white paper circle. Turn the circle and draw another set of eyes. Give your witch different eyes with each turn.

YARN HAIR WIG
(one knee-high stocking, large beverage container, yarn, crochet hook)

1. Pull a knee-high stocking, inside out, over your hair. Tie a knot close to your head in the extra stocking hanging loose. Take off the stocking and turn it right-side out. Stretch the stocking over a large beverage container.

2. Cut pieces of yarn 16 to 20 inches long. Hold a small pinch of stocking in your fingers. Gently poke a crochet hook through the stocking. Place a piece of yarn on the hook and pull it through the hole. Tie a knot in the yarn.

3. Continue to cover the stocking with pieces of yarn.

Special Costumes

BOX ROBOT
(a small and a large cardboard box, aluminum foil, construction paper, permanent markers)

1. To make the head, remove the flaps from a small cardboard box that fits on your shoulders. Cover the box with glue and aluminum foil. Cut out holes for the eyes and a mouth.

2. For the body, remove the flaps from a large cardboard box. Cut a hole in the bottom of the box for your head to fit through. Cut a square on each side of the box for your arms. Cover the box with glue and foil.

3. Decorate with construction paper and permanent markers. Twist together foil antennae, and tape them to the head.

CEREAL-BOX CLOWN
(family-sized cereal box, yarn, construction paper, tissue paper)

1. Cut off the back and the top sections of a family-sized cereal box. When placed on your head, it should almost touch your shoulders. Cover the box with glue and white paper. Cut out holes for eyes and a mouth. Cut and glue decorations from construction paper. Glue paper ears to the box sides.

2. Cut and glue loops of yarn to the box top to create hair. Make a hat by cutting out a paper circle. Make a slit to the center of the circle, pull the paper into a cone shape, and tape. Glue it on top of the hair.

3. Poke a hole in each side of the box behind the ears. Tie a piece of yarn from each hole to hold the mask on.

4. Make a collar by cutting a strip of paper long enough to go around your neck. Glue on gathered tissue paper and other decorations. Place the collar around your neck and tape in place.

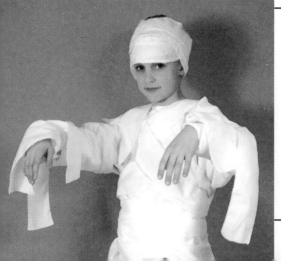

MUMMY
(old white sheet or fabric, white tape)

1. Wear a white or light-colored sweat suit. Cut strips from an old white sheet or other scrap fabric.

2. Tape one end of a strip to your clothes. Wrap the strip around your body, not too loose and not too tight. Tape the end of the strip to hold in place. Let some of the ends hang. Continue to wrap your body.

3. Wrap a strip around just the top of your head. Don't cover your face.

FLOWER
(poster board, yarn, tissue paper)

1. Cut three different petal sizes. Hold the petals together, and punch two holes so they will match from petal to petal.

2. To join together, work from left to right. Place a small petal on top of a large petal and thread a piece of yarn through the left holes of the petals. Place a medium petal between the large and small with the right hole of the large and small petals and the left hole of the medium petal lining up. Thread the yarn through the holes. Then place a large petal with its left hole, the medium petal with its right hole, and a small petal with its left hole lined up and thread the yarn through. Continue, then tie a knot at each end, leaving a piece of yarn to tie later.

3. For the center, cut a 2-inch strip of poster board, and staple to form a ring. Cut a tissue-paper circle larger than the ring. Glue it to the inside of the ring. Cut small circles of tissue paper. Place your finger in the middle of each circle and gather the paper around it. Glue the tip to the cap.

4. Tie the petals around your shoulders, and place the flower center on your head.

LION
(heavy paper plate, yarn, poster paint, felt)

1. To make the face, paint the outside bottom of a heavy paper plate. Draw and cut out holes for the eyes and a mouth. Decorate with yarn and a red-felt tongue.

2. To make the mane, cut pieces of yarn. With the lion's face down, glue the yarn on the rim of the paper plate.

3. Paper punch two holes close together on each side of the plate rim. Tie a piece of yarn to each hole to hold the mask in place.

BALLERINA
(seven chenille sticks, glitter)

1. Bend five 10-inch-long chenille sticks in half, then twist a 1/2-inch loop at the top. Lay the five pieces together in a row. Join them together, as shown. Make a loop at each bottom end. Attach these ends to a 3-inch-diameter ring made from a chenille stick.

2. For the top of the crown, bend one 12-inch chenille stick in half, twist a 1/2-inch loop at the top, and twist two extra side loops, as shown.

3. Make a loop at each bottom end. Fasten to the center of the crown. Dab glue over the crown, and sprinkle on glitter.

ASTRONAUT
(rectangular cardboard box, aluminum foil, large paper bag, fabric)

1. Tape or glue a piece of aluminum foil on one of the large sides of a rectangular cardboard box. Have an adult help you cut four slits, as shown. Slide a long strip of cloth through the slits and tie the ends so that the box can be worn as a backpack. Tape foil around the rest of the box.

2. To make a helmet, cut out a circle on one side of a paper bag for your face. Cut away about half of each side of the bag so that it fits over your shoulders. Cover the bag with foil using tape or glue. Cut the foil into pie-shaped wedges over the face hole and fold them inside.

3. Complete your costume by wearing boots and a pair of large gloves.

AUTOMOBILE
(corrugated cardboard box, poster paint, five large paper plates, small paper plates, fabric)

1. Open all the flaps on a corrugated cardboard box. Use poster paint to decorate sides of the cardboard to resemble a car.

2. Glue small paper plates to the front and back of the car to make headlights and tail lights. Glue four large paper plates to the car to make wheels. Staple a fifth large paper plate to the car to make a steering wheel.

3. Cut two long strips of fabric. Staple them to the top in the front and in the back of the car. Step into the car, and place the straps over your shoulders to carry the car.

RABBIT
(poster board, headband, paper clips, cotton balls, construction paper, large paper plate, yarn, elastic)

1. Fold a piece of white poster board in half. Cut out the ears, as shown. Place a headband inside the fold of each ear and glue them together, holding with paper clips until dry. Cover the headband and ears with glue and small cotton balls, adding pieces of pink construction paper.

2. Place a large paper plate in front of your face with the bottom facing out. Using a crayon, have a friend carefully mark on the outside of the plate where the eyeholes should be. Remove the plate and cut out the eyeholes.

3. Draw an outline around the eyes, and draw a nose and a mouth. Cut a tongue from paper. Glue on cotton balls, and add yarn whiskers. Staple elastic on opposite sides of the head to hold the mask in place.

4. Cover a round piece of poster board with cotton balls, and tape to the seat of your pants.

LADYBUG
(corrugated cardboard, poster board, black ribbon, paper towels, red tissue paper, mask)

1. Ask an adult to help cut a large oval, about the size of your back, from a piece of corrugated cardboard. Cover one side with red poster board, and cover the other side with black poster board. With an adult's help cut four slits, as shown. From the black side, insert a piece of black ribbon into each set of slits. Glue about 2 inches of the ribbon ends to the red side.

2. Cover the red side with crumpled paper towels glued in place to form a mound. Cover the mound with red tissue paper and glue at the edges. Cut and glue on yellow spots from poster board. Cut and staple six legs from black poster board.

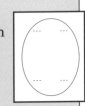

PRINCE
(poster board, glitter, fabric, ribbon)

1. Draw a crown shape on a piece of poster board, as shown, and cut it out. Draw designs with glue and sprinkle them with glitter. Glue on ribbon and fabric pieces. Roll the cutout shape into the form of a crown. Leave the opening large enough to fit your head. Staple the ends together.

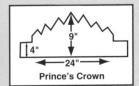
Prince's Crown

2. Cut a rectangular piece of fabric for a cape. Fold it in half, and cut a small section in the middle large enough for your head to go through.

3. Draw designs on the cape with glue and sprinkle them with glitter. Add ribbon and fabric pieces to match the crown. Let dry. Wear the cape over your clothes.

PRINCESS
(poster board, glitter, fabric, lace)

Princess's Hat

1. Draw a hat shape on a piece of poster board, as shown, and cut it out. Draw designs with glue and sprinkle them with glitter. Glue on ribbon and fabric pieces.

2. Roll the cutout into the shape of a cone to fit your head, and staple it in place. Leave a small opening at the top. Staple streamers of ribbons and fabric to the top of the hat. At the bottom, staple ribbon to hold the hat in place.

3. Follow step 2 and step 3 of the Prince costume to make a cape.

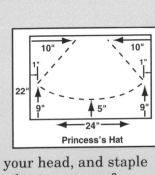

THREE-HEADED MONSTER
(four heavy cardboard paper plates, elastic, paint, paper, poster board)

1. To make the masks for your hands, cut one plate in half. Place one of the halves on a whole plate, face to face, and glue together at the rim. This forms a pocket for your hand. Repeat this for the second mask. To make the mask for your face, use one plate.

2. Punch holes at the top of each mask, and tie yarn for hair. Add other features with paint, paper, or poster board.

3. To wear the face mask, punch a hole on opposite sides of the plate, and tie a piece of elastic to each hole.

CHRISTMAS PACKAGE
(large cardboard box, gift wrap, small paper plate, ribbon)

1. Remove the top flaps from a large cardboard box so the top of the box will be open. Cut a hole in the bottom of the box large enough for your head to fit through.

2. Cut two holes on opposite sides of the box, large enough for your arms to fit through and for the box to rest on top of your shoulders. Decorate the box with gift wrap and ribbon.

3. Tape pieces of ribbon to the center of a small paper plate. Punch a hole on each side of the plate, and thread a piece of ribbon through the holes. Wear the plate on your head as the bow on top of the package.

LITTLE LEPRECHAUN
(poster board)

1. Cut hair and a beard from a piece of orange poster board. Draw a circle for your face in the middle and cut it out.

2. Draw and cut out a hat from green poster board. Glue the hat on top of the hair. Decorate the hat with a shamrock.

3. To make a pot of gold, cut out a large pot shape from a piece of black poster board. Cut small gold coins, and glue them around the top of the pot.

LADY AND GENTLEMAN
(old clothes and accessories)

1. Ask an adult to let you use some of his or her old clothes and accessories to play dress-up. Use your imagination to mix and match pieces of clothing, ties, hats, shoes, and old jewelry to make your own characters.

FIVE OF HEARTS
(four sheets of white poster board, red felt, red ribbon)

1. To make the front and back of a playing card, glue two sheets of white poster board together for one side of your body and two sheets together for the other side of your body.

2. To make the front side of the playing card, cut five large red-felt hearts, and glue them in place. Draw the numeral 5 in opposite corners of the card. Cut two small hearts from felt, and glue one below each number. Draw designs on the back side of the playing card.

3. Have someone help you hold up the card sections to the top of your shoulders, front and back. Cut strips of ribbon to fit over your shoulders, and staple them to the front and back of the card sections with the red hearts facing out for the front and the design facing out for the back.

4. Cut four strips of ribbon, and staple two of them to each side of the cards below your elbow. Tie the strips together in a bow to help hold the card in place on your body.

5. To make a hat, cut a long strip of poster board with a large heart in the middle. Cut out a red-felt heart, and glue it in the middle of the white one. Staple or tape the ends of the strips together to fit your head.

SURPRISE JACK-O'-LANTERN
(orange cellulose sponge, permanent marker, felt, chenille stick, flashlight)

1. Cut a pumpkin shape from a dry orange cellulose sponge (the kind that has irregular holes).

2. Draw lines on the pumpkin with a permanent marker. Cut out pieces of felt for the eyes, nose, and mouth, and glue them to the pumpkin.

3. Cut a small piece of chenille stick and loop it to form a stem. Glue it to the top of the pumpkin.

4. What's the surprise? Place a flashlight behind this jack-o'-lantern, and watch it glow in the dark!

TRICK-OR-TREAT TOTE
(large cereal box, half-gallon milk carton, construction paper, yarn)

1. Cut off the two long top flaps of a large cereal box. Fold back and glue the two small top flaps to each narrow side of the outside of the cereal box. These will be reinforcements for the handle.

2. Cut a half-gallon milk carton in half. Cover the milk carton and the cereal box with glue and black construction paper. Glue them together.

3. Draw and cut out ghost shapes from paper and glue them to the tote-box. Add yarn around the top edges.

4. Poke a small hole on each narrow side of the cereal box. Thread the ends of a piece of yarn through the holes from the outside of the box, and tie the yarn into knots on the inside of the box.

HALLOWEEN BANNER
(paper)

1. To create the word "HAPPY," you will need a piece of paper that measures 5 by 15 inches. You may need to tape pieces of paper together.

2. Starting at the narrow end, fold over 3 inches of the paper and continue to fold into accordion pleats until the whole piece is pleated.

3. With a pencil, lightly sketch a ghost, as shown in the diagram, on the top of the folded paper. Cut around the ghost shape, but don't cut on the folds. You should have five ghosts. Write one letter of the word "HAPPY" on each ghost.

4. To create the word "HALLOWEEN," follow steps 1, 2, and 3, using a piece of paper measuring 5 by 27 inches.

POP-OUT GHOST

(plastic container with snap-on lid, construction paper,
small plastic-foam ball, tissue paper, thread)

1. Cover a plastic container with strips of gray construction paper.
Cover the snap-on lid with a circle of paper. With a marker, draw
stones on the paper.

2. Cut two strips of paper 1 inch wide. Fold the strips over each other,
as shown in the diagram on page 27, to form a long spring. The spring,
when flattened, should be the height of the can. Glue one end of it to
the inside bottom of the container.

3. Cover a small plastic-foam ball with white tissue, and secure with
thread at the neck. Add eyes and a mouth to the ghost. Spread out the
ghost body and glue the bottom of the ball to the other end of the
spring.

4. Push the ghost inside the container and close the lid. Surprise a
friend by opening the lid. See the ghost pop up and down.

GOBLIN CUP

(plastic-foam cup, construction paper)

1. Tape or glue construction paper to the outside of a
plastic-foam cup.

2. Add features such as ears, eyes, a mouth, and a nose
from paper to create your goblin.

SPIDER HAT

(paper plates, yarn, chenille sticks, 2 1/2-inch plastic-foam ball, paper)

1. Cut the center from one paper plate without cutting through
the rim. Cut another paper plate, from the edge to the center.
Staple this plate into a cone shape.

2. Glue the cone to the rim. Use a paper punch to punch a hole
on each side of the hat, and add yarn for ties.

3. Draw a spider web on the cone. Spread glue and pieces of yarn
over the web. Color a 2 1/2-inch plastic-foam ball with a marker.
Push chenille sticks into the ball for legs. Add paper eyes.

4. Glue the spider to the top of the hat, attaching his legs
somewhere on the web.

PAPER-PLATE PUMPKIN
(two 9-inch paper plates, construction paper, string, poster paint)

1. Glue two 9-inch paper plates right sides together. Place a green stem cut from construction paper and a piece of string in between the plates at the top before the glue dries.

2. Paint the plates orange and let dry.

3. To make the face, cut features from paper, and glue them onto the front of the pumpkin.

HAPPY HALLOWEEN BASKET
(plastic food containers, bathroom tissue tube, paint, paper, self-adhesive stars)

1. Paint a happy face on an upright bathroom tissue tube and let it dry. Cut a strip of paper, decorate it, and glue each end to the inside of the tube for a handle.

2. Glue the tube in the center of a plastic margarine container. Add self-adhesive stars around the outside.

3. Fill the basket with treats.

DANCING GOBLIN
(cardboard egg carton, poster paint, yarn, construction paper, two marbles)

1. Cut four identical cup sections from a cardboard egg carton.

2. To make the head, glue two of the cups together and let dry. Cover with paint and let dry again. Cut eyes, a nose, and a mouth from construction paper, and glue them to the cup for the face. Glue short pieces of thin yarn to the top of the head for hair.

3. To make the feet, poke a hole in each of the two remaining cups. Paint the cups and let them dry. Cut two pieces of thick yarn about 7 inches long, and thread one piece into each hole. Tie a knot at the ends so the yarn won't come out of the cups.

4. Attach the feet to the head by poking a hole on each side of the head and gluing the ends of the yarn into these holes.

5. Glue a marble inside each foot for weight. Hold the goblin with your fingers, and tilt his head back and forth quickly to make him dance.

WOODEN-STICK MUMMY
(five ice-cream sticks, gauze, paper, string)

1. Glue five ice-cream sticks together, as shown, to make the body.

2. Cut a head shape from paper and glue it to the body.

3. Cut strips of gauze. Spread some glue along the sticks and head and wrap the gauze around them.

4. With a paper punch, punch out two paper eyes and glue them to the head. Glue a string loop to the back of the mummy for a hanger.

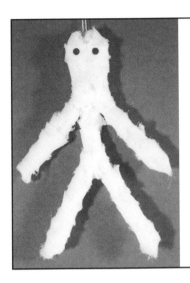

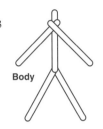

Body

GHOSTLY GAME
(shoe box and lid, poster paint, large thread spool, white paper, three Ping-Pong balls)

1. Remove the lid from an empty shoe box. Paint the inside of the lid with black poster paint and let dry. Paint three Ping-Pong balls black and let dry.

2. Draw a ghost shape on a piece of white paper to fit the inside of the lid. Cut out the ghost and glue it inside the lid.

3. To make the eyes and mouth, place a large thread spool on the face and trace around the spool. Cut out along the outline. Turn the shoe box upside down, and hold the lid against the bottom. Trace around the holes for the eyes and mouth, then cut along the outlines.

4. Glue the lid to the bottom of the box, matching the holes. Cut out sections of the sides of the shoe box to make legs.

5. Drop the three balls onto the lid. Hold the box in your hands, and roll the balls around until you have filled the holes.

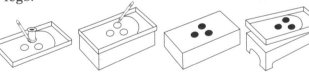

FUZZY SPIDERS
(four black chenille sticks, one large four-hole button, construction paper)

1. Cut four black chenille sticks about 6 inches in length.

2. Push a chenille stick through each hole of a large four-hole button. Bend and shape the sticks to look like legs.

3. To make the spider's head and body section, cut a piece of black construction paper. Glue it to the top of the button. Add paper eyes.

GHOSTLY HAND PUPPET
(white paper, yarn, black crayon)

1. Cut two identical ghost shapes, larger than your hand, from white paper.

2. Hold one ghost on top of the other. With a paper punch, punch holes around the sides and tops.

3. Cut a long piece of yarn. Lace the front and back together by going in and out of the holes. Tie a knot in the ends of the yarn.

4. Draw a ghost face with black crayon. Place your hand in the puppet, and say "Boo!"

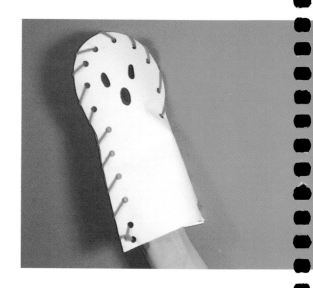

FUNNY-FACE PUMPKIN
(construction paper)

1. Cut out three identical paper pumpkin shapes with straight bottoms.

2. Fold each pumpkin in half and then open up. Draw a different face on each paper pumpkin, using the fold as a guide to center the face.

3. Add glue to one half of the back of two pumpkins, and glue these together. Then glue the third pumpkin to the remaining back sections.

TREAT BAGS
(small white paper bags, construction paper)

1. Decorate one side of a small white paper bag with cutout pieces of construction paper. Glue them in place.

2. Make Halloween cats, witches, goblins, or other creatures. Let your imagination loose.

3. Place treats inside each bag for your friends.

HALLOWEEN HOUSE
(construction paper)

1. Fold a square piece of paper into sixteen squares, as shown in the diagram. Cut on the solid lines (Fig.1).

2. Fold B over C and staple (Fig. 2). Fold F over G and staple.

3. Bring A and D together, overlapping slightly, and staple (Fig. 3). Do the same with E and H.

4. Draw doors and windows, and decorate the house as you wish.

Fig. 1

Fig. 2

Fig. 3

THREE-D CAT
(heavy cardboard, poster paint)

1. From heavy cardboard, cut out the body, front legs, back legs, and head. Make slits in these four parts, as shown.

2. Slide the legs and head into the body slits to be sure that the parts fit properly. Take apart.

3. Paint the parts with poster paint, adding features. Let dry, then put the parts back together.

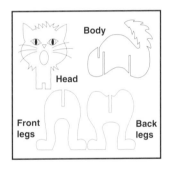

Body

Head

Front legs

Back legs

TONGUE DEPRESSOR FINGER PUPPETS
(permanent markers, watercolor or tempera paint, tongue depressors, felt, lightweight cardboard)

1. Paint a face on a tongue depressor with permanent marker, watercolor, or tempera paint. Features can be added with pieces of felt.

2. Glue a lightweight piece of cardboard in the shape of a ring to the back of each tongue depressor. When dry, place the puppets on your fingers.

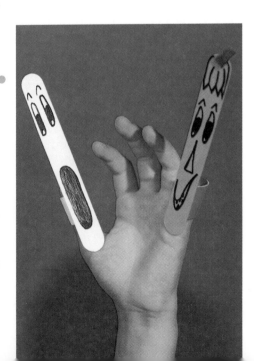

OWL NAPKIN HOLDER
(bathroom tissue tube, poster paint, construction paper)

1. Draw two V shapes, one at each end of a bathroom tissue tube, and cut them out. Glue the V shapes to each side of the tube for ears.

2. Paint the tube and let dry. Cut out eyes and a beak from paper and glue in place.

3. Place a rolled napkin inside the tube and stand the owl up.

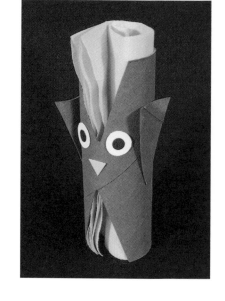

TRICK-OR-TREAT FUN BOX
(small cardboard gift box, construction paper, poster board)

1. Cover the lid of a small cardboard gift box with construction paper. Tape the ends inside the lid.

2. Cut the face of a witch from white paper, and glue it to the top of the lid. Draw on facial features with a marker.

3. Cut a poster board hat, and glue it to the witch. Fill the box with treats for a friend.

EERIE HOUSE CARD
(construction paper)

1. Fold a piece of dark blue construction paper in half for the card. On the outside write this message: "Dear _____, On Halloween will you help me haunt a house? Look inside."

2. On black construction paper, draw a house that will fit inside the card. Add windows and a door with a marker or a crayon. Cut out the house.

3. From white paper, cut out a ghost shape longer than the height of the house. On the bottom of the ghost print "PUSH UP."

4. Inside the card, put the house in place with the ghost behind it. Put glue on the back of the house but only at the sides. Be sure the ghost moves freely.

5. Pull the ghost down so that it is invisible until your friend follows the instruction "PUSH UP."

GOBLIN TREE

(cream containers, construction paper, tree branch,
plastic food container, modeling clay, fabric, yarn, string)

1. For each goblin, glue together two small cream containers. Cut features from paper to decorate each goblin.

2. Stick a fallen tree branch into a plastic food container filled with modeling clay. Cut a circle of fabric. Wrap it around the container and tie it together with yarn.

3. Glue a piece of string to the top of each goblin, and tie the goblins to the branches.

BLACK CAT MOBILE

(plastic food container, yarn, cardboard egg carton, poster paint, construction paper)

1. For the top section, cut a ring from a plastic food container. Punch four evenly spaced holes near the top of the ring. Insert a piece of yarn through each hole, tying a knot at the end. Gather the four pieces at the top, and tie them together into one knot.

2. Cut out five egg-carton sections and make them into the shapes of cats' heads, as shown. Paint them black. Add whiskers and eyes with paper and glue. Poke a hole in the top of each cat's head.

3. On the bottom of the ring, punch five evenly spaced holes. Thread a piece of yarn through each cat's head and through a hole in the ring. Tie a knot at each end.

4. Glue a piece of black paper to cover the back of each head. Add paper ears.

PUMPKIN PIN

(frozen-juice pull-top lid, felt, safety pin)

1. Place a frozen-juice pull-top lid on a piece of felt, and trace around it with a pencil. Do this again and cut out the two circles.

2. Glue one felt circle to each side of the lid.

3. Cut out a mouth, a nose, eyes, and a stem from pieces of felt, and glue them in place.

4. On the other side, glue or tape a safety pin.

BAT ERASER
(pencil, rubber eraser cap, permanent marker, construction paper)

1. Place a rubber eraser cap on the top of a pencil. With scissors, cut out a small notch at the top of the eraser to form two pointed ears.

2. Color the eraser black with a permanent marker.

3. Cut out bat wings from construction paper. Glue the wings to the back of the eraser and let dry. Cut out small paper eyes, and glue them to the bat.

FLASHY JACK-O'-LANTERN
(brown paper bag, flashlight)

1. Place a brown paper bag on a table, with the open end at the bottom.

2. Draw and cut out a pumpkin face on the bag.

3. At night, place the bag over a small flashlight. See the pumpkin glow in the dark!

SCARECROW
(one medium and one small brown paper bag, newspaper, straw hat, construction paper)

1. For the body, use a medium-size brown paper bag. For the arms, roll a few sheets of newspaper into a tube. Poke a hole in each side of the bag near the top, and push the arms through. Stuff the body with crumpled newspaper, fold the opening closed, and staple it shut.

2. For the head, use a small paper bag stuffed with newspaper. Twist and tape the bag shut. Make a small hole in the body and insert the twisted end of the head into the hole. Use tape to hold it in place.

3. Roll a few sheets of newspaper into two small tubes for the legs. Poke two holes in the bottom of the body and insert the legs. Add tape to hold them in place.

4. Glue on cut paper for features and patches. Cut and glue paper hay for the feet, hands, neck, and head. Add an old straw hat.

GHOSTLY GREETINGS
(black construction paper, white crayon, white plastic bread wrapper)

1. Fold a piece of black construction paper into quarters to make a card.

2. Use white crayon to draw the outline of a ghost on the front of the card. Open the card and cut the ghost outline out of the card.

3. Tape a piece of white plastic cut from a bread wrapper behind the cutout ghost so that when the card is refolded the white plastic shows through the front of the card. Cut black paper dot eyes and a mouth and glue to the ghost.

4. On the front of the card, use white crayon to write "Boo!" On the inside of the card, write a message and your name.

SPIN-A-WEB BRACELET
(wide plastic ribbon holder, felt, yarn, sequins, heavy black thread on a spool)

1. Glue a piece of white felt around a wide plastic ribbon holder.

2. Cut the body of a spider from felt. Glue on yarn legs. Add sequins for eyes. Glue the spider on the white felt.

3. Tape the end of heavy black thread to the inside of the holder. Holding the spool of thread in your hand, wrap thread around the inside and outside of the holder to look like a spider's web. Cut the thread and tape the end.

COLONIAL WIG
(brown paper bag, cotton balls, ribbon)

1. Find a brown paper bag that will fit on your head.

2. Cut the bag in the shape of a wig, as shown. Cut out a ponytail from the leftover paper, and glue it to the back of the wig.

3. Spread some glue over a section of the wig, and press cotton balls into it until the wig and ponytail are covered.

4. Tie a piece of ribbon around the ponytail and make a bow.

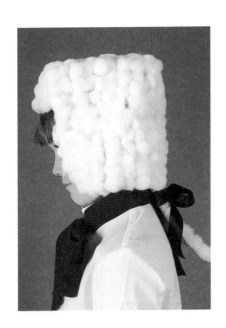

EGG-CARTON WITCH
(cardboard egg carton, construction paper, yarn)

1. For the witch's head, cut four adjoining sections from a cardboard egg carton.

2. Using the inside of the carton as the face, glue on eyes, a mouth, and a wart. Add a black construction-paper hat to the back of the cardboard egg carton.

3. Glue long pieces of black yarn over the top of the witch's head, letting it hang down around her face.

4. Add a yarn hanger to the back of the witch.

GHOST-IN-A-BOX
(cotton balls, facial tissue, rubber band, metal bandage box, paper)

1. To make the ghost, center two or three cotton balls in two facial tissues. Place a small rubber band around the bottom of the tissue ball to form the ghost's neck. Draw a face with a marker.

2. Place the ghost's body into a metal bandage box. Tape the back of the ghost's head to the inside lid of the box. Close the lid gently, tucking the head into the box.

3. Decorate the outside of the metal bandage box with paper to give the ghost a home. Pull open the lid and the ghost will pop up.

OWL TREE
(plastic food container, tree branch, clay, small stones, paper, hemlock pinecones, plastic food wrap)

1. Place a fallen tree branch into a plastic food container filled with small stones and clay. Decorate the outside with paper.

2. To make owls, decorate the hemlock pinecones with paper eyes and beaks.

3. Glue the owls to the fallen tree branch. To help hold them in place, wrap a small piece of plastic food wrap around them. Remove the wrap when almost dry.

JUMPING CRITTER
(cardboard egg carton, dried beans, poster paint, paper, elastic, button)

1. For the body, cut two egg cups from a cardboard egg carton. Glue the two cups together with a few dried beans inside.

2. Paint the body with poster paint and let dry. Add eyes, a nose, a mouth, and hair from pieces of paper.

3. Glue a long piece of elastic to the top. Thread the other end through the holes of a button and tie a knot. Slip the button between your fingers and make the critter jump.

HALLOWEEN CAT
(construction paper)

1. Cut a piece of black construction paper about 5 inches by 8 inches. Measure 2 inches down on the long side and draw a line across the paper.

2. In the center above the 2-inch line, draw the head of a cat. Cut along the line and the outline of the cat. Roll the paper cat into a tube and tape the edges together.

3. Cut and glue on eyes, a nose, a mouth, and whiskers. Cut claws and two paws from paper and tape them to the bottom of the paper tube.

4. For the tail, glue the ends of two long, narrow strips of paper together at a right angle, as shown. Then fold one strip across the other alternately, as shown by the arrows.

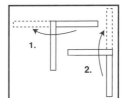

Continue until almost at the end, then cut tiny strips for fringe. Glue the other end to the cat.

PUMPKIN BOOKMARK
(construction paper)

1. Cut a long stem from green construction paper.

2. Cut small orange pumpkins, and glue them on the stem.

3. On a pumpkin, write the name of a book you have read during the Halloween season. Add a book title to each pumpkin after you have read other books.

Papier-Mâché Masks

These masks are created with papier-mâché. Simply mix flour and water together until it is the consistency of ketchup. Tear strips of newspaper or paper towel and dip them into the mixture. Pull them through your fingers to remove excess mixture. Layer the strips to create the mask. Allow a day or two for the papier-mâché to dry before painting.

CAT
(large heavy paper plate, lightweight cardboard, papier-mâché, poster paint, elastic)

1. Facing the outside bottom of a large heavy paper plate, trim the plate to form the cat's head. Cut ears from lightweight cardboard and staple in place. Cover with papier-mâché.

2. To make the nose and cheeks, cover small wads of paper with papier-mâché. Add a small papier-mâché tongue. Let dry.

3. Add features with poster paint. Cut out eyeholes, and staple elastic to opposite sides of the mask to fit around your head.

SUN
(large heavy paper plate, lightweight cardboard, papier-mâché, poster paint, elastic)

1. Use the outside bottom of a large heavy paper plate for the sun. To make rays, cut triangular pieces from lightweight cardboard, and staple them around the sun.

2. Cover the entire sun with papier-mâché, adding rolled pieces of papier-mâché to create eyebrows and a mouth. Let dry.

3. Paint with poster paint and let dry. Cut out eyeholes. Staple a piece of elastic to opposite sides of the mask to fit around your head.

ALIEN
(cardboard cereal box, small boxes, thread spool, papier-mâché, poster paint, toothpicks, paper, elastic)

1. Remove the back and bottom sections from a cardboard cereal box. Tape the top flaps closed. Tape on small boxes to form features. Add a thread spool for a nose. Cover with papier-mâché and let dry.

2. Paint with poster paint. Add toothpicks to the nose and curled pieces of paper for hair. Cut out eyeholes, and staple a piece of elastic to opposite sides of the mask to fit around your head.

BEAR
(large heavy paper plate, lightweight cardboard, small heavy paper bowl, papier-mâché, poster paint, elastic)

1. To make the snout of the bear, turn over a small heavy paper bowl, and place on top of the outside bottom of a large heavy paper plate. Tape it on the plate. Cut small ears from pieces of lightweight cardboard, and staple them to the plate.

2. Cover with papier-mâché, adding rolled pieces of papier-mâché to form the eyebrows. Let dry.

3. Paint and let dry. Add features with poster paint. Let dry. Cut out eyeholes. Staple a piece of elastic to opposite sides of the mask to fit around your head.

WITCH
(cardboard candy box, papier-mâché, poster paint, elastic)

1. Use the outside of a cardboard candy box with a lid to create the witch. Cut and tape together, as shown.

2. Cover the box and lid with papier-mâché. To make the nose, cover a wad of paper with papier-mâché. Add strips of papier-mâché to create eyebrows and a mouth. Fold a strip of papier-mâché for cheeks.

3. Paint the features with poster paint and let dry. Cut out eyeholes. Staple a piece of elastic to opposite sides of the mask to fit around your head.

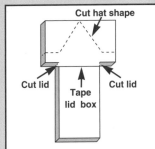

MOUSE
(large heavy paper plate, three small paper plates, papier-mâché, poster paint, elastic)

1. Use the outside bottom of a large heavy paper plate for the face of the mouse. To make ears, staple two small paper plates, right-side up, to the large plate.

2. To make the nose, cut a small section from a small paper plate, as shown. Bend it to form the point of a nose, and tape it in place on the face. Cover the nose, ears, and face with papier-mâché and let dry.

3. Decorate with poster paint, adding features, and let dry. Cut out eyeholes. Staple a piece of elastic to opposite sides of the mask to fit around your head.

Cut on dotted line.

FLYING BAT
(black poster board, black elastic, heavy black thread)

1. Fold a large piece of black poster board in half.

2. With the board folded, draw and cut out half a bat shape.

3. Staple the end of a piece of black elastic, like the kind used on masks, to each wing. Tie a piece of heavy black thread to the middle of the elastic.

4. Bounce the bat to make it "fly."

BIG EYES
(7-inch paper plates, construction paper, frame from an old pair of plastic eyeglasses)

1. Glue and tape two 7-inch paper plates together, side by side. Cut large eyes and eyelids from construction paper, and glue them in place.

2. Hold the paper-plate eyes up to your face and have an adult help mark a place for your eyes. Remove from your face. Cut or punch eyeholes on the marks.

3. Tape a frame from an old pair of plastic eyeglasses to the back of the big eyes so they will be easy to wear.

PARTY HAT
(10-inch heavy paper plate, poster paint, yarn)

1. Cut from the edge to the center of a 10-inch heavy paper plate. Pull one cut edge over the other to form a cone-shaped hat. Staple in place.

2. Paint Halloween decorations on the hat and let dry.

3. Cut twenty to thirty short pieces of yarn. Tie together in the center. Glue to the top of the hat for a pompon.

4. Punch one hole on opposite sides of the base of the hat, and attach a piece of yarn for a tie.

HALLOWEEN CANDY HOLDER
(round cardboard food container with plastic lid, aluminum foil, construction paper, small aluminum pie tin, brass fastener, chenille stick)

1. Remove the plastic lid from a round cardboard food container. Cover the container with aluminum foil. Decorate it with pieces of construction paper.

2. Using a brass fastener, attach the center of a small aluminum pie tin to the center of the plastic lid.

3. To make a flower, cut circles of different-colored paper. Hold them together and punch two holes in the center, like a button. Thread a chenille stick through the holes, and twist in the back to make a stem.

4. Punch two holes in the side of the aluminum pie tin, and fasten the stem of the flower.

5. Fill the cardboard container with candy. Put some candy in the aluminum pie tin, and place the lid on top of the container.

HALLOWEEN GOURD
(small gourd, construction paper, yarn, pompon)

1. Wash and dry a small gourd. Cut and glue on pieces of construction paper to create a face on the lower half.

2. Spread a line of glue around the gourd above the face. Cut small pieces of black yarn. Press the yarn into the glue to create hair.

3. Glue a black pompon at the tip of the gourd. Add a loop of yarn for a hanger.

SPIDER CARD
(white poster board, black yarn, construction paper)

1. Fold a 6-by-8-inch piece of white poster board in half to make a card. With the fold at the top, find the center of the front of the card. Draw a circle, 1 1/2 inches in diameter, and cut it out.

2. With the card still folded, draw around the circle, making an outline on the inside of the card.

3. Open the card. Spread glue in the circle, and cover it with yarn by going around in a spiral until the circle is covered. This is the spider's body.

4. Add eight legs to the body using pieces of yarn. Add a paper head and eyes. Write "HAPPY HALLOWEEN." Close the card, and all you will see is the spider's body.

SPOOKY PLACE CARD
(paper, permanent marker, pennies, drinking straw)

1. Draw and cut out a ghost shape from paper. Draw eyes and a mouth. Outline the edges of the ghost with a permanent marker. Punch a hole in the mouth of the ghost.

2. Glue a penny under each "hand."

3. Put the straw through the ghost's mouth, letting the body of the ghost rest on the rim of the glass.

HALLOWEEN PLACE MAT
(white poster board, clear self-adhesive paper)

1. Cut a large rectangle from a piece of white poster board. With markers, draw a Halloween scene.

2. Have an adult help you cover your scene with clear self-adhesive paper. Fold the extra paper to the back of the board or trim at the edges.

3. Reuse your place mat by cleaning it with a damp cloth.

WITCH PIN
(cardboard, yellow and black felt, dried grass, sequin, safety pin)

1. Cut out two 2 1/2-inch circles, one from lightweight cardboard and one from black felt. Glue them together.

2. Cut a slightly smaller circle from yellow felt and glue it to the center of the black circle.

3. From black felt, draw and cut out a witch that will fit on the yellow felt circle.

4. Use pieces of dried grass to make a broom and glue it to the yellow circle. Glue the witch on top of the broom.

5. Add a sequin eye. Glue a small safety pin to the back.

TUBE GHOST FAMILY

(corrugated cardboard, paper, paper towel tubes, facial tissue)

1. To make the base, cut out a piece of corrugated cardboard. Trace around the shape on a piece of black paper and cut it out. Glue the paper on top of the cardboard.

2. For each body, cut a paper towel tube in a different length. Glue or tape white paper around each tube.

3. For each head, roll facial tissue into a small ball. Place two facial tissues over the ball as smoothly as possible, and tape together at the bottom of the ball.

4. Glue the heads to the bodies. Add black paper eyes and mouths.

BLACK-BEAN CAT

(poster board, black beans, kidney beans, pumpkin seeds, dried green peas, broom straw, yarn)

1. Draw and cut out a cat shape from black poster board. Glue black beans on it for the body.

2. Add pumpkin seeds and dried green peas for eyes. Use a pumpkin seed for a nose and two kidney beans for the mouth. Cut small pieces of broom straw for whiskers.

3. After all the seeds and beans have dried, glue the cat on a large piece of orange poster board. Add a yarn hanger to the back.

BONE NECKLACE

(2 cups flour, 1 cup salt, 1 cup cold water, bowl, spoon, waxed paper, plastic drinking straw, cookie tray, oven mitts, shoestring)

1. In a bowl, stir together the flour, salt, and water. Knead, or work the mixture together with your hands, until it forms a smooth dough.

2. Place a small amount of flour on a piece of waxed paper. Roll some of the dough into small balls. Press to flatten them slightly. Use a plastic drinking straw to poke a hole in the center of each shape. Shape larger dough pieces, poking holes in some of them.

3. Have an adult help you dry the dough pieces in a 325°F oven for one to two hours or until they feel hard to the touch. Remove from the tray, and place them on a wire rack to cool.

4. Tie a large-shaped bone in the middle of the shoestring, and string smaller ones on each side of it. Tie a bow at the ends.

53

SCARECROW PUPPET
(three plastic drinking straws, tongue depressor, felt, straw)

1. Cut three plastic drinking straws in half. Glue three pieces to a tongue depressor vertically for the body and three horizontally for the arms. Leave space at the top of the tongue depressor for a head and space at the bottom for feet.

2. Fold a piece of felt in half, and cut out a coat shape. Cut a small slit in the fold for a neck opening, and slip the coat over the head of the body. Glue the coat in place, stuffing a few pieces of straw at the hands and feet. Add felt buttons.

3. Cut a felt hat and a round piece of felt for the head. Glue in place. Add a few pieces of straw, and draw on a face with a marker.

CREPE-PAPER BUG
(crepe paper, thread, poster board, sequins)

1. Wrap a 1 3/4-by-6-inch piece of crepe paper around a pencil, and glue in place. Let dry.

2. Push the ends of the paper toward the center of the pencil to crush. Remove the pencil. At one end, tie off a head section with thread. Stuff a small ball of crepe paper in this part for the head, and glue to close.

3. Cut a strip of poster board as long as the bug from neck to tail. Cut legs from both sides of the strip and bend down. Glue the body to the legs.

4. Add sequins to the body and to the head for eyes.

TUBE SURPRISE
(bathroom tissue tube, tissue paper, yarn, paper)

1. Place some wrapped candies inside a bathroom tissue tube.

2. Cut a piece of orange tissue paper so it will measure at least 3 inches beyond each tube end.

3. Wrap the tissue paper around the tube, and close the ends with pieces of yarn.

4. Cut a bone shape from paper, and glue on the tube.

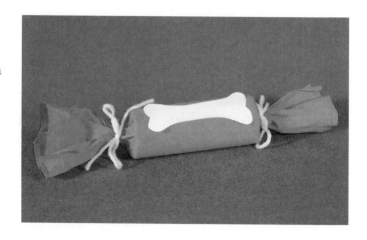

HOLIDAY PLATE COVER
(two heavy paper plates, poster paint, cotton balls, construction paper, moveable plastic eyes)

1. Paint the outside of one heavy paper plate with poster paint and let dry.

2. Glue cotton balls on top to make ghosts. Add moveable plastic eyes.

3. Cut pieces of construction paper to make pumpkins with cutout faces and leaves.

4. Place cookies or other treats on the undecorated paper plate. Use the decorated plate to cover the treats.

PUMPKIN-SEED BOX
(small cardboard jewelry box, pumpkin seeds, clear nail polish)

1. Glue pumpkin seeds around the outer edge of the box lid to form a design. Glue seeds to the top of the box lid, again forming a design.

2. After the seeds have dried, cover them with a coat of clear nail polish to give them a nice shine.

PUMPKIN TREAT HOLDER
(small cardboard food container with lid, construction paper, chenille stick)

1. Glue orange construction paper to the outside of a small cardboard food container and its lid. Cut out paper features for a jack-o'-lantern face, and glue them to the container.

2. Add a green leaf to the middle of the lid. Punch two holes in the lid, making it look like a button, and insert a chenille stick. Twist it together to form a stem.

3. Store treats inside the holder.

BLACK-CAT STICK PUPPET
(ice-cream stick, construction paper, yarn)

1. Cut four identical circles from black construction paper. Glue two circles to one side of an ice-cream stick and two to the other side to form the body and head of the cat.

2. Cut ears, eyes, and a mouth from paper, and glue to the head.

3. Glue pieces of black yarn to the face to make whiskers, and add a piece to the back of the cat for a tail.

WITCH'S HAT
(black poster board)

1. Draw a large circle about 14 to 18 inches in diameter on a piece of large black poster board. Draw a circle in the center about 5 to 8 inches in diameter. (The size really depends on how large your head is.)

2. Cut out the small center circle. Cut tabs along the inside edge, as shown.

3. Draw another circle about 9 to 12 inches in diameter on black poster board. Cut a section from the circle, as shown in the diagram. Roll the section into a cone shape, fitting it over the tabs of the brim.

4. Use transparent tape to hold the cone shape together. Tape the tabs to the inside of the cone.

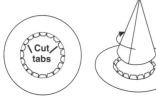

JACK-O'-LANTERN SPECTACLES
(poster board, chenille sticks)

1. For the lenses of the spectacles, cut two circles from a piece of orange poster board. Draw two off-center circles on the lenses for the eyes, and cut them out.

2. Draw black triangle-shaped eyes, a nose, and a big smiling mouth in the area next to each eyehole.

3. Cut a small piece of chenille stick, and glue it to the lenses to make the nosepiece.

4. For the earpieces, punch a hole on opposite sides of the spectacles. Insert a chenille stick into each hole. Twist the ends together. Be sure they are long enough to fit comfortably over your ears.

GHOST STATIONERY

(potato, table knife, black construction paper, white paint, white crayon)

1. Wash and dry a potato. Cut the potato in half. Trace around the potato half, with the cut-side down, on a piece of paper. Cut it out. Draw a ghost on the potato tracing and cut it out.

2. Place the ghost pattern on the cut-side of the potato. Have an adult help you use the table knife to cut away the area around the ghost, leaving it about 1/2 inch higher than the rest of the potato.

3. Paint the ghost design with white paint, and press it onto a piece of black construction paper. Repeat the painting and printing until you have the design you want. Let dry.

4. Write a message with a white crayon.

PUMPKIN DECORATION

(two heavy paper plates, poster paint, tissue paper, felt, plastic-foam tray)

1. Draw eyes, a nose, and a mouth, making a pumpkin face on one heavy paper plate. Cut them out. Place the paper plate on top of the second plate, trace around the openings, and cut them out.

2. Paint the outside of each plate orange, and glue a piece of yellow tissue over the facial features on the inside of the plates. Glue the plates together, rim to rim with the painted sides facing out.

3. Make a slot in a green plastic-foam tray. Stand the pumpkin in the tray. Add glue and let dry.

4. Add a felt stem to the top of the pumpkin, and glue leaves around the base.

5. Place the pumpkin where light can shine through it.

REFLECTIVE HALLOWEEN WAND

(aluminum pie pan, wooden dowel, paper)

1. Punch a hole in the side of an aluminum pie pan. Push a wooden dowel through the hole and to the other side. Glue or tape the dowel in place.

2. Decorate the bottom of the pie pan with paper to create a black cat. Add paper-punch dots around the rim of the pie pan.

NAPKIN HOLDER
(plastic food container, construction paper)

1. Cut a 2-inch section, starting at the top, on each side of a plastic food container, as shown.

2. Use pieces of construction paper to make the outside of the holder look like a pumpkin.

3. Place paper napkins in the cutout section.

LEAF PICTURE
(fallen leaves, construction paper)

1. Select various kinds of leaves, and glue them on a piece of construction paper.

2. Use markers to draw lines around the leaves to create witches, cats, or other Halloween things, and finish the scene.

OWL MOBILE
(lightweight cardboard, brown paper bag, construction paper, yarn, pinecones)

1. Cut an owl head from lightweight cardboard. Cover it with a piece of brown paper bag. Trim around the edges. Add two big round eyes and a triangular beak from construction paper.

2. Punch a hole at the top between the eyes, and add a loop of yarn for a hanger.

3. Glue eyes and a beak on each of four pinecones to make little owls. Glue a piece of yarn to the top of each one.

4. Punch two holes on each side of the big owl's beak. Tie a little owl to each hole.

TRICK-OR-TREAT BAG
(construction paper, large brown paper bag)

1. Glue a half-sheet of construction paper on each wide side of a large brown paper bag, as shown. Let dry.

2. Draw a handle on each piece of paper, across the center of the bag. Cut around the outside and inside of the handles and around the sides of the bag.

3. Use crayons, markers, cut paper, or stickers to decorate the outside of the bag.

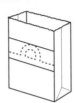

TRIANGLES-AND-CIRCLES WITCH
(construction paper, yarn)

1. Cut a triangle from black paper for the witch's body. Cut a circle from light-colored paper for the head.

2. Use a marker to draw a face. Glue on some yarn hair, and glue the head to the body.

3. Cut a smaller black triangle for the hat and glue it on.

4. Cut a big circle from yellow paper for the moon, and glue it in back of the witch.

HOLIDAY PIN
(lightweight cardboard, felt, small bottle tops, safety pin)

1. Cut a shape from lightweight cardboard. Cover it with glue and a piece of felt. Let dry and trim around the edge.

2. Glue small bottle tops on top of the felt. Use felt to decorate the bottle tops as holiday characters.

3. Glue or tape a safety pin to the back.

Paper-Bag Masks

These masks are simple to make using large paper bags. Put your imagination to work, and create something funny or scary, or a favorite animal.

CHICK
(large paper bag, construction paper)

1. Measure about 6 inches from the opening of a large paper bag, and cut around the entire bag. Set aside the cut section.

2. Put the bag on your head. Using a crayon, have a friend carefully mark where the eyeholes should be on the outside of the bag. Remove the bag.

3. Cut out and glue facial features on the chick, but make large eyes. Cut out holes for the eyes. Add curled strips of paper to the top of the chick head.

PUPPY DOG
(large paper bag, construction paper, yarn)

1. Cut off 6 inches from the opening of a large paper bag. Glue construction paper to one large side of the bag.

2. From paper, cut out and glue a head, a nose, a mouth, and two eyes. Add yarn whiskers.

3. Put the bag on your head. Have a friend mark with a crayon where the eyeholes should be. Remove the bag and cut out the eyeholes.

CLOWN
(large paper bag, construction paper, heavy paper plate, poster paint, large plastic bottle top, old newspaper)

1. Cut off 6 inches from the opening of a large paper bag. Set aside the cut section.

2. Put the bag on your head. Using a crayon, have a friend carefully mark where the eyeholes should be on the outside of the bag. Remove the bag. Cut and glue pieces of construction paper to make eyebrows, large eyes with glasses, a nose, a mouth, ears, and a beard. Cut out the eyeholes.

3. Glue a large plastic bottle top in the middle of a painted heavy paper plate. Glue on top of the clown's head.

HIPPOPOTAMUS
(large paper bag, construction paper, crayons, markers)

1. Measure down about 6 inches from the opening of a large paper bag, and cut around the entire bag. Set aside the cut section.

2. Using a piece of light-colored construction paper about the same size as one side of the paper bag, draw the opened mouth of a hippopotamus. Color it with crayons and markers.

3. Glue the hippopotamus face to the paper bag. Put the bag on your head. Using a crayon, have a friend carefully mark where the eyeholes should be on the outside of the bag. Remove the bag and cut out the eyeholes.

4. Add cut-paper flowers around the hippopotamus's head. Trim the bag around the bottom of the head and mouth with scissors.

FROG
(large paper bag, construction paper)

1. Measure about 6 inches from the opening of a large paper bag, and cut around the entire bag. Set aside the cut section.

2. Cover one large side of the paper bag with construction paper, gluing it in place.

3. To make the frog and lily pad, draw and cut pieces from construction paper and glue them in place.

4. Put the bag on your head. Using a crayon, have a friend carefully mark where the eyeholes should be on the outside of the bag. Remove the bag and cut out the eyeholes.

GOBLIN
(large paper bag, rubber band, yarn, construction paper)

1. Cut through the center of the bottom of a large paper bag and along the sides, as shown. Open the flaps. Make fringe with scissors by cutting strips to the folds. Secure the bag below the strips with a rubber band and tie on pieces of black yarn.

2. From construction paper, cut and glue facial features and fringe. With the bag on your head, have a friend carefully mark where the eyeholes should be. Remove the bag and cut out the eyeholes.

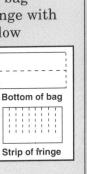

Bottom of bag

Strip of fringe

MATERIAL INDEX

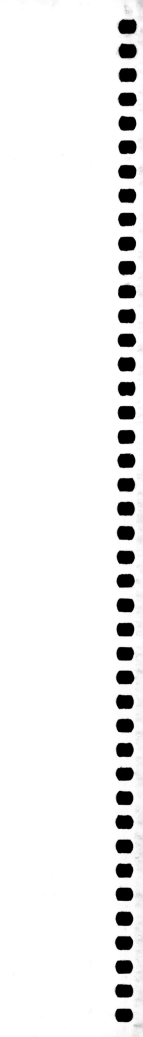

175 Easy-to-Do
THANKSGIVING
CRAFTS

Edited by
Sharon Dunn Umnik

175 Easy-to-Do THANKSGIVING CRAFTS

Edited by Sharon Dunn Umnik

BOYDS MILLS PRESS

Inside this book...

you'll find a fabulous assortment of crafts made from recyclable items and inexpensive things found in or around your house. Have pencils, crayons, scissors, tape, paintbrushes, and other supplies for craft making close by. —*the Editor*

Published by Bell Books
Boyds Mills Press, Inc.
A Highlights Company
815 Church Street
Honesdale, Pennsylvania 18431
Printed in China

Publisher Cataloging-in-Publication Data
175 easy-to-do Thanksgiving crafts : creative uses for recyclables / edited by
Sharon Dunn Umnik.—1st ed.
[64]p. : col. ill. ;   cm.
Summary : Includes step-by-step directions to make craft items such as
Pilgrims, holiday-table accessories, turkeys, and more.
ISBN 1-56397-374-X
1. Thanksgiving Day—Juvenile literature. 2. Handicraft—Juvenile literature.
[1. Thanksgiving Day. 2. Handicraft.]
I. Umnik, Sharon Dunn. II. Title.
745.59—dc20   1996   CIP
Library of Congress Catalog Card Number 95-80773

First edition, 1996
Book designed by Charlie Cary
The text of this book is set in 11-point New Century Schoolbook

10 9 8 7 6 5

Craft Contributors: Patricia Barley, Laura G. Beer, B.J. Benish, Beverly Blasucci, Linda Bloomgren, Judy Burke, Norma Jean Byrkett, G.L. Carty, Jeanne Corrigan, Linda Douglas, Linda Faulkner, Virginia Follis, Sandra Godfrey, Mavis Grant, Paula Hamilton, Edna Harrington, Amanda Hepburn, Olive Howie, Garnett Kooker, Chris R. Kueng, Twilla Lamm, Lee Lindeman, Agnes Maddy, John McDowell, June Rose Mobly, Betsy Ochester, Joan O'Donnell, Helen M. Pedersen, James W. Perrin Jr., Luella Pierce, Louise Poe, Simone Quick, Linda Rindock, Kathy Ross, Helen R. Sattler, Karen Bornemann Spies, June Swanson, Beth Tobler, Sharon Dunn Umnik, Jean White, Janine M. Williams, and Rebecca D. Zurawski.

Table Dress-ups

Add a festive touch to your Thanksgiving table with these apple harvest decorations.

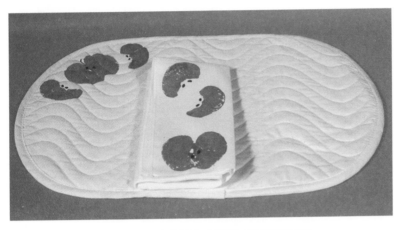

PLACE MAT AND NAPKIN
(old newspaper, apple, table knife, fabric paint, paper plate, white fabric place mat and napkin)

1. Cover your work surface with old newspaper. Cut an apple in half using a table knife. Then cut one half into quarters.

2. Squeeze some fabric paint onto a paper plate. Brush paint on one side of a quarter piece of apple or on an apple half.

3. Press the painted side of the apple section on a white fabric place mat and napkin, creating a decorative print.

4. Wash your brush. Follow the directions on the fabric-paint label for drying.

CENTERPIECE
(two apples, two candles, plastic lids, table knife)

1. *Ask an adult to help you* cut a hole from the center of two apples, large enough to hold a candle.

2. Cut feathers from different-colored plastic lids. Use a table knife to cut small slits in the apples, and insert the feathers to create a tail.

3. For each apple, draw and cut out a neck, head, and wattle from a plastic lid. Add features. Cut slits and insert the heads.

4. Place the turkeys in the center of your holiday table.

NAPKIN RING
(cardboard tube, tempera paint, poster board)

1. To make the ring, cut a 1-inch section from a cardboard tube. Paint it to look like tree bark.

2. Draw and cut out an apple from red poster board. Add a green leaf. Glue the apple to the ring and let dry.

3. Place a napkin through the ring.

HARVEST WREATH
(sixteen ice-cream sticks, watercolors, construction paper, string)

1. Paint sixteen ice-cream sticks with brown watercolor. Let dry. Glue the sticks together in pairs to form X shapes.

2. Arrange the Xs in a wreath shape and glue them together, end to end.

3. Glue a cut-paper bow, fruit, and vegetables to the wreath.

4. Tie a piece of string on the back of the wreath as a hanger.

THANKSGIVING CARD
(poster board)

1. Fold a piece of poster board in half. Place your hand on the board with the longest finger touching the fold.

2. Trace around your hand with a pencil. Leaving the connection at the longest finger, cut out the hand shape.

3. Write a holiday message on the inside or the front of the hand. Stand the card up.

PUMPKIN PIE GAME
(paper plate, one die, paper, pencil)

1. Color a paper plate to look like a pumpkin pie. Cut the pie into six equal pieces, and number each piece from one through six.

To play: The first player throws the die three times. After each throw, the player removes the numbered piece of pie that matches the number on the die. Add the numbers of the pieces removed, and write the total on a score sheet. If the player rolls a duplicate number, the turn is over and the player gets no points in that round.

  After each player's turn, put the pie back together. The player with the highest score after four rounds is the winner.

RING TURKEY
(cardboard tubes, poster paint, construction paper)

1. Cut seven rings from a cardboard tube, each about 1/2 inch wide, to make the feet and tail feathers.

2. Cut another section about 2 1/2 inches wide for the body and one about 1 inch wide for the head.

3. Paint the cardboard sections. Glue them together, as shown. Cut eyes, a beak, and a wattle from construction paper. Glue them onto the turkey.

FEEDING STATION FOR BIRDS
(one-liter plastic beverage bottle, pencil, paper, bird seed, string)

1. On each side of the bottom plastic section of a one-liter plastic beverage bottle, cut a tab about 1 inch wide with scissors. Bend down the tabs, and using a paper punch, make a hole in the center of each one. Push a pencil through the holes for a perch.

2. To make the feeding holes, press a crease along each side of the bottle above the two ends of the pencil perch. Hold the crease in place, and punch a hole on the crease about 2 or 3 inches above the perch.

3. Roll a piece of paper into a cone shape, and place it in the top of the bottle to use as a funnel. Add seeds to the bottle and cap it tightly.

4. Knot string several times around the lip of the bottle just below the cap. Tie the feeder to a tree branch.

LEAF DISH
(white paper, plastic bowl, paint, permanent marker, floor wax, soft cloth)

1. Draw and cut out a large leaf shape from white paper. Trace around it, making three more leaves, all the same size. Glue all four leaves on top of one another, with the edges touching.

2. While the glue is still damp, center the leaf over an upside-down plastic bowl. Gently press the sides around the bowl to form a shallow dish. Let dry.

3. Paint the dish in fall colors. Draw dark veins, as shown, with a permanent marker.

4. *Ask an adult to help you* rub a thin coat of floor wax on the dish to make it shine. Polish with a soft cloth.

TURKEY NAPKIN HOLDER
(half-gallon milk carton, construction paper)

1. Cut off the top, bottom, and one side of an empty half-gallon milk carton. Glue brown construction paper to the outside of the carton. Then staple a strip of paper to each open end.

2. Cut out the turkey's head and feathers from colorful paper. Glue them in place on one side of the holder. Use a marker to add details to the face.

3. Place napkins inside the holder.

PILGRIM BOY AND GIRL
(construction paper, yarn)

1. To make the boy, cut three large strips from construction paper for his body. Cut a circle for his head, and glue it to the top of the body. Add hands, boots, collar, hat, and buttons made from paper. Cut pieces of yarn for hair and glue them to his head. Draw facial features with markers.

2. To make the girl, cut a large triangle from paper for her body. Cut a circle for her head, and glue it to the top of the body. Add arms, hands, boots, hat, and a bib-apron from paper. Draw facial features with markers.

3. Attach a yarn hanger to the back of the girl and the boy.

PARCHMENT PAPER
(bowl, warm tap water, two tea bags, white paper, paper towels, ribbon)

1. Add warm tap water to a bowl. Place two tea bags in the water until it has turned a dark color, then remove the bags.

2. Gently crumple a piece of white paper. Place it in the bowl, using a spoon to hold it down in the tea-colored water. Let the paper soak about fifteen minutes until it becomes a light brown color.

3. Carefully pour the water in a sink and remove the paper, letting the water drip off. Place the paper on paper towels and let it dry thoroughly. The color should vary throughout the paper when dry.

4. Write your message on the paper. Then roll it up, and tie it with ribbon.

NUTTY NOTEPAD
(tan and brown paper, cardboard, white paper)

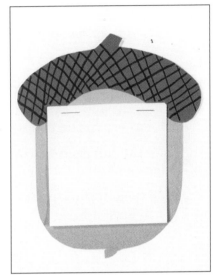

1. Glue tan paper onto a piece of cardboard, and cut it to measure 5 inches square.

2. Draw an acorn shape on the square with a pencil, and cut it out. Draw and cut out an acorn-cap shape from brown paper, and glue it to the acorn. Add lines to the acorn cap with a marker.

3. Cut ten or more 3-inch squares of white paper to fit onto the acorn shape. Stack the papers together, put them in the center of the acorn, and staple in place.

AN AUTUMN DISPLAY
(round cardboard container, paper, old magazine, dried flowers and weeds)

1. Spread glue on the outside of a round cardboard container, such as one that holds oatmeal, and cover with paper.

2. Turn the bottom right-side up. Decorate the container with a picture cut from an old magazine.

3. Poke small holes in the bottom, and place dried flowers or dried weeds into the holes.

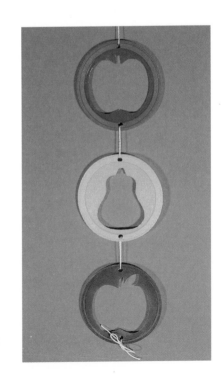

FRUIT WALL HANGING
(plastic lids, string)

1. Draw apple and pear shapes on different-colored plastic lids. Bend the lids slightly in half and carefully cut out the fruit shapes.

2. Punch a hole in each lid above and below the shape. Tie the lids together with pieces of string.

3. Attach a long string at the top for a hanger. Tie a string bow in the bottom hole of the last fruit shape. Hang the decoration on a wall.

TISSUE TURKEY
(paper plate, construction paper, tissue paper, yarn)

1. Cut out the center of a 9-inch paper plate, leaving a 2-inch rim. Turn the rim over so the bottom faces up.

2. Draw and cut out a turkey's head and feet from construction paper. Glue these to the rim.

3. To make the tail section, cut round pieces of different-colored tissue paper and glue them onto the rim.

4. Punch a hole in the rim, thread a piece of yarn through it, and tie a knot to form a hanger.

LEATHER-LIKE JOURNAL
(cardboard, masking tape, soft cloth, brown shoe polish, paper, leather shoelace)

1. To make the front and back of the journal, cover both sides of two 8 1/2-by-11-inch pieces of cardboard with small torn pieces of masking tape. Using a soft cloth, rub brown shoe polish over the masking tape, giving it a rough, leather-like look.

2. With a paper punch, punch two holes in each cover, as shown. Punch holes in several 8 1/2-by-11-inch pieces of paper, making sure all the holes line up.

3. Place the sheets of paper between the covers. Thread a leather shoelace through the holes and tie a bow.

4. Make an entry every day in your journal. Add more sheets of paper as you need them.

FRUIT BOWL
(round cardboard container, construction paper, cardboard-box lid, paper doily)

1. To make the bowl, cut a round cardboard container in half lengthwise, including the lid and bottom. Cover the container with glue and construction paper.

2. To make the base, cover a cardboard-box lid with construction paper.

3. Decorate the bowl and base with pieces from a paper doily. Glue the bowl and base together and let dry. Fill the bowl with fruit, and set it in the middle of your table.

EGG-CARTON HEADS
(cardboard egg carton, poster paint, construction paper, yarn)

1. Cut the cups from a cardboard egg carton. Glue two together to make each head. Glue another to the bottom for the shoulders. Paint them and let dry.

2. Cut facial features from construction paper, and glue in place. Add a yarn bow and a white paper shirt.

3. Glue on yarn hair. Cut hats from other parts of the carton. Paint them and attach with glue.

FABRIC-LEAF MOBILE
(fabric, poster board, string, fallen tree branch)

1. Glue different colorful fabrics to both sides of white poster board. Let dry.

2. Draw and cut out leaf shapes from the different fabrics. Use a paper punch to punch a small hole in each leaf. Tie a string through each hole.

3. Tie the other ends of the strings to a small fallen tree branch. Attach another string to the center and hang the mobile where the leaves will catch the breeze and flutter.

MILK CARTON COW
(one-pint milk carton, white glue, water, bowl, paper towels, four ice-cream sticks, paper)

1. Close the top of a one-pint milk carton. Secure with staples.

2. Mix an equal amount of white glue and water in a bowl. Brush some of the mixture on the carton. Press on pieces of paper towel, adding more mixture to the pieces with a brush. Cover the entire carton and let dry.

3. Cut four slits in the carton and glue one ice-cream stick in each for a leg. Let dry.

4. Paint the body and the legs. Draw and cut out horns, ears, eyes, a nose, and a tongue from paper. Color with markers and glue in place. Add a paper tail and udders.

TURKEY NUT CUP
(plastic cup, felt, ice-cream stick, rubber band, nuts)

1. Use a plastic cup for the body of the turkey. Cut wings and tail feathers from different-colored pieces of felt. Glue them on the outside of the cup.

2. Cut one piece of felt for the neck and head. Add eyes, a beak, and wattle from felt.

3. Glue an ice-cream stick to the back of the head. Then glue the stick to the outside of the cup. Hold in place with a rubber band until dry.

4. Fill the cup with nuts.

CLAM-SHELL PLANTER
(half-gallon milk carton, construction paper, clam shells)

1. Measure up about 5 inches from the bottom of a half-gallon milk carton. Cut off the top and discard it.

2. Cover the carton with glue and construction paper.

3. Glue clean clam-shell halves in a decorative design onto one side of the carton. Let dry before adding shells to another side.

4. Place a plant inside the planter.

THE MAYFLOWER
(paper plate, paper)

1. Fold a paper plate in half so the bottom is facing you. Open the plate and draw waves with a marker on the bottom half.

2. On a piece of paper, draw a ship to represent the Mayflower. Cut it out. Fold the plate and glue the Mayflower along the top of the fold. Let dry.

3. Gently push on one end of the fold, and watch the Mayflower rock back and forth.

HAND-PAINTED TURKEY PAPER
(old newspaper, poster paper, tempera paint, paper plate)

1. Cover the floor with old newspaper. Cut a section from a roll of poster paper. Hold it in place on the newspaper with small pieces of tape in each corner.

2. Squeeze some tempera paint on a large paper plate. Place your hand in the paint until your palm and fingers are covered. Let the excess paint drip off your hand.

3. Carefully place your hand on the poster paper with your fingers spread open. Make several handprints and let dry.

4. With a black marker, add legs, a beak, and an eye to each hand, creating a turkey.

5. Use the paper to wrap holiday gifts.

STRIP PUMPKIN
(construction paper, brass fastener)

1. Cut eight strips of orange construction paper 1 inch wide and 18 inches long. Punch a hole at both ends of each strip with a paper punch.

2. Do the same with one 1-by-9-inch strip and fold it in half. This will be the stem.

3. Place the eight long strips on top of each other, as shown in the diagram. Staple in the center. Bring the ends together so the strips form a pumpkin shape. Place the stem on top. Hold everything together with a brass fastener, running through all the holes.

4. Cut and glue green paper leaves around the stem.

OAK-LEAF PIN
(poster board, felt, safety pin, acorns)

1. Draw and cut out an oak leaf from poster board to use as a pattern. Place the pattern on a piece of felt. Trace around it with a marker and cut it out. Glue the felt leaf on top of the pattern.

2. Glue an opened safety pin to the back of the leaf. Then glue a small strip of felt across the opened pin and let it dry.

3. Place three acorns on top of the leaf and attach with glue. Let dry for a day.

HOLIDAY GIFT BOX
(paint, small cardboard box, pumpkin seeds, clear nail polish)

1. Paint the outside of a small cardboard box and lid.

2. Glue pumpkin seeds in a decorative design on top of the lid. Let dry.

3. Cover the pumpkin seeds with a coat of clear nail polish to give them a glossy look.

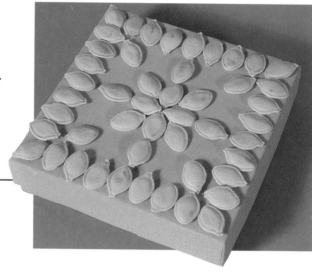

PINECONE TURKEY
(pinecone, paper plate, poster board, kernel corn)

1. Glue a pinecone to the center of a paper plate.

2. Draw and cut out colorful tail feathers and a head with a wattle and a neck from poster board. Glue the tail feathers to the flat end of the pinecone and the head to the other end.

3. Dot glue on the plate around the turkey, and add kernels of corn.

STANDING DEER
(paper, poster board)

1. On paper, draw the front section of a deer, including the antlers, head, chest, and front legs; the body, including the tail; and the hind legs. Cut out these three sections and use as patterns.

2. Place the patterns on poster board and trace around them. Cut out the sections. Add features from cut paper and glue them in place. Add other details with a marker.

3. Cut slits, as shown. Slide the legs onto the body section. You may need to adjust the slits to balance the deer.

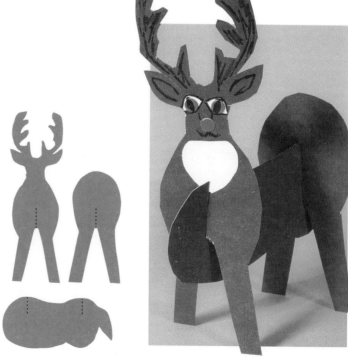

APPLE HOT PAD
(corrugated cardboard, rubber bands, paint, poster board)

1. Cut several long strips of corrugated cardboard, about 1 inch wide. Put glue on one side of a strip and wind it tightly into a coil.

2. Keep winding strips around the coil until the hot pad is as large as you would like it. Hold the strips in place with rubber bands and let dry.

3. Cover the hot pad with paint and let dry. Cut a stem and leaf from poster board. Glue them to the back of the hot pad.

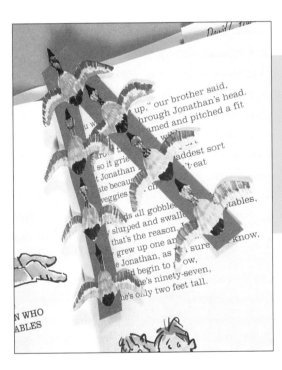

GEESE BOOKMARK
(construction paper)

1. Cut a V shape from a piece of construction paper for the base of the bookmark.

2. Draw and cut out geese from white paper. Color them with markers. Glue them along the V shape as if they were flying together.

FALL PLANTER
(cardboard food container, felt, sand, dried grasses and flowers)

1. Use a clean cardboard food container such as one in which peanuts are packaged. Measure the container and cut a piece of felt to fit around it. Glue the felt in place.

2. Cut out leaves from different-colored pieces of felt. Glue them onto the outside of the container. Add felt acorns.

3. Fill the container with sand. Arrange dried grasses and flowers in the container.

FRUIT-BOWL PICTURE
(construction paper, poster board, string)

1. Cut different colors of construction paper into long strips about 1/2 inch wide.

2. Bend and curl the strips to form shapes of a bowl and fruit. Glue the shapes onto poster board. Add strips for leaves. Let dry.

3. Cut around your design to make an attractive shape. Glue this onto poster board of a contrasting color.

4. Attach a string to the back for a hanger.

HARVEST BASKET
(construction paper, cardboard, twine, paper towels)

1. Glue construction paper on top of a sheet of cardboard. Draw a basket design on the paper with a pencil.

2. Cut and soak a piece of long twine in warm water so it will be easy to work with. Remove the twine from the water, and dry it with a paper towel. Squeeze glue on the outline of the basket, and press the twine into it.

3. Spread glue on the inside of the basket. Cut some dry twine into tiny pieces, and press them into the glue. Glue short pieces of twine in a crisscross design on top.

4. Cut fruit shapes from construction paper, and glue them at the top of the basket. Add a loop of twine to the back for a hanger.

PILGRIM CARD
(construction paper)

1. Fold a sheet of construction paper to form a card.

2. Draw a Pilgrim boy's face on another piece of paper, and cut it out. Glue it to the inside of the card, centering it on the fold.

3. Cut the top of a hat from black paper. For the brim, cut a small strip of black paper and make accordion pleats along the strip.

4. Glue the top of the hat to the card, centering on the fold. Glue one end of the accordion-pleated brim to each side of the fold.

5. Write "Happy" on the front of the card and "Thanksgiving" on the inside.

HARVEST PHOTO FRAME
(four tongue depressors, poster board, yarn, photograph)

1. Glue four tongue depressors together to form a square frame. Let dry.

2. Decorate the front of the frame by creating two ears of corn from yellow and green poster board. Add details with a black marker. Glue the corn to opposite sides of the frame.

3. Cut a piece of poster board to cover the open section of the frame. Glue it to the back. Cut and glue a yarn loop for a hanger.

4. Select a photograph. Trim if necessary and glue it onto the front.

WREATH
(heavy paper plate, large brown paper bag, construction paper, yarn)

1. To make the wreath base, cut a 7-inch circle from the center of a 10-inch heavy paper plate. Discard the circle.

2. Cut along one side and around the bottom of a large brown paper bag to make a large sheet of paper. Cut paper strips 3 inches wide.

3. Glue one end of a paper strip to the wreath base. Wrap the strip around the base, glue the end, and continue with another strip until the base is covered.

4. Cut leaves and acorns from construction paper. Add veins with a marker. Glue the paper cutouts to the wreath. Add a yarn hanger to the back.

TURKEY TREAT HOLDER
(plastic bottle, construction paper)

1. For the holder, cut a 3-inch bottom section from a plastic bottle. Discard the top.

2. Draw and cut out a head, feet, and wings from construction paper. Add cut-paper features to the head. Glue the head, feet, and wings to the holder.

3. To make the tail, draw a fan shape on colored paper and cut it out. Glue this to another sheet of colored paper. Trim away the extra paper, leaving a border. Continue to do this until the tail has as many colors as you want. Glue the tail in place.

4. Fill the holder with treats.

FALL PLACE MAT
(construction paper, tempera paint, paper towels, fallen leaves, clear self-adhesive paper)

1. Under a sink faucet, wet one side of a large sheet of white construction paper. Using paintbrushes, drop yellow, green, and red tempera paint here and there onto the wet paper.

2. Tip the paper back and forth over the sink until the colors run across the paper. Let the paper dry on a bed of paper towels.

3. On a black sheet of paper, trace around a variety of fallen leaves. Carefully poke your scissors into each leaf shape and cut it out.

4. Glue the black paper over the painted paper to see the autumn leaves. *Ask an adult to help you* cover your place mat with clear self-adhesive paper.

BOX TURKEY
(two gelatin boxes, toothpaste boxes, construction paper)

1. To make the turkey's body, tape two gelatin boxes together. To make the feet and the head, cut sections from toothpaste boxes. Cover the boxes with construction paper and glue them together.

2. To make the tail feathers, cut feather shapes from several colors of construction paper and glue them together, as shown. Glue the tail feathers to the back of the turkey.

3. Cut wings, eyes, a beak, and a wattle from construction paper, and glue onto the turkey.

Glue tail feathers

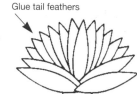

MAYFLOWER'S CROW'S NEST
(heavyweight paper, ice-cream stick, plastic-foam cup)

1. Draw and cut out a Pilgrim boy from heavyweight paper. Add features with markers. Glue the boy to one end of an ice-cream stick.

2. Push the other end of the ice-cream stick through the bottom of a plastic-foam cup so the boy is inside. Draw railings around the outside of the cup.

3. Hold the stick with one hand and the cup with the other. Make the Pilgrim boy pop up and down as he looks over the rail of the crow's nest.

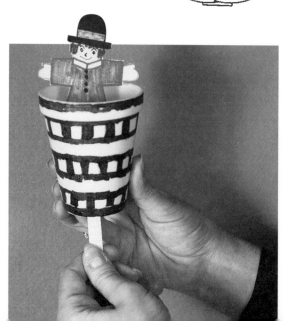

CHANCE OF FLURRIES
(paper, glitter, string)

1. Tape two sheets of paper together to form a long sheet. Starting at the short side of the paper, fold accordion pleats. Staple the folded paper in the middle.

2. Cut the two ends at an angle. Cut through all the folds to make small triangles.

3. Spread open the folds until the ends meet, forming a circle. Tape the ends together.

4. Add dabs of glue and sprinkle with glitter. Let dry. Glue a piece of string for a hanger.

STUFF-THE-TURKEY GAME
(one large brown paper bag, two small brown paper bags, old newspaper, tissue paper)

1. Fold down 4 inches of a large brown paper bag, keeping the fold inside. Gather the corner edges together so the opening of the bag is a little smaller, and staple in place. Push out the corners to round out the body of the "turkey."

2. Stuff two small brown paper bags with old newspaper. Twist the bags to form "drumsticks." Cut strips of red tissue paper and glue around the ends to make frills. Glue the "drumsticks" to opposite sides of the body.

3. For "bread stuffing," wad up sheets of newspaper. Cover them with white tissue paper and hold together with pieces of tape.

To play: Players take turns tossing the "stuffing" into the "turkey" from a distance of four to five feet. See who can get the most "stuffing" into the "turkey."

MILKWEED-POD MOUSE
(milkweed-pod half, construction paper, moveable plastic eyes,
sewing needle, black thread)

1. Select a dried milkweed-pod half with a stem, which will be used as a tail for the mouse.

2. Cut two ears, two eyes, and a nose from construction paper and glue in place. Glue moveable plastic eyes on top of the paper eyes.

3. Thread a sewing needle with black thread. Carefully poke the needle and thread through the nose area of the milkweed pod. When through, cut the thread to look like a whisker. Do this several times.

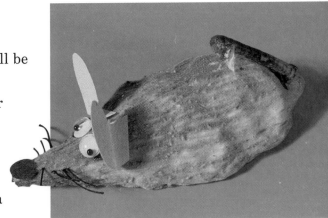

CORNUCOPIA

(old T-shirts or socks, needle and thread, cotton, felt, yarn, paper plate)

1. Using old T-shirts or socks, cut long, narrow, and wide rectangles to make different vegetables and fruits.

2. Fold each rectangle in half. With a needle and thread, sew up all but one short side. Turn the shape inside out, and stuff with cotton.

3. Sew up the fourth side, and add leaves made of felt or yarn.

4. Roll a paper plate into the shape of a cornucopia, and staple the ends together. Place the fruits and vegetables inside.

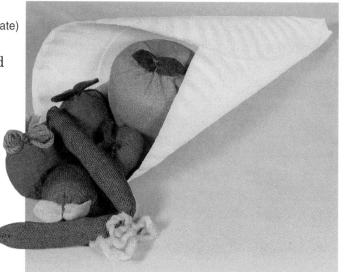

DOORKNOB TURKEY

(construction paper, yarn)

1. Draw and cut out a turkey shape from construction paper. Color the turkey with crayons, as shown.

2. Punch two holes in the tail area, and tie a loop of yarn for a hanger.

3. Place the turkey on a doorknob in your home.

PILGRIM BOOKENDS

(two half-gallon milk cartons, construction paper, rocks)

1. Cut two half-gallon milk cartons in half and discard the tops. Glue construction paper around each carton.

2. Draw and cut out a Pilgrim boy and Pilgrim girl from paper. Glue them to one side of a carton.

3. Place rocks inside the cartons so they will be heavy enough to hold books in place.

PUMPKIN CRUMBER
(two heavy paper plates, poster paint, ribbon)

1. Cut a heavy paper plate in half. Cover it with orange poster paint and let dry.

2. Cut a stem and leaf from another heavy paper plate. Paint them and let dry. Glue the stem and leaf to one plate half so when the other half is joined it looks like a pumpkin.

3. Glue a piece of orange ribbon along the bottom of the pumpkin's top half. Let this dry.

4. Gently sweep the top half of the pumpkin over your holiday tablecloth, brushing the crumbs from the table into the bottom half of the pumpkin. Discard the crumbs.

APPLE WALL HANGING
(felt, three brass fasteners, three plastic lids, paper, metal ring)

1. Cut a strip of felt 3 by 30 inches. Cut each end to a point. Push a brass fastener through the center of each of the plastic lids. Attach the lids to the felt strip.

2. Draw pictures on round pieces of paper, and glue them to the centers of the lids. Glue a metal ring at the top for hanging.

LEAF NAPKIN RING
(paper, felt, permanent marker)

1. To make a pattern, draw and cut out an oak leaf shape from paper, as shown.

2. Pin the paper leaf on felt and cut around the pattern. Do this twice, using two different-colored pieces of felt. Draw veins on the leaves with a permanent marker.

3. Glue the stems of the leaves together. Cut a slit in one leaf just above the stem. Pull the uncut leaf through the slit, forming a ring with the stems.

4. Place a napkin in the ring.

LEAF-TURKEY PICTURE
(paper, fallen leaves)

1. Cut the body of the turkey from a piece of paper. Glue it onto another piece of paper.

2. Collect different kinds of fallen leaves for the tail feathers. Glue the leaves in place.

3. Add features with pieces of cut paper and attach with glue.

SQUIRREL NUT BOX
(fabric, small jewelry box, acorns)

1. Cut and glue small strips of fabric around the lid and the bottom of a small jewelry box.

2. Place four acorns in the center of the lid and attach with glue. Let dry for about a day.

3. Store little keepsakes in the box.

PAPER CHAIN
(construction paper)

1. Cut strips of construction paper measuring 3 by 18 inches. Fold over 3 inches of one strip at one end, making a 3-inch square. Continue to fold into accordion pleats until the whole strip is pleated.

2. On the top square, draw a pumpkin shape with the edges touching the folds.

3. Keeping the strip folded, cut out the pumpkin. Do not cut through the folded paper at the edges. Unfold the paper. Use five pumpkins and write one letter of the word "Happy" on each pumpkin.

4. To create the word "Thanksgiving," follow steps 1, 2, and 3, but tape two strips together at one end to make twelve pumpkins.

CORNFIELD BOWLING
(ten one-quart milk cartons, brown wrapping paper, construction paper, rubber ball)

1. Fold over the tops of ten one-quart milk cartons and seal with tape. Cover each carton with brown wrapping paper.

2. Draw ten ears of corn on white construction paper and color with markers. Glue an ear of corn to one side of each milk carton.

3. Cut ten kernels of corn from yellow paper and number them 1 through 10. Glue a kernel to the top of each milk carton.

To play: Set up the ten ears of corn like pins in bowling. Using a rubber ball, bowl over as many ears as you can and total the number of points scored. Each player gets one turn. The player with the highest score wins.

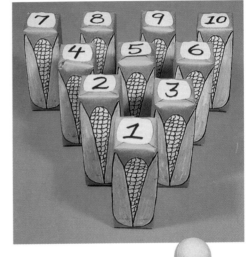

FINGERPRINT STATIONERY
(paper, tempera paint)

1. Select paper for your stationery.

2. Using tempera paint, brush a small amount of paint on your fingertip. Practice making fingerprints on a piece of scrap paper.

3. Make fingerprints in various places on the stationery. With markers, add feathers, eyes, a beak, and feet to each fingerprint, making little turkeys.

FALL BANNER
(felt, fabric glue, wooden dowel, decorative trim)

1. Lay four pieces of felt vertically, overlapping the edges about 1 inch. Glue them together with fabric glue.

2. Fold the top edge of the first piece of felt over a small wooden dowel and hold in place with glue. Let dry.

3. Cut fall symbols such as leaves, a turkey, a pumpkin, and corn from pieces of felt and glue onto the panels.

4. Glue or staple decorative trim around the ends of the wooden dowel for a hanger.

BEAN NECKLACE
(plastic lid, dried beans and lentils, ribbon)

1. Spread glue around the inside of a plastic lid. Place a variety of dried beans and lentils in the glue, making a decorative design. Let dry.

2. Cut a long piece of ribbon. Glue the ribbon around the outside rim of the lid, leaving two equal ends of ribbon to tie around your neck.

BASKET OF GOURDS
(cardboard, felt, wicker basket, ornamental gourds)

1. Draw and cut out different types of leaves from cardboard to use as patterns. Trace around the patterns on felt. Cut out the leaves.

2. Glue the leaves on the outside of a wicker basket and let dry.

3. Place a variety of ornamental gourds in the basket. Set the basket in the center of a table.

GRANDPARENT HOLIDAY CARD
(poster board, felt, photographs)

1. Cut a rectangle from a piece of white poster board. Draw and cut out a cornucopia from a piece of brightly colored felt.

2. Glue the cornucopia on the poster board. At the opening of the cornucopia, glue photographs of your family.

3. Write a message such as "Happy Thanksgiving to Grandma and Grandpa from all of us!"

TURKEY PLACE CARD
(two tongue depressors, construction paper, one toothpick, cotton ball, corn kernels)

1. Glue the bottom edge of one tongue depressor to the back edge of another tongue depressor. Let dry. Cut a small piece of construction paper and write a guest's name on it. Glue it on a tongue depressor, as shown.

2. Color a toothpick with a marker, and break it in half for the turkey's legs and feet. Glue the toothpicks into a cotton ball. Cut and glue paper tail feathers and a head onto the cotton ball. Add a wattle to the head.

3. Attach the turkey to the tongue depressor by gluing the legs in place. Glue a few corn kernels onto the flat tongue depressor.

4. Make a place card for each dinner guest.

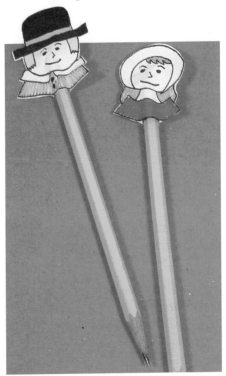

THANKSGIVING PICTURE PUZZLE
(paper, poster board, markers)

1. Draw a holiday picture on a piece of paper using markers.

2. Glue the picture on a piece of poster board that is a little larger than the picture. Let dry.

3. Turn the picture over and lightly draw lines to create puzzle pieces. Cut along the lines.

PENCIL PILGRIMS
(paper, markers, pencils)

1. Draw a Pilgrim boy and a Pilgrim girl on a piece of paper, making sure they will be large enough to go around the top of a pencil, as shown. Cut out the shapes.

2. Trace around the boy and girl on a piece of paper, making a front and a back for each. Cut out the shapes and color with markers.

3. With a pencil in the middle, glue a front and a back shape together for each Pilgrim.

PLYMOUTH ROCK DOORSTOP
(stones, cereal box, construction paper)

1. Put some clean stones inside a cereal box for weight. Tape the flaps closed. Cover the cereal box with construction paper.

2. Draw and cut out a rock to represent the famous Plymouth Rock. Glue the rock to one side of the cereal box. Add a sign.

3. Place the doorstop by a door.

THANKSGIVING CENTERPIECE
(old newspaper, large brown paper bag, string, thin cardboard)

1. Crumple sheets of old newspaper into balls and place them in a large brown paper bag until full. Tie the top closed with string.

2. Draw a turkey head, tail, wings, and feet on thin cardboard. Cut them out and color with markers or crayons.

3. Flatten the top of the bag and glue the head in place. Glue on the tail, wings, and feet.

VASE OF CHRYSANTHEMUMS
(construction paper)

1. Use a 12-by-18-inch piece of construction paper for the background. Cut out and glue on a vase from paper.

2. Cut circles measuring 7, 5 1/2, 4 1/2, and 2 1/2 inches for each flower. Cut slits around the outer edges to make fringes. Curl the fringes around a pencil.

3. Glue the largest fringed circle to the construction paper, then add the other circles. End with the smallest in the center. Add paper stems and leaves.

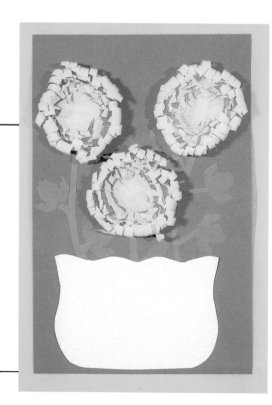

AUTUMN GREETING
(pear, tempera paint, paper)

1. *Ask an adult to help you* cut a pear in half. Paint the cut side of the pear with tempera paint. Press it onto a sheet of white paper. Let the print dry.

2. Fold a piece of colored paper in half to make a card. Glue the white-paper print onto the front of the card.

3. Write a message inside.

PIGGY MAGNET
(frozen-juice pull-top lid, construction paper, buttons, moveable plastic eyes, chenille stick, magnetic strip)

1. Trace around a frozen-juice pull-top lid on a piece of pink construction paper. Cut out the circle and glue it to the lid.

2. Glue a large button nose to the center of the lid. Add a smaller button in the center of the larger one. Add moveable plastic eyes, button ears, and button feet.

3. Cut a small piece from a chenille stick, curl it around a pencil, and glue it to the back of the lid for the tail.

4. Glue a small magnetic strip to the back of the lid.

FEED THE TURKEY
(large cardboard box, brown wrapping paper, construction paper, poster board, fabric, dried beans, rubber bands)

1. Remove the flaps from one end of a large cardboard box. Cover the rest of the box with brown wrapping paper, leaving the open end uncovered. Place the box on your work surface with the opened end as the bottom.

2. Make eyes, eyelashes, and a large beak from construction paper. Glue them onto the front of the box. Cut tail feathers from poster board, and tape them onto the back of the box.

3. *Ask an adult to help you* cut a large hole under the beak.

4. To make large kernels of corn, cut out three circles about 7 inches in diameter from yellow fabric. Place dried beans in the center of each circle and gather the edges. Hold together with rubber bands.

5. See who can toss the most kernels into the turkey's mouth.

PAPER ACORN WREATH
(paper plate, brown wrapping paper, gold wrapping paper, ribbon, yarn)

1. Cut the center from a paper plate. Use the outer ring as the base for the wreath.

2. Cut a piece of brown wrapping paper about 7 by 3 inches. Leaving about 1 inch in the center uncut, cut slits in both short ends of the strip to make fringes. Curl the fringes around a pencil. Glue this to the wreath base. Make more sections until the wreath is filled.

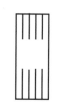

3. To decorate, draw and cut out acorn shapes from gold wrapping paper. Glue them around the wreath. Add a ribbon.

4. Glue a yarn loop to the back for a hanger.

PILGRIM HOUSE
(paper, construction paper, yarn)

1. Draw a Pilgrim house on a piece of paper with markers or crayons. Trim around the picture.

2. Place the picture on a large piece of construction paper. Punch a hole in the middle of the picture near the top, and tie a loop of yarn for a hanger.

TUBE TURKEY
(bathroom tissue tube, tempera paint)

1. Cut sections from one end of a bathroom tissue tube for feet, as shown.

2. At the front of the turkey, cut two 3-inch slits, about 1 inch apart, starting at the top of the tube. Trim this 1-inch section, making the turkey's neck and head. Cut the tube near the base of the neck, as shown, to form the tail. Round the corners.

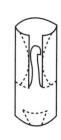

3. Decorate with tempera paint.

FRUIT COASTERS
(felt, plastic lids)

1. Cut circles of felt and glue them on the insides of plastic lids.

2. Draw and cut out fruit shapes, such as apples or pears. Glue them on top of the felt

GIFT BAG
(brown paper bag, construction paper, ribbon)

1. Fold over the top flap of a brown paper bag about 3 inches. Cut pieces of construction paper to make a Pilgrim girl's head, including the collar. Glue onto the bag.

2. With the bag folded, punch a hole on each side of the collar and through the layers of the bag. Thread a piece of ribbon through the holes and tie a bow. This will hold the bag closed.

3. Decorate the rest of the bag with paper, making the girl's hands, dress, and apron.

CLOTHING TRUNK
(shoe box, brown wrapping paper, ribbon, gold wrapping paper)

1. Cover a shoe box and lid separately with brown wrapping paper.

2. Cut and glue pieces of ribbon as strapping around the box. Do the same with the lid, matching the strapping on the box.

3. To make hinges in the back, cut two pieces of ribbon. With the lid on the box, glue each piece of ribbon over the strapping, connecting the lid and the box together. Let dry.

4. Add a decorative latch cut from gold wrapping paper. Glue diamond shapes to the hinges.

WHEAT BOOKMARK
(poster board, broomstraw)

1. Draw and cut out a wheat shape from poster board. Decorate with markers.

2. Glue pieces of broomstraw to the back of the bookmark.

TURKEY TISSUE BOX
(box of facial tissues, brown wrapping paper, construction paper)

1. Cover a box of facial tissues on three sides with brown wrapping paper. On the fourth side, cover the box only up to the slot through which the facial tissues will be removed.

2. Cut tail feathers from construction paper, and tape them around the slot.

3. Decorate the front of the box with paper eyes, a beak, a wattle, a beard, and feet. Add paper wings to the sides of the box.

PLANTER
(half-gallon milk carton, ice-cream sticks, construction paper)

1. Cut away the top of a half-gallon milk carton so the bottom is slightly shorter than an ice-cream stick.

2. Glue ice-cream sticks on each side of the carton. Let each side dry before starting another side.

3. Cut apple shapes from construction paper, and glue them to the sides. Add paper leaves.

4. Place a potted plant inside.

RECIPE CARDS
(tempera paint, paper plate, plain index cards)

1. Squeeze drops of tempera paint onto a paper plate. Dip a fingertip in one color and press it in a corner of an index card.

2. Clean your fingertip before using a different color on another card.

3. Decorate the fingerprints with markers, creating holiday figures or scenes.

APPLE MOBILE
(two tongue depressors, felt, five frozen-juice pull-top lids, yarn)

1. Glue two tongue depressors in the shape of an X and let dry.

2. Draw and cut out two apple shapes from red felt for each juice lid. Cut a green stem and leaf for each apple.

3. Cut lengths of green yarn. Glue the end of a piece of yarn on one side of a lid. Add a felt apple on top. Glue a felt apple on the other side of the lid. Add a stem and a leaf to each apple. Let dry. Do this for each apple.

4. Tie one apple to the center of the X. Tie the other four apples to the ends of the tongue depressors. Add glue to the tied ends. Tie yarn in the center to hang.

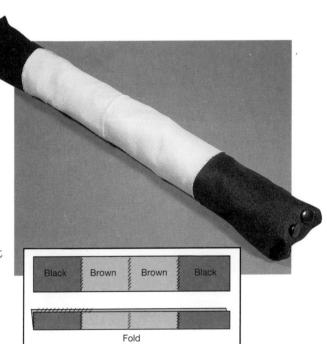

WOOLLY-BEAR DRAFT STOPPER
(felt, needle and thread, old rags or cotton batting, buttons)

1. Sew two brown-felt rectangles together. Then sew a black rectangle to each end.

2. Fold the right sides together and sew along the long side using brown and black thread where needed. Stitch one end closed.

3. Reach your hand inside, grab the end, and turn the felt right-side out. Stuff with old rags or cotton batting. Sew the open end closed. Add button eyes.

4. Place the woolly bear at the bottom of a door to stop any draft from coming in.

| Black | Brown | Brown | Black |

Fold

STRAW BRUSH
(broomstraw, fallen tree branch, rubber band, ribbon)

1. Cut pieces of broomstraw from an old broom.

2. Gather the straw around a piece of a fallen tree branch. Hold in place with a rubber band.

3. Trim the broomstraw ends evenly with scissors. Tie a ribbon on top of the rubber band.

SHAPE TURKEY
(construction paper)

1. From different colors of construction paper, cut circles about 7 inches, 6 1/2 inches, 4 inches, 2 1/2 inches, and 1 1/2 inches wide.

2. Cut feet for the turkey to match the color of the largest circle. Place the circles as shown.

3. From paper, cut out a neck and a small circle for the face. Add a beak, eyes, wattle, and beard

4. Glue the turkey to a large sheet of paper.

PAPER-BAG PILGRIM MASK
(large brown paper bag, construction paper)

1. Measure about 6 inches from the opening of a large paper bag, and cut around the entire bag.

2. Cover the front of the bag with construction paper. Put the bag on your head. Using a crayon, have a friend carefully mark where the eyeholes should be on the outside of the bag. Remove the bag.

3. Cut out the eyeholes. Cut out and glue pieces of paper to make eyebrows, a moustache, and hair.

4. To make the collar, cut a strip of white paper. Fold it in accordion pleats. Open it up and glue it in place.

5. Draw and cut out a black hat from paper. Add a brown-paper band. Glue the hat to the top of the head.

BOOKREST
(corrugated cardboard)

1. For the bookrest, cut a piece of corrugated cardboard to measure 12 by 18 inches.

2. Cut a strip of corrugated cardboard 1 by 18 inches for the ledge. Glue it to the bottom edge of the rest.

3. Cut two pieces of corrugated cardboard, as shown, for the stands. Glue them to the bottom of the bookrest.

4. Use markers to draw a wood-like grain on the bookrest.

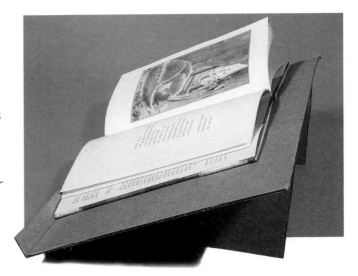

SUET HOLDER FOR BIRDS
(plastic-mesh vegetable bag, suet, string, ribbon)

1. Reuse a plastic-mesh vegetable bag by filling it with suet, purchased from the supermarket, for the birds to eat.

2. Gather the opened end and tie it closed with string, wrapping the string around several times before knotting. Leave the ends of the string long so the holder can be tied to a tree limb. Add a ribbon.

3. Tie a ribbon at the bottom.

THREE-DIMENSIONAL FISH
(poster board, tissue paper, paper plate, yarn)

1. Cut a rectangular piece of poster board. Make a decorative border around the edges with a marker. Lightly sketch a fish shape in the middle.

2. Tear colored tissue paper into little pieces. Squeeze a small amount of white glue onto a paper plate.

3. Dip the pieces of tissue paper into the glue and place them inside the fish drawing, making a textured effect. Continue to fill the drawing.

4. Tape or glue a piece of yarn in the back for a hanger.

Travel Helpers

Create these playful travel accessories to make your holiday trip even more fun.

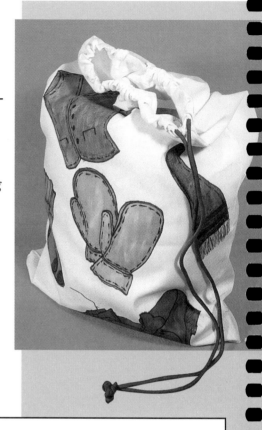

PILLOWCASE TOTE
(white pillowcase, cardboard, permanent markers or fabric paint, decorative cording)

1. Place a white pillowcase on a flat work surface. Insert a piece of cardboard inside. (This will protect the markers or paint from going through to the back of the pillowcase.)

2. With permanent markers or fabric paint, draw on pictures of clothing you might put in the tote.

3. Cut a small slit in the hem on each side of the seam near the opening of the pillowcase. Insert decorative cording in one slit, pulling the cord through the hem and out the second slit. Tie the ends of the cord together.

4. Close by pulling the cord and tightly gathering the pillowcase top.

CAN OF FUN
(cardboard container with lid, paper)

1. Cut a piece of paper the correct size to cover the outside of a tall, round cardboard container.

2. Write "Can of Fun!" in the center of the paper. Draw pictures on it. Glue the picture around the container.

3. Place pencils, pens, markers, small pieces of note paper, scissors, and tape inside.

LUGGAGE TAG
(corrugated cardboard, paper, yarn)

1. Cut a small rectangle from a piece of corrugated cardboard. Glue a piece of bright paper to both sides.

2. Using a paper punch, punch holes around the edges.

3. Weave a long piece of yarn through the holes and tie together at the end. To place the tag on your luggage, loop the yarn over a handle and pull the tag through the loop.

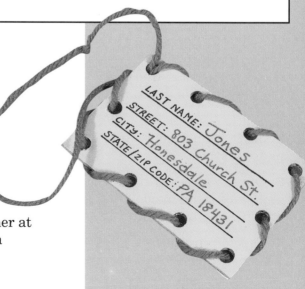

GOOD-GROOMING TRAVEL KIT
(felt, fabric place mat, fabric glue, rickrack, ribbon)

1. Cut felt squares and rectangles to hold the shapes of the items you will place in the kit, such as a brush, comb, shampoo, toothpaste, and soap. Place the pocket shapes on the place mat, making sure each item will fit its pocket. Put fabric glue on the bottom and the sides of each pocket. Press the pockets onto the place mat. Decorate with pieces of rickrack. Let dry overnight.

2. Place the toiletries in their pockets. Tightly roll up the place mat. Cut two pieces of ribbon long enough to fit around the rolled place mat. Tie the ribbons, as shown, to hold the kit together.

3. When you open the kit, place the ribbons in one of the pockets so they don't get lost.

PERSONAL PET BOX
(shoe box, paper, two plastic containers, one plastic bottle, sandwich bags)

1. Decorate the outside of a shoe box with paper cutouts of paw prints and biscuits.

2. Use two plastic containers, one for food and one for water, as feeding dishes for your pet. Extra water can be stored in a plastic bottle. Treats can be placed in a sandwich bag.

3. Store other items such as a toy and a leash.

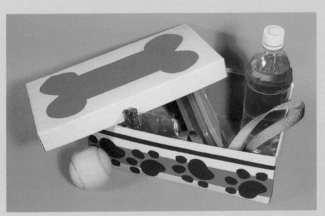

TRAVEL ACTIVITY BOX
(cardboard candy box, brown wrapping paper, felt)

1. Cover the outside of an empty cardboard candy-box lid with brown wrapping paper. Cut and glue pieces of felt on the lid, making a scene.

2. Glue a piece of felt inside on the bottom of the box. Use this as your activity board.

3. Cut various objects from felt. Place the cutouts on the felt inside the box to create different scenes. Cut two white strips, five red circles, and five green circles from felt to play tic-tac-toe. Store the felt pieces in the box.

GLOVE TURKEY PUPPET
(brown cotton glove, felt, moveable plastic eye)

1. Place a brown cotton glove with the palm side facing up. Cut a beak, a wattle, and an eye from felt and glue onto the thumb. Add a moveable plastic eye to the felt eye.

2. Cut tail feathers from felt and glue one feather to each of the four fingers. Cut out a wing from felt and glue on the palm.

3. Insert your hand in the glove and make your turkey run.

BLACK CROW
(two index cards, penny, yarn)

1. Draw a crow flying with its wings extended on one index card. Draw a crow on another index card with its wings in another flying position.

2. Glue a penny to the middle of the back of one card to add weight so it will spin.

3. Cut a 36-inch piece of yarn, double it, and knot the ends. Find the middle of the doubled yarn, and glue it to the back of one of the cards.

4. Glue the cards together with the pictures outside and with the yarn extending from the right and left sides. Wind the card by holding the ends of the yarn and spinning the card. Firmly pull the ends of the yarn away from the card and watch the crow fly.

CORN-CHIP BASKET
(fabric, plastic berry basket)

1. Cut long strips of yellow fabric wide enough to be woven in and out of sections of a plastic berry basket.

2. Weave one strip per section, as shown. Tie the ends into a bow. Fill the basket with corn chips.

PAPER-BAG PILGRIMS
(tempera paint, two small brown paper bags,
old newspaper, paper)

1. For the bodies, paint two small paper bags with tempera paint and let dry. Wad up old newspaper and stuff each bag. Fold back the top corners and fold the opening back twice. Glue in place.

2. Cut out arms and shoes from paper and paint them the same color as the bodies. When dry, glue to the bodies.

3. To make a Pilgrim man and woman, draw and cut out paper heads. Add features. Draw and cut out hats and details for the clothing and glue in place.

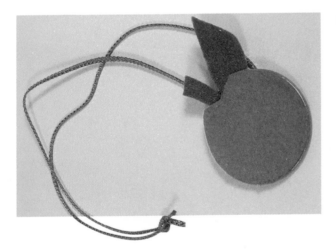

APPLE NECKLACE
(felt, frozen-juice pull-top lid, cording)

1. Draw and cut out an apple, stem, and leaf from felt. Glue them to a frozen-juice pull-top lid.

2. Cut a piece of cording long enough for a necklace. Knot the ends. Find the middle of the cording, and glue it to the back of the lid.

LITTLE WHITE CHURCH CARD
(brown paper bag, pencil)

1. Cut a piece of brown paper bag 9 by 12 inches. Fold it in half (6 by 9 inches), then fold in half again the other way (6 by 4 1/2 inches).

2. On the inside fold line, draw a church, making sure the center of the church is on the fold line. Cut through only one layer of paper along the roof and the bottom of the church, as shown. With a pencil, pull the church forward and reverse the fold.

Cut
Cut

3. Close the card, press down, and reopen. Your church now stands out.

4. Color a scene around the church.

Fold out

TURKEY-FOOT PLACE MAT
(poster board)

1. Draw and cut out the shape of a turkey footprint from a large piece of poster board.

2. Draw and cut out the talons from another piece of poster board and glue them onto the place mat.

3. Make one place mat for each guest.

PAPER-TUBE TURKEY
(paper towel tube, poster paint, brown paper bag, construction paper)

1. Cut a paper towel tube on a slant and make slices about 3/4 inch wide. Paint the slices bright colors and let them dry.

2. Cut out the turkey's body and feet from a brown paper bag, and glue them to a large sheet of construction paper.

3. For the tail feathers, glue the slices to the body with the holes facing up. Add a cut-paper beak and wattle.

WREATH OF LEAVES
(poster board, yarn, glitter, fabric)

1. Cut a doughnut shape from poster board to make the base of the wreath. Wrap yarn completely around it.

2. Draw and cut out leaves from colored poster board. Spread glue around the edges of the leaves and sprinkle them with glitter. Let dry.

3. Glue the leaves to the wreath. Cut a strip of fabric and make a bow. Tie it to the wreath. Attach a loop of yarn to the back for a hanger.

RAINBOW TURKEY
(cardboard box, construction paper, paper plate)

1. To make the body of the turkey, cover a cardboard box with construction paper.

2. To make the tail, cut a paper plate in half. Divide the front and back of one plate half into sections. Color each section with a crayon or marker. Glue the tail to the back of the box.

3. To make the wings, cut the remaining half of the paper plate in half. Divide the front and back of each half into sections. Color both sides. Glue the wings to the sides of the box.

4. Draw and cut out a head and neck from paper. Add features. Glue the shape to the front of the box.

PHOTO ALBUM
(three-ring binder, scrap wallpaper, poster board)

1. Cover a three-ring binder with scrap wallpaper.

2. Make a label from poster board and glue it to the front of the album.

WALNUT-MICE RACERS
(walnut halves, tempera paint, construction paper, moveable plastic eyes, yarn, marbles)

1. Cover two walnut halves with different-colored tempera paint and let dry.

2. Cut and glue paper ears on each walnut half. Add paper noses and moveable plastic eyes. Paint whiskers around the noses. Glue small pieces of yarn for tails.

3. Place a small marble under each mouse. Set them on a board. Tilt the board so the mice race down it.

PILGRIM PLACE CARD
(poster board)

1. Draw a Pilgrim boy from the waist up on a piece of poster board. Color with markers.

2. Cut out the boy, as shown, making a long tab. Fold at the dotted lines so he will stand.

BAKING-CUP TURKEY CAN
(paper baking cup, construction paper, round cardboard container with lid)

1. Spread open a paper baking cup. Cut the cup in half. Cut out the half-circle of one cup half and shape the pleated section into two wings.

2. Use the other half for the fan-shaped tail, cutting small slashes in it. Cut a body and feet from construction paper and color with markers. Glue all the parts in the center of a piece of paper.

3. Cover a round cardboard container with construction paper. Glue the turkey picture onto the container.

PIN THE TAIL ON THE TURKEY
(white paper, poster board, corrugated cardboard, yarn, pushpins)

1. Draw a large picture of a turkey on white paper. Cut out the drawing, and glue it in the center of a large piece of poster board.

2. Glue the poster board on a sheet of corrugated cardboard. Punch two holes, one at each corner, and tie a piece of yarn for a hanger.

3. Cut tail feathers from poster board, using a variety of colors. Press a pushpin in the base of a tail feather.

To play: Hang the turkey on a wall. All players receive a tail feather with a pushpin. Blindfold the players when it's their turn. Spin the players around, point them in the direction of the turkey, and let them pin their tail feathers on the turkey.

MILKWEED-POD BOX

(pinking shears, construction paper, white gift box, dried milkweed-pod halves, lentils)

1. Using pinking shears to give a saw-toothed design, cut a piece of construction paper to fit the top of a white gift box. Glue the paper to the top of the box.

2. Arrange a design of dried milkweed-pod halves as flower petals and lentils for the flower's center. Glue in place and let dry.

OWL GIFT BAG

(construction paper, brown paper bag, chenille stick)

1. Cut two hearts, about 6 inches square, from construction paper.

2. Cut paper wings and glue them to one of the hearts. Add paper feet. Glue the heart to the front of a brown paper bag, 1 inch down from the opening.

3. To make the head, fold down 3 inches of the second heart. Cut and glue paper eyes and a beak to the folded flap. Cut paper triangles for ear tufts and glue them under the flap, just below the fold, so they stick out at the sides.

4. Open the folded heart and spread glue below the fold. Press it against the back side of the bag so the fold is even with the top of the bag.

5. To make a handle, bend a chenille stick in a horseshoe shape, with 2 inches at each end bent toward the center. Tape the ends inside the fold.

6. Close the bag by folding the flap down. Draw curved lines on the owl to make feathers.

CORNUCOPIA WALL HANGING

(plastic-foam trays, poster board, rickrack, yarn)

1. Draw and cut out a cornucopia shape from a large plastic-foam tray. Glue it on a piece of poster board.

2. Draw and cut out various fruit and vegetable shapes from different-colored plastic-foam trays. Glue them at the opening of the cornucopia.

3. Glue a strip of rickrack across the top and bottom of the poster board. Punch two holes at the top and tie a yarn hanger.

TUBE PILGRIMS
(bathroom tissue tubes, brown paper bag, poster paint, paper)

1. Use a bathroom tissue tube for each body. To make arms, cut circles from a brown paper bag, slit to the center, shape into cones, and glue. Cut a man's hat from brown paper. Paint the body, arms, and hat with poster paint and let dry.

2. For the heads, cut two 1 1/2-inch-wide rings from a bathroom tissue tube. Paint them and let dry.

3. Glue the arms, heads, and the man's hat to the bodies. Add cut-paper features to each head. Cut out a hat and glue onto the woman. Add other paper features.

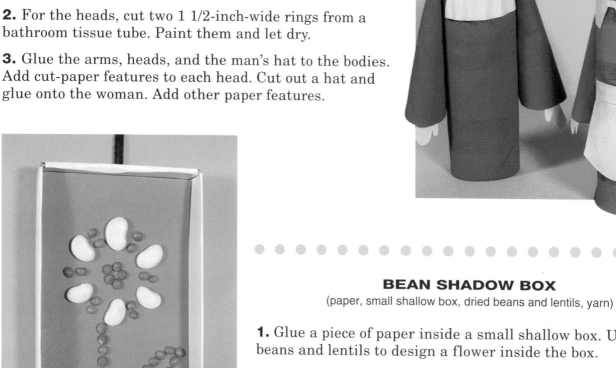

BEAN SHADOW BOX
(paper, small shallow box, dried beans and lentils, yarn)

1. Glue a piece of paper inside a small shallow box. Use dried beans and lentils to design a flower inside the box.

2. Squeeze dabs of glue on the paper and place the beans or lentils in the design.

3. Cut and glue a loop of yarn to the back of the box for a hanger.

TURKEY PAPERWEIGHT
(rock, construction paper, cardboard egg carton, poster paint)

1. Find a rock that looks like a fat turkey body. Wash and dry the rock.

2. From construction paper, cut feathers of different sizes for the tail. Cut paper wings. Glue them to the rock body.

3. Cut a cup from a cardboard egg carton and cover with poster paint. Let dry. Add paper eyes and a beak. Glue the head on the body.

HAIR CLIP
(3-inch metal barrette base, cardboard, ribbon, rubber band, poster board)

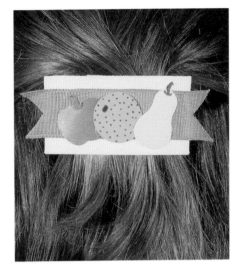

1. Recycle a metal barrette base by removing the old ribbon.

2. Cut a 3-inch-long piece of cardboard the width of your ribbon. Glue a piece of ribbon around the cardboard, securing the ends underneath it. Glue the cardboard to the top of the barrette. Hold it in place with a rubber band and let dry.

3. Glue a smaller ribbon of another color on top of the first ribbon, as shown. Draw and cut out fruit shapes from poster board. Add details with a marker. Glue them on top of the ribbon.

WISHBONE WELCOME
(paper, string, ribbon)

1. Cut a wishbone shape from a piece of paper. Punch a hole at the top and tie a piece of string for a hanger.

2. Punch two holes just below the hanger and tie a bow from ribbon. Punch a hole at each end of the wishbone.

3. Make a sign on a rectangular piece of paper. Write "Welcome, we wish you a happy Thanksgiving."

4. Punch a hole at the top corners of the sign to line up with the holes at the ends of the wishbone. Tie the sign to the wishbone with string.

RECIPE HOLDER
(small cardboard box, 4-by-6-inch index cards, fabric, felt)

1. With tape, close the opening of a small cardboard box, such as one that holds cookies.

2. *Ask an adult to help you* cut off one side panel. A 4-by-6-inch index card should fit inside.

3. Spread glue on the outside and 1 inch inside the box opening. Cut out a piece of fabric and press it into the glue, covering the box.

4. Cut out letters from felt to spell the word "Recipes." Glue the letters to one side of the box. Fill the box with recipes written on the index cards.

POTATO TURKEY
(potato, poster board, table knife, bathroom tissue tube)

1. Wash and dry a potato that looks like a fat turkey body.

2. Cut tail and wing feathers and a head and neck from poster board.

3. *Ask an adult to help you* make small slits at the front, back, and sides of the potato with a table knife. Gently slide the head and neck into the front slit. Slide the tail and wing feathers into the back and side slits. Add glue.

4. Cut a 2-inch ring from a bathroom tissue tube, paint it, and let it dry. Place the potato turkey on top of the ring.

THANKFULNESS CARD
(poster board, fallen leaf, construction paper)

1. Fold a piece of poster board in half. On the front, trace around a fallen leaf. Tear scraps of construction paper into small pieces, and glue them to fill the leaf shape.

2. Inside the card, write a message such as "Thank you for being there when I need you."

PILGRIM PUPPET
(small brown paper bag, paper)

1. Flatten a small brown paper bag. With paper and glue, make the girl's head, starting from her top lip to her hat, on the bottom of the paper bag.

2. Lift up the bag bottom. Cut and glue features for the bottom half of her hat, her mouth, and the rest of her body.

3. Place your hand inside the bag, and curve your fingers over the fold to move the puppet's head.

PHOTO MOUSE
(paper, photograph)

1. Cut out a 4-by-5-inch piece of paper. Cut the paper into three equal sections, as shown.

2. Fold the top section forward. Cut in 1/2 inch on the fold from each side (between the top and middle sections). With the top still folded forward, fold the curved ends up to meet in the center to form the head. Add eyes and a nose with a marker.

3. Cut paper whiskers, half-circles for inside the ears, and a strip for the tail. Glue them in place. Roll the end of the tail around a pencil to curve it.

4. Cut a paper circle for the mouse's belly. Glue it in place. Glue a photo to the center of it.

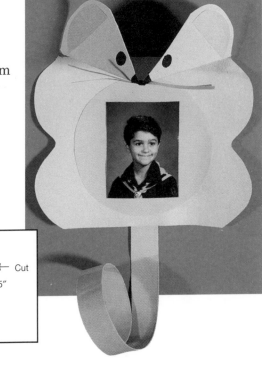

POPCORN HOLDER
(felt, round cardboard container with lid, rickrack)

1. Cut yellow felt and glue onto a round cardboard container. Cut out and glue other pieces of felt to create an ear of corn for a decoration.

2. Add rickrack around the top and bottom of the container.

3. Store kernels of popcorn in the container.

TALL TURKEY
(toothpaste box, brown wrapping paper, construction paper)

1. Cover a long toothpaste box with brown wrapping paper.

2. Cut eyes, a beak, a hat, and feet from construction paper. Attach them with glue.

3. Cut tail feathers from construction paper and glue to the back of the box.

HARVEST GARLAND
(paper, felt, straight pins, fabric glue, cotton balls, twine)

1. Draw vegetable and fruit shapes on paper and cut them out. Pin the shapes on pieces of felt with straight pins, and cut around them. Cut two pieces of felt for each fruit or vegetable shape.

2. Spread glue on the edges of one felt shape, and place a few cotton balls in the center. Place the second piece of felt on top of the first, pressing the pieces together at the edges. Add green felt pieces for leaves.

3. Glue or staple the decorations to a long piece of twine. Hang the garland over a door or window.

ICE-CREAM-STICK PUZZLE
(ice-cream sticks, masking tape, markers or crayons)

1. Place several ice-cream sticks together on your work surface. Place a strip of masking tape across all the sticks. Number the sticks in order, left to right.

2. Turn the sticks over. Draw a picture on them with markers or crayons. Remove the tape.

3. Mix up the sticks, and try to put the picture back together without looking at the numbers on the back.

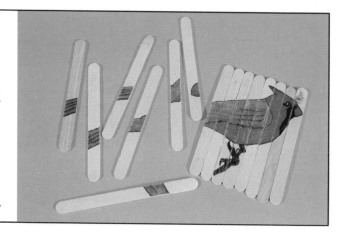

THANKSGIVING FAVOR
(paper towel tube, treats, brown wrapping paper, ribbon, cotton ball, construction paper)

1. For each favor, cut a 5-inch section from a paper towel tube. Place treats inside the tube.

2. Cut a piece of brown wrapping paper about 8 by 10 inches. Wrap the paper around the tube. Gather the ends and tie with a ribbon. Cut slits in the ends, making fringe. Glue a cotton ball for a head. Add features from construction paper.

3. For the tail, cut different-sized circles of yellow, black, and red construction paper, as shown. Fringe the edges of the circles and glue the circles on top of each other. Cut about 1/4 inch off the bottom so the tail is even. Glue the tail to the tube.

PORCUPINE
(3-inch plastic-foam ball, table knife, ice-cream stick,
2-inch plastic-foam ball, poster paint, sponge, felt, toothpicks)

1. To make the body, cut a 3-inch plastic-foam ball in half with a table knife. Place one of the halves in your supply box to use another time.

2. To make the head and neck, break an ice-cream stick in half. Put glue on one end of the stick, and push it into a 2-inch plastic-foam ball. Put glue on the other end of the stick and push it into the body.

3. Cover the body with poster paint, using a small piece of sponge. When dry, place the body on a piece of felt, and trace around it. Add four feet and a tail. Cut out the felt shape, and glue it to the body.

4. Break off the ends of one ice-cream stick. Paint them black. When dry, add glue and insert them in the head for ears. Cut out felt eyes and a nose, and glue to the head. Draw a mouth with a marker.

5. Paint some toothpicks black and let dry. Break them in half and insert them in the body. Add toothpick whiskers.

FESTIVE FRUIT CUP
(plastic cup, paper)

1. Create fruit designs, such as grapes, apples, and pears, on a plastic cup with cutout paper. Attach with glue.

2. Make a cup with different fruit on it for each dinner guest.

TONGUE DEPRESSOR PUPPET
(tempera paint, tongue depressor, permanent marker,
two moveable plastic eyes, construction paper, lightweight cardboard)

1. Paint a turkey body on a tongue depressor. Add a beak and feet with a permanent marker. Glue two moveable plastic eyes on the turkey.

2. Cut tail feathers from construction paper, and glue them to the back of the tongue depressor.

3. Glue a lightweight piece of cardboard in the shape of a ring to the back of the tongue depressor. When dry, place the puppet on your finger.

CHRYSANTHEMUM SCULPTURE
(poster paint, bathroom tissue tubes, yarn, paper)

1. Paint two bathroom tissue tubes and let dry.

2. For each tube, begin by cutting 1/2 inch from the end of the tube. Continue to cut around in a coil shape toward the other end of the tube. Bend the two ends of the coil together, and tie with a piece of yarn to form one flower.

3. Glue the flowers to a piece of paper. Add painted stems and leaves.

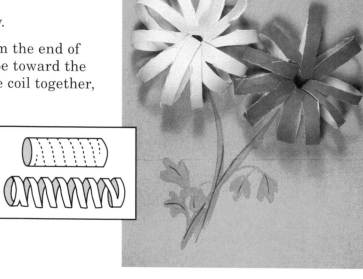

EGG-CARTON TURKEY
(cardboard egg carton, poster paint, lightweight cardboard, construction paper)

1. To make the body, cut two cups from a cardboard egg carton and glue them together. Paint when the glue is dry.

2. To make the tail feathers, cut another cup from the egg carton. Carefully cut a zigzag edge around the rim. Paint tail feathers. When dry, glue it to the body.

3. Cut out the neck and head from lightweight cardboard. Add details with paint. Cut a small slit in the body and glue the shape in place.

4. Add construction paper wings and feet.

SALT-AND-PEPPER PILGRIMS
(cardboard salt-and-pepper shakers, paper)

1. Decorate the sides of cardboard salt-and-pepper shakers with cut pieces of paper to make features and clothing for a Pilgrim boy and a Pilgrim girl.

2. Use markers to add eyes, noses, and mouths.

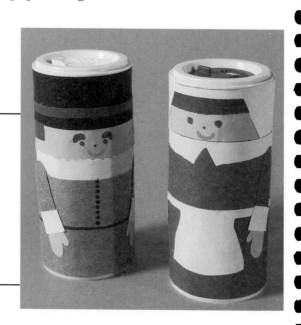

MARBLE BEETLE BUG
(heavyweight paper, small marble)

1. Draw a 4-inch-long shape, as shown, on heavyweight paper. Fold up the sides on the dotted lines. Overlap and tape the tabs together.

2. Roll each end of the center strip around a pencil to curve it. Wrap one end of the strip around the overlapped tabs. Tape in place.

3. Place a small marble inside. Wrap the other end of the center strip around the shape and tape in place. Decorate with markers. Give the bug a little push, and it will wobble back and forth.

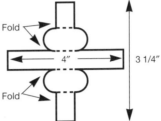

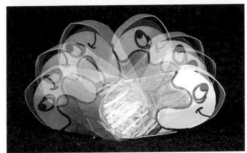

HOLIDAY GROCERY ENVELOPE
(envelope)

1. On the front of an envelope, draw a holiday design and straight black lines in the center, as shown.

2. List your holiday groceries on the lines. Place coupons inside the envelope.

SCARECROW WREATH
(fallen leaves, magazine, paper plate, ice-cream sticks, brown paper bag, yarn, fabric)

1. Place fallen leaves between magazine pages to press and dry for a few days. Cut the center from a paper plate, leaving a ring. Glue the dried leaves around the ring.

2. To make the scarecrow's body, glue two ice-cream sticks in an X shape. Glue another stick across the front of the X for arms. For the face, cut a circle from a brown paper bag. Glue yarn pieces to the ends of the arms and legs and to the head.

3. To make clothes, glue fabric around the legs for pants. Cut out a shirt. Glue it to the body.

4. To make a hat, cut a circle and a strip from the paper bag. Roll the strip and glue it to the center of the circle.

5. Glue the scarecrow to the wreath. Add a yarn hanger to the back.

WOODEN-SPOON PILGRIM
(paper, wooden spoon, fabric, yarn)

1. To make the head, cut eyes, a mouth, and hair from paper. Glue them to the inside of a wooden spoon. Cut a bonnet from paper and glue it to the outside of the wooden spoon.

2. To make the dress, cut an A-shaped piece of fabric and glue it around the spoon handle. Cut fabric arms and glue them to the back.

3. Add a collar, cuffs, hands, and apron from paper. Cut a small piece of yarn and make a bow. Glue it to the collar.

4. Attach a small piece of yarn to the back of the bonnet for a hanger.

TURKEY FOOD CLIP
(spring-type clothespin, paper)

1. For the head, cut a small circle from paper. Add paper eyes, a beak, and a wattle. Glue the head to one side of a spring-type clothespin.

2. Cut another small circle from paper. Add paper tail feathers around the edge. Glue the tail to the other side of the clothespin.

3. Cut a body from paper and glue it under the head. Draw legs and feet with a marker.

HOLIDAY POSTCARD
(paper, poster board)

1. Draw a fireplace scene similar to the way the Pilgrim home may have looked. Write a message such as "Good Wishes for Thanksgiving Day" in the lower corner.

2. Glue the picture on a piece of poster board that is slightly larger than the drawing to form a border. (The postal minimum size is 3 1/2 by 5 inches, the maximum size is 4 1/4 by 6 inches.)

3. On the back of the picture, draw a line to create a message area and address section. Add a stamp in the upper right-hand corner of the postcard.

STUFFED TURKEY
(brown paper bag, construction paper, yarn, cotton balls, chenille stick)

1. Cut two 8-inch circles from a brown paper bag. Cut a slit in the middle of one circle. Insert a turkey's head made of construction paper. Tape in place.

2. Place the second circle behind the first circle. Punch holes around the edge of the circles, about 1 inch apart. Lace the circles together with a piece of yarn, leaving an opening. Stuff the turkey with cotton balls. Finish lacing, and tie the ends of the yarn together.

3. Cut tail feathers from construction paper, and glue them between the circles. Staple pieces of a chenille stick for feet.

PLASTIC-BOTTLE VASE
(plastic bottle, fabric)

1. Cut the top from a plastic bottle. Discard the top. Cut a curved edge on the bottom section.

2. Cover the outside of the bottle with scraps of fabric attached with glue.

FABRIC CAT
(paper, straight pins, fabric, needle and thread, cotton balls, permanent markers)

1. Draw a simple cat design on paper. Cut it out. Use straight pins and pin the paper pattern on a folded piece of light-colored fabric. Cut around the pattern.

2. With the right sides of the fabric facing each other, sew around the edges, using a straight stitch. Leave the bottom open. Turn the fabric cat right-side out. Stuff the cat shape with cotton balls. Sew the bottom closed.

Straight stitch

3. Using permanent markers, lightly draw details on the fabric.

DRUMSTICK BOOKMARK
(paper)

1. Draw and cut out a turkey-drumstick shape. Color it with markers to create a "roasted" look.

2. Use the drumstick to keep your place in a recipe book.

THANKSGIVING BASKET
(brown paper bag, paper)

1. Place a folded brown paper bag flat on the table with the folded bottom of the bag facing up. Place your hand flat against the bag, with your wrist at the upper edge of the bag bottom. Trace around your hand onto the bag.

2. Without cutting the bottom of the bag, cut in from the sides of the bag to meet the wrist. Then cut around the traced hand (through both thicknesses of the bag).

3. Decorate the bag with markers.

4. Open the bag. To form handles, glue together the fingertips to make praying hands. Fill the bag with slips of paper listing things for which you are grateful.

ICE-CREAM-STICK TURKEY
(2-inch plastic-foam ball, tempera paint, 3-inch plastic-foam ball, ice-cream sticks, yarn, chenille stick, felt)

1. To make the head, cover a 2-inch plastic-foam ball with brown tempera paint. To make the body, cut a 3-inch plastic-foam ball in half and cover one half with brown paint. Save the other half for another project.

2. Insert 1 inch of an ice-cream stick into the center of the head. Poke 1 inch of the other end into the curved side of the body. Glue yarn around the stick.

3. Cut a 3-inch piece of chenille stick. Fold it in half and push the folded end into the face for a beak. Add felt eyes and a wattle.

4. Paint ice-cream sticks in different colors and let dry. Put glue on one stick end and insert them in the body for the tail feathers.

BLACK-BEAR SOCK TOY
(black sock, cotton balls, needle and thread, felt, buttons)

1. Cut off the leg of a black sock at the heel and discard. Stuff the foot portion with cotton balls and sew the bottom closed.

2. Shape the toe of the sock into a small ball. Tie a piece of thread at the bottom of the ball, forming the head and neck of a bear. With a needle and thread, stitch some of the head area together to form a snout. Glue a small piece of felt onto the end of the snout.

3. Sew two buttons to the head for eyes. Cut and sew two small felt ears. Cut out felt legs. Glue them to the bear.

PEAR-SHAPE TWIG WREATH
(twigs, rubber band, ribbon)

1. Take one long twig and bend it around in a pear shape. Hold it together with a small rubber band. Wrap other twigs around the pear frame, building up the wreath.

2. Wrap a long piece of ribbon around the wreath. Add a bow at the top. Attach a loop of ribbon for a hanger.

PLACE CARD
(cardboard egg carton, lightweight cardboard, tempera paint, chenille stick)

1. Cut a cup from a cardboard egg carton. Make the cut edges even.

2. Cut a head and tail shape from lightweight cardboard. Cut a slit in the bottom of the cup and insert the head in the slit.

3. Bend one chenille stick into a U shape. Glue the chenille stick to the bottom edge of the tail with the legs extending below. Then glue the cup to the tail, over the chenille-stick legs. Paint the turkey with tempera paint.

4. For the card, cut a rectangle from lightweight cardboard and paint it. Shape part of the chenille stick into feet. Glue the feet on top of the card.

5. Write a guest's name on the card.

SCRIBBLE TURKEY
(paper, cardboard egg carton, two beans)

1. On a sheet of paper, scribble circles with crayons of different colors to make one big semicircle. Leave room at the bottom of the paper.

2. Cut one cup from a cardboard egg carton. Glue the cup in the center of the bottom of the semicircle, as shown.

3. Cut a circle from paper and glue it onto the cup. Glue two beans for eyes. Add details with a marker. Cut a paper beak and wattle and glue in place. Draw legs and feet with a marker.

SQUIRREL NUT HOLDER
(half-gallon milk carton, paper)

1. Measure 2 inches from the bottom of a half-gallon milk carton, and draw a line around the outside of the carton. Cut along the line to make a small square box.

2. Glue paper to the outside of the box and about 1 inch inside the box. Draw and cut out a squirrel and glue it to the outside of the box. Fill with peanuts.

TURKEY GOBBLER
(paper towel tube, two paper plates, paper)

1. Hold one end of a paper towel tube against a paper plate, and trace around it. Cut out the circle on the plate. Lay the plate on top of another plate, trace around the hole, and cut out the circle on the second plate.

2. Cut five slits in the end of the paper towel tube, and bend the pieces flat. Slip the tube through the hole in one paper plate, and tape the bent pieces tightly to the plate, as shown in the diagram.

3. Using the hole as the turkey's mouth, add cut-paper eyes, a beak, and a wattle to the back of the second paper plate. Cut and glue tail feathers around the rim of the plate. Add legs and feet.

4. Place the second paper plate over the first one, with the holes lining up. Staple the rims together.

5. Put the paper towel tube to your mouth, and gobble like a turkey.

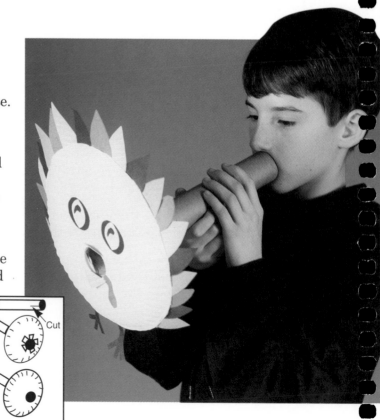

HORN OF PLENTY
(small brown paper bag, modeling clay, paper)

1. Roll down the top few inches of a small brown paper bag. Twist the paper bag tightly from bottom to top. At the top, gently open the bag to form a cone shape.

2. Use modeling clay to mold various fruits and vegetables. Cut different-colored fall leaves from paper.

3. Lay the bag on its side in the middle of a table. Place the fruits and leaves in the opening of the bag.

BRAIDED COASTER
(yarn, thread, straight pins)

1. Cut nine lengths of yarn, three each of three different colors, about a yard long. Group the same colors together. Lining them up lengthwise, tie the groups together with thread at one end, as shown.

2. Braid by folding Group 1 over Group 2, and then Group 3 over Group 1, as shown. Continue until the whole length is braided. Glue the ends together.

3. Starting at one end, curl the braid into a flat coil. As the coil is being formed, add small amounts of glue to the edges of the braid to hold it. Use straight pins to help keep the coil together until it is dry.

PINE SACHET
(fresh pine, fabric, pinking shears, rickrack)

1. *Ask an adult to help you* pick some small sprigs or needles of fresh pine.

2. Cut two 5-inch-square pieces of fabric with pinking shears to get a saw-toothed effect.

3. Place the pine in the center of one square. Squeeze glue around the edges of the fabric. Place the second piece of fabric on top and press the fabric into the glue.

4. Cut pieces of rickrack and glue to one side of the sachet for decoration.

HARVEST BREADBOARD
(corrugated cardboard, tempera paint)

1. Cut a breadboard shape from heavy corrugated cardboard, as shown. Cover it with brown tempera paint.

2. Paint the word "Harvest" on the bottom of the board. Add harvest decorations such as wheat, a pumpkin, and apples.

3. Punch a hole at the top of the board to hang.

FALL-TREE CARD
(paper, old newspaper, sponge, tempera paint)

1. Fold a piece of paper in half to make a card. Spread old newspaper on your work surface. Open the card.

2. Cut a soft sponge into small pieces. Dip pieces of the sponge in various colors of tempera paint. Lightly touch the paper with the sponges to create a fall tree on the front of the card.

CLAY-POT PLANTER
(clay flower pot and base, acrylic paint;
high-gloss, waterbased crystal-clear glaze)

1. Cover a clay flower pot and base with a white acrylic paint. Let dry overnight.

2. Lightly sketch wheat around the flower pot. With a brush, paint the wheat a golden color. Paint a ring around the base. Let dry.

3. To protect the flower pot, *ask an adult to help you* cover it with a clear glaze, following the package directions.

PERKY TURKEY
(bathroom tissue tube, tempera paint)

1. Cut 2 1/2-inch-deep slits, spaced about 1/4 inch apart, around a bathroom tissue tube. Leave the last two spaces wider with 3-inch-deep slits for the legs.

2. Cut 1 inch from each leg, then cut talon shapes on the ends. Bend the talons at right angles, then bend the feet as shown, 1/2 inch from the end. Spread out the slit sections to form tail feathers.

3. Cut 3/4-inch slits on the front of the tube at the center top and bottom. Draw and cut out a cardboard head. Insert it into the slits.

4. Cover the turkey with tempera paints.

HOLIDAY HAND TOWEL
(terry-cloth hand towel, rickrack, fabric glue, felt, needle, embroidery floss)

1. Decorate a terry-cloth hand towel by attaching rickrack with fabric glue along the flat woven band on the towel. Let dry.

2. Cut a felt apple, leaf, and pear. Attach the felt pieces to the towel with fabric glue. Let dry.

3. With a needle and embroidery floss, sew a single featherstitch design, as shown, around the outside of the felt pieces.

Single featherstitch

CLOTHESPIN PILGRIMS
(paint, clothespins, paper)

1. Paint the very top of two clothespins with facial features of a Pilgrim man and Pilgrim woman.

2. Paint arms and clothing details on the rest of the clothespins. Paint the tips of the clothespins to make shoes.

3. To make the man's hat, cut a small black-paper circle. Cut a small strip of paper and glue the ends together to form a ring. Glue the ring on its edge to the circle.

4. To make the woman's bonnet, cut a small white rectangle and glue it to her head.

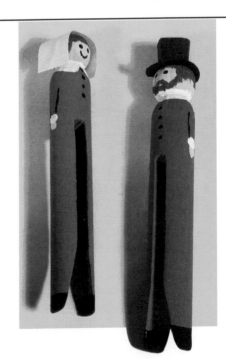

PILGRIM HARVEST CENTERPIECE
(cookie sheet, construction paper, nuts, vegetables, fruits, berries, twigs, walnuts, yarn)

1. Line the bottom of a cookie sheet with green construction paper. Arrange nuts, vegetables, fruits, and berries along the edges of the sheet. Place leaves cut from construction paper on the sheet.

2. Break twigs into small pieces. Glue them together for a "cookfire" in the center of the sheet. Cut and glue red and orange flames to the twigs.

3. To make the Pilgrim bodies, cut a paper circle. Make a slit to the center of the circle and pull the ends together to form a cone.

4. To make the heads, decorate walnuts with markers, yarn, and paper. Let the ridge dividing the halves be the nose. Glue the heads to the top of the cones. Place the Pilgrims around the fire.

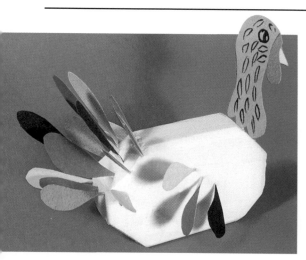

SOAP TURKEY
(bar of soap, table knife, construction paper, toothpicks)

1. For the body of the turkey, *ask an adult to help you* round off each corner of a bar of soap with a table knife. The bottom should be flat.

2. Cut wing and tail feathers from construction paper and glue each feather to a toothpick. When dry, stick the toothpick feathers in place on the turkey body.

3. To make the head, cut two turkey shapes from construction paper. Glue them together with a toothpick neck between the two shapes. Stick the head and neck on the body.

THANKSGIVING PLACE CARD
(small paper cup, tempera paint, construction paper, index card)

1. Cover a small paper cup with brown tempera paint. Cut two side-by-side slits, 1/2 inch apart, in the bottom of the cup.

2. Cut rows of connected feathers from red, orange, and yellow construction paper, making each row a different size. Glue the largest feathers to the back of the cup. Glue the base of the medium-sized feathers in the slit nearest the back. Glue the base of the smallest feathers in the other slit.

3. Draw and cut out a paper turkey's head. Add eyes and a beak with a marker. Glue the head to the front of the cup.

4. Glue the turkey to an index card on which you've written the name of the person the turkey is for. Add something about that person for which you're thankful.

POTATO BAG
(fabric, needle and thread, felt, string, safety pin)

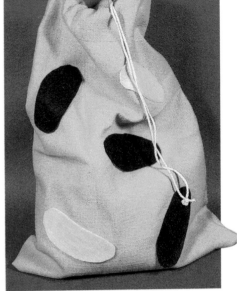

1. Cut a piece of fabric. (See Diagram 1.)

2. Open the fabric and fold over a hem of 2 inches. With a needle and thread sew a running stitch along the hem. (See Diagram 2.)

3. Fold the fabric wrong-side out with the edges touching and the hem at the top. Then sew along the bottom and up the side just to the hem. (See Diagram 3.)

4. Turn the bag right-side out. Cut a piece of string three times the width of the bag. Attach a large safety pin to one end of the string. Thread it through one opened end of the hem and come out the other end. Remove the safety pin and tie the ends of the string together. (See Diagram 4.)

5. Cut and glue felt potatoes on the bag. To close the bag, pull the string toward you and push the fabric away from you.

Running stitch

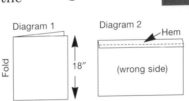

Diagram 1 — Fold — 14" — 18"

Diagram 2 — Hem — (wrong side)

Diagram 3 — (wrong side)

Diagram 4 — (right side)

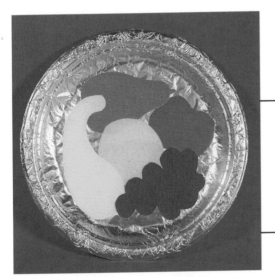

HOLIDAY SERVING PLATE
(heavy paper plate, aluminum foil, paper)

1. Cover a heavy paper plate with aluminum foil. Cut fruit and vegetable shapes from paper. Glue the shapes onto the center of the plate.

SUNFLOWER SPINNER
(poster board, paper plate, sunflower seeds, yarn)

1. Draw and cut a flower from yellow poster board. Cut two circles from the poster board and glue them to the center on each side of the flower.

2. Squeeze a little glue on a paper plate. Holding the pointed end of a sunflower seed, dip the flat end in the glue. Place the seed upright on the circle. Fill the circle with seeds, let dry, then fill the circle on the other side with seeds.

3. Punch a hole in one petal of the flower. Tie a piece of yarn for a hanger. Hang the flower where it can spin around.

HARVEST BRACELET
(plastic ribbon ring, fabric ribbon, poster board)

1. For the bracelet, use a plastic ring that holds ribbon. Cover the outside of the ring with glue and fabric ribbon for the base. Cover this with another color of fabric ribbon.

2. Cut various fruits from poster board and glue on top of the ribbon.

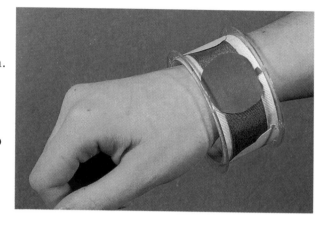

GOURD PILGRIM
(ornamental gourd, paper)

1. Look for an ornamental gourd that could be made into a head of a Pilgrim.

2. Cut a hat, as shown, and glue in place. Cut paper eyes and a mouth. Glue to the gourd. One of the bumps on the gourd could be the nose.

RING THE GOOSE
(corrugated cardboard, fuzzy white fabric, moveable plastic eyes, string, plastic lid)

1. Draw and cut a goose shape from a piece of corrugated cardboard. Place the goose on a fuzzy white fabric and trace around it twice. Cut out the two geese. Glue one to each side of the cardboard goose. Attach a moveable plastic eye to each side of the goose's head with glue.

2. Punch a hole in the breast of the goose. Tie a long string to the hole.

3. Cut the center from a plastic lid, leaving a ring. Attach the other end of the string to the ring.

4. Hold the tail of the goose and try to swing the ring up and around the goose's neck.

TURKEY CENTERPIECE
(two paper plates, construction paper)

1. Fold a paper plate in half. Color it with markers or crayons to look like a turkey's body. Draw and color wings.

2. Using another paper plate, cut as shown, creating a tail-feather section. Color feathers on both sides of the plate. Make the center section of the plate brown.

3. Cut two heads from construction paper. Glue them together and add eyes, a beak, and a wattle. Slide the head into a 1-inch slit along the fold line of the body and add glue.

4. Two inches from the back of the body, cut a slit, slanting it toward the front. Insert the tail in the slit.

JACK FROST
(fallen leaf, paper plate, yarn)

1. To make the body, glue an autumn leaf to the center of a paper plate. Add arms, legs, and a face with markers.

2. Glue the tip of a second autumn leaf to the top of the head for a cap.

3. Add a yarn bow tie and a loop of yarn glued to the back of the paper plate for a hanger.

LEAF SWEAT SHIRT
(cardboard, white sweat shirt, fabric paint)

1. Draw and cut out a leaf shape from the center of a piece of cardboard, making a stencil. Create several different leaf stencils.

2. Lay a washed sweat shirt flat on your work surface. Put a large piece of cardboard inside the sweat shirt.

3. Think of a design you want, and tape a stencil on one section of the sweat shirt. Paint the inside of the stencil with fabric paint. Gently lift the stencil from the fabric. Select another stencil and another color of paint and repeat. Continue until the sweat shirt is covered with leaves.

4. Follow the directions on the paint bottle for drying time.

Corn Creations

Corn was a staple of the Pilgrims' diet and was served during their first Thanksgiving. Here are holiday decorations you can create with it.

DOOR DECORATION
(ornamental corn, string, ribbon, poster board)

1. Gather small ears of corn with their husks still attached, and tie them into bunches with string. Leave a loop of string in the back.

2. Tie a large ribbon over the string.

3. Cut various colored leaves from poster board. Glue them within the ribbon folds. Attach the corn to a door with the string loop.

KERNEL SIGN
(poster board, corn kernels, yarn)

1. Cut a piece of poster board and scallop the edges. Cut another piece of poster board of a different color and glue onto the first. Glue a small leaf cut from poster board in the center.

2. Lightly sketch the letters on the poster board to spell "Happy Autumn." Glue corn kernels on top of the letters. Let dry.

3. Tape a piece of yarn to the back and hang the sign.

DRIED-HUSK FLOWER
(dried cornhusk, green poster board, dried corn silk, dried corn kernels)

1. Glue dried pieces of cornhusk on a piece of green poster board in a flower design.

2. In the center of the flower, glue dried corn silk. Using dried corn kernels, glue them in the center of the corn silk, making a design. Let dry overnight.

3. Trim around the flower with scissors, cutting a flower design in the poster board. Place the flower in the center of a table.

WOVEN MAT
(dried cornhusks, warm water, paper towels, poster board)

1. To make dried cornhusks easy to handle, soak them in warm water for about five minutes. Remove and drain. Place them on paper towels to dry slightly.

2. Cut a piece of poster board about 8 1/2 by 11 inches. Cut and glue sections of cornhusk together, making long strips, as shown.

3. Glue one cornhusk strip vertically and one horizontally in the corner of the poster board. Add more strips, weaving them over and under each other. Cut and glue down the ends of the strips.

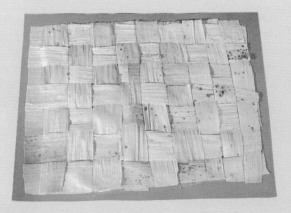

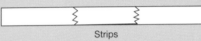

Strips

CORNHUSK BRACELET
(dried cornhusks, warm water, paper towels, leather shoelace)

1. To make dried cornhusks easy to handle, soak them in warm water for about five minutes. Remove and drain. Place them on paper towels to dry slightly.

2. Cut and glue sections of cornhusks together, making long strips. Let dry.

3. Tie the ends of three strips together with a small piece of leather shoelace. Braid the cornhusk strips by folding 1 over 2, and then 3 over 1, as shown. Continue until the whole length is braided. Tie the other end together with another small piece of leather shoelace.

4. To wear the bracelet, tie the laces together.

CORNHUSK PILGRIM
(dried cornhusks, yarn, dried corn silk, paper, felt)

1. To make the body, gather dried cornhusks together. Tie a piece of yarn around them about 2 1/4 inches down from one end.

2. Glue dried corn silk to the top for hair.

3. Cut a piece of felt and glue it around the cornhusks to form a dress. Add a paper collar, apron, and hat. Cut two felt arms. Add paper cuffs. Cut hand shapes from cornhusks and glue in place.

4. Add cut-paper features to the face.

MATERIAL INDEX

175 Easy-to-Do
CHRISTMAS CRAFTS

Edited by
Sharon Dunn Umnik

175 Easy-to-Do
CHRISTMAS
CRAFTS

CREATIVE USES · FOR RECYCLABLES

Edited by Sharon Dunn Umnik

BOYDS MILLS PRESS

Inside this book...

you'll find a fabulous assortment of crafts made from recyclable items and inexpensive things found in or around your house. Have pencils, crayons, scissors, tape, paintbrushes, and other supplies for craft making close by. —*the Editor*

Copyright © 1996 by Boyds Mills Press

Published by Bell Books
Boyds Mills Press, Inc.
A Highlights Company
815 Church Street
Honesdale, Pennsylvania 18431
Printed in China

Publisher Cataloging-in-Publication Data
175 easy-to-do Christmas crafts : creative uses for recyclables / edited by Sharon Dunn Umnik.—1st ed.
[64]p. : col. ill. ; cm.
Summary : Includes step-by-step directions to make Christmas ornaments, decorations, cards, and more. Also includes instructions for making crèches.
ISBN 1-56397-373-1
1. Handicraft—Juvenile literature. 2. Christmas decorations—Juvenile literature. 3. Recycling (Waste)—Juvenile literature. [1. Handicraft. 2. Christmas decorations. 3. Recycling (Waste).] I. Umnik, Sharon Dunn. II. Title.
745.5941—dc20   1996   CIP
Library of Congress Catalog Card Number 94-79156

First edition, 1996
Book designed by Charlie Cary
The text of this book is set in 11-point New Century Schoolbook

10 9 8 7

Craft Contributors: Sharon Addy, Martha Utley Aitken, Karen Wellman Banker, Doris Bartholme, Katherine Corliss Bartow, Beverly Blasucci, Linda Bloomgren, Betsy Jane Boyd, Doris D. Breiholz, Dorothy Anderson Burge, Frances M. Callahan, Wilma Cassel, Lydia Cutler, Ronni Davis, Ruth Dougherty, Donna Dowdy, Kathryn H. Dulan, N.D. Dunlea, Kathy Everett, Susan M. Fisher, Dorothy L. Getchell, Eugenie Gluckert, Edna Harrington, Mark Haverstock, Zelma Hinkel, Isabel K. Hobba, Carmen Horn, Rebecca Hubka, Lola J. Janes, Ellen Javernick, Helen Jeffries, Murley K. Kight, Roseanne Kirby, Garnett C. Kooker, Lillian Koslover, Denise Larson, Jean LaWall, Lee Lindeman, M. Mable Lunz, Agnes Maddy, Paula Melillo, Dorothy Scott Milke, Blanche B. Mitchell, Joan O'Donnell, Helen M. Pedersen, James W. Perrin Jr., Jane K. Priewe, Simone Quick, Roni Reschreiter, Kim Richman, Kathy Ross, Becky Sawyer, Lois Saxelby, Jane Scherer, Dorothy Snethen, Carle Statter, Jean B. Taylor, Beth Tobler, Sharon Dunn Umnik, Evelyn E. Uyemura, Deirdre B. Watkins, Agnes Choate Wonson, and Rebecca D. Zurawski.

Crèches

"Silent night, holy night"... Here are simple Nativities you can make from recycled greeting cards, spice bottles, and a shoe box.

CARD CRÈCHE
(paper towel tube, old greeting cards, heavy cardboard; dried grass, hay, or straw)

1. Using a ruler, mark off 1-inch sections along a paper towel tube. Cut the sections, making 1-inch rings.

2. Cut out figures from old greeting cards. Glue them to the 1-inch tube rings so the figures stand up.

3. Cover a heavy piece of cardboard with glue and dried grass, hay, or straw. Glue the figures in place to form the Nativity scene.

SHOE BOX CRÈCHE
(shoe box and lid, construction paper, poster board, clear plastic wrap)

1. Remove the lid from a shoe box. Glue construction paper to the inside of the box. Cut a 1-inch eyehole in one end of the box.

2. Create Nativity figures from pieces of cut paper. Attach each figure to the box bottom with folded strips of poster board. Keep the figures toward the back half of the box.

3. Cut away one half of the box lid, leaving the rim uncut. Tape clear plastic wrap inside the lid to cover the opening.

4. Cut a small paper star and a strip of poster board. Glue the star to half of the strip. Bend the strip in two and tape the other half to the plastic wrap, above the Nativity figures.

5. Put the lid on the box, and view the scene through the eyehole.

SPICE BOTTLE NATIVITY
(two spice bottles, felt, paper, yarn, cording, jewelry box, cardboard, cotton)

1. To make the heads for Mary and Joseph, trace around a spice-bottle top two times on beige felt and cut out the circles. Glue them to the bottle tops. Cover the sides of the tops with strips of beige felt. Glue on paper eyes and mouths. Add yarn for hair and let dry.

2. To make clothes, glue large strips of felt around the bottles. Cut sleeves and glue at the sides. Place cording for a sash around the waist areas. Add felt hands and feet.

3. For Mary, cut a rectangular shape for the cape, mold it to her body, and glue in place. For Joseph, cut an oval piece of felt and glue it to his head. Add a piece of cording.

4. To make the manger, cover the bottom of a jewelry box with felt. To make the Christ Child, cut a small piece of cardboard. Glue on some cotton. Cover it with felt, making the head and swaddling clothes of Jesus. Add paper eyes and a mouth.

STANDING REINDEER

(bathroom tissue tube, construction paper, yarn, fallen twigs)

1. Cut four sections from one end of a bathroom tissue tube to form the reindeer's four legs.

2. Cut eyes, a nose, and hoofs from construction paper, and glue them in place. Tie a yarn bow around the deer's neck.

3. Using a paper punch, punch a hole on each side of the reindeer's head. Push small twigs through the holes for antlers.

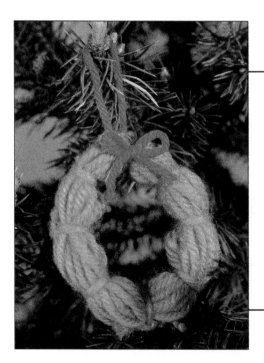

YARN WREATH ORNAMENT

(yarn)

1. Loosely wrap green yarn around your hand about twenty times to form a circle.

2. Cut eight pieces of yarn, each about 6 inches long. Tie each piece, evenly spaced, around the wreath to hold it together. Knot the ends, and trim them with scissors.

3. Decorate the wreath with a red yarn bow. For a hanger, make a loop from a piece of yarn.

EGG-CARTON ANGEL

(cardboard egg carton, poster paint, 1 1/2-inch plastic-foam ball, yarn, paper)

1. Cut out a small, a medium, and a large pillar section from a cardboard egg carton, as shown.

2. Glue all three sections together for the body, with the largest on the bottom and the smallest on the top.

3. Cut wings from the lid, and glue them to the body. Cover the body with white poster paint and let dry.

Cut →
Cut →
Cut →

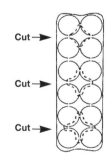

4. For the head, glue a 1 1/2-inch plastic-foam ball. Glue on yarn hair and features cut from paper.

PINECONE PLACE CARDS
(pinecones, green paper, glitter, ribbon)

1. Collect one pinecone for each family member. Rinse the pinecones with water, and let them dry on a paper towel.

2. Cut a holly-leaf shape from green paper for each pinecone.

3. Print each person's name on a leaf. Squeeze white glue around the edge, and sprinkle it with glitter.

4. Glue each holly leaf into a pinecone. Add a ribbon bow at the top.

JINGLE-BELL SHAKER
(large thread spool, construction paper, felt, pencil, bells, yarn, white tape)

1. Trace around the top of a large thread spool two times on construction paper. Cut out the circles and glue one on each end of the spool. Let dry.

2. Cut holly leaves and berries from pieces of felt. Glue them on the sides of the spool.

3. Poke a pencil through the paper at each spool hole. String three bells on a 12-inch piece of yarn. Put the two ends of the yarn through the holes in the spool.

4. Hold the yarn ends with one hand and push a pencil into the bottom of the spool for a handle. Tie the yarn ends around the pencil, forming a bow. Wrap the pencil completely with white tape.

SANTA MAILBAG
(construction paper, 6-by-12-inch brown paper bag, cotton balls, self-adhesive reinforcement rings, ribbon)

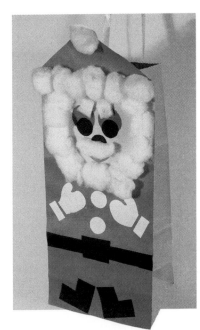

1. Cut and glue red construction paper to cover the lower three-fourths of a 6-by-12-inch brown paper bag.

2. Cut a 4-inch circle of paper for the face, a red triangle for the hat, and a small white circle and strip for the trim on the hat. Glue in place. Glue cotton balls on the trim of the hat.

3. Add eyes, a nose, and a mouth from paper. Glue on cotton balls for eyebrows, a mustache, and a beard. Glue paper mittens, buttons, a belt, and boots in place.

4. On the back of the bag near the top, place two self-adhesive reinforcement rings about 2 inches apart. Make a hole through the centers, and string a ribbon through for hanging.

CHRISTMAS TREE CARD
(plastic-foam tray, poster board, construction paper)

1. Wash and dry a small plastic-foam tray. Draw a picture of a tree on the tray, and cut it out.

2. Glue the tree to the front of a folded piece of poster board.

3. Glue paper-punch dots to the tree.

CLOTHESPIN BIRD ORNAMENT
(paper, paint, spring-type clothespin)

1. Place two sheets of paper one on top of the other. Draw the side view of a bird on the top piece. Holding both sheets, cut around the bird. Decorate the edges with a marker.

2. Paint a spring-type clothespin to match the color of your paper and let it dry.

3. Glue the birds across from each other, one on each side of the clothespin. Let dry.

4. Clip the bird onto a branch of your Christmas tree.

SANTA DECORATION
(wire clothes hanger, construction paper, three plastic bottle caps, string)

1. Pull down the bottom of a wire clothes hanger until the hanger is diamond-shaped.

2. To form Santa's hat, cut two pieces of red construction paper into triangles slightly wider than the top half of the hanger. Glue the edges of the triangles together, leaving an opening at the very top and bottom. Slip the hat over the hanger, with the hook poking through the opening at the peak. Glue on white pieces of paper to decorate the hat.

3. Fold an 18-by-8-inch piece of white paper in half for the beard. Cut slits through both thicknesses to about 2 inches from the fold. Roll the strips around a pencil to curl them. Hang the paper over the bottom of the hanger, and attach it with glue.

4. For the eyes and nose, tie and glue a long string around each plastic bottle cap and tape each string to the inside of the hat. Make a mustache from white paper, and glue it to the beard. Use a marker to draw on a mouth.

DOORKNOB WREATH
(felt, cardboard, glitter, sequins)

1. Cut out a 4-inch circle from a piece of red felt and a thin piece of cardboard. Glue them together.

2. Make a dot in the center of the cardboard. Draw an X through the dot. Cut along the lines of the X.

3. Cut several holly leaves from green felt, and cut berries from red felt. Glue the leaves around the outside edge of the circle, then add the berries. Glue on sequins and glitter.

4. Slip the wreath over a doorknob.

JIGSAW PUZZLE
(old greeting card, poster board, envelope)

1. Choose an old greeting card that has a festive holiday scene on it. Cut a piece of poster board the same size as the greeting card.

2. Spread a thin layer of glue on the poster board and glue the greeting card to it. Let dry.

3. On the back of the poster board, draw a pattern for the puzzle pieces, dividing the board into about twelve pieces. Carefully cut along the lines of the pattern.

4. Put the puzzle pieces in an envelope and give to a friend.

GLITTER-STAR ORNAMENT
(waxed paper, white glue, glitter)

1. Place a piece of waxed paper on your work surface.

2. Draw a star shape on the waxed paper using white glue. Add a loop at one point.

3. Sprinkle glitter onto the glue. Let dry.

4. Gently peel the paper away from the star. Hang the star by the loop on your holiday tree, or attach a ribbon to the loop and hang the star in your window.

SLEIGH CARDHOLDER
(cereal box, paint, poster board)

1. Cut a section from a cereal box to make the holder. Cover the cutout section with red paint and let it dry.

2. Draw runners for the sleigh on black poster board. Cut out the runners and glue them in place.

3. Fill the sleigh with holiday cards.

EVERGREEN BALL
(apple, ribbon, wooden skewer, evergreens)

1. Tie a ribbon around a firm apple, the way you would tie a package, so that the apple can be hung.

2. Collect several different kinds of evergreens. Poke holes in the apple using a small wooden skewer. Push a piece of greenery firmly into each hole.

3. Continue until the apple is covered. The juice from the apple will keep the evergreens fresh. Hang the evergreen ball in a window or a doorway.

PAPER-PLATE ANGEL
(paper plate, quarter, glitter, string)

1. Divide a paper plate into four parts, as shown. On the center line, below the rim, trace around a quarter to make the head. Draw the body and arms, as shown.

2. Cut the plate apart along the dotted lines. The shaded areas are left over but will be used later.

3. Tape the narrow ends of the arms behind the body, with the backs of the plate facing outward. Glue the wing sections the same way, with half of each wing visible.

4. To make the halo, cut a curved piece from one of the leftover pieces and glue it to the top of the head. Add hands and feet.

5. Spread glue and add glitter. Glue a loop of string to the back of the head.

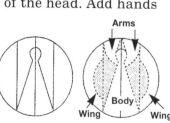

FILM CANISTER ORNAMENT
(old greeting cards, 35mm plastic film canister, ribbon, rickrack)

1. Cut out holiday pictures from old greeting cards. Trim them to the size of a 35mm plastic film canister.

2. Glue the pictures to the outside of the canister.

3. To make the hanger, glue a piece of ribbon underneath the lid. When it is dry, replace the lid on the canister.

4. Decorate the canister with rickrack.

TREE SKIRT
(fabric)

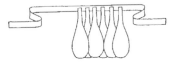

1. Draw and cut out a teardrop-shaped pattern on an 18-by-7-inch piece of paper.

2. Place the pattern on a piece of fabric 2 yards wide and 20 inches long. Pin to hold. *Ask an adult to help you* cut around the pattern, using sewing scissors or a pair of pinking shears for a saw-toothed edge. Cut ten to twelve teardrop shapes.

3. Cut a strip of fabric about 3 1/2 inches wide and 2 yards long. Staple the narrow end of one teardrop shape to the center of the strip of cloth. Continue to staple the teardrops on either side of the center, overlapping each teardrop halfway.

4. Place the skirt around the base of your tree, and tie the ends of the strip into a bow.

CANDLE HOLDER
(two baby-food jars, sand, twine, felt, glitter, candle, salt)

1. Wash and dry two baby-food jars. Fill one jar with sand and attach the lid.

2. Spread glue, starting at the edge of the lid. Place an end of twine in the glue and wrap the twine around the jar. Add more glue and continue until the jar is completely covered. (Do not cover the top or the bottom of the jar.) Cover the other jar, without a lid, in the same way.

3. Glue the two jars together, keeping the one filled with sand on the bottom. Decorate with a poinsettia flower made from felt. Add glitter.

4. Place a candle in the jar, and pour salt around it to hold it in place.

PAPER-PLATE CHRISTMAS TREE
(two 9-inch paper plates, watercolors, poster board,
self-adhesive reinforcement rings, glitter, yarn)

1. Paint two 9-inch white paper plates with green watercolor.
Cut both plates in half, then cut one section in half again.

2. On a square piece of red poster board, arrange the plate
pieces to form a tree shape, and glue in place. Attach a
brown-paper tree trunk.

3. Color self-adhesive reinforcement rings with markers.
Place the rings on the tree. Drop glue inside each hole, and
sprinkle it with glitter.

4. Add a glittery star to the top of the tree. Then glue a piece
of yarn to the back for a hanger.

FRAMED ORNAMENT
(frozen-juice pull-top lid, old greeting card, ribbon)

1. Wash a frozen-juice pull-top lid and let dry.

2. Place the lid on a design of an old greeting card, and trace
around it. Cut a little inside the traced line. Glue the design
inside the rim of the lid.

3. Glue a thin piece of ribbon to the back of the ornament for
a hanger.

PRINCE OF THE KINGDOM OF SWEETS
(46-ounce beverage can, construction paper, cardboard, poster paint,
2-liter beverage bottle, yarn, old newspaper)

1. Use a 46-ounce beverage can for the prince's body. Glue on pieces
of construction paper to decorate.

2. For the feet, trace around the bottom of the can on a piece of
cardboard. Draw feet that stick out from the circle and cut them out.
Paint the feet black and, when they are dry, glue them to the can.

3. For the hat, remove the black plastic bottom from a 2-liter beverage
bottle. To make a strap, tape the ends of a piece of yarn to the inside.
Crumple up some old newspaper and stuff it into the hat so it doesn't
fall down over the prince's eyes.

4. Place the hat on top of the prince and adjust the yarn so it goes
across where his mouth would be.

SANTA DOOR DECORATION
(corrugated cardboard, fabric, white plastic table cover, acrylic paint,
1 1/2-inch plastic-foam ball, string)

1. For Santa's body, cut a large triangle from corrugated cardboard. Starting at the point of the triangle, staple or tape red fabric for the hat, beige fabric for the head, and red fabric for the body.

2. Cut a cardboard strip and cover it with white plastic for the brim of the hat. Staple it to the hat.

3. Cut a cardboard beard shape and cover it with white plastic. Cut strips of plastic, loop them, and staple them to the beard.

4. Add paper eyes and eyebrows. For the nose, paint a 1 1/2-inch plastic-foam ball and glue it in place. Cut boots from cardboard and cover with black fabric.

5. Glue a loop of string to the back. Hang your Santa where he won't get wet.

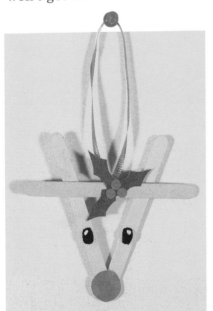

A REINDEER
(three ice-cream sticks, construction paper, ribbon)

1. Glue three ice-cream sticks together in an A shape and let dry.

2. Turn the A shape upside down. Decorate with a paper nose, eyes, holly leaves, and berries.

3. Add a piece of ribbon to the back with glue, and hang the reindeer on your holiday tree.

NOTE PAD
(old greeting card, cardboard, paper)

1. Cut around a picture from an old greeting card to make the front of the note pad.

2. Place the picture on a piece of cardboard and trace around it. Cut out the cardboard to use as the back of the note pad.

3. Stack some sheets of white paper. Place the picture on the top sheet of paper and trace around the picture. Holding the sheets of paper together, cut out the shape.

4. Place the sheets of paper between the picture and the cardboard back. Staple together at the top.

EGG-CARTON CAROLERS
(gift wrap, plastic-foam egg carton, construction paper, yarn)

1. Glue gift wrap to the top of a plastic-foam egg carton, tucking the edges inside the carton. Turn the carton over.

2. With a paper punch, punch pieces of construction paper for eyes and mouths, and glue them to the twelve egg sections. Cut bow ties from paper and glue them in place.

3. For the hair, glue strands of yarn to the top of each head. Draw on noses.

4. Write the name of your favorite Christmas carol on a strip of paper and glue it to the front.

SANTA SNOWBALL TOSS
(cardboard box, construction paper, three 2-inch plastic-foam balls)

1. Cover the bottom and sides of a rectangular cardboard box with construction paper.

2. On a piece of paper, draw a Santa face with a large mouth. Paint or color the face with markers. Glue it to the box and cut out the large mouth.

To play: Place Santa against a wall. Give each player three tries at throwing 2-inch plastic-foam balls into Santa's mouth. See who can get all three into Santa.

THREE-IN-ONE BELL
(construction paper, string)

1. Glue two contrasting colors of construction paper together. Fold the paper in half, and cut a large bell (number 1) on the fold.

2. Starting at the lower part of the bell, cut two additional bells (number 2 and 3), leaving 1/2 inch at the top of the bells uncut.

3. Open the bells. On the right side of the bell cut directly to the fold. On the left side cut diagonally to the fold. Turn the bells to go in different directions.

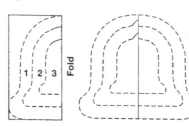

4. Attach a string to the bell and hang the decoration.

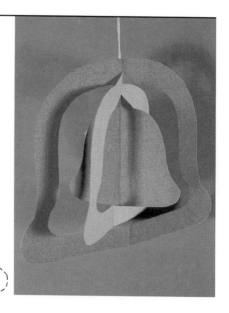

REINFORCEMENT RING CARD
(construction paper, self-adhesive reinforcement rings)

1. Fold a piece of construction paper in half, forming a card. On the front of the card, place self-adhesive reinforcement rings in a holiday shape.

2. Add a colorful bow for decoration. Write a message inside.

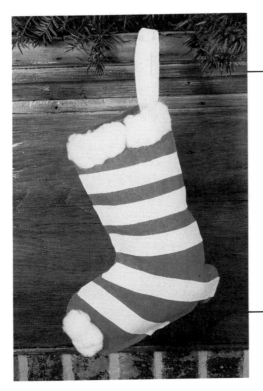

CHRISTMAS STOCKING
(lightweight cardboard, felt, cotton)

1. Draw a stocking pattern on a piece of cardboard and cut it out. Trace around the pattern on two pieces of felt. Cut out the stockings.

2. Spread glue around the edges of one stocking. Place the other stocking on top and let it dry.

3. Decorate the front with other pieces of felt and cotton. Staple a loop of felt to the stocking to make a hanger.

ICICLE ORNAMENTS
(clear plastic lids, white tissue paper, water, white glue, cup, ribbon)

1. Cut icicle shapes from large clear plastic lids. Cut or tear white tissue paper into small pieces.

2. Mix even amounts of water and white glue in a small cup. Brush a small amount of the glue solution on the icicle and press pieces of tissue paper into the glue, giving the icicle texture. Repeat until you have covered the entire icicle, back and front. Let dry.

3. Punch a small hole at the top of each icicle and tie a loop of ribbon.

SNOWMAN CARD
(white paper)

1. Cut a piece of white paper 10 by 8 inches. Fold it in half to measure 5 by 4 inches.

2. Draw a snowman starting with the top of his hat at the fold line, and work down to the bottom of the paper.

3. Cut along the drawing of the snowman, but do not cut along the fold at the top of his hat.

4. Decorate the snowman with markers and write a message inside.

PLASTIC-FOAM ORNAMENT
(cookie cutter, plastic-foam tray, ball-point pen cap, ribbon)

1. Press a holiday cookie cutter on a flat, clean, white plastic-foam tray. Cut out the shape following the pressed line.

2. Use the open end of a ball-point pen cap and press circles into the ornament, making a design. Poke out the center of each circle with a pencil.

3. Punch a hole at the top of the ornament, and tie a ribbon for a hanger.

WALNUT-SHELL CRADLE
(walnut-shell half, cotton, fabric, button, paper)

1. Use a walnut-shell half for the cradle. Stuff a bit of cotton into the shell. Lay a small piece of white fabric over the cotton to serve as a bottom sheet. Tuck the edges in and add glue to hold in place.

2. Glue a piece of paper on top of a button. Draw on facial features with a marker. Glue the button face partly on the sheet and partly on the walnut-shell edge.

3. Cut a piece of white fabric for the top sheet and a piece of colored fabric for the blanket. Tuck the edges in and add glue.

4. Make a hanger by adding a loop of yarn to the cradle bottom.

FABRIC WREATH
(wire clothes hanger, fabric)

1. Bend and shape the triangular section of a wire clothes hanger into a circle.

2. Cut fabric into strips about 5 inches long and a 1/2 inch wide.

3. Tie the strips to the hanger. The more strips you use, the fuller the wreath will become.

4. Add a bow cut from fabric.

CHRISTMAS FRAME
(four tongue depressors, acrylic paint, poster board, ribbon, string, photo)

1. Glue four tongue depressors together to form a square frame.

2. Paint the frame with a couple of coats of acrylic paint, letting each coat dry before adding another.

3. Cut four small squares from poster board. Decorate them with ribbon to look like packages. Glue one package to each corner.

4. Glue a string hanger to the back and let dry. Cut a photo to fit the frame and tape it on the back.

SANTA CLAUS MASK
(large paper bag, construction paper)

1. Measure about 4 inches from the opening of a large paper bag, and cut around the entire bag. Glue a piece of construction paper on the front side of the bag.

2. Put the bag on your head. Using a crayon, have a friend carefully mark where the eyeholes should be. Remove the bag. Cut out the eyeholes.

3. To make a hat, glue a large piece of red paper from the front to the back of the bag. Add facial features from paper and glue in place. Add a white paper beard. Cut slits into the bottom and sides of the paper. Curl the edges of the beard by rolling them around a pencil.

4. Add small strips of paper to trim the hat. Wear a red sweat shirt when you put on the mask.

HAND AND FOOT ANGEL
(poster board, cardboard, chenille stick, paper, ribbon, glitter, large paper clip)

1. To make the angel body, place your foot on white poster board with cardboard underneath the poster board. Trace around your foot with a pencil, and cut out the shape.

2. To make the wings, trace around your hands on yellow poster board. Cut out the shapes, and glue one to each side of the body.

3. To make the halo, form a circle with a chenille stick. Glue it to the back of the angel. Create a face with markers and paper cutouts. Use ribbon for hair. Spread glue on the wings, and sprinkle them with glitter.

4. Bend open a large paper clip, and tape it to the back as a hanger.

SILVER DOOR BOW
(three 8-inch aluminum pie tins, chenille stick, ribbon, string)

1. Cut off and discard the heavy outer rim of three 8-inch aluminum pie tins. Cut each tin into one long, continuous strip, about 1/4 inch wide, starting at the outer edge, continuing around, and ending at the tin's center.

2. To create the bow, make a loop for one side of the bow, then another loop for the other side, holding the strip firmly at the center. Continue making these loops from one side to the other, reaching the curl that was the center of the tin. Let this end hang down for the bow end. Twist a chenille stick around the center to hold.

3. Following step 2, create a bow with each of the other two strips of foil. Fasten all three bows together to form one large bow with a chenille stick in the center.

4. Add green and red ribbon to the foil. Add a string loop to hang.

HOLLY CHAIN
(green and red construction paper)

1. Fold a 3-by-4-inch piece of green construction paper in half, the long way. Draw half of a double holly leaf and cut it out along the dotted lines, as shown.

2. Fold back the center of the leaf at the solid line. Cut several leaves. Hook each leaf underneath the next one to make a chain.

3. Cut and glue red berries along the holly.

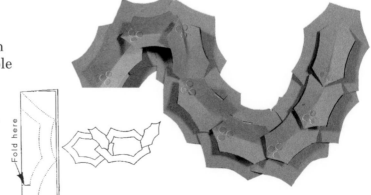

THREE-DIMENSIONAL CARD
(small gift box, paper, green poster board)

1. Use a small white gift box, or cover a small box with white paper. Draw and cut out a tree shape from the center of the lid. Discard the cutout tree and keep the lid.

2. Glue green paper inside the box. Glue red strips of paper on the green paper. Glue the lid on the box. Add paper cutouts.

3. Write a greeting on the lid with a marker. Glue the box to a piece of green poster board that is larger than the box.

YARN SNOWFLAKES
(old newspaper, disposable container, yarn, large plastic lid, glitter, heavy thread)

1. Cover your work space with old newspaper. Squeeze white glue into a disposable container. Dip pieces of yarn in the glue. Press the pieces of yarn through your fingers to remove excess glue.

2. Place pieces of the glue-covered yarn on a large plastic lid, creating snowflake shapes. Let dry.

3. Peel the shapes away from the lid. Brush a little glue on each snowflake and sprinkle them with glitter. Let dry.

4. Add a thread-loop hanger.

CHRISTMAS CORSAGE
(poster board, ribbon, two 1-inch plastic-foam balls, table knife, yarn, sequins, moveable plastic eyes, chenille stick)

1. Cut a large bow shape from a piece of poster board for the base of the corsage. Add pieces of cut ribbon.

2. Cut two 1-inch plastic-foam balls in half with a table knife. Glue three halves on top of the ribbon. (Save the leftover one for another project.)

3. Glue pieces of yellow yarn for hair. Add sequin mouths and moveable plastic eyes.

4. To make halos, cut three pieces from a chenille stick and glue them in place.

NAPKIN RING
(red and green felt)

1. For the ring, cut a rectangular shape about 3 inches wide and 6 inches long from red felt.

2. For the leaf, cut a 4-inch square from green felt. For the flower, cut two 3-inch squares from red felt.

3. Trim the shapes, as shown. Cut a slit in the middle of the leaf and flowers.

4. Slip the ends of the ring shape first through the leaf and then through the two flowers.

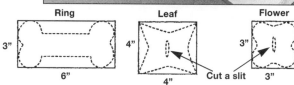

Ring   Leaf   Flower

3"   6"   4"   4"   Cut a slit   3"   3"

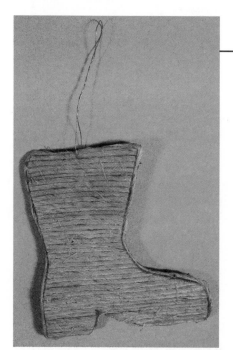

TWINE ORNAMENT
(heavy cardboard, twine, sewing needle, thread)

1. Cut out an ornament shape from heavy cardboard.

2. Cover one side with glue. Press pieces of twine into the glue and let dry. Trim away the excess twine when dry. Glue twine to the other side of the ornament in the same way.

3. To outline the ornament, soak twine in warm water so it will be easy to work with. Remove the twine from the water and dry it off with a cloth.

4. Spread glue around the edge of the shape and press the twine into it. Use a needle and thread to make a loop hanger.

MRS. CLAUS PUPPET
(small soup box, construction paper, cotton balls, paper doily, small ornaments)

1. Secure the top of a small soup box with tape, and cover the box with construction paper.

2. Cut through the box at the center, leaving the back uncut. Cut and glue paper features for the face, using the cut at the center as the mouth. Add cotton for eyebrows and hair. Glue on a paper collar and a piece of doily for trim.

3. Make a hat from paper and add cotton for the trim. Glue the hat in place. Add small ornaments as earrings.

4. Cut two small holes through the back, one at the top for your index finger and one at the bottom for your thumb to fit into. Work the puppet with your fingers inside the holes.

RING WREATH

(cardboard, paper towel tubes, poster paint, beads, paper, tissue, string)

1. To make the base for the wreath, *ask an adult to help you* cut a 7-inch-wide circle from cardboard. Measure 2 inches from the outer edge and draw a smaller circle inside. Cut out a 3-inch circle from the center.

2. Cut off ten 1-inch rings from cardboard tubes. Cut a zigzag or scalloped edge on one side of each ring. Glue the flat side of the rings onto the base of the wreath and let dry.

3. Paint the rings and the base green and let them dry. Add another coat of paint.

4. Add beads and cut-paper holly leaves to the edge of the wreath. Wad up some tissue and glue it in one of the rings, filling it. Glue a paper bow on top of the tissue. Add a loop of string to the back for a hanger.

BELL COOKIE-CUTTER ORNAMENT

(string, bell, metal cookie cutter, ribbon)

1. Tie one end of a piece of string to a small bell. Tie the other end of it to a bell-shaped cookie cutter so the small bell hangs in the center of the cookie cutter.

2. Cover the outside of the cookie cutter with ribbon, making a loop at the top for a hanger. Let dry.

REINDEER CUTOUTS

(paper)

1. Cut a strip of paper about 16 inches long and 3 1/2 inches wide. Fold it in half three times.

2. With the folds at the sides, draw a reindeer's head. Bring the tip of the nose and two antlers to the edge of the right side, and two antlers to the edge of the left side, as shown in the diagram.

3. Keeping the paper folded, cut out the reindeer. Do not cut on the fold. Open the chain. Color the noses and draw eyes.

RECYCLED CARD
(white paper, ribbon, old greeting card)

1. Fold a sheet of 8 1/2-by-11-inch paper in half twice, forming a card.

2. Cut pieces of ribbon and glue around the edges of the front of the card.

3. Cut out a design from an old greeting card and glue it in the middle of the ribbon border.

4. Write a message inside.

QUILTED ORNAMENT
(fabric, 3-inch plastic-foam ball, table knife, straight pin, ribbon)

1. Cut small pieces of fabric in different shapes. Place one piece on a 3-inch plastic-foam ball. Gently press the corners of the fabric into the ball with a table knife.

2. To place the second piece of fabric, overlap one edge of the first piece of fabric, and press in. Continue until the entire ball is covered.

3. Fold a piece of ribbon so the ends overlap. Stick a straight pin through the overlap, and pin the ribbon to the quilted ball so the ornament can be hung.

SANTA CANDY HOLDER
(poster board, white paper, cardboard egg carton)

1. Cut a large half circle, about 12 inches across, from red poster board. Cut a smaller half circle, about 6 inches across. Form each into a cone and staple the ends.

2. Cut a piece of white paper for the face. Fringe and curl the edges of the paper to make a beard, and add eyes and a nose. Glue the face to the larger cone.

3. To make a tassel, poke some thin white strips of paper through the top of the small cone, and glue them in place. Glue the small cone on top of the larger one.

4. Cut cups from a cardboard egg carton and glue around the bottom of the Santa. Fill the cups with treats.

THE CHRISTMAS MOUSE
(construction paper, yarn)

1. Cut three large circles from gray paper and three smaller circles from pink paper. Glue a pink circle in the middle of each gray circle.

2. Glue the three circles together to form the head and ears of the mouse. Draw facial features with a marker.

3. Cut two small holly leaves from green paper and berries from red paper. Glue them to the mouse's head.

4. Glue a loop of yarn behind the head for a hanger.

HOLIDAY SWEAT SHIRT
(cardboard, white sweat shirt, green fabric paint, sewing needle, embroidery floss, buttons)

1. Draw and cut out a tree shape from the center of a piece of cardboard, making a stencil.

2. Lay the sweat shirt flat on your work surface. Place another piece of cardboard inside the sweat shirt. Tape the stencil on the front of the sweat shirt. Paint the inside of the stencil with green fabric paint. Follow the directions on the paint bottle for drying time.

3. With a needle and embroidery floss, sew different-colored buttons of different sizes all over the tree as ornaments.

COTTON-BALL SNOWMAN
(poster board, felt, cotton balls, fabric, yarn)

1. From poster board, cut the shape of a snowman wearing a hat. Cover the hat with glue and a piece of felt. Trim around the edges with scissors. Add felt decorations.

2. Glue cotton balls over the body of the snowman. Glue pieces of felt for the face and buttons. Tie a strip of fabric around the neck for a scarf.

3. Use a small piece of yarn for a hanger, and glue it to the back of the snowman's hat.

YARN CHRISTMAS BELLS
(different-sized plastic cups, yarn, bells)

1. Cover the outside of three cups with glue, and wind yarn around each cup. Poke a small hole in the bottom of each cup with a pencil.

2. Cut three long pieces of yarn. Attach a bell to the end of each piece. Make a knot about 1 to 2 inches above each bell.

3. Thread the loose ends of yarn through the cup holes. Tie the cups together at different lengths.

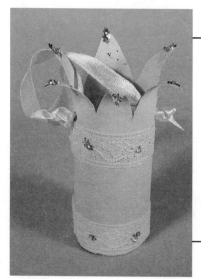

TUBE ORNAMENT
(bathroom tissue tube, poster paint, glitter, lace, ribbon)

1. Cut the ends of a bathroom tissue tube into fringes, scallops, or points. Cover the tube with poster paint and let dry.

2. Decorate with glue, glitter, and lace. Punch a hole on opposite sides of the tube and tie a piece of ribbon for hanging.

FELT HANDPRINT
(felt, poster board, old newspaper, tempera paint, paper plate, cording, sequins)

1. Cut a piece of felt about 8 by 11 inches. Glue it to a piece of poster board and trim around the edges with scissors.

2. Cover your work area with old newspaper. Pour a small amount of white tempera paint onto a large paper plate. Place your hand in the paint until your palm and all of your fingers are covered. Let the excess paint drip off your hand.

3. Carefully place your hand on the felt. (Do not wiggle your hand or you will smear the print.) Then slowly lift your hand, holding the felt down with your clean hand. Let dry.

4. Punch a hole in each top corner and tie a piece of cording from one hole to the other for a hanger.

5. Using a marker, print "Merry Christmas" across the top of the handprint. Sign your name at the bottom. Decorate with sequins. (Add the date if you wish.)

SANTA NAPKIN HOLDER
(felt, red napkin)

1. To make each napkin holder, cut a beard shape from white felt, as shown. Fold a red napkin.

2. Place the felt piece on top of the napkin. Fold the ends behind the napkin and glue or staple them together.

3. Add eyes and a mouth from felt and glue in place.

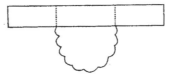

CANDY-CANE REINDEER
(candy cane, moveable plastic eyes, pompon, chenille stick, felt, string)

1. Hold a candy cane so that its curved top faces you. This part will be the reindeer's face. Keeping the wrapper on the candy cane, glue moveable plastic eyes and a red pompon to the reindeer's face.

2. Twist a brown chenille stick around the top of the head, and bend to create antlers. Add smaller pieces of chenille stick to make points on the antlers.

3. Cut a piece of felt in the shape of a bow tie. Glue onto the neck.

4. Tie a loop of string behind the antlers, and display the reindeer on your tree.

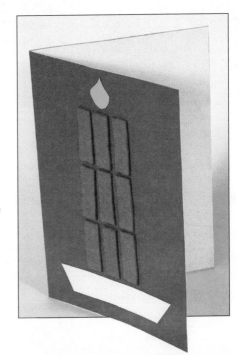

CANDLE CARD
(white poster board, paper, felt)

1. Fold a piece of white poster board to form a card. Cut and glue a piece of paper on the front of the card.

2. Cut 1-inch-square pieces of felt. Cut these into smaller pieces and glue them to the front of the card, creating a candle shape.

3. Add a paper base and flame to the candle. Write a greeting inside the card.

CHRISTMAS CARD HOLDER
(cardboard, burlap, felt, paper, cotton, spring-type clothespin, yarn)

1. Cut a 10-inch-square piece of cardboard. Cut a piece of burlap about a 1/2-inch larger than the cardboard. Glue it on top of the cardboard. Pull a few strands of the burlap to fringe the edges.

2. To make Santa, cut a cardboard triangle. Cut and glue black-felt boots to the bottom of the triangle. Glue red felt on top of the triangle. Add paper eyes and cotton hair, beard, and trim for the hat.

3. Glue one side of a spring-type clothespin in the center of the burlap square. (Keep the closed end facing downward.) Glue the Santa on the other side of the clothespin with the boots at the closed end of the clothespin.

4. Glue a piece of yarn to the back for a hanger.

"GINGERBREAD-BOY" ORNAMENT
(corrugated cardboard, paper, yarn)

1. Draw a gingerbread boy shape on a piece of corrugated cardboard. Cut out.

2. Glue pink yarn around the edges to look as if he is trimmed with frosting.

3. Punch circles of colored paper to make buttons, cheeks, and eyes. Glue them in place.

4. Punch a hole in the top of the boy, and tie a piece of yarn for a hanger.

NOEL PLAQUE
(heavy cardboard, fabric, decorative trim, old greeting card, glitter)

1. Cut a rectangular shape from heavy cardboard. Glue fabric on the front and wrap the excess on the back. Attach decorative trim at the top and bottom edges.

2. Select the front of an old greeting card and glue to the fabric. Write the word "Noel" on the fabric with white glue and carefully sprinkle glitter. Let dry.

3. Glue a piece of decorative trim on the back as a hanger.

STRING AND TISSUE FUN
(waxed paper, white glue, disposable container, water, tissue paper, white string)

1. Cover your work space with waxed paper. Squeeze white glue in a disposable container and stir in a little water. Place a piece of colored tissue paper on top of the waxed paper.

2. Dip pieces of white string in the glue. Pull the pieces of string through your fingers to remove excess glue.

3. Place the glue-soaked strings on the tissue paper, making a shape. Carefully place another piece of tissue paper on top of the shape. Press down gently along the string. Let dry.

4. Trim the tissue paper close to the dried string.

THE NUTCRACKER
(paper, 12-inch paper towel tube, fuzzy fabric)

1. To make boots, cut a strip of black paper 2 1/2 by 6 inches. Start at one end of a 12-inch paper towel tube and glue the paper around the tube. Cut a small section from the center.

2. Cut a strip of yellow paper 2 by 6 inches. Glue it above the boots to make pants. Cut a strip of red paper 1 by 6 inches. Glue it above the pants to make the bottom of the jacket.

3. Cut a strip of black paper 1 by 6 inches. Glue it above the jacket bottom for a belt. Cut a strip of red paper 2 1/2 by 6 inches for the top of the jacket.

4. Cut a strip of gold paper 1/4 by 6 inches. Glue it above the jacket for the collar. Cut and glue a strip of brown paper to cover the rest of the tube. Cut a strip of paper with saw-toothed edges and glue at the top for a crown.

5. Cut a hole for the mouth. Cut and glue strips of paper for arms. Add black gloves and gold paper trim. Add facial features from cut paper. Use pieces of fuzzy fabric for hair, eyebrows, and a beard.

PACKAGE PIN
(cardboard, fabric, ribbon, safety pin)

1. Cover a small square of cardboard with fabric. Glue a ribbon around it to look like a package.

2. Glue a safety pin to the back and wear it on a shirt or sweater.

ANGEL
(paper plate, chenille stick, aluminum foil, ribbon, thread)

1. To make the angel's shape, cut a paper plate, as shown. Fold the plate back to make the angel's body. Fold the plate forward to make the angel's wings.

2. To make the angel's hair, wrap a chenille stick around a pencil. Slide the curled stick off the pencil, and glue it around the angel's face. Add features to the face with markers.

3. For the gown, glue on a piece of aluminum foil. Add a bow made from ribbon.

4. Tie a piece of thread through the top of the hair for a hanger.

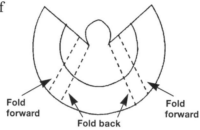

Fold forward

Fold back

Fold forward

PATCHWORK ORNAMENTS
(plastic-foam trays, scrap fabric, thread)

1. Cut ornament shapes from plastic-foam trays.

2. Glue patches of scrap fabric onto the ornaments until they are completely covered.

3. Poke a hole at the top of each ornament and attach a thread-loop hanger.

HOLIDAY POSTCARDS
(old greeting cards)

1. Use the picture panels of old greeting cards to create holiday postcards. Cut the picture panel from the verse panel. (The postal minimum size is 3 1/2 by 5 inches, the maximum size is 4 1/4 by 6 inches.)

2. On the back of the picture panel, draw a line to create message and address sections.

3. Attach a stamp in the upper right-hand corner of the postcard.

NAPKIN HOLDER
(plastic detergent bottle, felt, lace, sequins)

1. On each side of a clear plastic detergent bottle, draw the shape shown, starting an inch up from the bottom. Cut along the line and discard the top and side parts.

2. Cut and glue a piece of felt to cover the front and back of the holder. Glue a lace ruffle around the bottom.

3. Cut and glue a felt tree to each side of the holder. Decorate with sequins and let dry.

SANTA TISSUE BOX
(red tissue paper, unopened box of facial tissues, cotton ball, white paper)

1. Use a double-folded sheet of red tissue paper that is long enough to cover an unopened box of facial tissues and to extend beyond it for the hat, as shown. Cover three sides. Cover the fourth side only up to the slot through which the facial tissues will be removed. This will be the back.

2. Gather the hat into a point and staple. Glue on a cotton ball.

3. For the face and beard, cut three pieces of white paper to cover the front and to overlap 1 1/2 inches on each side. Scallop the bottoms with scissors and glue the pieces on separately. Add eyes and a mouth from paper.

4. Glue a white-paper band around the base of the hat and coat. Trim at the bottom of the box. Add a black belt and white buckle.

GIFT WRAP PHOTO FRAME
(lightweight cardboard, gift wrap)

1. Cut two rectangular pieces of lightweight cardboard the same size, one for the back section and one for the front section. Cut out from the front section an area large enough to fit a photo.

2. Cover the pieces of cardboard with gift wrap and tape down. To cut out the section for the photo, cut an X from corner to corner and fold back the paper, trim, and glue.

3. Place a photo in the opening, and tape it to the back of the front section. Glue the two cardboard sections together.

4. Cut a small piece of cardboard, and cover it with paper. Glue it in the middle of the back of the frame so it stands up.

ANGEL MOBILE
(poster board, string, plastic-foam trays, bells)

1. Cut a large star shape from a piece of yellow poster board. Holding the star with two points up, punch a hole between the two points and tie a long string for a hanger.

2. Draw an angel pattern on paper and cut it out. Trace and cut out three angels from plastic-foam trays. Punch a hole at the top and bottom of each one.

3. Punch a hole at the tip of three points of the star. With string, tie one angel to each point of the star.

4. Tie a bell to the bottom of each angel. Hang the mobile in a window or doorway.

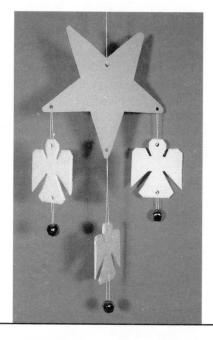

STAND-UP GREETING
(poster board)

1. Fold a long piece of poster board in half. Open the card, and draw a stocking on the front. Write the name of a family member or friend at the top of the stocking.

2. Cut around the stocking outline just to the fold of the poster board. Fold the card so the stocking will stand up.

3. Write a greeting inside.

LACY TREE ORNAMENT
(waxed paper, four ice-cream sticks, paint, paper doily, string)

1. Place waxed paper on your work surface. Paint four ice-cream sticks. Let dry between two coats of paint.

2. Glue the sticks together in the centers, one on top of the other. Place a piece of waxed paper and a heavy object on top of the sticks to press them together.

3. After they have dried, decorate with pieces cut from a white paper doily. Add a loop of string for a hanger.

PINECONE CHRISTMAS TREE
(aluminum foil, construction paper, large paper bag, pinecone)

1. Using scraps of aluminum foil or construction paper, punch out circles with a paper punch, letting them fall into a large paper bag.

2. Brush glue onto a pinecone's "branches." Place the pinecone into the bag of paper circles, close the bag, and shake.

3. Gently remove the decorated cone from the bag, and let it dry.

SANTA'S HELPER
(cardboard egg carton, poster paint, moveable plastic eyes, paper, yarn)

1. Cut two cups from a cardboard egg carton for the body. Cut a pillar for the head and one for the hat. Cut arms and legs from the lid of the carton.

2. Glue the arms and legs in between the two cups and let dry. Paint the body. Add black gloves and boots.

3. Paint one pillar for the head. When dry, glue it to the body. Glue moveable plastic eyes and a paper mouth to the face.

4. Cut the second pillar to fit on top of the head. Paint and glue it in place for the hat.

5. Add a loop of yarn to the back for a hanger.

UNDER-THE-TREE SURPRISE
(quart-size milk carton, paper, tissue paper)

1. Wash and dry a quart-size cardboard milk carton. Measure 2 1/2 inches from the bottom and draw a line around the carton on three sides. Cut on the line and up the sides of the carton, leaving the fourth panel, as shown.

2. Cut a piece of paper the same size as the fourth panel above the 2 1/2-inch base. Draw and cut out a picture of Santa. Glue it to the panel with the open carton in front. Trim around the edges of the drawing.

3. Decorate the bottom of the carton with paper to look like a chimney. Place red tissue paper in the carton. Fill with treats.

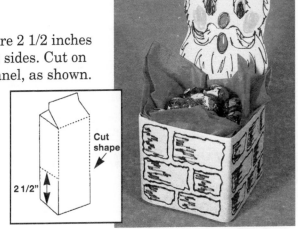

Cut shape

2 1/2"

STAINED-GLASS WINDOW

(white shelf paper, crayons, paper towels, cotton balls, baby oil, poster board)

1. Cut a piece of white shelf paper to fit in a window. Sketch a drawing on the panel in pencil. With black crayon, draw heavily over the lines about a quarter of an inch in width, creating the "leading."

2. Color each area within the leading, pressing hard on the crayon to get as deep a color and as opaque a covering as possible.

3. Turn the panel face down on a paper towel-covered surface. Dip a cotton ball in baby oil and rub the back of the paper. The oil gives a translucent effect of stained glass.

4. Wipe off any excess oil and let dry. Cut strips of poster board and glue together to form a frame. Tape the stained-glass picture in the frame.

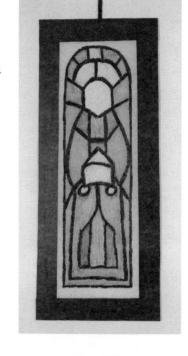

FOIL TASSEL
(aluminum foil, ribbon)

1. Tear a piece of aluminum foil the length you would like the tassel to be.

2. Cut long slits across the width of the foil, leaving a solid band at the top to hold fringe together, as shown.

3. Roll the band around a pencil very carefully. Remove and hold the top of the tassel together. Press the band together and bend the end to form a hook.

4. Decorate the hook with ribbon.

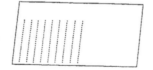

HOLIDAY FLOWER POT
(clay flower pot and base, acrylic paint; high-gloss, waterbased crystal-clear glaze)

1. Cover a clay flower pot and base with an acrylic paint and let dry. Paint on a holiday design.

2. When dry, *ask an adult to help you* cover the flower pot and base with a clear glaze, following the package directions.

PAPER DOILY CARD
(paper, paper doily, self-adhesive stars)

1. Cut and fold a piece of paper to fit a 4-by-9 1/2-inch envelope.

2. Create trees by cutting cone-shaped pieces from paper doilies. Arrange them in a row on the card and glue in place. Add self-adhesive stars and a tree base cut from paper.

3. Write a Christmas greeting inside the card.

CHOIR BOY AND GIRL
(cardboard string spools, paint, two 1 1/2-inch plastic-foam balls, yarn, paper)

1. Cover two cardboard string spools with two coats of paint, letting them dry between coats.

2. Glue a 1 1/2-inch plastic-foam ball to the top of each spool for a head. When dry, spread glue and place pieces of yarn for hair. Add paper eyelids and mouths.

3. Cut and glue long white collars from paper. Add paper bows and hymnals.

SANTA'S HOUSE
(shoe box and lid, construction paper, felt, white cardboard)

1. Cover the outside top and sides of a shoe-box lid with construction paper. Cut a large hole in the top of the lid. Cover the outside of the shoe box with paper.

2. Inside the box, cut and glue white paper to the bottom and the two short sides. Cut and glue felt to one of the long sides to make a rug.

3. Lay the box on its side with the "rug" down. Draw and cut out a window and a door and glue them on the back "wall."

4. Draw and cut out a Santa, Christmas tree, Rudolph, and other objects from white cardboard, leaving a tab at the bottom of each.

Color them. Bend the tabs back and glue them inside Santa's house.

5. Glue the lid on the shoe box and place it on a table for decoration.

Christmas Trees

These tabletop Christmas trees are easy to make. Use them to decorate your home, or give them as gifts.

● ● ● ● ● ● ● ● ● ● ●

PINECONE TREE
(plastic-foam cone, felt, pinecones, ball ornaments)

1. Cover a plastic-foam cone with felt and let dry.

2. Starting at the bottom of the cone, glue on small pinecones. Continue around the cone, adding some shiny ball ornaments. You may want to let a small section dry before you continue.

3. When you reach the top of the cone, add a larger pinecone.

GLITTER TREE
(poster board, old newspaper, glitter)

1. On a 12-by-18-inch piece of poster board, draw and cut out a large half-circle. Draw four smaller half-circles on it, as shown.

2. Draw and cut out a small V-shape pattern from poster board that will fit between the half-circles. Trace around the pattern, drawing V shapes about an inch apart, all pointing outward. Cut the sides of each V shape to form a small tab.

3. Cover your work area with old newspaper. Squeeze glue on the half-circles and on the tabs. Sprinkle with different colors of glitter and let dry.

4. Shake off the excess glitter and pull the half-circle into a cone shape. Tape or staple the overlap. Bend out the tabs.

PAPER TREE
(poster board, construction paper, self-adhesive stars)

1. To make the tree trunk, color a piece of white poster board brown, or cut a strip of brown poster board to measure 4 by 27 inches. Fold 2 inches in from each narrow end. Overlap the folded pieces and tape together, forming a triangular shape that will stand.

2. To make tree branches, cut pieces of green construction paper and glue to the trunk. Place self-adhesive stars over the tree. Add a paper star to the top.

SEQUIN TREE

(lightweight cardboard, felt, rickrack, sequins, ball ornament)

1. Cover both sides of two pieces of lightweight cardboard with green felt. Draw and cut out a Christmas tree from a third piece of lightweight cardboard. Trace around the tree on each felt-covered board and cut them out.

2. On one tree, cut a slit in the center, beginning at the bottom and extending halfway up the tree. The slit width should be slightly more than the thickness of the cardboard. On the second tree, cut a slit in the center, beginning at the top and extending halfway down the tree.

3. Slip the two trees together to form a three-dimensional tree. Add some glue at the seams and let dry.

4. Glue rickrack along the tree edges and let dry. Glue a variety of sequin shapes to decorate the tree. Add a small ball ornament to the top.

TISSUE TREE

(poster board, plastic-foam tray, tissue paper, paper plate)

1. Cut a half-circle from a piece of poster board. Place the half-circle on top of a piece of plastic-foam tray to protect your work area. With a pencil, carefully poke holes through the half-circle, about 1 inch apart. Discard the plastic-foam tray. Roll the half-circle into a cone and staple or tape it together.

2. Cut circles, about 3 inches in diameter, from tissue paper. Pinch the center of one of these circles into a point.

3. Squeeze some glue onto a small paper plate. Place the point of the tissue into the glue and insert it into one of the holes on the cone. Repeat until the whole tree is covered.

RIBBON TREE

(cereal box, construction paper, old ribbon bows)

1. Cut the top flaps from a cereal box. Cut sections from the front and back of the box, as shown.

2. Tape the sides and the triangular sections on the front and back together to form a tree shape. You may need to trim the top points evenly.

3. Lay the different sides of the tree on construction paper and trace around each side. Cut out the traced sections of paper and glue them to the tree.

4. Glue or tape old ribbon bows to the tree.

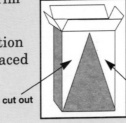

cut out   cut out

SANTA CARDHOLDER
(two 9-inch heavy paper plates, paint, construction paper, cotton balls)

1. Cover the top of one heavy paper plate with red paint and let dry. Cut the other paper plate in half. (Save one half for other crafts.)

2. With the bottom facing upward, place the half plate on top of the painted plate. Staple around the edges, leaving the cut edge open.

3. For the face, cut out construction paper eyes and mouth. Glue these to the plate half. Add cotton balls for the hair, the mustache, and the beard.

4. Add cotton balls to the edge of the red plate to decorate the hat. Glue a yarn loop to the back for a hanger. Fill with cards.

POINSETTIA CARD
(construction paper, glitter)

1. Fold a sheet of construction paper to make a card.

2. Cut out petals from red paper. Glue the petals to the front of the card. Spread glue in the center and sprinkle on gold glitter. Let dry.

3. Shake off the excess glitter. Write a holiday message inside the card.

CHRISTMAS CHAIN
(corrugated cardboard, paint, long sewing needle, string)

1. Cut several 2 1/2-inch circles from corrugated cardboard. Paint the circles, making designs on both sides.

2. When dry, hold them together by threading a long sewing needle with string through the corrugated sections of the cardboard.

3. Hang the chain or tie it to your tree.

FELT ORNAMENT
(felt, rickrack, string of craft pearls, sequins, string)

1. Draw and cut out two identical circles from felt. Glue the circles together.

2. Cut and glue pieces of rickrack, a string of craft pearls, and sequins to decorate.

3. With a paper punch, punch a hole and tie a string for a hanger.

SANTA COOKIE CAN
(cardboard container, construction paper)

1. Use a cardboard container that has a plastic snap-top lid and is at least 3 inches in diameter.

2. Cover the outside of the container with construction paper. Create your Santa with cut pieces of construction paper.

YARN WREATH
(cardboard, yarn, plastic-foam trays, acrylic paint, glitter, ribbon)

1. To make a wreath, cut a doughnut shape from cardboard about 9 inches in diameter. Tape the starting end of a ball of green yarn to the cardboard. Wrap the yarn around the cardboard until it is covered. Tuck the finished end under the wrapped yarn.

2. Draw and cut out three bells from white plastic-foam trays. Paint the bells with gold and silver acrylic paint. Sprinkle them with gold and silver glitter while the paint is wet and let dry.

3. Make a bow, following directions on page 60, and glue it to the top of the wreath. With a paper punch, punch a hole at the top of each bell and glue a piece of ribbon.

4. Glue the bells to the wreath. Add a piece of yarn to the back of the wreath for a hanger.

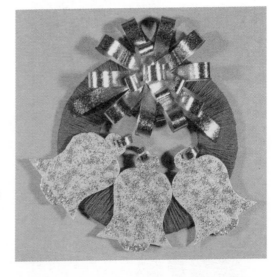

EGG-CUP ORNAMENT
(cardboard egg carton, string, paint, glitter)

1. Cut two cups from a cardboard egg carton. Place a string in between the cups and glue the cups together.

2. Paint the ornament and sprinkle with glitter. Let dry.

RED BERRIES
(paper towel tube, paint, string)

1. Cut 1-inch rings from a paper towel tube. Paint the inside and outside of three rings with red paint and let dry. Paint two rings green and let dry.

2. Glue the three red rings together, forming berries. Press the green rings together to form leaves and glue them to the berries. Hold the rings in place with paper clips if needed.

3. Glue a loop of string in between the leaves for a hanger.

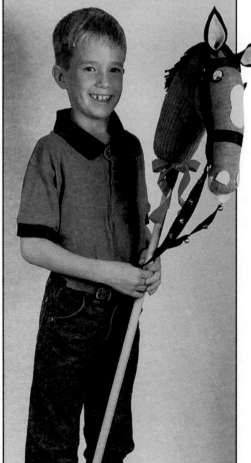

HOBBYHORSE
(old sock, rags, wooden dowel, heavy-duty tape, large-eyed needle, heavy thread, ribbon, silver buttons, D rings, bells, black buttons, felt, yarn)

1. Stuff an old sock with rags. Put one end of a wooden dowel into the sock as far as the heel. Stuff rags around the dowel, then tape the end of the sock to the dowel.

2. Using a large-eyed needle and heavy thread, sew pieces of ribbon to make the bridle. (You may want to *ask an adult to help you.*) Sew on silver buttons for decoration. Sew two D rings to the ends of the ribbon near the mouth area for the bit ends. Sew each end of a long piece of ribbon to the D rings for the reins. Sew bells to the reins.

3. Sew on two black buttons for eyes, adding pieces of felt for details. Sew two felt ears and a blaze in place. Glue pieces of felt to make the nostrils, mouth, and tongue of the horse.

4. To make the mane, cut pieces of yarn 2 to 3 inches in length. Tie four to six pieces together in the middle with another piece of yarn. Sew the center of each bunch to the sock. Sew one bunch between the ears for the forelock.

EASY TREE CARD
(poster board, construction paper)

1. Cut a piece of poster board 7 by 8 inches. Fold it so the card is 4 by 7 inches.

2. From construction paper of two different colors, cut triangles of different sizes. Arrange them to form tree shapes.

3. Cut a paper base for the tree. Glue the base and the triangles, creating a tree shape on the front of the card.

● ●

"GINGERBREAD" CHARACTERS
(light brown paper)

1. Cut a strip of light brown paper about 18 by 3 1/2 inches. Fold one end of the strip to make a rectangle about 2 1/2 by 3 1/2 inches. Fold the rest of the strip back and forth under the first rectangle, making each section the same size as the first.

2. On the first rectangle, draw a gingerbread character with the hands touching the folds and the legs reaching the bottom of the paper.

3. Keeping the paper folded, cut out the character. Do not cut through the folded paper at the end of the hands. Unfold the paper.

4. The characters should be in a row, holding hands. Decorate them with markers.

DEER FINGER PUPPET
(old brown cotton glove, paper, ribbon)

1. To make the puppet, cut off a finger from an old brown cotton glove. With a paper punch, punch out two white paper dots for eyes and a red paper dot for the nose. Glue these to one side of the fingertip to form the facial features.

2. From light brown paper, cut out antlers and glue them to the back of the fingertip. Make a bow tie from a piece of ribbon and paper, and glue in place.

3. Place your finger in the glove finger, and work your deer puppet.

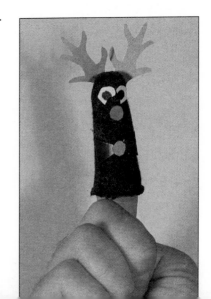

CHRISTMAS ANGEL
(construction paper, tinsel garland)

1. From construction paper, cut a head, a body, arms, hands, and wings. Place the pieces on a table to form an angel, and staple all the pieces together.

2. Draw hair, eyes, a nose, and a mouth on the face. Add pieces of tinsel garland for a halo and on the bottom of the angel's skirt.

3. Attach a piece of yarn at the top to hang the angel on a wall or in a window.

STAR GLUE ORNAMENT
(cardboard, plastic wrap, white glue, yarn, paper plate, food coloring)

1. Draw the outline of a star with a loop on a piece of cardboard. Place a piece of plastic wrap on top. Squeeze white glue on the outline. Press two strands of yarn in the glue.

2. On a paper plate, mix a few drops of food coloring with white glue. Pour the colored glue inside the star design. Dry for several days.

3. Peel the star from the plastic wrap and hang it on your tree.

PINECONE CANDLE HOLDER
(corrugated cardboard, felt, decorative trim, small wooden candle holder, pinecones, ball ornaments, candle)

1. Cut a 5-inch circle from corrugated cardboard. Trace around the circle on red felt. Cut out the felt circle and glue it on top of the cardboard. Add decorative trim around the edge.

2. Glue a small wooden candle holder in the center. Glue pinecones around the candle holder along with ball ornaments.

3. Place a candle in the holder.

BELL NECKLACE
(empty thread spools, fabric, bells, cording)

1. Place thread spool ends on fabric and trace around them with a pencil. Cut out the circles of fabric and glue them on the spool ends. Cut an X through the center holes.

2. Glue fabric around the spools and let dry.

3. Thread the spools and bells on a piece of cording long enough to hang loosely around your neck. Tie a bow at the ends.

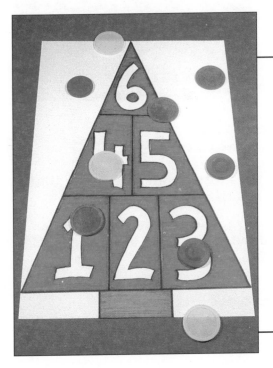

CHRISTMAS-TREE GAME
(two white poster boards, plastic lids)

1. Tape two white poster boards together end to end on one side. Turn the boards over. Using a yardstick and pencil, draw a tree shape, including its trunk.

2. Divide the tree into sections using a black marker. Draw a number in each section. Color the tree green, leaving the numbers white. Color the trunk brown.

3. Place the tree on the floor. Give each player a turn at throwing three plastic lids on the playing board. Total each player's score after three throws. See who can get the highest number of points.

NORTH POLE EXPRESS
(individual-sized cereal boxes, construction paper, plastic tops, cardboard, string)

1. Close the flaps of individual-sized cereal boxes with tape. Cover with glue and construction paper.

2. Decorate the car and caboose with paper windows. Draw children looking out. Add a sign that says "North Pole Express." Decorate the engine with paper windows. Add the engineers.

3. Glue various types of plastic tops to the engine and caboose. Cut out cardboard wheels and glue them to the train.

4. Attach the cars together with pieces of string and glue.

HOLLY DECORATION

(green poster board, paper, cording)

1. From green poster board, cut out five holly leaves. Outline their edges with a marker. Glue the leaves together to form a body.

2. Cut out a circle and glue it to the body for the head. Cut out a holly leaf, outline its edge, and glue it in place for a hat.

3. From paper, add facial features, berries on the hat, and red circles near the hands and feet. Attach a loop of cording at the back to hang the decoration.

CRÈCHE TREE ORNAMENT

(three ice-cream sticks, brown shoe polish, paper, string)

1. Rub three ice-cream sticks with brown shoe polish. Glue the sticks together to form a triangle.

2. Cut colorful pieces of paper, and glue them together to create Joseph, Mary, and the Christ Child in a manger. Add details with a marker. Glue the family to the bottom of the triangle.

3. Attach a piece of string to the back.

HOLIDAY PLACE MAT

(poster board, construction paper, clear self-adhesive paper)

1. Cut a piece of white poster board the same size as a large sheet of construction paper. Gently fold the construction paper in half and cut around the inside to form a curved frame. Glue the frame on top of the poster board.

2. On the poster board, draw a picture and write a holiday greeting with colored markers.

3. Cut a piece of clear self-adhesive paper a little larger than the place mat. *Ask an adult to help you* separate the adhesive paper from its backing. Cover the front of the place mat and overlap the edges.

4. Keep the place mat clean with a damp cloth.

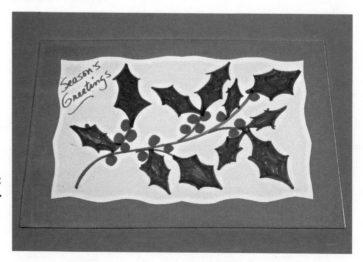

SILVER BELLS
(cardboard egg cartons, acrylic paint, glitter, string, bells)

1. To make the bell shapes, cut three pillars from a cardboard egg carton. Cover them inside and out with acrylic paint. Sprinkle them with glitter and let dry.

2. Attach a string to a metal bell and tie a knot about an inch above it.

3. Poke a small hole in the cardboard bell and pull the string through the hole until the knot is against the inside of the cardboard bell. Tie a knot in the string on top of the cardboard bell.

4. Follow step 2 and 3 for the other two bells. Gather all the strings together and tie a knot. Hang the bells in a window or on a door.

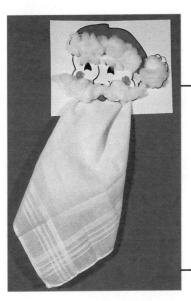

SANTA HANKY
(poster board, cotton balls, white handkerchief)

1. Draw and paint a Santa face on a 6-by-8-inch piece of poster board. Make a cut along the bottom of the moustache. Add cotton balls to the hat, eyebrows, and moustache.

2. Fold a white handkerchief in half. Make pleats along the fold, and insert half of the handkerchief in the slit under the moustache.

ADVENT CENTERPIECE
(corrugated cardboard, paper, felt, rickrack, five bathroom tissue tubes, pompons)

1. To make the base for the centerpiece, cut an 8-inch circle from corrugated cardboard. Lay the base on a piece of paper, trace around it, and cut it out. Do the same with a piece of white felt. Glue the paper and then the felt on top of the base. Glue rickrack around the edge.

2. To make the candles, cut and glue purple felt around three bathroom tissue tubes. Glue light purple felt on one tube and red felt on another. Glue the tubes to the base.

3. Decorate around the candle bases with holly leaves cut from green felt. Add red pompons for berries. Cut pieces of yellow felt for the candle flames. Roll pieces of tape to attach a flame to each appropriate candle.

(Attach a flame to one purple candle for each of the three Sundays before Christmas. Light the light purple one on the fourth Sunday. Light the red candle on Christmas Day.)

MOUSE RIBBON HOLDER
(paper towel tube, cardboard, felt)

1. For the body, cut a piece of gray felt and glue it around a paper towel tube. Cut the head and ear shapes from cardboard. Cover both sides with felt. Glue the head to one end of the tube with the ears in between. Let dry.

2. Draw and cut legs and feet from cardboard. Cover both sides with felt. Glue them in place on the body.

3. For the tail, cut a long, thin piece of felt and glue it in place.

4. Wrap loose ribbon around the body of the mouse and tape the end securely until needed.

FOLDED BELL CARD
(construction paper, ribbon)

1. Cut two pieces of white construction paper about 3 inches square. Fold them in half. Draw a half bell at the folded edge. Cut out the two bells.

2. Using a paper punch, hold the bells together and punch a hole at the top of the bells. Tie the bells together with a piece of ribbon. Write a message on the top bell.

3. Cut a piece of construction paper 9 by 5 inches. Fold it in half to 4 1/2 by 5 inches.

4. Glue the back of the bottom bell to the center of the card. Glue only the fold line of the top bell to the bottom bell, making a three-dimensional effect.

GROCERY BAG STOCKING
(large brown paper bag, yarn, paper)

1. Cut down the seam of a large brown paper bag and cut out the bottom. Cut out two stocking shapes from the paper.

2. Hold the two stockings together and punch holes about 1 inch apart. Lace the two stockings together with yarn. Make a loop at the end.

3. Cut white paper for the stocking cuff. Write a name on it, and glue it to the top of the stocking. Decorate the rest of the stocking with a snowman or other holiday figure.

TABLE ANGEL

(bathroom tissue tube, gold gift wrap,
2-inch plastic-foam ball, lightweight cardboard,
glitter, tinsel garland, cotton ball, paper)

1. For the body, cover a bathroom tissue tube with gold gift wrap. For the head, glue a 2-inch plastic-foam ball on one end of the tube and let dry.

2. Draw and cut out wings from lightweight cardboard, as shown. Glue gold gift wrap to each side of the wings, and trim the edges with scissors. Add dabs of glue, sprinkle with glitter, and let dry. Glue the wings to the body.

3. For the base, draw and cut out a 6-inch circle from heavy cardboard and cover it with gold gift wrap. Glue the body to the base. Add tinsel garland for decoration.

4. For hair, glue on pieces of a cotton ball. Add cut-paper facial features.

5. For a halo, cover a small piece of lightweight cardboard on both sides with gold gift wrap. Cut out a small strip and a circle. Cut the center from the circle. Glue the halo to the strip. Glue the strip to the back of the angel.

CUTOUT ORNAMENT

(bathroom tissue tube, poster paint, string)

1. Using a paper punch, punch holes around each end of a bathroom tissue tube in a decorative pattern. Cut out small oval sections within the tube.

2. Cover the tube with poster paint. Decorate with another color and let dry. Tie a string to the ornament and hang on your Christmas tree.

FABRIC WALL DECORATION

(fabric, embroidery hoop, rickrack, cardboard, cotton batting)

1. Place a piece of fabric in an embroidery hoop. Trim around the edge. Glue rickrack around the rim of the hoop and let dry.

2. Cut pieces of cardboard to form a house shape that will fit inside the hoop area.

3. Glue one layer of cotton batting on top of the cardboard pieces. Cut fabric a little larger than the cardboard pieces, and wrap it around the cardboard. Glue the extra fabric to the back.

4. Glue the house to the fabric in the hoop. Decorate with pieces of fabric to make windows and a door. Add rickrack to the roof.

YARN HOLIDAY CARD
(construction paper, yarn)

1. Fold a piece of construction paper in half to make a card.

2. On the front of the card, draw the outline of the design you want.

3. Squeeze glue on the outline. Press yarn into the glue and let it dry.

4. Write a holiday greeting inside.

STRING ORNAMENT
(white glue, water, disposable container, balloon, string, glitter)

1. Mix equal amounts of white glue and water in a disposable container.

2. Blow up a small round balloon and knot the end. Tie a piece of string around the knot.

3. Dip pieces of string into the glue mixture. Wrap the strings around the inflated balloon. Sprinkle on some glitter and let dry.

4. Pop the balloon and pull it out from between the strings.

PAPER PINECONES
(brown paper bag, white paint, yarn)

1. Cut a square from a brown paper bag. Roll it tightly around a pencil and fasten the rolled-up paper with tape. Remove the pencil.

2. Cut many oval-shaped pieces from the same paper bag. Curl one end of each over a closed pair of scissors. Glue them to the rolled paper, starting at one end. Glue on more rows, overlapping each row, until the roll is covered.

3. Brush a little white paint at the tip of each scale to look like snow. Add a yarn loop to the top of the cone, and hang on your Christmas tree.

BELL PICTURE FRAME
(paper, photograph, plastic-foam tray, acrylic paint, decorative trim)

1. Draw and cut out a bell shape from paper, large enough for the photograph you have selected. Trace the bell pattern on a plastic-foam tray and cut it out. Cut out an oval shape in the center of the bell to fit the photograph.

2. Paint the bell with an acrylic paint and let dry. Cut a small tab from another plastic-foam tray. Paint it and let dry.

3. Tie a bow of decorative trim and glue to the top of the bell. Glue some trim around the oval opening.

4. Tape your photo to the back of the frame, centering the picture in the oval. Tape the tab to the back so the frame will stand.

SANTA CANDY BOX
(paper, empty candy box)

1. Cut and glue bright paper to the top of an empty candy box.

2. Draw and cut out a Santa pattern from white paper. Trace around the pattern on white paper, making two more Santas. Cut out the Santas and color them with markers.

3. Glue the Santas on the box top. Cut out three white caption balloons and write "Ho!" in each one. Glue one next to each Santa.

HOLLY NAPKIN RINGS
(empty adhesive-tape rings, ribbon, felt)

1. Cover the outside of empty adhesive-tape rings with glue and ribbon.

2. Cut holly leaves and berries from felt. Glue them to the rings.

3. Place a napkin in each ring for your dinner guests.

MILK-CARTON CHURCH

(half-gallon milk carton, white tape, construction paper)

1. Wash and dry an empty half-gallon milk carton. Staple the top closed. Cover the carton with pieces of white tape.

2. To make the roof, cut out two pieces of black construction paper and glue to each side of the top of the carton, extending a little over the edge. Cut small slits along the edge.

3. To make windows, cut shapes from black paper. Fold them and cut out little sections. Unfold and glue pieces of different-colored paper over the cutout sections. Glue the windows in place on the church.

4. Cut a door from red paper and add black trim. Draw a cross on black paper. Cut it out and glue it to the top.

ACTION CARD

(poster board, plastic lid, yarn)

1. Draw an outdoor scene on a 3-by-4-inch piece of white poster board. On another piece of poster board, the same size, draw lots of fluffy snowflakes.

2. Glue a 1-by-2-inch piece of plastic lid to the middle of the back of each card to add weight so it will spin.

3. Cut a 36-inch piece of yarn, double it, and knot the ends. Find the middle of the doubled yarn, and glue it to the plastic on the back of the snowflake card.

4. Glue the cards together with the pictures outside and the yarn extending from the right and left sides. Print a greeting on the card and sign your name.

5. Place a note in with your card that says "Wind card by holding the ends of the yarn and spinning the card. Firmly pull ends of yarn away from the card and watch snowflakes fall on the scene."

FABRIC ORNAMENT

(fabric, 2 1/2-inch plastic-foam ball, yarn)

1. Cut 1-inch squares from scraps of different-colored fabric.

2. Place a small drop of glue on a plastic-foam ball. Center a fabric square over the glue. Push the fabric into the ball with a dull-pointed pencil. Repeat until the ball is covered.

3. Knot the ends of a 6-inch piece of yarn together. Place glue on the knot, and push it into the ball between two pieces of fabric. Let dry.

SANTA'S SNACK TRAY
(9-inch-round aluminum tin, gift wrap, clear self-adhesive paper, ribbon, paper)

1. Trace around the outside of a 9-inch-round aluminum tin on a piece of gift wrap and a piece of clear self-adhesive paper. Cut out the circles.

2. First glue the gift-wrap circle in the tin. Then you may want to *ask an adult to help you* separate the adhesive paper from its backing and place the adhesive-paper circle on top of the gift wrap.

3. Glue a piece of ribbon around the outer edge of the aluminum tin. Add a ribbon bow. Staple a paper note that says "To Santa" on the edge.

4. Fill the tin with cookies and milk for Santa on Christmas Eve.

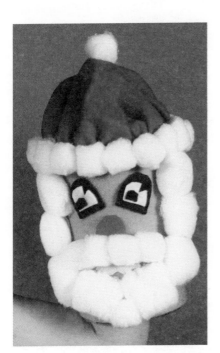

SANTA PUPPET
(round cardboard food container, felt, cotton balls)

1. Wash and dry a round cardboard food container such as one in which snacks are packaged.

2. To make the head, measure the container and cut a piece of felt to fit around it. Glue the felt in place.

3. To make the hat, cut out a circle of red felt larger in diameter than the container. Turn the container upside down so the bottom faces upward. Spread glue around the outside bottom edge. Place the edge of the felt in the glue, gathering the felt together if needed. Hold in place with a rubber band and let dry.

4. Glue a cotton ball to the top of the hat, and add some around the bottom. Make eyes, a nose, and a mouth from felt. Attach them with glue. Add cotton balls for hair, a beard, and a moustache.

5. Place your arm and hand inside the container to move your puppet.

HOLIDAY ACTIVITY BOARD
(heavy corrugated cardboard, gift wrap, ribbon, cording)

1. Cut two 12-inch squares from heavy corrugated cardboard. Glue or tape them together. Cover the cardboard with gift wrap, taping the extra paper on the back like a package.

2. Glue ribbon around the front and the back of the board. Let dry.

3. *Ask an adult to help you* poke two holes at the top of the board. Thread a piece of cording through the holes to hang the activity board.

HEART ORNAMENT
(cookie cutter, cardboard, acrylic paint; dried beans, peas, and barley, string)

1. Place a heart-shaped cookie cutter on a piece of cardboard and trace around it with a pencil. Cut out the heart.

2. Paint both sides of the heart with acrylic paint and let dry. Use a paper punch to punch a hole near the top of the heart.

3. Glue different kinds of dried beans, peas, and barley on one side of the heart. Let dry.

4. Place a loop of string through the hole to hang the ornament on your tree.

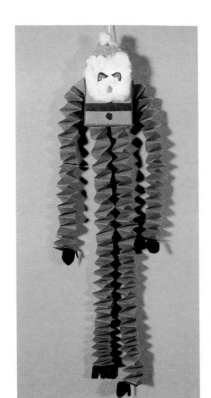

BOUNCING SANTA
(individual-sized cereal box, construction paper, cotton balls, yarn)

1. Close the flaps of an individual-sized cereal box with tape. Cover with glue and red construction paper.

2. Add a triangle of red paper for the hat. Add facial features with paper. Glue cotton balls for hair, a beard, and a moustache.

3. Cut long strips of red paper and fold, as shown, to make arms and legs that will spring. Glue in place. Add boots and mittens from black paper.

4. Glue a yarn loop at the top of the head behind the hat. Let dry. Jiggle the loop, and watch Santa jiggle like a bowl full of jelly.

HOLIDAY HUMMER
(gift wrap, cardboard tube, waxed paper, rubber band, pen or pencil)

1. Glue gift wrap around a 4 1/2-inch cardboard tube.

2. Cut a 4-inch-square piece of waxed paper. Place it over one end of the tube and hold it in place with a rubber band.

3. *Ask an adult to help you* make two or three holes along the side of the tube, using a pen or pencil.

4. Hum into the open end of the tube, and "play" the hummer by covering and uncovering the holes with your fingers.

RIBBON BARRETTE
(3-inch metal barrette base, cardboard, ribbon, bell)

1. Recycle an old metal barrette base by removing the old ribbon.

2. Cut a 3-inch-long piece of cardboard the width of your ribbon. Glue an 8-inch-long piece of red ribbon around it, gluing the ends underneath. Glue the cardboard to the top of the barrette. Hold it in place with rubber bands and let dry.

3. Cut three 8-inch pieces of ribbon. Glue the ends of each ribbon together to form three loops. Glue the center of each loop to the center of the barrette, as shown. Let dry.

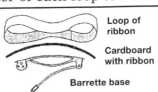

Loop of ribbon

Cardboard with ribbon

Barrette base

4. Glue a bell to the center of the ribbon loops. You may need to tape the bell lightly to hold in place until the glue dries.

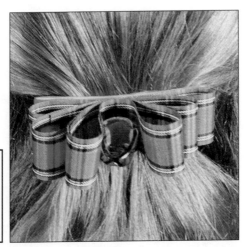

PAPER-PUNCH CARD
(construction paper)

1. Fold a piece of construction paper to form a small card. Cut a holiday design from a piece of paper and glue it to the front of the card.

2. Use a paper punch to punch dots from different-colored paper. Arrange them on the holiday design and glue in place.

3. Write a message inside.

THREE WISE MEN
(paper, gift wrap, self-adhesive stars, bottle cap, lipstick tube top, cardboard)

1. Draw two 10-inch paper circles. Cut them in half. Glue three half-circles into cone shapes for the gowns, leaving a small opening at the top.

2. From paper, cut three heads with long necks. Add eyes and mouths. Stick the necks into the cones and tape underneath. Cut arms from paper and glue to the sides.

3. Make collars by cutting small circles of gift wrap. Cut a small hole in the center and a slit from the outside edge to the center hole. Slip the collars over the heads and glue in place.

4. Cut and glue pieces of gift wrap to make crowns and to decorate the gowns. Add self-adhesive stars.

5. To make the gifts, glue a bottle cap, a lipstick tube top, and cardboard covered in gift wrap to the ends of the arms. Add stars.

THE CHIMNEY GAME
(paper, plastic berry basket, string, Santa ornament)

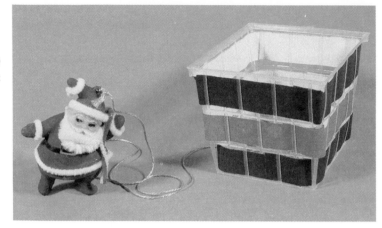

1. To make the chimney, cut strips of paper to weave in and out through sections of a plastic berry basket. Overlap the ends and glue together.

2. Attach a piece of string from the outside bottom of the basket to a non-breakable Santa ornament.

3. Hold the chimney in your hands and try to swing Santa into the chimney.

HOLIDAY BANNER
(felt, fabric glue, wooden dowel, decorative trim)

1. Place four pieces of felt vertically. Overlap the edges about 1 inch and glue together with fabric glue. Fold the top edge of the first panel over a small wooden dowel and glue in place. Let dry.

2. Cut Christmas symbols such as a candle, a bell, a tree, and a dove from pieces of felt and glue onto the panels.

3. Glue or staple decorative trim around the ends of the dowel for a hanger.

MISTLETOE BALL
(3-inch plastic-foam ball, lace, ribbon, plastic mistletoe, straight pin)

1. Place a 3-inch plastic-foam ball in the center of a 14-inch circle of lace.

2. Gather the lace around the ball and tie a piece of ribbon tightly to hold the lace together. Make loops from a second piece of ribbon and attach them to the first ribbon, making a knot. Leave the ribbon ends loose.

3. Poke pieces of plastic mistletoe in between the holes of the lace. Add glue to hold the leaves in position if necessary.

4. To make a hanger, cut a long piece of ribbon. Place a straight pin through the ends. Push the pin into the top of the ball.

PERSONALIZED SLED
(ice-cream sticks, cardboard, paint, paper, string)

1. Glue five ice-cream sticks together for the sled frame. Cut a piece of cardboard to look like a short ice-cream stick, and glue it to the sled for the handles.

2. Glue two ice-cream sticks to the bottom of the sled for runners.

3. Paint the sled and let dry. Add your name with paint and let dry. Add paper gloves and boots. Glue a piece of string for a hanger.

BAG-IT SNOWMAN
(plastic-mesh vegetable bag, cotton balls, string, ribbon, cardboard, paint, 35mm plastic film canister, paper, button, twigs)

1. Fill a plastic-mesh vegetable bag with cotton balls. Gather at the top and tie a piece of string to hold closed. Tie a piece of ribbon around the center, forming a head and a body.

2. To make a hat, cut and paint a small circle of cardboard. Then glue a black 35mm plastic film canister on top. Glue the hat in place.

3. Add paper eyes and a button nose. Cut out paper boots and glue in place. Add twigs for arms.

THE NORTH POLE
(two rectangular tissue boxes, construction paper, poster board, one individual-sized cereal box, one toothpaste box, cotton balls)

1. To make the house shape, tape together two rectangular tissue boxes. Cover them with construction paper.

2. To make the roof, fold a piece of poster board in half. Cut it the same width as the house. Tape one edge of the roof to one side of the box and tape the other edge to the other side. To make the sides of the roof, place the side of the house on a piece of poster board and trace around the open area. Cut out the shape and tape it in place. Do the same to the other side.

3. Cut several 1-inch strips of black paper. Cut slits along one edge. Glue the uncut edges of the strips to the roof. Bend the slits up slightly to look like shingles.

4. To make the chimney, cover an individual-sized cereal box and a toothpaste box with paper. Glue it to the side of the house. Draw bricks on the chimney and stones on the house.

5. Add cut-paper windows, a door, signs, and icicles. To make snow, pull sections from cotton balls and glue across the roof, chimney, and the front of the house.

HOLIDAY BOOKMARK
(plain ribbon, plaid ribbon, old greeting card)

1. Glue a narrow piece of plain ribbon on top of a wide piece of plaid ribbon about 10 inches long. Cut a V shape from each end.

2. Cut a holiday scene from an old greeting card and glue it on top of the ribbons. Let dry.

HAND WREATH
(10-inch and 6-inch plates, poster board, construction paper, yarn)

1. Trace around a 10-inch and a 6-inch plate, as shown. Cut out the circles, making a doughnut shape.

2. Trace around your hand on different-colored construction paper. Cut out the hands. Glue the hands around the doughnut.

3. Add a paper bow. Glue a loop of yarn to the back for a hanger.

SNOW-JAR PAPERWEIGHT
(baby-food jar, plastic or ceramic ornament, adhesive cement, water, glitter, ribbon)

1. Wash and dry an empty baby-food jar. Select a small plastic or ceramic Christmas ornament to fit inside the jar. *Ask an adult to help you* glue the ornament to the center of the underside of the lid with an adhesive cement. Let dry overnight.

2. Add water to the jar, almost filling it. Add some glitter. Place the lid tightly on the jar. Glue ribbon around the lid.

3. Turn the jar upside down and watch the snow fall.

KITCHEN-SPOON ELF

(wooden spoon, paint, felt, sequins, decorative trim, yarn)

1. To make the face, cover the inside of a wooden spoon with paint and let dry. Add eyes, a nose, and a mouth from felt. Add sequins to the eyes.

2. Cut a felt hat and glue to the top of the head. Add pieces of yarn for hair.

3. Using decorative trim, tie a bow around the spoon, under the chin. Add a felt body and hands.

4. Add a loop of yarn to the back and hang the elf in your kitchen.

MOUSE'S HOUSE DOORSTOP

(stones, large cereal box, construction paper)

1. Place some stones inside a large cereal box for weight. Tape the top flaps closed.

2. Cover the box with construction paper. Draw and cut out a mouse hole from black paper and glue in place. Draw and cut out a mouse and glue in front of the door.

3. Add a sign decorated with pieces of holly cut from paper. Write "Mouse's House" on the sign.

4. Place the doorstop by your front door.

BELL-CLUSTER ORNAMENT

(ribbon, bells)

1. Cut a piece of green ribbon about 14 inches long and fold in half. Measure 2 inches down from the fold, and glue the rest of the ribbon together, leaving the 2-inch loop at the top.

2. Tie a knot about 2 inches up from the bottom of the ribbon.

3. Cut four pieces of red ribbon. String one bell on each piece of ribbon, and tie in a bow to the green ribbon above the knot.

4. Slide the bells down to the knot, forming a cluster.

WOODEN BLOCK ORNAMENT
(wooden block, acrylic paint, string)

1. Using a pencil, draw features on a small wooden block to represent a house.

2. Paint the house. Add details such as candles and ribbons to the windows.

3. Form a piece of string into a loop and glue it onto the top of the house for a hanger. You can write the date and your name on the bottom of the ornament.

WINTER SCENE
(paint, heavy paper plate, construction paper, string)

1. Paint the inside and outer edge of a heavy paper plate, making the background for a scene.

2. Cut a snowman, hat, and scarf from construction paper. Glue them onto the scene. Cut tiny pieces of white paper for the snowflakes and glue them around the outer edge of the plate.

3. Glue or tape a loop of string to the back for a hanger.

CHRISTMAS GREENS BASKET
(cardboard box lid, construction paper, greens, pinecones)

1. Cover the inside of a shallow box lid with red construction paper. Cut holly leaves from green paper and glue them onto the sides and the handle. Add red paper berries.

2. Fill the basket with greens and pinecones.

TUBE SURPRISE
(bathroom tissue tube, tissue paper, candies, ribbon, stickers)

1. Cover a bathroom tissue tube with tissue paper that is wider than the tube. Stuff little candies inside.

2. Gather the tissue at each end of the tube and tie with several pieces of different-colored ribbon.

3. Add stickers to the outside for decoration.

Wrap yarn

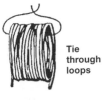

Tie through loops

Cut loops

SNOWMAN HAT
(cardboard, yarn, needle and thread, knit cap, moveable plastic eyes, fabric glue, felt)

1. Cut a piece of cardboard 1 1/2 by 2 inches. Wrap white yarn around it, as shown, about forty-five times, or more for a fuller pompon.

2. Carefully slip the yarn from the cardboard, and tie a piece of yarn tightly through the loops. Cut through the loops at the other end. Fluff up the yarn.

3. Sew the white pompon to the cuff of a knit cap. Sew or glue moveable plastic eyes in place. Add a felt hat and a mouth.

DOVE CARD
(poster board, plastic-foam trays, construction paper)

1. Fold a piece of poster board 8 1/4 by 10 3/4 inches in half to form a card.

2. Draw and cut out a dove pattern from paper. Place it on a plastic-foam tray. Trace around the pattern with a pencil, and cut out the dove. Do this again, but turn the pattern over first.

3. Have the doves face each other on the front of the card and glue in place. Add paper holly leaves and berries.

4. Write a holiday message inside.

CORNUCOPIA
(old greeting card, paper clip, paper doily, ribbon)

1. Use an old greeting card and cut the card 6 inches square with the corners at the center top, bottom, and sides of the picture.

2. Roll into a cone. Glue down the long edge, using a paper clip to hold in place.

3. Fold a paper doily in half. Roll it into a cone and place inside the card. Dab some glue around the inside edges to hold the doily in place.

4. With a paper punch, punch a hole at the back of the cone and insert a narrow ribbon as a hanger. Place small gifts or treats in the cornucopia, and hang the decoration on a doorknob or tree.

MATCH-MAKING GAME
(frozen-juice pull-top lids, gift wrap, resealable sandwich bag)

1. Clean the metal lids from several frozen-juice containers.

2. Decorate one side of two lids so they match, using paper cutouts from gift wrap. Decorate the remaining lids in pairs so that each lid has a match.

3. To play, turn the lids facedown. Each player turns over two lids at a time, trying to find a match. The player with the most matches wins.

4. Store the game in a resealable sandwich bag.

CANDY CANE FOREST
(floral foam block, gift wrap, ribbon, cellophane-covered candy canes, cotton balls, paper)

1. Cover a floral foam block with gift wrap. Tape two pieces of ribbon around the sides for decoration.

2. With a pencil, gently poke holes in various places on the foam block. Insert cellophane-covered candy canes in the holes.

3. To make snowmen, glue two cotton balls on top of each other. Add paper eyes, a mouth, and a hat to each one. Glue them near the candy canes.

4. Place the decoration on a table. Replace the candy canes as they are eaten.

HOLIDAY RECIPE BOX
(medium-weight cardboard box, construction paper, cookie cutters)

1. Cut a small section from a medium-weight cardboard box, as shown. The box should be able to hold 4-by-6-inch index cards.

2. Cover the outside of the box with construction paper.

3. Place cookie cutters on colored paper. Trace around the cookie designs. Cut out the designs and glue them on the box.

4. Decorate the designs with paper and markers. Write "Holiday Recipes" on the front of the box.

Cut

DECORATIONS FOR THE BIRDS
(large-eyed needle, string, unsalted popcorn, unsalted unshelled peanuts, wire, yarn, dog biscuits, cookie cutter, stale bread, plastic straw, outdoor tree)

1. With a large-eyed needle and string, thread popped popcorn, making a long garland.

2. Using the needle, thread about twelve unshelled peanuts on a 15-inch piece of wire. Twist the ends together, forming a clothes hanger-like hook. Cut the excess wire.

3. Tie a piece of yarn around one end of a dog biscuit, leaving a loop for a hanger. Make several.

4. Using a cookie cutter, cut shapes from stale bread slices. Make a hole at the top with a plastic straw, and thread a yarn loop for a hanger.

5. Hang the garland, peanuts, dog biscuits, and bread ornaments on an outdoor tree for the birds to eat. Add a bow to the top.

RECTANGLE SANTA CLAUS
(construction paper, cotton balls)

1. Cut two large and two small rectangles from red construction paper.

2. Glue or staple these together so that the two larger rectangles hang down for Santa's legs and the smaller rectangles stick out on each side for his arms.

3. Cut a head and hands from construction paper and attach them in place. Give Santa a red hat and black boots and belt.

4. Draw his face, then give him a cotton-ball beard. Trim his suit and hat with cotton balls.

REINDEER SOCK PUPPET
(paper, spring-type clothespins, sock, pompon, ribbon, bell)

1. To make the antlers, trace around your hands on paper. Cut out the antlers and add details with markers. Glue each to a spring-type clothespin.

2. Lay an old sock on a table. Cut out eyes, eyelashes, and a mouth with a tongue from paper. Glue them to the bottom of the sock. Add a red pompon for a nose.

3. Glue a ribbon with a bell on the leg area of the sock. Place your hand inside the sock, and clip on the antlers at the heel of the sock.

HOLIDAY "COOKIE" MOBILE
(two tongue depressors, bead, string, cookie cutters, poster board)

1. Glue two tongue depressors together at the center. Add a bead at the center. Let dry. Place a string loop through the bead.

2. Trace around cookie-cutter shapes on poster board, making two of each shape. Cut them out. With a paper punch, punch a hole in the top of each shape. Color the shapes with markers.

3. Tie a string from each shape to a tongue depressor. If you hang the same shapes opposite each other, using the same length of string, the mobile will be easier to balance.

PAPER BAG VILLAGE
(paper bags, poster board)

1. Cut 2-inch slits along the four corners of the open ends of brown and white paper bags. When those 2 inches are turned out flat, the bags will stand upright.

2. Flatten each bag again and draw windows and doors on the bags. Make houses, apartment buildings, or stores. Add Christmas decorations to the buildings.

3. Glue the bags to a large piece of poster board. Add streets, sidewalks, lawns, shrubs, cars, and people.

CHRISTMAS CARD ADDRESS BOOK
(cardboard, index cards, fabric, ribbon)

1. To make the front and the back of the book, cut two pieces of cardboard 6 1/2 by 4 1/2 inches. Using a paper punch, punch a hole 1 1/2 inches in from the long sides and 3/4 inch in from the narrow sides, as shown.

2. To make the inside pages, place a 4-by-6-inch index card over the cardboard and mark the holes on the card. Place this card on top of several other cards, and punch out the holes. Create more inside pages, making sure all holes line up.

3. Cut holiday fabric to cover one side of the front and back cardboard pieces. Tape the edges on the other side. Feel the holes in the cardboard underneath the fabric, and punch out the holes.

Trim with scissors. Glue a punched card over the taped fabric, lining up the holes.

4. Place the cards inside the covers. Thread a piece of ribbon through the holes in the back cover, the cards, and the front cover. Tie the ribbon into a bow.

SNOWMAN ORNAMENT
(three plastic beverage caps, poster board, paper, string)

1. Glue three white plastic beverage caps in a row onto a piece of poster board and let dry. Trim around the edges with scissors.

2. Add paper features to make a snowman. Glue a string to the back for a hanger.

ANGEL PLACE CARD
(paper, self-adhesive stars, ribbon, two plastic-foam cups)

1. To make the angel wings, cut a piece of paper 4 inches square. Make accordion pleats, as shown. Dab glue along the center within the folds, and press together.

2. To make the body, cut a piece of paper 4 by 6 inches and pleat parallel to the 6-inch side of the paper. Dab glue about 2 inches from one end within the folds, and press together.

3. Glue the wings to the body. Cut out a paper circle for the head and glue in place. Add self-adhesive stars for a halo. Cut out paper eyes and a mouth. Tie a ribbon around the waist. Glue an ice-cream stick to the back of the angel and let dry.

Accordion pleats

4. Place one plastic-foam cup inside another and glue together. Add a ribbon around the rim. Cut a small slit in the bottom of the cup and insert the ice-cream stick. Cut a paper heart and write a guest's name on it. Glue it on the cup.

Holiday Wrap-ups

Make your gift giving special by creating your own packaging.

TWO EASY BOWS
(ribbon, cardboard, wire)

1. Wrap ribbon around a 2-by-6-inch piece of cardboard. Cut notches at the center of both sides of the ribbon. Remove the cardboard. Twist wire around the notches. Spread out the ribbon, forming a bow.

2. Cut 8-inch strips of ribbon. Glue the ends of the strips together, making loops. Press and glue each loop in the center. Layer the loops on top of each other, and glue. Glue a small circle of ribbon in the center.

HOLIDAY STENCIL PAPER
(old newspaper, poster paper, poster board, cellulose sponge, watercolors)

1. Cover your work surface with old newspaper. Cut a large piece of poster paper and tape the corners down so the paper is flat on the newspaper.

2. To make stencils, draw and cut out holiday designs from 6-inch-square pieces of poster board, as shown. Hold a stencil on the poster paper. Dip a small piece of cellulose sponge in watercolor and dab the inside of the stencil.

3. Let the designs dry. Use the paper to wrap holiday gifts.

POTATO-PRINT SACK
(paper bag, potato, table knife, paint, ribbon)

1. Before you decorate your sack, be sure your gift will fit inside.

2. Wash and dry a potato half. Draw a simple design on a piece of paper and cut it out. Place the design on the cut side of the potato. Using a table knife, cut away the area around the design, leaving the design about a 1/2 inch above the rest of the potato.

3. Paint the potato design and press it onto the paper bag. Repeat the painting and printing. Let the paint dry before you put the gift inside.

4. Fold over the top of the sack, and punch two holes through the flap. Thread a ribbon through and tie it into a bow.

RUDOLPH GIFT BOX

(cardboard box with lid, paper, four cellophane-covered candy canes, ribbon)

1. Cover the top and sides of a box lid with paper.

2. Cut out a head for Rudolph from paper. Glue on cut-paper features. Arrange the cut-paper head and the cellophane-covered candy canes on the lid. Glue in place. Add a ribbon bow to the top of his head.

3. Cut and glue a small paper caption balloon. On it, write the word "To:" and the name of the person receiving the gift.

CUT-PAPER SURPRISE BAG

(paper bag, paper, self-adhesive reinforcement rings, yarn)

1. Before you decorate your bag, be sure your gift will fit inside.

2. Create a colorful scene by drawing and cutting out pieces of paper and gluing them to the front of the bag. Near the top, place two self-adhesive reinforcement rings. Use a paper punch and punch out the holes in the rings.

3. Close the top of the bag. Punch through the front holes to the back of the bag. Add two self-adhesive rings to the back holes. Thread a piece of yarn through the holes to make a handle.

ORNAMENT-TAGS

(plastic-foam tray, poster board, moveable plastic eyes, paper, ribbon, cookie cutter, felt, buttons, rickrack)

1. To make the Santa, cut a circle from a plastic-foam tray. Add a hat from poster board. Add moveable plastic eyes and a paper mouth and nose. Cut pieces of ribbon, curl around a pencil, and glue in place to make a beard.

2. With a paper punch, punch a hole at the top of the hat and tie a loop of ribbon.

3. To make the "gingerbread" character, place a gingerbread cookie cutter on a piece of brown poster board and trace around it. Draw another line about 1/4 inch from the traced outline and cut out the character.

4. Place the gingerbread cookie cutter on a piece of felt and trace around it. Cut out the design. Glue the felt piece on top of the poster board.

5. Add button eyes, a mouth, and buttons down his body. Add rickrack for trim. Punch a hole at the top and add a loop of rickrack. Add a sign from poster board with the recipient's name on it.

(Use these gift tags as ornaments after the presents are opened.)

MATERIAL INDEX

175 Easy-to-Do
VALENTINE
CRAFTS

Edited by
Sharon Dunn Umnik

VALENTINE

175 Easy-to-Do VALENTINE CRAFTS

CREATIVE USES · FOR RECYCLABLES ·

Edited by Sharon Dunn Umnik

BOYDS MILLS PRESS

Inside this book...

you'll find a fabulous assortment of crafts made from recyclable items and inexpensive things found in or around your house. Have pencils, crayons, scissors, tape, paintbrushes, and other supplies for craft making close by. *—the Editor*

Published by Bell Books
Boyds Mills Press, Inc.
A Highlights Company
815 Church Street
Honesdale, Pennsylvania 18431
Printed in China

U.S. Cataloging-in-Publication Data
(Library of Congress Standards)

175 easy-to-do valentine crafts : creative uses for recyclables / edited by Sharon Dunn Umnik.—1st ed.
[64] p. : col. ill. ; cm.
Includes index.
Summary: Includes step-by-step directions to make decorations, gifts, and greeting cards for Valentine's Day.
ISBN 1-56397-672-2
1. Valentine decorations. 2. Handicraft. 3. Recycling (Waste, etc.).
I. Umnik, Sharon Dunn. II. Title.
745.594/ 1 21   2001   CIP   AC
00-109926

First edition, 2001
Book designed by Charlie Cary
The text of this book is set in 11-point New Century Schoolbook.

Visit our Web site at www.boydsmillspress.com

10 9 8 7 6 5 4 3 2

Craft Contributors: Patricia Barley, Frances Benson, Linda Bloomgren, Deborah Bowen, Beverly Swerdlow Brown, Judy Burke, Martha Carpenter, Karen Lee Davidow, B. J. Deike, Ruth Dougherty, Jean E. Doyle, Doris D. Engles, Anita Fitz-Gerald, Clara Flammang, Tanya Turner Fry, Elsa Garratt, Isabel Joshlin Glaser, Nora Grubmeyer, Janice Hauter, Juanita Havill, Loretta Holz, Marjorie Homonoff, Carmen Horn, Ellen Javernick, Helen Jeffries, Jacqueline Koury, Twilla Lamm, Ella L. Langenberg, Lee Lindeman, Miriam Twyman Lister, M. Mable Lunz, Clare Mishica, June Rose Mobly, Dorice Moore, Miranda Murphy, Anita Page, Evelyne Good Pearson, Beatrice Bachrach Perri, James W. Perrin, Jr., Dora M. Prado, Erma Reynolds, Joyce Rinehart, Kathy Ross, Audrey A. Scannell, Jane Scherer, Barbara J. Smith, Sylvia W. Sproat, Margaret Squires, Sally E. Stuart, June Swanson, Helen A. Thomas, Sharon Dunn Umnik, Jan M. Van Pelt, Jean Vetter, Agnes Choate Wonson, Patsy N. Zimmerman.

Valentine Holders

The custom of exchanging greeting cards called valentines with sweethearts, friends, and family members may have begun as early as the 1400s. Place the valentines you receive in one of these special holders.

PAPER-PLATE HOLDER
(two heavy paper plates, thick yarn, construction paper)

1. Cut a small section from two heavy paper plates.

2. Glue the paper plates together rim to rim with the bottoms facing out. Leave the cut section open for a pocket.

3. Cut a long piece of thick yarn for a hanger and glue it around the outer edges of the plates. Knot the yarn ends together at the bottom. Glue other yarn pieces around the top of the pocket.

4. Decorate the front of the holder with hearts cut from construction paper. Hang the holder on a doorknob.

PAPER-BAG HOLDER
(lunch bag, cardboard, construction paper)

1. Fold down the top of a lunch bag about 1 to 2 inches. Write your name across the folded top.

2. Cut out a piece of cardboard to fit in the bottom of the bag to help it stand.

3. Draw and cut out a heart shape from construction paper. Glue it to the front of the bag.

MAIL-TRUCK HOLDER
(construction paper, yarn)

1. Fold a sheet of white construction paper in half lengthwise, keeping the fold at the bottom.

2. Cut a section from the top right corner to make the truck shape. Glue a piece of blue paper even with the fold on the white paper, making the bottom of the truck. Add a red stripe in the middle. Cut out and glue on red paper circles for wheels.

3. Write "U.S. Mail" on the white portion of the truck. Glue on paper hearts. Staple the edges of the truck, leaving the top of the truck open.

4. Using a paper punch, punch a hole at the front and back of the truck. Tie a piece of yarn for a hanger.

"KNOTS ABOUT YOU" WREATH
(plastic-foam tray, fabric, lace)

1. To make the wreath base, cut out a large heart from a plastic-foam tray. Draw a smaller heart inside the large heart. Cut out the center heart.

2. Cut fabric into strips about 1/2 inch wide and 5 inches long. Tie each strip in a half-knot around the heart-shaped wreath base until it is covered.

3. Wrap a piece of lace around your hand four times, slide it off, and tie another piece of lace around the center of the wrapped lace to make a bow. Glue the bow to the wreath.

4. Glue a piece of lace to the back of the wreath for a hanger.

VALENTINE MOUSE CARD
(construction paper)

1. Fold a large sheet of construction paper in half. Cut out a large half-heart shape from one side of the folded paper.

2. With the heart folded, glue on a heart-shaped paper ear, nose, and eye. Add whiskers and a tail.

3. Write a greeting inside.

SWEETHEART HAT
(poster board, paper, glitter, paper doily)

1. Cut a large heart from red poster board. Draw a small heart in the center of the large heart and cut it out.

2. Glue white paper to the back of the cutout heart section. Turn the heart right side up and draw a letter on the white heart with glue. Sprinkle it with glitter and let dry.

3. Glue the heart to a round paper doily. Cut a strip of white poster board and glue the doily and the heart to the center of the strip. Staple the ends of the strip together so that it fits around your head.

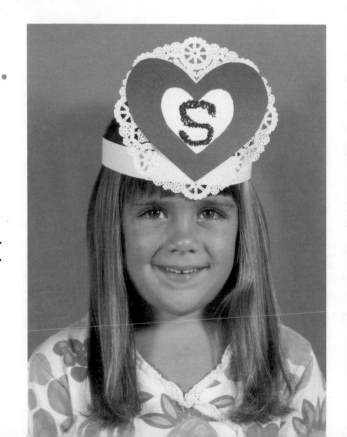

KEY CHAIN
(plastic lid, felt, metal book ring)

1. Cut away the rim from a small plastic lid.

2. Cut two circles of felt to fit the center of the lid. Glue one piece of felt to each side of the lid.

3. Draw and cut out hearts from another color of felt and glue to the center.

4. Using a paper punch, punch a hole near the edge. Attach a metal book ring through the hole. Keys can be attached to the ring.

SWEET-SMELLING VALENTINES
(felt, fabric, lace, cotton balls, dried herbs or flowers, yarn)

1. Cut out two identical shapes from a piece of felt. Glue them together at the edges, leaving an opening at the top.

2. Decorate with pieces of fabric and lace. Fill with cotton balls and a dried herb or flower, such as mint or lavender. Glue shut.

3. Glue yarn around the edges, leaving a loop for a hanger.

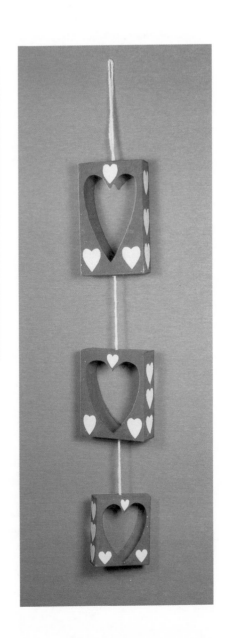

VALENTINE MOBILE
(three different-sized cardboard boxes, poster paint, paper, yarn)

1. Collect three different-sized cardboard boxes. Draw and cut out hearts from each large side of the boxes.

2. Cover the boxes with red poster paint. Let dry. Decorate them with white paper hearts.

3. Poke a small hole in the top and bottom of each box. Place white yarn through the holes and make knots, tying the boxes together.

4. Tie a loop at the top for a hanger.

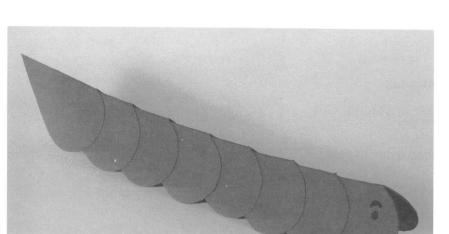

WORM CARD
(construction paper)

1. Cut out eight identical red hearts from construction paper. Fold each heart in half. Glue them on top of each other, overlapping them a bit.

2. Draw an eye and a mouth with a marker. Open the worm and write "I'd like to worm my way into your heart."

SWEETHEART BASKET
(tissue paper, plastic berry basket, chenille sticks, paper doilies, ribbon)

1. Tape red tissue paper onto the outside of a plastic berry basket.

2. To make the handle, twist two chenille sticks together and poke the ends through each side of the basket. Twist the ends of the chenille sticks, attaching them to the basket.

3. Decorate the basket with sections cut from paper doilies and ribbons.

4. Fill the basket with snacks.

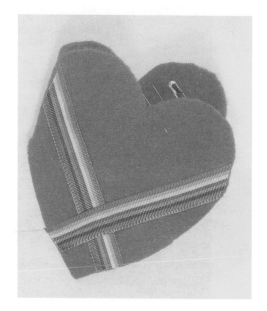

SEWING NEEDLE CASE
(paper, felt, ribbon)

1. On a 3 1/2-inch square piece of paper, draw and cut out a heart.

2. Cut a piece of felt 3 1/2 inches by 7 inches. Fold it in half with the short sides together.

3. Pin the paper heart on the felt so the left edge of the heart overlaps the fold about 1/4 inch. Trace around the heart with a pencil. With the felt folded, cut along the pencil line, leaving the hearts connected by the fold as shown.

4. Decorate the heart with ribbon. Store sewing needles and safety pins inside.

  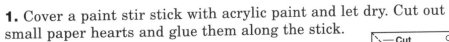

SPINNING HEARTS
(paint stir stick, acrylic paint, construction paper, thumbtack, bead)

1. Cover a paint stir stick with acrylic paint and let dry. Cut out small paper hearts and glue them along the stick.

2. Cut out a 9-inch square piece of paper. Draw a diagonal line from each corner as shown. Cut a 4-inch slit from the corner toward the center on each diagonal line.

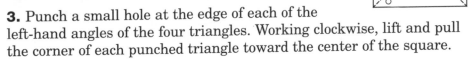

3. Punch a small hole at the edge of each of the left-hand angles of the four triangles. Working clockwise, lift and pull the corner of each punched triangle toward the center of the square.

4. Insert a thumbtack through the holes, the center of the square, and a small bead. Push the thumbtack into the paint stir stick. Glue on paper hearts.

VALENTINE RING
(two paper plates, paper, string)

1. Cut the centers out of two paper plates. Using red paper, cut a heart shape that will fit in the center of the plate rims.

2. Tie a long string to the heart and glue the two plates rim to rim, with the string between them. Use the extra string for a hanger.

3. Decorate with markers and cut-paper letters and hearts.

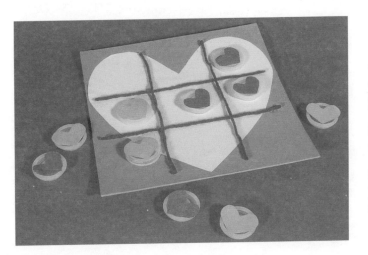

VALENTINE TIC-TAC-TOE
(cardboard, paint, paper, yarn, ten plastic caps)

1. Cut a square piece of cardboard and cover it with paint. When dry, glue a large paper heart in the center.

2. Glue on pieces of yarn to form the lines of the playing board.

3. Gather ten plastic caps. Cut out five pink paper hearts and five red paper hearts. Glue one heart on top of each cap.

"BEE" MINE, VALENTINE
(cardboard egg carton, yarn, chenille sticks,
waxed paper, paper, cardboard)

1. Cut out one cup section from a cardboard egg carton. Cover it with glue and wind brown yarn around it to look like a beehive.

2. Wrap a yellow chenille stick around your finger to make the body of a bee. Wrap a shorter piece of black chenille stick around the bee to make stripes. Glue the bee to the hive. Cut wings from waxed paper and eyes from paper. Glue them to the bee.

3. Draw and cut out a large heart shape from cardboard. Cover it with paper. Glue the hive to the center of the heart.

4. Write the message "Will you (bee) mine, Valentine?"

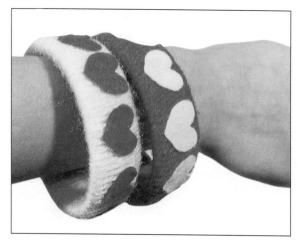

VALENTINE BRACELETS
(plastic-foam cups, yarn, felt)

1. Draw a line about 1 inch down from the top edge of two plastic-foam cups. Cut around the cups on the lines, making the bracelet forms.

2. Wrap pink or red yarn around each bracelet. Glue the ends to the inside of the bracelet.

3. Decorate the bracelets by gluing on hearts cut from pink, red, or white felt.

SURPRISE VALENTINE TUBE
(paper towel tube, yarn, red tissue paper, aluminum foil,
paper, snack food)

1. Cut a section from a paper towel tube to make it a little shorter. For a hanger, tape the ends of a piece of yarn to the inside of each tube end.

2. Cut and glue a folded strip of red tissue paper around the edge of each end of the tube. Cut slits in the tissue for fringe.

3. Cover the tube with glue and aluminum foil. Glue on cut-paper hearts. Place bite-sized snacks inside the tube. Stuff the tube ends with crumpled tissue paper.

PEANUT VALENTINE
(construction paper)

1. Fold a piece of light-brown construction paper in half. Draw the shape of a large peanut, with one side of the peanut on the fold.

2. Cut out the peanut along the dotted line, being careful not to cut the fold as shown. Decorate the peanut with black dots.

3. Inside write "I'm nuts about you, Valentine!"

I'M "NUTS" ABOUT YOU, VALENTINE!

PLANTER OF LOVE
(clay flowerpot and base; acrylic paint; paper;
high-gloss, water-based crystal-clear glaze)

1. To decorate a plain clay flowerpot and base, cover them with white acrylic paint. Let dry overnight.

2. Cut a heart-shaped pattern from paper. With a pencil, lightly trace around the heart on the pot, making a design. Paint the hearts, adding other details with paint. Let dry.

3. To protect the clay pot, *ask an adult to help you* cover it with a clear glaze, following the package directions.

VALENTINE WAND
(paper, paper doily, wooden dowel, permanent marker, yarn)

1. Cut two hearts the same size from red paper. Glue a paper doily between the two hearts. Insert a wooden dowel between the two hearts at the bottom before the glue dries.

2. Color the stick with a red permanent marker.

3. Decorate the wand with more hearts and a yarn bow.

PATCHWORK CARD
(construction paper, fabric)

1. For the card, fold a piece of construction paper in half. Fold it over in half again the other way. Then unfold the card. Draw a heart in the lower right-hand square. Cut out the heart.

2. Fold the paper together so the heart opening is on the top layer and the fold is on the left. With a pencil, trace through the heart shape onto the square beneath.

3. Unfold the card again and glue on small pieces of different-colored fabric, side by side, to fill the traced heart shape. Some fabric may extend beyond the shape.

4. Dot glue around the fabric heart edges. Refold the card, pressing the cutout section over the fabric heart.

5. Draw a border on the front of the card. Write a message inside.

"I LOVE YOU" BOOKMARK
(yarn, paper)

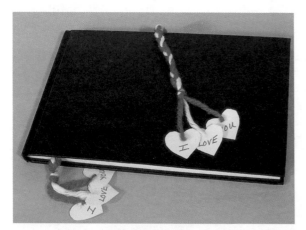

1. Cut three lengths of yarn—two of the same color and one of a different color—each about a foot long. Line up the pieces of yarn and tie them together into a knot about 1 inch from one end.

2. Braid by folding A over B and then C over A as shown in the diagram. Continue until the yarn is braided. Tie the strands into a knot again about 1 inch from the end.

3. Cut six small hearts from white paper. Write a three-word message on three hearts, writing one word on each heart. Write the same message or a different one on the other three hearts. Glue the hearts to the ends of the braid.

DOVE DOOR DECORATION
(construction paper, plastic-foam "peanuts," yarn)

1. Draw and cut out two doves from white construction paper. Glue them onto a large heart cut from pink paper.

2. Spread glue over the doves and press small plastic-foam "peanuts" into the glue. For the eyes, glue on black paper circles.

3. Cut out small hearts from red paper. Write valentine messages on them and glue them next to the doves' beaks.

4. For a hanger, thread a piece of yarn through two punched holes at the top of the decoration.

VALENTINE PALS
(old socks, cotton balls, thread, felt, construction paper)

1. Stuff an old clean sock as far as the heel with cotton balls. Twist the rest of the sock and wrap it with thread to make the tail.

2. Tie thread around other parts of the sock to shape a head and feet.

3. Cut ears and other heart-shaped features from felt or construction paper and glue them in place.

THE HEARTS GAME
(white poster board, permanent red marker, four plastic caps)

1. Draw four hearts of different sizes on a large piece of white poster board as shown. Add color with a permanent red marker.

2. Draw and cut out four small hearts from white poster board. Give each one a point value from 1 to 4. Glue one numbered heart to each heart on the board.

To play: Place the board on the floor. Players take turns tossing four plastic caps onto the board. The player with the highest number of points wins.

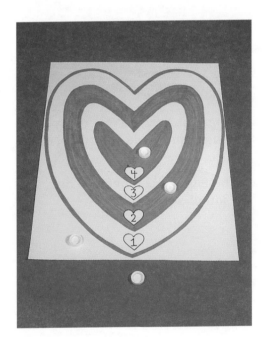

SENTIMENTAL SLATE
(four ice-cream sticks, yarn, black paper, white paint)

1. Form a square frame with four ice-cream sticks. Glue the sticks together at the corners and let dry.

2. Attach a piece of yarn to one stick for a hanger.

3. Cut a piece of black paper to fit the square frame, making a slate. Paint a message on the black paper using white paint. Let dry.

4. Glue the slate to the square frame.

TWIRLING HEART MOBILE
(paper, glitter, string, poster board)

1. Cut four strips of paper in different lengths and widths. Spread a thin layer of glue on one side of each strip. Sprinkle glitter on the glue. Let dry.

2. Fold each strip in half, with the glitter facing out. Curve the ends to form a heart shape. Spread glue on one outside end. Place a piece of string between the ends and glue them together.

3. Cut a large arrow from poster board. Add a piece of paper with a message. Tape the string ends to the back of the arrow, leaving the hearts hanging at different lengths and twirling in the air.

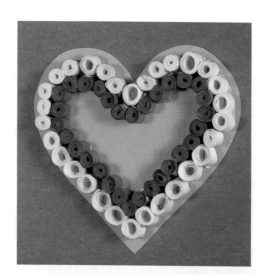

ROLL-A-HEART VALENTINE
(paper)

1. Cut a piece of paper in the shape of a heart.

2. Cut red and white paper into long narrow strips. Roll the strips around a pencil, glue the ends, and slide the rolls off the pencil.

3. Glue the white rolls around the edge of the heart. Then glue the red rolls inside the section of white rolls.

VALENTINE CARRIER
(construction paper, cereal box)

1. Glue red construction paper around the sides of a cereal box.

2. Fold a piece of paper in half, and cut a heart shape almost as wide as the box and about half as tall.

3. To make the handle, place the heart on the front of the box and trace around it with a pencil. Do the same on the back. Carefully cut out the area around the heart shapes as shown in the diagram. Cut a smaller heart out of the middle of both heart shapes.

4. Decorate the carrier with other hearts. Place your valentines inside, and hand them out to your family and friends.

FOUR-LEAF CLOVER VALENTINE
(thread spool, construction paper)

1. Cover a thread spool with glue and red construction paper. Cut four identical heart shapes from green paper. On one heart write "There's a secret message inside for you." Glue the hearts to the top of the spool to form a four-leaf clover.

2. Cut a long strip of paper the same width as the spool. Draw a heart and write a message or poem on it.

3. Roll the paper tightly and slip it into the hole in the bottom of the spool.

VALENTINE DANCER
(2-inch plastic-foam ball, plastic spice bottle, fabric, bottle cap,
moveable plastic eyes, ribbon, chenille stick)

1. To make the head, use a table knife to cut a small section from a 2-inch plastic-foam ball. Use a plastic spice bottle for the body and glue the cut side of the head on top of the spice bottle cap.

2. Cut a small circle of fabric and glue it to the top of another bottle cap, forming a hat. Glue the hat to the top of the head. Add moveable plastic eyes and a fabric mouth.

3. Glue a piece of ribbon around the side of the spice bottle cap. Cut a piece of fabric for a dress to fit around the bottle. Put glue on the bottle below the ribbon and press the fabric into it.

4. To make the arms, cut two pieces from a chenille stick and insert them under the glued fabric of the dress. Add fabric gloves.

LACY BAG
(felt, lace, cording, beads)

1. From a large piece of felt, cut an 18-inch circle. Cut flower designs from a piece of lace and glue them near the center of the circle.

2. Using a paper punch, punch a hole about every other inch around the edge of the felt circle.

3. Lace one piece of cording in and out through the holes on one half of the circle, leaving the ends hanging loose. Lace another piece of cording through the other half.

4. At one half of the circle, thread a bead on two ends of cording and knot the ends together. Do the same for the other half.

5. Hold the cording ends in one hand. Push the fabric on the cording away from you with the other hand to form the bag.

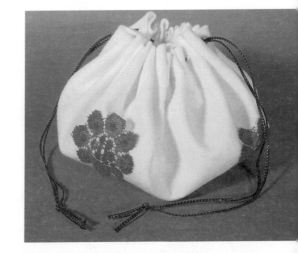

ROCK PAPERWEIGHT
(smooth rock, acrylic paint, fabric, fabric flower)

1. Wash and dry a smooth rock. Cover it with acrylic paint. Let dry.

2. Cut and glue a fabric strip around the rock, forming loops on top. Glue a small fabric flower in the center of the loops.

RAINBOW HEART HANGER
(paper, string)

1. Make a pattern by folding a sheet of paper in half and cutting out a heart. Then cut a heart out of the middle of the first heart, leaving a border heart.

2. Trace around the inside and outside of the border-heart pattern on black paper. Cut out the hearts, making several border hearts.

3. Trace around the outside of the heart border on white paper. Make half as many hearts as borders, and cut out the hearts. Color both sides of the hearts with markers.

4. Glue one colored heart in between two black border hearts along with a piece of string. Glue all the hearts together on a string.

VALENTINES FROM THE GARDEN
(construction paper, old seed catalog or magazine)

1. Fold a piece of construction paper in half. Fold it in half again the other way. Open the paper and lay it flat. Draw a heart in the lower right-hand square. Cut out the heart.

2. Fold the paper together so the heart opening is on the top layer and the fold is on the left.

3. Cut a flower picture from an old seed catalog or a magazine. Glue the picture behind the cutout heart. Write a message to go with your picture. For example, "My heart grows for you."

HEART NUT BOX

(half-gallon milk carton, construction paper, white glue and water, rickrack, tissue paper, nuts)

1. Measure 2 1/2 inches from the bottom of a half-gallon milk carton. Cut off the top of the carton and discard.

2. Tear red and pink construction paper into small pieces. Brush the pieces of paper with a mixture of white glue and a little water. Overlap the pieces on the box. Let dry.

3. Glue strips of rickrack and paper hearts around the box. Put tissue paper and nuts inside.

TISSUE FLOWERS

(tissue paper, chenille sticks, buttons)

1. To make the petals for each flower, cut eight circles of tissue paper, each about 4 inches in diameter. Poke a small hole through the middle of all the circles.

2. To make the stem and flower center, push a chenille stick through all the holes. Thread one end of the chenille stick up through one button hole and down through the other button hole, twisting the end around the stick just under the button.

3. Add a dab of glue at the flower center just under the button. Gather the tissues to create a conelike shape. Place a small piece of tape around the bottom of the cone and chenille stick stem.

HEART PIN GIFT AND CARD

(paper, felt, safety pin)

1. To make the card, fold a piece of white paper in half. Write a message and draw a border, leaving room for the heart pin in the center of the card.

2. Cut two matching hearts from red felt. Glue them together. The heart should fit on the front of the card.

3. Glue a safety pin in the middle of the heart. Glue a small strip of felt across the opened pin. Let dry.

4. Pin the heart to the front of the card.

SIGNED, "I LOVE YOU"
(paper, poster board)

Many people who have hearing difficulties use sign language to communicate. The sign language symbol for "I Love You" combines the letters *I*, *L*, and *Y* into one symbol.

1. Trace around one of your hands on a piece of paper. Cut out the tracing.

2. From poster board, draw and cut out a heart large enough to fit the hand in the center. Glue the hand to the heart, leaving the ring and middle fingers unglued. Curl the two unglued fingers forward and glue the fingertips to the palm of the hand.

3. Cut another heart, larger than the first, from poster board and glue the first heart in the center. Write the message "I Love You!"

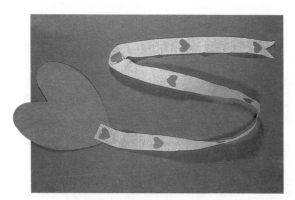

FLUTTERING HEART
(construction paper, crepe paper)

1. Draw and cut out a large heart from construction paper.

2. Cut a tail about one yard long from a roll of crepe paper. Staple the tail to the point of the heart.

3. Draw and cut out small hearts and glue them along the tail.

4. Go outdoors. Hold onto the tail and run. The heart will flutter in the wind.

VALENTINE BUTTERFLY MESSAGE
(construction paper, paper doily, poster paint, spring-type clothespin, chenille stick)

1. Cut a butterfly shape from red construction paper and decorate it with pieces from a paper doily.

2. Paint a spring-type clothespin red and let it dry. Glue the butterfly on one side of the clothespin. Add antennae made from a chenille stick.

3. Write a valentine greeting on a small, heart-shaped piece of paper, and glue it to the other side of the clothespin.

4. Clip the butterfly where it will surprise the person who is to receive it.

PET DISH
(plastic food container, fabric, rickrack)

1. Glue fabric from the top to the bottom on the outside of a plastic food container.

2. Cut out small fabric hearts from another piece of fabric and glue them around the sides of the container.

3. Add rickrack along the top and bottom as shown.

VALENTINE CANDY HOLDER
(plastic laundry detergent bottle, yarn, felt, candy)

1. *Ask an adult to help you* thoroughly clean a plastic laundry detergent bottle and to draw and cut out the shape shown in the diagram.

2. Use a paper punch to make holes around the edge of the plastic holder. Start at the center of the heart and loop yarn around the edge and through the holes, ending where you started. Tie the yarn ends into a bow.

3. Cut a strip of felt and glue it around the outside of the holder. Add a felt heart. Place wrapped candy inside the holder.

HEART HOTPAD
(paper, denim fabric, clear-drying glue, needle and embroidery floss, cotton)

1. Draw and cut out a large heart pattern from a piece of paper 8 inches square. Trace two of these hearts onto a piece of denim fabric.

2. Spread a clear-drying glue around the inside edge of each heart. Let dry, then carefully cut out each heart. (The glue will help keep the fabric from fraying.)

3. Start at the top of the heart. Sew the hearts together with an embroidery needle and six-strand embroidery floss, using a running stitch. Leave an opening.

4. Stuff some cotton between the two hearts, spreading the cotton evenly inside. Sew the opening shut.

5. Tie a bow at the top of the heart with the remaining floss.

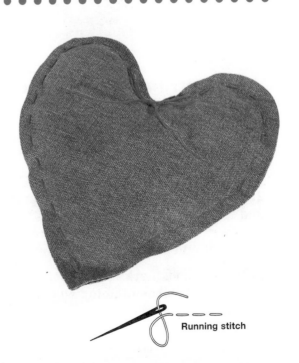

Running stitch

PAPER-DOLL VALENTINE
(construction paper)

1. Starting at the narrow end of a 5-by-12-inch piece of paper, fold over 1 1/2 inches of the paper. Continue to fold into accordion pleats until the whole piece is pleated.

2. Using a pencil, lightly sketch half of a doll shape. Be sure the center of the doll is on the fold and that the hands come out to the end of the paper.

3. Cut out the dolls with the paper folded. The dolls will be holding hands. On the front of each doll, glue a cutout paper letter, spelling *L O V E*.

VALENTINE NECKLACE
(white glue, aluminum foil, yarn)

1. Draw the shape of a heart with white glue on a piece of aluminum foil.

2. Press pieces of yarn into the glue-shaped heart, making a colorful design. Add a yarn loop. Brush the top of the yarn with glue and let dry completely.

3. Gently peel the heart away from the foil. Cut a long piece of yarn and thread it through the loop for the necklace. Tie the ends together.

VALENTINE MOUSE BOOKMARK
(construction paper, yarn)

1. Cut a rectangle from a piece of black construction paper. Fold one end of the rectangle.

2. Cut out and glue a red paper heart to the fold for a head. Add big ears, eyes, a nose, and whiskers to the head. Glue a piece of yarn to the other end of the rectangle for a tail.

3. Put the bookmark into a book, keeping the mouse's head above the top edge of the pages so it can "peek" at you.

VALENTINE PORTRAIT
(poster board, construction paper, flashlight)

1. Fold a vertical strip of poster board into three equal sections. Cut two pieces of white construction paper to fit the middle section.

2. Put a lit flashlight on a table in a dark room. *Ask permission* to lightly tape one paper to a wall. Sit between the flashlight and the paper so your profile fits on the paper. Have a partner trace the outline of your silhouette on the paper.

3. Remove the paper from the wall and cut out the silhouette. Trace around the silhouette on a piece of black paper and cut it out. Glue the black silhouette to the second piece of white paper and then to the middle section of the poster board. Write your name and date below the silhouette.

4. Glue a heart at each corner. Make one more fold in the third section of poster board. Place the top of the first section in the fold and tape it so the portrait will stand up.

TREE OF SWEETHEARTS
(poster paint, poster board, construction paper)

1. Paint a tree trunk and limbs on a large piece of white poster board. Let dry.

2. Cut out hearts from construction paper. Write the name of a friend, a classmate, or a family member on each heart. Glue them to the tree.

3. Hang it on a bulletin board.

PIGGY-BANK VALENTINE CARD
(construction paper)

1. Draw and cut out a large circle for the pig's body and a small circle for the pig's head from construction paper. Glue them together.

2. Cut out ears, eyes, a nose, legs, and a tail from paper, and glue them to the pig's body. Draw on a mouth.

3. Decorate the pig by gluing on small red paper hearts. Draw a slot at the top of the pig.

4. Write this message on the back of the pig: "You can bank on me to be your Valentine!"

LACY RING VALENTINE
(construction paper, self-adhesive reinforcement rings)

1. To make the card, fold a piece of red construction paper in half. Draw and cut out a heart shape from pink paper and glue it onto the front of the card.

2. To make the lacy border, cut self-adhesive reinforcement rings in half. Remove the backing and place them around the pink heart.

3. Write a message inside the card.

HEART TOSS GAME
(February calendar page, construction paper, five candy hearts)

1. Glue a February calendar page on a piece of construction paper, or draw one yourself.

To play: Place the calendar in the center of a table. Standing a few feet away from the table, players take turns tossing five candy hearts onto the page. Add up the numbers in the boxes where the candies land. The player with the most points is the winner.

EGG CARTON JEWELRY BOX
(cardboard egg carton, fabric ruffle, lightweight cardboard, fabric, string of craft pearls)

1. Use a pink-colored cardboard egg carton for the jewelry box. Glue a 1 1/2-inch white fabric ruffle around the top edge of the lid.

2. Turn the box over and trace around the lid on a piece of lightweight cardboard. Cut out the cardboard. Cover one side of the cardboard with fabric, gluing the excess fabric on the underside.

3. Glue the covered cardboard on top of the jewelry box lid. Add a fabric-covered cardboard heart in the center.

4. Decorate the heart by gluing a string of craft pearls around the heart's edge.

THREE-SIDED HEART PICKS

(construction paper, round toothpicks, cake)

1. To make each heart pick, cut out three small hearts, one each from white, pink, and red construction paper.

2. Glue a round toothpick to the center of one heart. Fold the other two hearts in half. Glue one half of each heart to each side of the first heart at the back. Then glue the remaining two halves together.

3. Place the heart picks into a cake, making a design.

(Be sure to remove all the heart picks before cutting and serving the cake.)

VALENTINE RABBIT

(poster board, construction paper, cotton balls)

1. Fold a piece of white poster board in half to form a card.

2. Draw and cut out hearts of different sizes, shapes, and colors from construction paper to create a rabbit as shown.

3. Pull bits of cotton from cotton balls and glue to the ears, paws, legs, and tail of the rabbit.

4. Write a message inside such as, "I'm 'hopping' you will be my Valentine."

SWEETHEART PHOTO FRAME

(plastic-foam trays, paper, table knife, rickrack, construction paper, yarn)

1. Use a white plastic-foam tray for the base of the photo frame. Trim away the curved edges of a pink plastic-foam tray to fit inside the base.

2. Draw and cut out a heart shape from paper, making it small enough so that two hearts will fit on the pink section of the frame. Trace two hearts on the pink section, and carefully cut them out with a table knife. Tape a photo in each heart.

3. Glue the pink section to the base. Add rickrack and cut-paper hearts for decoration.

4. Poke two holes at the top of the frame and tie a piece of yarn through for a hanger.

HEART NOTEPAD
(poster board, paper, paper doily, ribbon)

1. To make the front and back cover of the notepad, fold a 7-by-14-inch piece of poster board in half. Draw a heart shape as shown in the photo and cut it out.

2. Trace the heart shape on a piece of white paper. Cut out the heart shape, trimming it slightly smaller so it will fit inside the notepad.

3. Cut out about twenty white paper hearts. Place them inside the notepad and staple them together at the top.

4. Decorate the cover of the notepad with pieces cut from a paper doily. Use a paper punch to punch a hole in the corner of the front cover. Tie on a piece of ribbon.

THREE-D VALENTINE CARD
(poster board, crayons)

1. Fold a piece of white poster board in half to make the card.

2. Cut out a heart shape from white poster board, color it with crayons, and write a message on it. Fold the heart in half with the message on the outside. Then fold the outside edges of the heart forward.

3. Glue the folded edges of the heart to the inside of the card, centering the fold of the heart on the fold of the card.

4. Open the card, and the heart will "pop out."

HEART CANDY BOX
(construction paper, small paper cup)

1. Cut two hearts from construction paper, making them slightly larger than the diameter of a small paper cup. Glue one heart to the bottom of the cup.

2. Draw and cut out a strip of paper for a hinge. Glue one end of the hinge to the side of the cup and one end to the second heart for a lid.

3. Lift the lid and place candies or other treats inside.

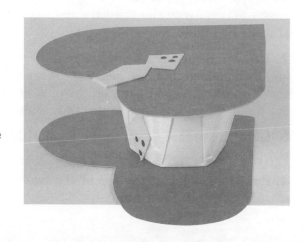

POTATO PRINT STATIONERY
(potato, table knife, poster paint, envelope and writing paper)

1. Cut a clean potato in half. With a pencil, draw a different-sized heart on each half.

2. *Ask an adult to help you* use a table knife to cut away the area around the hearts, leaving them about 1/2 inch higher than the rest of the potato.

3. Cover the hearts with poster paint, and press them onto a piece of writing paper or an envelope. Repeat until you have the design you want. Let dry.

FABRIC FLOWERS
(thin wire, small bottle, paper plate, lightweight fabric, chenille sticks, white tape, permanent marker)

1. To make each petal, wrap a 3-inch thin, flexible wire around a small bottle that is about 1 1/2 inches in diameter. Twist the ends of the wire together and slide it off the bottle. Bend the ends upward so the wire looks like an egg holder. Repeat this process six times.

2. Squeeze some white glue on a paper plate. Hold the wire ends and dip the petal in the glue. Place each petal on a piece of lightweight red fabric with the wire ends up and let dry.

3. To make the stamens, cut 2-inch pieces from a white chenille stick and bend them in half. For the stem, use a long green chenille stick. Wrap one end of the stem around the stamens and twist to hold.

4. With scissors trim the fabric around the outer edge of each petal. Straighten the wire ends. Cut two leaves with long stems from green felt.

5. Use a permanent marker to color the white tape green. Place three petals and one leaf on each side of the flower stem. Wrap the wire ends and leaves with the tape. Bend the stem in a spiral shape until the flower will stand.

A VALENTINE MOBILE
(wire clothes hanger, yarn, Valentine cards)

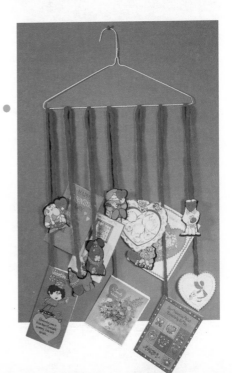

1. Cut a long piece of yarn for every two Valentine cards you have received.

2. Tie the pieces of yarn onto the crossbar of the hanger, leaving all the ends hanging at different lengths.

3. Tape one card to each end of yarn. Spread the tied yarn sections out evenly across the crossbar.

SWEETHEART HOUSE
(construction paper, large facial tissue box, paper, fabric ruffle, bead, half-gallon milk carton, toothpaste box, cotton ball)

1. To make the base of the house, glue white construction paper around the outside of a large, rectangular facial tissue box. Decorate the box with paper and markers. Glue pieces of ruffle at the windows for curtains. Glue a bead to the door for a doorknob.

2. For the roof, measure 5 inches from the bottom of a half-gallon milk carton. Cut off the top and discard. Draw a line diagonally across the bottom of the carton. Cut on the line and up each side seam, making two triangular sections. Place the sections together, overlapping a little to fit the length of the top of the house. Glue the sections together where they overlap and let dry. Cover the roof with paper and draw shingles with a marker. Glue the roof to the top of the house and let dry.

3. To make the chimney, glue paper around a toothpaste box and decorate with paper and markers. Use some cotton from a cotton ball for smoke. Glue the chimney to the side of the house.

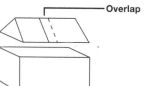
Overlap

PENCIL VALENTINE
(paper, pinking shears, poster paint, pencil)

1. Draw and cut out two identical paper hearts. Use pinking shears for a saw-toothed edge.

2. Paint "Be Mine" in the center of one heart.

3. Glue the two hearts together with the pencil in between. Let dry.

VALENTINE CROWN
(construction paper)

1. Cut out and tape together a 2-inch-wide strip of red construction paper to fit around your head.

2. Cut two strips of paper, each 1 inch by 12 inches. Fold one strip in half and make a 2-inch slit in the center. Glue the strip from one side of the headband to the other.

3. Glue the second strip so the headband is divided into quarters. Tuck and glue the center of the second strip into the slit of the first. Cut out a paper heart and glue it in the center where the two strips cross.

4. Add white cut-paper hearts to the crown.

CHENILLE-STICK DOLL

(three chenille sticks, construction paper, yarn, buttons, moveable plastic eyes)

1. To make the body and legs of the doll, place two long chenille sticks next to each other and twist them together from one end about three quarters of the length of the sticks. Spread the two untwisted ends apart for legs.

2. To make arms, wrap one chenille stick around the middle of the body.

3. Cut two identical hearts from construction paper for the body. Then cut sets of two smaller hearts for the head, shoes, and hands. Glue the hearts together with the chenille sticks in between them. Glue a piece of yarn between the hearts at the top of the head.

4. Add details with buttons, markers, cutout paper hearts, and moveable plastic eyes.

VALENTINE DESIGN

(poster board, tissue paper, white glue and water)

1. Cut a rectangular piece of white poster board.

2. Cut several hearts the same size from various colors of tissue paper.

3. Make a mixture of half white glue and half water. Brush the mixture on each heart and arrange them on the poster board.

VALENTINE GARLAND

(construction paper, pinking shears, string)

1. Cut out pairs of different-colored construction paper hearts of various sizes, using scissors to make straight or scalloped edges and pinking shears for a saw-toothed edge.

2. Glue the heart pairs together with a long piece of string between them. Let dry.

3. Hang the valentine garland over a doorway or a window.

HEART COASTERS
(clear plastic lids, heavy white paper, old flower catalog)

1. For each coaster, trace around a clear plastic lid on heavy white paper. Cut out the circle and trim so it fits snugly inside the lid. Remove the paper circle.

2. Find a flower picture in an old flower catalog. Trace the paper circle around the picture. Cut out the flower circle and then cut it into a heart shape. Glue the heart on top of the paper circle.

3. Press the paper circle, with the flower facing up, inside the clear plastic lid.

GLITTERING HEART PIN
(poster board, glitter, safety pin)

1. Draw and cut out a heart shape from a piece of poster board.

2. Spread one side of the heart with glue and sprinkle it with glitter. Let it dry and then shake off any loose glitter.

3. Tape a safety pin to the back of the heart.

A BIG VALENTINE HUG
(paper plate, yarn, paper doily, construction paper)

1. Draw a face on a paper plate and glue cut pieces of yarn around the plate rim for hair. Cut a paper doily in half and glue it to the bottom of the back of the paper plate for a collar.

2. Tape pieces of construction paper together, making a long strip for arms. Glue the head in the middle of the arms. Draw and cut out paper hands and glue them to the ends of the arms.

3. Cut two small paper doilies in half and glue them to both arms for cuffs.

4. Write a valentine message below the collar so that the arms, when folded, will cover your message.

A Great Big Valentine Hug! Love, Sue

VALENTINE RECIPE CARDS
(index cards, permanent markers)

1. Decorate index cards by drawing a border of hearts along the edges using different-colored permanent markers.

2. Make a set of cards, writing your favorite "sweet" recipes to give to a relative or a friend.

DOORKNOB DECORATION
(fabric, pinking shears, cotton balls, yarn)

1. Cut four identical hearts from colorful fabric. Use pinking shears for a saw-toothed edge.

2. Glue cotton balls in the center of two of the hearts. Squeeze some glue around the edges of the hearts.

3. Cut a piece of yarn and place one end in the center of each heart. Put the remaining two fabric hearts on top of the yarn and cotton balls. Press the edges together and let dry.

4. Use the yarn to hang the hearts on a doorknob.

PLASTIC BIRDHOUSE
(2-liter plastic beverage bottle with black base, felt)

1. *Ask an adult to help you* cut the top off a 2-liter plastic beverage bottle.

2. Look at the base of the bottle. There should be three small holes in the base. If there aren't any, *ask an adult to help* poke a hole in the base.

3. Cut hearts and rectangles from pieces of felt. Glue them to the outside of the bottle.

4. *Ask an adult to help you* hang the birdhouse outside by mounting the base on a nail under a roof eve as shown.

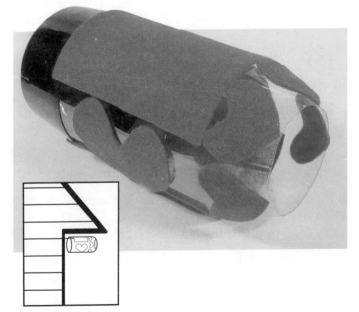

HEART-IN-HAND VALENTINES
(construction paper, buttons, lace, fabric)

1. With a pencil, trace around your hand and wrist on construction paper. Repeat for as many valentines as you wish to make. Cut along each hand outline. Draw and cut out a heart and glue it onto the palm of each hand.

2. Draw and cut out rectangular pieces of paper and glue them on each wrist for a cuff. Add buttons and pieces of lace and fabric.

3. Write a message on the back of each paper hand and give it to someone special.

HEART-SHAPED PINECONE WREATH
(cardboard, waxed paper, paper plate, pinecones, ribbon, heavy white paper, plastic-foam tray, large needle)

1. Draw and cut out a heart shape from cardboard to make the base of the wreath as shown in the diagram.

2. Cover your work space with waxed paper. Squeeze glue onto a paper plate. Using pinecones that have flat tops, dip each top in the glue and place it on the wreath base until the base is covered. Let dry for at least one day.

3. Tape ribbon to the back of the wreath and wrap it around the pinecones. Make a bow and tie it to the wreath. Glue a loop of ribbon to the back for a hanger.

4. Cut hearts from heavy white paper. Place each heart on a plastic-foam tray. Using a large needle, punch a design on the hearts. Glue them to the wreath.

SECRET HEARTS VALENTINE
(construction paper, old flower catalog)

1. Fold a large sheet of construction paper in half. Keeping the paper folded, cut out half of a heart. Open to find a large heart.

2. Refold the heart and glue pictures cut from an old flower catalog around the edge of the half heart. In the center write "Roses are red...violets are blue..."

3. Cut out a small heart pattern. Open the large heart. Trace around the small pattern five times on the right half of the inside of the card. Cut out the hearts.

4. Fold the card and turn it over. Trace through the five cutout hearts to make five hearts on the left inside the large folded heart. Open the card. Write one word inside each heart: "Hey, Valentine, I like you."

5. Trace around the small heart pattern, making several more hearts around your valentine message. Write a word inside each heart.

6. Open the card. Draw a dotted line down the center fold. Write "Fold here to read a secret message for you."

CUPID POP-UP
(plastic-foam cup, tongue depressor, construction paper, paper bag, gift wrap)

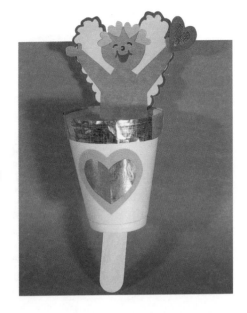

1. In the bottom of a plastic-foam cup, cut a slit just big enough to fit a tongue depressor through.

2. To make Cupid, draw and cut out construction paper wings that will fit inside the cup. Cut out a head, arms, and body half in one piece from a paper bag. Glue the shape on the wings. Add features with markers and paper. Glue Cupid to the tongue depressor.

3. Decorate the outside of the cup with pieces of gold gift wrap and paper.

BOOK OF HEARTS
(cardboard, fabric, construction paper, ribbon, felt)

1. Cut two pieces of cardboard slightly larger than a sheet of construction paper for the front and back cover of the book.

2. Glue fabric to one side of each cardboard, wrapping and gluing the excess fabric around to the back. Let dry.

3. With a paper punch, punch two holes in each cover. Punch holes in several sheets of construction paper, making sure all the holes line up.

4. Place the paper between the covers. Thread a piece of ribbon through the holes and tie a bow. Cut out heart-shaped pieces of felt and glue them to the front cover.

5. Glue or tape the valentines you receive inside the book.

VALENTINE RINGTOSS
(paper towel tube, poster paint, ribbon, plastic scoop, construction paper, heavy paper plate, three plastic lids)

1. Cover a paper towel tube with pink poster paint and let dry. Glue a piece of red ribbon around the tube as shown. Cut the handle off a clear plastic scoop from a dry beverage-drink mix, and push the scoop over one end of the tube. Add a construction paper heart to the top.

2. Glue the open tube end to the center of a heavy paper plate and let dry. Decorate the plate with hearts cut from pink and red paper.

3. Cut the centers out of the three plastic lids, leaving the rims, to make rings.

To play: Place the plate a few feet from you on the floor. Have each player take a turn tossing three rings onto the tube. Make the game more challenging by moving farther from the plate.

Special Valentines

Create unique keepsake valentines for those people who are special to you.

JUST FOR MOM
(three plastic berry baskets, yarn, large-eyed needle, paper)

1. Cut the bottom sections from three plastic berry baskets that have a square design. Cut out areas from the basket to form the block letters *M O M* as shown.

2. Thread a piece of yarn on a large-eyed sewing needle. Weave the yarn around the edges of each letter, tying the ends together when finished.

3. Tie each letter one above the other with yarn. Add a piece of yarn to the top of the first letter *M* for a hanger.

4. Draw and cut out a paper heart. Write "I love you, Mom!" on it. Punch two holes in the heart and tie it to the bottom of the second letter *M*.

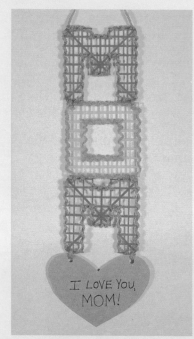

LOLLIPOPS FOR SISTER
(five lollipops, tongue depressor, fabric, yarn, paper, felt, chenille stick)

1. Glue five lollipops to a tongue depressor, making legs, arms, and a head. Let dry overnight.

2. Cut pieces of fabric and wrap around the tongue depressor and lollipop body. Glue in place. Add a yarn belt.

3. Add paper eyes and a felt mouth. Glue pieces of a chenille stick to the top of the head for hair.

4. From fabric and paper, make a square sign that says "Sister, you're sweet!" Glue the sign to a piece of chenille stick and glue the stick to a lollipop arm.

CITYSCAPE FOR DAD
(poster board, plastic-foam tray, acrylic paint)

1. Cut a rectangle about 6 inches by 13 1/2 inches from poster board. Fold in half to measure 6 inches by 7 inches.

2. Draw and cut out a city skyline from a black plastic-foam tray. Glue it to the front of the card. Add "lit" windows with acrylic paint and let dry. Cut and glue a crescent moon in place.

3. Inside the card, write "Dad, you're one in a million! Happy Valentine's Day!" and add your signature.

A BAT FOR BROTHER
(poster board, masking tape)

1. Draw and cut out a baseball bat shape about 17 inches long from a piece of orange poster board. Wrap masking tape around the handle area. Fold the baseball bat into three equal sections.

2. Cut out a circle from white poster board and draw on baseball stitching with a marker. On the ball write "Brother, you're an MVP." Glue it on the end of the bat as shown.

3. Open the sections of the bat, and write inside "My Valentine Pal!" and add your signature.

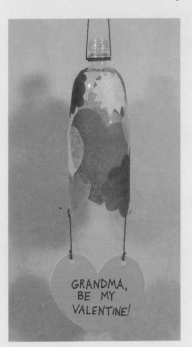

SUN CATCHER FOR GRANDMA
(1-liter plastic bottle, tissue paper, yarn, paper)

1. Cut off the bottom curved section of a 1-liter plastic bottle and discard. Carefully cut shapes from colorful tissue paper. Brush a little glue on them and arrange them on the bottle.

2. Tie two pieces of yarn at the neck of the bottle opposite each other for a hanger. Knot the ends together.

3. Using a paper punch, punch two holes opposite each other near the bottom edge. Cut a heart from paper and write "Grandma, be my Valentine!" Punch two holes in the top of the heart. Tie the heart with yarn to the two holes at the bottom of the bottle.

MEET THE BEST GRANDPA
(poster board, old magazines, aluminum foil)

1. Cut a 10-by-20-inch rectangle from poster board and fold it in half to make a 10-inch square card.

2. Decorate the front of the card with magazine cutouts of grandpa-like pictures from around the world. Add two paper hearts. Write "OPEN to meet the best grandpa in the WORLD!"

3. Open the card. On the left side, cut and glue a heart with the message "Happy Valentine's Day!" On the right side, cut and glue a large aluminum-foil heart in the center. Add a small paper heart in each corner.

4. Write the word "You!" above the foil heart. Sign your name under the heart.

Valentines You Can Wear

It's always fun to dress up on a special day. Create these festive clothes and accessories for yourself. Or make someone a gift to wear.

HAT AND GLOVE SET
(plastic-foam trays, toothpick, yarn, large-eyed needle, knitted hat and gloves)

1. Draw and cut out several hearts from clean white plastic-foam trays. Poke a hole in the top of each heart with a toothpick.

2. Thread a long piece of yarn through the needle.

3. Loosely attach each heart by threading the yarn through the hole, then through the knitted fabric. Tie a knot in the yarn and cut the ends.

4. Attach four hearts to the top of the hat and one to the side of each glove.

SWEETHEART SOCKS
(felt, socks, fabric glue)

1. Using three different colors of felt, cut three different-sized heart shapes.

2. Lay the socks flat with the cuffs folded down.

3. Glue the larger heart first to each cuff. Then add the others. Let dry.

VALENTINE FOOTWEAR
(paper, cloth sneakers, permanent or fabric markers)

1. Draw heart designs on a piece of paper and cut them out.

2. With a pencil, lightly trace the hearts on a pair of sneakers.

3. Trace around the hearts with markers. Don't press too hard, or the marker may spread over the cloth.

FLOWERED GARDEN GLOVES
(flowered fabric, fabric glue, cloth gloves, yarn,
needle and thread, permanent marker)

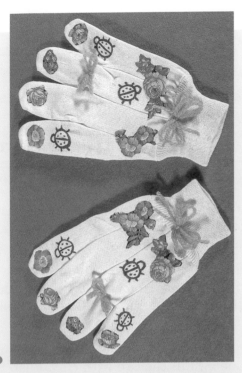

1. Cut out flowers from fabric. Use fabric glue to attach a flower to the end of each finger on a pair of cloth gloves. Add more flowers near the cuffs.

2. Cut two small pieces of yarn. Tie them loosely around the ring finger of each glove, making a bow. With a needle and thread, sew around the bow to hold it in place.

3. Wrap some yarn around four of your fingers. Pull the yarn off and sew around the center to make a bow. Attach a bow at each cuff.

4. Draw bugs on the gloves with permanent marker.

HEART PRINT SHIRT
(cardboard, cotton shirt, cellulose sponge, fabric paint, paper plate)

1. Place a large piece of cardboard inside a cotton shirt, stretching it tight.

2. Using scissors, cut a heart shape from a hard cellulose sponge.

3. Squeeze a small amount of fabric paint on a paper plate. Dip the sponge heart in the paint. Then press the heart on the front of the shirt, making a design. Let dry.

4. Repeat the process and add hearts to the sleeves or neck of the shirt.

BOLO TIE
(large button with shank, aluminum foil, construction paper, shoestring)

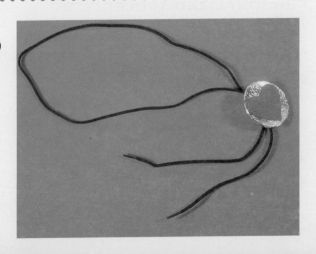

1. Cover a large button with aluminum foil, leaving the shank exposed.

2. Cut a heart from construction paper. Glue it on the button.

3. Fold a long shoestring in half. Thread the ends through the shank of the button.

4. Push the button up the shoestring near the neck of your shirt.

Table Decorations

Decorate the table for Valentine's Day with some heart-shaped accessories.

TABLETOP VALENTINES

(construction paper, glitter, paper doily, plastic straws, chenille sticks, felt, laundry detergent cap, ribbon, clay)

1. Cut hearts of different sizes from construction paper. Decorate them with other colors of paper, glitter, or a section from a paper doily. Glue them to plastic straws.

2. Twist a white and a red chenille stick together, then shape them into a heart. You can also make a heart from just one chenille stick. Glue the chenille-stick ends into one end of a plastic straw. Let dry.

3. Glue felt around the outside of a clean laundry detergent cap. Add ribbon. Fill the cap with clay. Push the straws into the clay.

FABRIC-HEART PLACE MAT
(paper, fabric, fabric ruffle)

1. Draw and cut out a large paper heart pattern about the size of a place mat and a smaller heart large enough to cover the handles of a fork, a knife, and a spoon.

2. Pin the heart patterns on fabric. Carefully trace around the hearts with fabric glue, being sure not to get glue on the paper. Remove the paper patterns. Let the glue dry overnight.

3. Cut around the fabric hearts close to the line of dried glue. (The glue will prevent the fabric edges from fraying.) Glue a fabric ruffle around the edge of the large fabric heart.

4. Glue the smaller heart on the left side of the large heart, leaving an opening at the top for the utensils.

PERSONALIZED TABLECLOTH
(paper tablecloth, poster board, old newspapers, permanent markers)

1. Cut a large paper tablecloth to fit your table.

2. Draw and cut out a place mat-sized heart pattern from poster board.

3. Place the tablecloth on old newspapers. Using permanent markers, trace around the heart pattern once for each place setting.

4. Add a name and features to each of the place settings, one for each guest.

FELT-HEART CENTERPIECE
(felt)

1. Cut six identical hearts from white, red, and pink felt.

2. Lay the hearts in a circle with the edges of the hearts overlapping slightly.

3. Glue the hearts together at the overlapped areas. Let dry.

SALT AND PEPPER SHAKERS
(cardboard salt and pepper shakers, paper)

1. Cover the outsides of cardboard salt and pepper shakers with white paper.

2. Cut out various-sized paper hearts and glue them to one side of each shaker, making a valentine character. Add a small heart to the top of each shaker, leaving the hole area open.

3. On the opposite side of the pepper shaker, glue a paper heart with the message "I'll pepper you with love!" On the salt shaker, glue a paper heart with the message "You're worth your salt to me!"

HEART NAPKIN HOLDER
(one-quart milk carton, construction paper)

1. Draw a pencil line 1 1/2 inches from the bottom around a one-quart milk carton.

2. Cut out a paper heart pattern. Place the point of the heart on one side of the carton, 1 inch up from the bottom, and trace around the heart. Do this again on the opposite side. Cut out as shown.

3. Cut out a 1-inch section or slot from the two carton sides without hearts.

4. Lay the carton on paper and trace around the heart and base of the carton. Cut out the tracing and glue it to the carton. Add more paper hearts.

5. Place dinner napkins in the slots.

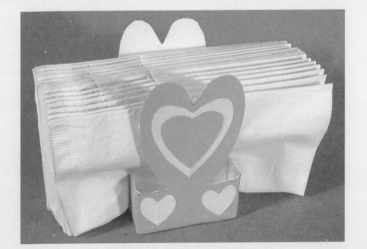

DOILY BASKET

(construction paper, paper doily)

1. On a sheet of construction paper, trace around a plate that is slightly smaller than the diameter of a paper doily. Cut out the circle.

2. Glue the paper circle in the center of the doily and let dry. Fold the circle in half with the doily on the outside.

3. Divide the fold line into thirds as shown in Diagram 1. Fold up a corner of the doily as shown in Diagram 2. Then fold each corner to the back of the doily along the same crease lines. Tuck the corners of the doily to the inside along the crease lines as shown in Diagram 3.

4. Staple a strip of paper to the inside of the basket for a handle.

Diagram 1   Diagram 2   Diagram 3

BUTTERFLY HEARTS

(poster board, construction paper, chenille stick, moveable plastic eyes)

1. Cut and fold a piece of poster board in half for a card.

2. Draw and cut out a butterfly's body from black construction paper. Glue it to the center of the front of the card. Add a small paper heart for a head.

3. Cut two pieces from a chenille stick for the antennae and glue them in place. Add two moveable plastic eyes.

4. Draw and cut out five paper hearts of various sizes and colors for each wing. Glue one heart on top of another, and then glue a wing to each side of the butterfly's body.

5. Write a message on the front of and inside the card.

VALENTINE'S DAY BANNER

(felt, fabric glue, wooden dowel, cording)

1. Cut three identical pieces of felt. Place them in a vertical position, overlapping the edges about 1 inch. Glue them together with fabric glue.

2. Fold the top edge of the first piece of felt over a wooden dowel. Glue in place and let dry.

3. Cut and glue felt flowers, stems, and leaves to the first section, a felt candy box to the second section, and a felt heart to the third section. Add pieces of yarn glued in place to spell "Be Mine."

4. Tie a piece of cording around each end of a wooden dowel for a hanger.

CUPID'S ARROW GAME
(round cardboard container, construction paper, poster board, wooden clothespins)

1. Cover a round cardboard container with pink construction paper.

2. Cut out a red heart from poster board and glue it to one side of the container. Draw and cut out a white arrow. Glue it on the heart as shown in the photo.

3. Draw and cut out four white arrows from poster board. Glue each one on a wooden clothespin with the point of the arrow at the opening of the clothespin.

To play: Stand with the container on the floor in front of you. Hold an arrow at chest height and drop it, trying to get it in the container. See who can get all of Cupid's arrows in the container.

YARN VALENTINE
(heavy white paper, yarn)

1. Fold a piece of heavy white paper to make a long vertical card. Scallop the edges with scissors.

2. With glue, draw a large heart with a smaller heart inside. Press a piece of yarn in the glue of each heart shape. Squeeze glue in the area between the two yarn hearts. Add small pieces of cut yarn.

3. Cut a long piece of yarn. Tie it into a bow and glue it to the top of the card and over the yarn-filled heart.

4. Write a message inside.

RED BIRD
(plastic cup, string, cellulose sponge, feathers, permanent marker, paper)

1. Use a ballpoint pen to make two small holes in the bottom of a plastic cup. Cut a 2-foot piece of string. Push one string end in each hole, tie a knot at one end, and let the string hang down inside the cup. Cut a 1-inch square of cellulose sponge. Tie it to the other end of the string.

2. Glue on a feather, covering the holes and string. Glue feathers to the sides of the cup for wings. Draw eyes with a permanent black marker. Cut a beak from black paper and glue in place.

3. To make the bird chirp, wet the sponge. Hold the cup in one hand. With your other hand, fold the sponge around the string. Slowly move the sponge down the string with a jerking movement to make the chirping noise.

VALENTINE BOOKMARK CARD
(construction paper)

1. To make the card, fold a piece of red construction paper in half. Cut a 3-inch slit in the middle of the front of the card.

2. Write on the card "Use my heart to mark your place." Write your name on the inside.

3. To make the bookmark, fold a 3-inch square of pink paper in half. Draw the outline of half a heart. Draw another smaller heart inside the first heart. Cut on both lines. Decorate the heart and slip it into the slit in the card.

VALENTINE SEQUIN PIN
(cardboard, tissue paper, sequins, ribbon, safety pin)

1. Cut a small heart shape from cardboard. Glue red tissue paper on both sides. Add sequins and let dry.

2. Cut a piece of ribbon, fold it in half, and glue the ends to the back of the heart. Tie a ribbon bow and glue it to the ribbon loop.

3. Attach a safety pin to the back of the ribbon loop.

YARN VASE
(plastic detergent bottle, yarn, felt)

1. *Ask an adult to help you* cut off the top of a small, clean plastic detergent bottle.

2. Start at the bottom of the bottle and spread a little glue around the outside. Press the end of a long piece of yarn into the glue. Continue until the bottle is covered.

3. Cut out a stem and leaves from pieces of yarn. Glue them to the vase. Add pieces of felt for a flower. Let dry overnight.

HEART ICE-CREAM-STICK HOLDER
(round cardboard container, ice-cream sticks, ribbon, felt, paper doily)

1. Cover the outside of a round cardboard container with glue and ice-cream sticks. Let dry.

2. Cut and glue a piece of ribbon at the top and bottom of the container. Cut hearts from felt and glue in place. Glue small hearts cut from sections of a paper doily on top of the felt hearts.

3. Fill the container with pencils, pens, markers, and other items.

FABRIC PHOTO FRAME
(cardboard, fabric, cotton balls, fabric ruffle)

1. Cut two 5-by-7-inch pieces of cardboard. Draw and cut out a heart shape from one cardboard so that a 3 1/2-by-5-inch photo will fill the shape.

2. To make the front of the frame, pull cotton balls apart and glue them around the cutout heart. Cover the cotton with fabric, gluing the fabric to the back of the cardboard. Carefully cut out the fabric from the center of the heart as shown. Glue the fabric tabs to the back of the cardboard.

3. To make the back of the frame, glue fabric to one side of the other piece of cardboard. Glue fabric ruffle around the edges and let dry.

4. Put the front and back of the frame together with the fabric facing out. Glue the sides and bottoms together, leaving the top of the frame open.

5. Cover a small piece of cardboard with fabric and glue it to the back for the stand. Slide a photo in the top of the frame to fill the cutout heart.

VALENTINE MOBILE
(construction paper, string)

1. Fold a sheet of construction paper in half, then in half again.

2. Following the diagram, draw the design along the two folded edges (the dotted lines) as shown. Cut along the solid lines only.

3. Unfold and pick up the outside strips at A and B, letting the rest drop down. Insert a piece of string for a hanger. Push out and press down the heart-shaped cutouts.

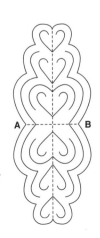

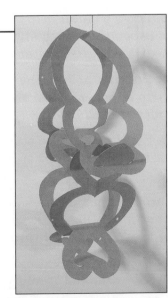

PUNCHED-CARD VALENTINES
(paper)

1. Fold a piece of paper in half to make a card. Keeping the card folded, punch holes with a paper punch all around the edges, leaving an unpunched section in the center.

2. Draw a picture or write a valentine message on the front. Open the card and write your name inside.

NECKLACE OF HEARTS
(string, construction paper)

1. Cut a piece of white string long enough to slip over your head with the ends tied together.

2. From red construction paper, cut pairs of identical hearts.

3. Glue one heart to the string. Glue the other heart on top of the first with the string in between. Continue until the string is covered with hearts.

VALENTINE KITE
(brown paper bag, old newspaper, poster paint,
self-adhesive reinforcement rings, two chenille sticks, cording, wooden dowel)

1. Draw a pencil line around a brown paper bag about 4 inches up from the bottom. Cut off the bottom section, and then cut a 1-inch strip from it. Glue the strip on the outside edge of the bag.

2. At the other end of the paper bag, draw a large heart on each large panel and a small heart on each side panel with the tops of the hearts on the bottom of the paper bag. Trim around the hearts as shown by the dotted line in the diagram.

3. Draw a small heart at the other end of the side panel, between the 1-inch strip and the other small heart. Paint the hearts with red poster paint. Let dry.

4. Punch a hole in the center of each panel through the 1-inch strip of paper. Place a self-adhesive reinforcement ring on both sides of each hole.

5. Staple a chenille stick inside the bag along each side panel on the 1-inch strip.

6. Cut four pieces of cording and tie one end of each piece through each of the four holes. Gather the other ends together and tie one long piece of cording around them. Tie the other end of the long piece of cording to one end of a wooden dowel.

7. Go outside. Holding the end of the wooden dowel, run or stand in the wind and watch your valentine kite flutter in the breeze.

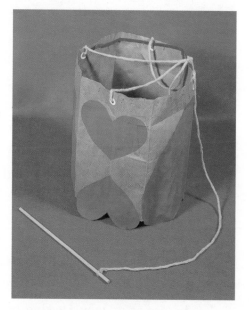

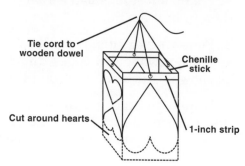

Tie cord to wooden dowel

Chenille stick

Cut around hearts

1-inch strip

BUTTON CARD
(poster board, construction paper, buttons)

1. Cut a piece of poster board slightly larger than a sheet of construction paper. Glue the paper in the center of the poster board. Fold in half, forming a card.

2. Cut the right edge of the card with scissors, making a scalloped design.

3. On the front of the card, arrange buttons of various sizes and colors in a heart shape. Glue them to the card.

4. Write a message inside.

PUFFY HEART MAGNET
(plastic lid, paper doily, cardboard, cotton balls, fabric, magnetic strip)

1. Cut out a heart shape from the center of a plastic lid. Trace around the plastic heart on a paper doily and cut out the heart. Glue the paper-doily heart on top of the plastic heart.

2. Draw and cut out a cardboard heart smaller than the plastic-lid heart. Glue cotton balls on one side. Cover the cotton balls with a heart-shaped piece of fabric, gluing it to the back of the cardboard.

3. Glue the fabric heart in the center of the plastic heart. Glue a magnetic strip to the back of the plastic heart.

CANDLE HOLDER
(tissue paper, white glue and water, glass bottle, nail polish, candle, sand)

1. Cut hearts from different-colored tissue paper. Brush a mixture of white glue and water on each piece. Press the pieces around the sides of a small glass bottle, overlapping some. Let them dry.

2. Paint the rim of the bottle with nail polish and let dry.

3. Stand a candle in the bottom of the bottle and pour sand around it to hold it in place.

DOORKNOB SURPRISE
(construction paper, yarn)

1. Cut a sheet of construction paper in half. Fold over 1 inch at the top. Using scissors, cut 1-inch slits at the bottom of the paper.

2. Cut a piece of white yarn about 1 1/2 feet long. Place the yarn in the fold at the top and glue in place. Tie the ends in a bow for a hanger.

3. Write a message with glue and press yarn into the glue. Add paper hearts. When dry, hang on a doorknob.

HEART SNACK HOLDERS
(plastic lids, permanent markers, spring-type clothespins)

1. Cut heart shapes from the centers of plastic lids. Decorate them with permanent markers. Write the name of the food or snack in the center of each lid.

2. Glue each plastic heart on a spring-type clothespin and let dry.

3. Place snacks in small bags and clip a heart holder to the top of each one to keep the bags sealed.

THREE-D FRAMED FLOWERS
(cardboard, picture frame, fabric, felt, button, fabric netting, chenille sticks, balloons, plastic cap, cardboard egg carton, candy, plastic berry basket, yarn, construction paper)

1. Cover a piece of cardboard from a picture frame with fabric. Place the cardboard in the frame. Cut a vase shape from felt and glue it in place, leaving the top open. Add fabric trim, making a flower with a button for the center.

2. Glue on a piece of fabric netting for the background. Cut and glue green felt leaves to green chenille sticks for flower stems.

3. Make one flower by gluing four balloons together with a plastic cap in the center. Create another flower using one cup section from a cardboard egg carton. Glue candy in the center.

4. Make a round-shaped flower by cutting a circle from the bottom of a plastic berry basket. Weave a piece of yarn in and out of the sections. Create another flower from construction paper.

HOLIDAY TISSUE BOX
(construction paper, 4 1/2-inch square tissue box, lace)

1. Cut and glue pink construction paper around all sides of a 4 1/2-inch-square vertical tissue box. Carefully trim around the tissue opening.

2. Draw and cut out two identical paper hearts for each side of the box. Glue one heart on top of the other in the center. Slightly curl up the edges of the top heart.

3. Cut small flowers from a piece of lace and glue one in the center of each heart. Add small paper hearts around the tissue opening.

NEEDLE-PUNCHED CARD
(construction paper, tracing paper, plastic-foam tray, large needle)

1. Cut a heart shape from a folded sheet of red construction paper so that the top of the heart is on the fold.

2. Lay tracing paper on the heart and print a message, such as "Be My Valentine?" Add a design around the edges. Turn the tracing paper over so the message is backward.

3. Place the double heart and tracing paper on a piece of plastic-foam tray. With a large needle, poke holes along the pencil lines through the tracing paper and both hearts.

4. Remove the tracing paper and turn the card over. The card will have an interesting raised-dot effect on the front.

HAIR CLIP
(2 1/2-inch metal barrette base, plastic lid, felt, fabric, ribbon, rubber bands)

1. Remove the old ribbon from a metal barrette base.

2. Draw and cut out a heart shape from a plastic lid. Cut a smaller heart from felt and glue it on top of the plastic. Cut a smaller heart from fabric and glue it on top of the felt.

3. Cut a piece of ribbon. Tie it into a bow and glue it on top of the fabric heart.

4. Glue the heart to the metal barrette base and hold in place with rubber bands until dry.

CATERPILLAR VALENTINE
(construction paper)

1. Draw and cut out a leaf shape from construction paper. Draw and cut out four small red paper hearts and one pink paper heart.

2. Glue the four red hearts right side up and slightly overlapping along the leaf to form the caterpillar's body. Glue the pink heart upside down at one end of the red hearts for the head.

3. Cut eyes and a mouth from paper and glue them on the head.

4. Write "Valentine . . . Don't ever 'leaf' me!" and add your signature.

POTTED PACKET
(plastic flowerpot and base, construction paper, potting soil, flower seed packet, tongue depressor)

1. Decorate the sides of a plastic flowerpot with cutout hearts from different-colored construction paper.

2. Fill the flowerpot with potting soil.

3. Tape a flower seed packet to a wooden tongue depressor. Decorate the seed packet with cutout paper hearts.

4. Press the end of the tongue depressor into the potting soil.

HEART BELL
(plastic-foam tray, string, bells)

1. Draw and cut out a large heart from a pink plastic-foam tray. Draw a smaller heart inside the larger one and carefully cut it out.

2. Punch a hole in the top center of the large heart and tie a string for a hanger.

3. Punch other holes along the inside top edge of the heart. Tie a string to a bell and then attach the other end of the string to a hole. Tie the bells at different lengths.

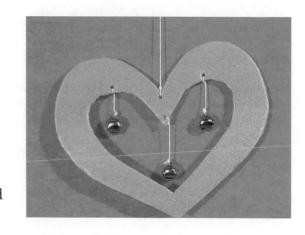

FABRIC JEWELRY BOX
(lightweight fabric, candy box with cardboard lid,
pinking shears, rickrack, lace)

1. Cut a piece of lightweight fabric big enough to cover the sides and top of a cardboard candy-box lid. Squeeze glue around the sides of the box and press the fabric in place.

2. Draw and cut out a heart shape with pinking shears from another piece of fabric and glue it in the middle of the lid. Glue rickrack around the edges.

3. Cut and glue lace around the edge of the box lid. Glue rickrack on top.

PAPER TREAT HOLDER
(construction paper)

1. Cut out a heart shape from a sheet of construction paper.

2. From another sheet of paper, cut a strip 2 inches wide. Draw a pencil line 1/2 inch from the edge of the strip. Make a fold on the pencil line. Open the fold and cut slits along the 1/2-inch section about 1/2 inch apart.

3. Spread glue along the clipped section and fit it around the bottom of the heart as shown. You may need to cut more than one strip to fit around the heart, depending on its size.

4. Decorate the outside of the box with paper hearts. Cut out and glue a heart with "Happy Valentine's Day" written on it. Fill the box with treats.

HEART GLASSES
(poster board, pink plastic wrap, self-adhesive stars)

1. Draw heart-shaped eyeglasses on pink poster board and cut them out along the dotted lines as shown in the diagram. (You can use a pair of old glasses to check the size.)

2. Cut and glue a piece of pink plastic wrap for the lenses. Add self-adhesive stars to decorate the front of the glasses.

3. Look through the glasses and see how everything looks "rosy."

GUESS WHO?
(construction paper, photograph)

1. Cut a square piece of construction paper. With a ruler, measure to find the center of each side of the square and draw a dot. Draw a straight line from one dot to the next as shown. Fold each corner into the center of the square.

2. Keeping the corners folded, write "Guess Who Loves You?" One word goes on each flap.

3. Open the flaps and glue a photograph of yourself in the center square. Write "I do!" under your picture.

4. Draw heart decorations around your photograph.

VALENTINE BOOKMARK
(paper doily, construction paper, clear self-adhesive paper, rickrack, yarn)

1. Cut small designs from a paper doily. Cut small hearts and arrows from construction paper.

2. Cut two identical shapes from clear self-adhesive paper for the bookmark. Carefully remove the backing from one bookmark shape, with the sticky side facing up. Press the hearts, arrows, and paper doily designs on the self-adhesive paper.

3. Place a strip of rickrack around the edge of the self-adhesive paper. Carefully remove the backing from the second bookmark shape. Place it on top of the first one, covering the cutout designs.

4. Punch a hole at one end of the bookmark and tie a piece of yarn through it.

PLASTIC HEART NECKLACE
(large clear plastic lid, nail polish, yarn)

1. Draw and cut out a heart shape from the center of a large clear plastic lid. Punch a hole at the top of the heart.

2. Paint a design on the heart with nail polish. You may want to let it dry, then put on another coat of polish.

3. Cut a piece of yarn long enough to fit over your head as a necklace. Thread the yarn through the hole and tie a knot.

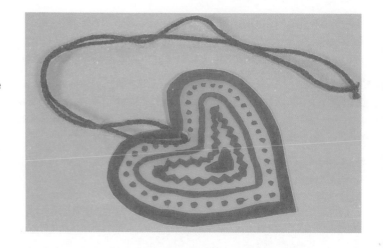

VALENTINE DOGGIE TREATS

(construction paper, two paper plates, yarn, dog biscuits)

1. Cut two heart shapes from construction paper, one larger than the other, and glue them together. Write a dog's name on the heart.

2. Cut away a small section of one paper plate as shown. Place the cut paper plate and a second paper plate face-to-face, making a pocket. Staple around the edges of the plates with the heart tucked in between them.

3. Glue on ears, eyes, eyelashes, a nose, and whiskers cut from construction paper. Punch two holes at the top and tie a piece of yarn for a hanger.

4. Place a few dog biscuits inside the pocket.

SACHET VALENTINE

(construction paper, paper doily, small white envelope, stickers, scented bath powder)

1. Cut a red paper heart and a white paper-doily heart the same size. Glue the paper doily heart on top of the red paper heart. Glue the heart to the front of a small white envelope.

2. Add cutout paper hearts and stickers to decorate the front of the envelope.

3. *Ask an adult* for some scented bath powder to put in the envelope. Seal the envelope and tape if necessary.

FROG HAS A MESSAGE

(construction paper, tracing paper, yarn, moveable plastic eyes)

1. Draw and cut out two frog shapes from green construction paper. Add details with markers from the mouth up on one frog and from the mouth down on the other frog.

2. Cut out the head and mouth of the first frog. Glue this shape on top of the second frog without gluing the mouth down. Fold the mouth open. Trace around the mouth shape on a piece of tracing paper and cut it out. Cut the same mouth shape from red paper and glue it inside the frog's mouth.

3. Draw and cut out a small white heart. Draw a fly on it with the message "You're a great catch!" Glue one end of a piece of yarn to the heart and the other end inside the frog's mouth so the heart hangs just below the mouth.

4. Glue moveable plastic eyes on the frog.

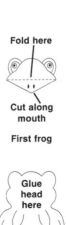

Fold here

Cut along mouth

First frog

Glue head here

Second frog

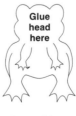

HEART HOT PAD
(waxed paper, twenty ice-cream sticks, felt)

1. Cover your work area with a sheet of waxed paper. Place ten ice-cream sticks next to each other with their sides touching. Squeeze glue on top.

2. Gently place the other ten ice-cream sticks in the glue crosswise on top of the first ten ice-cream sticks. Let dry.

3. Cut and glue a red felt heart in the center. Remove the hot pad from the waxed paper when dry.

HEART BANGLE BRACELET
(old newspaper, plastic ribbon ring, acrylic paint, nail polish)

1. Cover your work area with old newspaper. Paint the outside of an empty plastic ribbon ring with two coats of white acrylic paint, letting the first coat dry before applying the second one.

2. Carefully paint two coats of red nail polish on one outside rim, letting the first coat of polish dry before applying the second. Do the same to the rim on the opposite side.

3. Paint small hearts on the flat area of the ribbon ring. Let dry.

PLEATED VALENTINE
(construction paper)

1. Fold a sheet of red construction paper into eight accordion pleats.

2. On the top draw a half-heart shape, making sure the outline touches the left and right edges of the folded paper. Cut around the outline, but leave the right edge and a small area that touches the left side uncut.

3. Open the folded paper. It will form four hearts. Write a message on them and re-pleat. Give the folded valentine to a friend.

PENNANT MESSAGE
(felt, wooden dowel, construction paper)

1. Cut a pennant shape from felt. Glue one end of the pennant around a wooden dowel. Let dry.

2. Decorate the pennant with sports designs cut from construction paper.

3. Draw and cut out a paper megaphone and write the message "You are a good sport, Valentine!" Glue it to the pennant.

RAIN-OR-SHINE MOUSE
(bathroom tissue tube, cardboard, felt, paper plate, large-eyed needle, chenille stick, paper)

1. Place the end of a bathroom tissue tube on cardboard and trace two circles. Cut out the cardboard circles and glue one to each end of the tube. Cover the tube with glue and brown felt for the body of the mouse.

2. To make the head, cut a small paper plate in half. Roll it into a cone shape and tape it on the inside. Glue it to one end of the body and let dry.

3. Poke holes through the snout with a large-eyed needle and push pieces of chenille stick through the holes for whiskers. Draw on a mouth and eyes. Cut and glue on felt ears.

4. Draw and cut out an umbrella shape from a paper plate. Write "Rain or shine be my Valentine" on the umbrella. Bend and tape a chenille stick for the handle.

5. Cut out four foot shapes from felt. Glue them to the body. Glue a red paper heart to one foot and the umbrella to the opposite foot. Cut a felt tail and glue it to the body.

HAT STAND
(scrap wallpaper, round oatmeal container, ribbon, lace, construction paper)

1. Tape or glue a section of scrap wallpaper around a round oatmeal container.

2. Glue ribbon and lace around the bottom and top of the container for decoration. Add cut-paper hearts.

3. Place your valentine hat on top.

WREATH OF HEARTS
(large brown paper bag, gift wrap, ribbon)

1. Remove the bottom from a large brown paper bag. Cut up one side of the bag, making a large sheet of paper.

2. Measure 2 1/2 inches up along the longest edge and draw a line. Cut out the strip. Measure and cut another strip. Glue the two strips together, making a strip that measures 36 inches long by 2 1/2 inches wide.

3. Crush and twist the strip tightly so it looks like a rope. Shape the strip into a circle that is 3 inches across, wrapping the remainder of the strip around the circle. Staple the ends together.

4. Glue hearts cut from gift wrap onto the wreath. Add a ribbon bow.

POCKET VALENTINE
(construction paper, yarn)

1. Fold a rectangle of construction paper in half. With the fold at the bottom, fold down the top front of the paper and cut it to look like a pocket flap. Glue the flap in place. Glue the sides together to form a pocket. Decorate with cut-paper shapes.

2. Cut out a paper heart and write a message on it. Punch a small hole near the top and tie a piece of yarn through the hole.

3. Tuck the heart into the pocket with the yarn hanging out.

BLUE RIBBON VALENTINE
(felt, gift wrap, fabric, plastic cap)

1. Cut out a circle from blue felt, making a decorative edge. Cut two strips of felt for the tails and glue them to the back of the circle.

2. Draw and cut out a circle from gift wrap. Glue it in the center on the front of the felt circle. Cut and glue a small circle of fabric on top.

3. Cover the top of a plastic cap with gift wrap. Cut out a fabric heart and glue it on top of the gift wrap.

4. Glue the plastic cap in the center of the circle.

WINDOW FLOWER HEART
(clear self-adhesive paper, tissue paper, cardboard, chenille stick)

1. Cut two identical heart shapes from clear self-adhesive paper. Carefully cut out tissue-paper flowers and leaves.

2. *Ask an adult to help you* peel the backing from one heart. Place the heart with the sticky side up on a cardboard work surface. Use two small pieces of tape to secure the heart to the cardboard so it won't move.

3. Gently place the cutout flowers and leaves on the sticky surface, covering the heart. Peel the backing from the second heart and place it on top, sealing the tissue flowers inside. Remove the tape.

4. Poke a hole at the center of the top of the heart. Wrap one end of a chenille stick through the hole for a hanger.

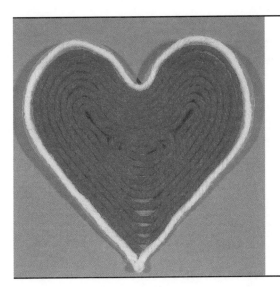

YARN-HEART COASTER
(clear plastic lid, waxed paper, fabric glue, yarn)

1. Cut a heart shape from a clear plastic lid. Place the heart on a piece of waxed paper.

2. Squeeze fabric glue around the outer edge of the heart. Press a long piece of white yarn into the glue outline.

3. Switch to red yarn and continue to add more glue and more yarn, working toward the center of the plastic heart. Let dry overnight.

SWEETHEART FAN
(five ice-cream sticks, ribbon, construction paper)

1. Place five ice-cream sticks in a fan shape. Glue the sticks, stacking one on top of the other at the bottom where they meet. Let dry.

2. Make a ribbon bow, and glue it to the bottom of the fan. Cut out two paper hearts. Write a message on the hearts and glue them to the middle of the fan.

3. Draw and cut out small hearts and glue them to the tips of the sticks. Add pieces of ribbon below the small hearts.

STAND-UP VALENTINE
(construction paper)

1. Cut two identical squares of construction paper, one red and one white. Cut the white square into a heart shape and draw a face on it.

2. Cut a strip of red paper the same length as the red square. Place the heart face down on the red square with about 2 inches of the top of the heart overlapping the edge of the square.

3. Glue one end of the strip to the red square and the other end to the back of the heart.

4. When the glue is dry, bend the strip back in the middle without creasing it, so that the heart stands up on the red square.

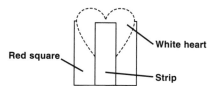

White heart
Red square
Strip

CUPID MAGNET
(red paper plates, white paper plate, moveable plastic eyes, magnetic strip)

1. Cut six hearts of various sizes from red paper plates. Use the largest heart for the body, the next largest for the head, and four small hearts for the arms and legs. Glue the hearts together to form Cupid.

2. To make wings, cut two small triangular sections from a white paper plate. Glue them to the back of Cupid.

3. Add moveable plastic eyes. Cut a nose and mouth from a white paper plate and glue in place.

4. Glue a magnetic strip to Cupid's back.

LACY VALENTINE
(paper doily, construction paper, white paper, needle and embroidery floss)

1. Glue a white paper doily on top of a sheet of red construction paper. When dry, cut out a large heart.

2. Cut out a small heart from white paper and glue it in the center of the large heart. Write a message on it.

3. Thread a large embroidery needle with six strands of red embroidery floss. Use a running stitch to stitch around the edges of both the small and large heart.

Running stitch

VALENTINE FISH MOBILE
(plastic milk jug, construction paper, yarn)

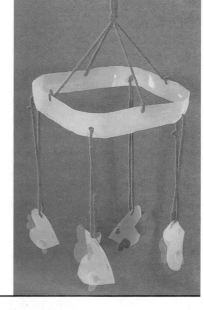

1. Cut four heart shapes from the sides of a clean plastic milk jug for the fish bodies.

2. Cut out three red paper hearts for each fish. Use one large heart for the tail, one medium heart for a fin, and one small heart for an eye. Glue the paper hearts on the fish. Punch a hole in the top of each fish.

3. Draw and cut a ring from the bottom of the plastic jug. Punch a hole in the center of each side section of the ring near the top. Cut four strands of yarn and tie one to each hole. Then tie the strands together at the top to form a hanger.

4. Punch four holes, one at each corner of the ring. Cut four strands of yarn. Tie one fish to each corner hole in the ring.

LICORICE HOLDER
(large frozen-juice container, fabric, rubber band, ribbon)

1. Turn a large frozen-juice container upside down. Place a piece of fabric over it, letting the fabric cover the container and leaving a few extra inches.

2. Pick up the upside-down container and gather the fabric near the opening. Place a rubber band around the gathered fabric about an inch below the top.

3. Tie a ribbon around the fabric-covered container on top of the rubber band. Use scissors to trim the fabric evenly above the container.

4. Place red licorice into the holder.

SPYGLASS VALENTINE
(paper towel tube, poster paint, paper)

1. Cover a paper towel tube with red poster paint and let dry.

2. Cut a paper label and write "Look Through This End." Add an arrow pointing to the left. Glue the label on the left end of the tube.

3. Cut out two paper hearts. On one write "To:" and add the name of the person who will receive the valentine. On the other heart write "From:" and add your name. Glue the hearts on the right end of the tube.

4. Place the right end of the tube on a piece of paper and trace around it, making a circle. Inside the circle draw a heart and write "Be Mine." Cut out the circle, making it about 1/2 inch larger, and place it over the opening of the right end of the tube with the writing on the inside. Glue the edges of the circle to the outside of the tube.

5. Hold the tube up to the light and look through the opened end. You should be able to read the message.

VALENTINE PUZZLE RACE
(corrugated cardboard, paint, permanent marker)

1. Draw and cut out two identical large corrugated cardboard hearts. Cover one heart with red paint and the other one with pink paint. Let them dry and add another coat of paint to each if needed.

2. Using a permanent marker, write "Be Mine, Valentine!" on one heart. On the other heart write "Don't Break My Heart!" *Ask an adult to help you* cut each heart into pieces.

To play: Starting at the same time, each player must try to put his or her heart puzzle together. The first player to complete the puzzle wins.

PLASTIC-FOAM NECKLACE
(plastic-foam trays, needle and thread)

1. Use a paper punch to punch dots from white and pink plastic-foam trays. Draw and cut out a heart shape from a white tray and decorate it with dots.

2. Cut a piece of heavy thread long enough to go over your head easily. Thread a sewing needle with the heavy thread, but do not tie a knot in the end. Make a necklace chain by sewing through the center of each white dot and sewing sideways through the pink ones.

3. Be sure to leave long ends of thread at each end of the chain. Sew the ends of the chain to the heart.

VALENTINE INVITATION
(construction paper, glitter)

1. Fold a piece of white construction paper in half for the card. Cut out a red paper heart and gently tear it down the middle. Glue it to the front of the card, leaving a little space between the torn edges.

2. Outline the edges of the heart and make a border on the card with glue and glitter.

3. Inside the invitation write "My heart will break
If you don't say
You'll come to my party
For Valentine's Day."

Add your name, address, phone number, and date and time of the party.

ALPHABET VALENTINES
(construction paper)

The secret to these valentines is that the first word of the message is the shape of the valentine itself.

1. Cut out a large letter from construction paper. Write a message to go with the letter. For example, cut the letter *B* from red paper. Write the words "My Valentine." Your real message is "Be My Valentine."

2. You can also make "words" with the letters *C, A, O, G,* and *U.* Think of others and write a message to go with each letter.

FLOWER BOUQUET
(food container with plastic lid, construction paper, plastic-foam egg carton, chenille sticks)

1. Cover a clean food container and its plastic lid with construction paper. Decorate the sides with cut-paper hearts.

2. From a plastic-foam egg carton, cut cup sections in flower shapes. Cut and glue paper hearts on the flowers.

3. With a pencil, poke a small hole in the bottom of each flower. Insert a long chenille stick through the hole for a stem.

4. Cut out paper hearts for leaves. Glue a small plastic-foam heart, cut from the lid of the egg carton, in the center of each paper-heart leaf. Glue the leaves on the stems and let dry.

5. *Ask an adult to help you* poke a hole in the center of the plastic lid. Place the flowers through the hole to make them stand up.

CAT TOY
(felt, paper, permanent markers, fabric glue, catnip)

1. Cut out two felt hearts the same size.

2. From paper, draw and cut out a cat's head that will fit on the heart shape. Pin the paper cat on a piece of felt and cut it out. Use fabric glue to attach the cat's head to one of the hearts. Add features with permanent markers.

3. Squeeze fabric glue around the edge of the plain heart. Cut out a felt tail and place it just inside the edge of the heart. Sprinkle a little catnip in the center of the heart.

4. Place the heart with the cat's head on top, pressing the edges together. Let dry.

MANY HEARTS VALENTINE
(construction paper, yarn)

1. Cut a 9-by-18-inch rectangle from red construction paper. Fold it in half, making a 9-inch square.

2. Cut a sheet of white paper into an 8-inch square. Fold the square in half. Cut out six small hearts as shown in Section 1. Open the paper and fold it in half the other way. Cut out six hearts as shown in Section 2.

3. Open the paper and fold it in half diagonally. Cut out eight hearts as shown in Section 3. Open the paper and fold it in half diagonally the other way. Cut out eight hearts as shown in Section 4.

4. Open the paper and glue it to the center of the 9-inch red square. Punch two holes close to the fold. Thread a piece of yarn through the holes and tie a bow. Write a message inside the card.

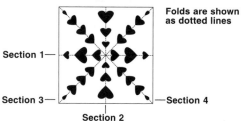

Folds are shown as dotted lines

Section 1 — Section 2 — Section 3 — Section 4

HEART RING
(lightweight cardboard, construction paper, chenille stick, beads)

1. Draw and cut out a small heart shape from lightweight cardboard. Trace around it twice on red construction paper. Cut out the hearts and glue one to each side of the cardboard heart.

2. Cut and glue a red chenille stick heart to the back of the cardboard heart.

3. Cut a piece of chenille stick to go around your finger. Glue it to the back of the cardboard heart. Let dry.

4. Put the ring on your finger and twist the ends of the chenille stick together. Remove the ring. Trim off any extra ends. Place the ring upright. Glue small beads around the edge of the heart. Let dry.

SECRET MESSAGE VALENTINE
(construction paper)

1. Fold a sheet of red construction paper in half the long way. Draw and cut three hearts almost all the way out, leaving about an inch at the top of each heart to hold the paper together.

2. Draw and cut out heart shapes along the sides as shown.

3. Glue the red paper on a sheet of white paper, attaching everything but the center row of hearts. Lift each of the center hearts and write your message on the white sheet underneath.

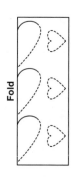

Fold

BE

MY

VALENTINE

BIRDSEED MOBILE
(waxed paper, plastic lids, ribbon, peanut butter, birdseed)

1. Cover your work surface with waxed paper. Cut out hearts from plastic lids. Punch a hole at the top and bottom of each heart.

2. Tie the hearts together with pieces of ribbon.

3. Spread one side of each heart with peanut butter. Then press each side in birdseed. Turn the hearts over and cover the other side.

4. Hang the mobile outside to give the birds a valentine treat.

LOLLIPOP PLACE CARD
(construction paper, flat lollipop, gumdrop)

1. Cut out a heart shape from construction paper for each place card. Make two slits in each one and insert a cut-paper arrow with a guest's name printed on it.

2. Glue the heart to the wrapper of a flat lollipop and stand it upright in a large gumdrop.

DESK DECORATION
(construction paper)

1. Use a sheet of red construction paper that measures 12 inches by 18 inches. Place it lengthwise in front of you. Draw vertical lines 10 1/2 inches long and 2 1/2 inches apart. With scissors, cut along the lines, making slits. Do not cut to the edges of the paper.

2. Cut strips of white paper, 2 1/2 inches wide by 18 inches in length. Weave them in and out of the slits on the red paper, making a checkerboard. Glue the ends of the strips.

3. Cut red paper hearts and glue them to the white squares.

CLOUD CUPID CARD
(construction paper, cotton balls)

1. Fold a sheet of light blue construction paper in half to form a card.

2. Draw and cut out Cupid from red paper. Add eyes and a mouth with a marker. Cut out a yellow paper sun.

3. Glue cotton balls on the card in a cloud shape. Add the sun and Cupid.

4. Write "Valentine . . ." on the front of the card. On the inside write "I'm floating on a cloud whenever you're around!"

VALENTINE COLLAGE
(lightweight cardboard, valentine cards, construction paper, yarn)

1. Cut out a large heart from a piece of lightweight cardboard. Glue some valentine cards on the heart.

2. Draw and cut out hearts of various colors and sizes from paper. Glue them onto the heart, overlapping the cards.

3. Squeeze glue around the edge of the large heart. Press a piece of yarn into the glue. Add a yarn bow. Let dry.

4. Tape or glue a loop of yarn to the back for a hanger.

GIFT OF FLOWERS
(construction paper, paper doily, ribbon)

1. Cut and glue a circle of red construction paper in the center of a round white paper doily.

2. Draw and cut stems and leaves from green paper. Cut out red and pink paper tulips. Glue the flowers to the stems. Then glue the flowers and leaves around the paper doily and let dry.

3. Fold the circle in half and glue it together. Punch a hole at the top. Thread a piece of ribbon through the hole and tie a pretty bow.

INCOMING MAIL

(shoe box, cardboard, one-pound coffee can with plastic lid, construction paper)

1. With the lid off, trace around one end of a shoe box on cardboard. Draw 2-inch flaps on the two long sides of the rectangle shape and cut it out. Fold up the flaps along the pencil lines. Staple this to one end of the shoe box with the flaps up.

2. Place the coffee can between the flaps. Tape the flaps to the can. Tape the ends of the can to the box. Cut off one end of the shoe-box lid. Close the shoe box and tape it shut.

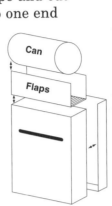

3. *Ask an adult to help you* cut a mail slot in the shoe box. Cover the mailbox with construction paper. Decorate the mailbox with cut-paper hearts.

4. To remove valentines from the mailbox, cut a door in the back of the box.

CLAY VALENTINE

(construction paper, greeting card box with clear acetate top, clay)

1. Cut and glue construction paper around the outside and inside of the bottom of a greeting card box that has a clear acetate top.

2. Press and mold clay inside the card box to look like a picture frame. Mold hearts of a different-colored clay and place them on the corners of the clay frame. Add a large clay heart in the center.

3. Roll thin strips of clay and form letters to spell the message "Be Mine." Add them to the large heart.

4. Place the clear acetate top on the box.

VALENTINE NOISEMAKER

(aluminum pie pans, yarn, dried beans, construction paper)

1. Place two small aluminum pie pans facing each other, rim to rim. Hold the rims together and, with a paper punch, punch holes around the edges so the holes line up.

2. Cut short pieces of yarn. Tie one piece of yarn through each set of holes, joining the two rims together. Before tying the last set of holes together, place a few dried beans between the pans. Tie pieces of yarn near each knot so they dangle around the noisemaker.

3. Cut paper hearts from construction paper and glue onto the pans.

Baskets and More

Give your gifts in a special way.

WRAPPING PAPER
(old newspaper, poster paper, poster board,
tempera paint, paper plate, old toothbrush)

1. *Ask an adult to help you* select a work area and cover it with old newspaper. Cut a section from a roll of poster paper. Tape each corner to the newspaper to hold it in place.

2. Draw and cut out hearts from poster board. Place the hearts onto the poster paper, holding them in place with small pieces of rolled tape on the backs.

3. Squeeze different colors of tempera paint onto a paper plate. Carefully dip the bristles of an old toothbrush in one color. Hold the brush in one hand close to the poster paper near a taped-on heart. With the other hand, run your finger sideways over the bristles, spattering paint onto the poster paper.

4. Continue to spatter paint lightly onto the poster paper until it is covered. Let dry. Carefully remove the taped-on hearts.

HEART BASKET
(eight ice-cream sticks, watercolor paint, construction paper, plastic berry basket)

1. Paint eight ice-cream sticks with green watercolor paint and let dry.

2. Cut out eight heart shapes from pink and red construction paper. Glue them to the ends of the sticks. Add smaller hearts to the centers of the larger hearts.

3. Weave the ice-cream sticks through the sides of a plastic berry basket. Put candy inside.

GIFT BAG
(small paper bag, poster paint, paper doily, paper, ribbon)

1. Cover the outside of a small paper bag with pink poster paint and let dry. Cut out a heart shape from a white paper doily. Glue it to the center of the bag.

2. Cut small red paper hearts and glue them along the bottom of the bag.

3. Holding the bag closed, punch a hole through all layers at the top. Open the bag and place a gift inside. Close the bag, thread a piece of red ribbon through the holes, and tie a bow.

WOVEN HEART BASKET
(construction paper)

1. Fold a sheet of white and a sheet of red construction paper in half the long way. Draw and cut out a large U-shape from each sheet of paper, and cut three slits as shown in the diagram.

2. Weave the four looplike sections as shown in the diagram. The first left white loop is inserted into the first red right loop, then over the second red loop. The second white loop is slipped over the first red loop and inserted into the second red loop.

3. Continue to weave until all the sections are woven together. Slide them together to fit snugly. Glue a paper handle onto the basket and fill with a snack.

GIFT BOX
(small gift box, poster paint, construction paper, yarn)

1. Draw and cut out a heart shape from the lid of a small gift box. Cover the lid with poster paint and let dry.

2. Turn the lid over on a piece of white construction paper and trace around the cutout heart shape. Draw red heart outlines on the white heart.

3. Cut out and glue a small red paper heart on top of a pink paper heart. Glue a ring of paper to the back of the hearts and glue them to the center of the white heart. Glue the white heart in the cutout center of the box lid. Glue yarn around the heart and the edge of the box.

4. Draw and cut out paper letters that spell "Be Mine" and glue them to the lid.

MINI CANDY BASKET
(cardboard egg carton, poster paint, construction paper)

1. Cut a cup section from a cardboard egg carton for the basket. Cover it with white poster paint and let dry.

2. Draw and cut out four red paper heart shapes. Cut out the centers. Glue pink paper on one side of the red hearts so the pink paper shows through on the other side.

3. Glue the hearts around the basket. Cut and glue a paper handle inside the basket on opposite sides. Fill the basket with candies.

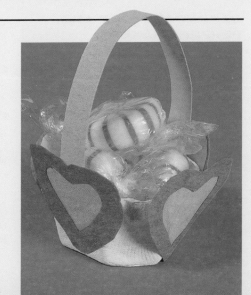

MATERIAL INDEX

175 Easy-to-Do EASTER CRAFTS

Edited by
Sharon Dunn Umnik

EASTER

175 Easy-to-Do EASTER CRAFTS

Edited by Sharon Dunn Umnik

BOYDS MILLS PRESS

Inside this book . . .

you'll find a fabulous assortment of crafts made from recyclable items and inexpensive things found in or around your house. Have pencils, crayons, scissors, tape, and other supplies for craft making close by. *– the Editor*

Copyright © 1994 by Boyds Mills Press
All rights reserved

Published by Bell Books
Boyds Mills Press, Inc.
A Highlights Company
815 Church Street
Honesdale, Pennsylvania 18431
Printed in China

Publisher Cataloging-in-Publication Data
Main entry under title :
    175 easy-to-do Easter crafts : easy-to-do crafts, easy-to-find things /
edited by Sharon Dunn Umnik.—1st ed.
[64]p. : col. photo. ; cm.
Includes index.
Summary : Includes step-by-step directions to make and decorate Easter
baskets, eggs, rabbits, place cards, greeting cards, and more.
ISBN 1-56397-316-2
1. Handicraft—Juvenile literature. 2. Easter decorations—Juvenile
literature. [1. Handicraft. 2. Easter decorations.] I. Umnik, Sharon Dunn.
II. Title.
745.59—dc20   1994   CIP
Library of Congress Catalog Card Number 93-70871

First edition, 1994
Book designed by Charlie Cary
The text of this book is set in 11-point New Century Schoolbook.

10 9 8 7 6 5

Craft Contributors: Jennifer and Caroline Arnold, Patricia Barley, Katherine Corliss Bartow, Linda Bloomgren, Barr Clay Bullock, Mary Caldwell, Catherine Carmody, Mindy Cheraz, Ann Clark, Mary Colarico, Carol Conner, Kathleen Conrad, Evelyn Cook, Paige Eckard, Laurie Edwards, Donna L. Eichler, Gladys Emerson, Virginia Follis, Dee Francis, Sarah T. Frey, Sandra Godfrey, Mavis Grant, Mildred Grenier, Norah Grubmeyer, Edna Harrington, Joann M. Hart, Ann Hatch, Kathryn Heisenfelt, Texie Hering, Loretta Holz, Carmen Horn, Olive Howie, Tama Kain, Virginia Killough, Garnett Kooker, Judith L. LaDez, Twilla Lamm, Sarah V. Lasher, Ruth E. Libbey, Lee Lindeman, Alvera M. Lundin, M. Mable Lunz, Agnes Maddy, Patricia A. McMillan, Ursula Michael, Patty S. Milton, June Rose Mobly, Judith Morgan, Ellen E. Morrison, Sister Mary Norma, Anita Page, Dorothe A. Palms, S. Peoples, Beatrice Bachrach Perri, James W. Perrin Jr., Luella Pierce, Ellen Plausky, Jane K. Priewe, Karla P. Ray, Terry A. Ricioli, Kathy Ross, Barbara Smith, Mary Collette Spees, June Swanson, Sister Mary Sylvia, V.S.C., Mildred G. Turner, Sharon Dunn Umnik, Jan J. Van Pelt, Bernice Walz, Jean White, Pamela Young Wolff, Agnes Choate Wonson, Jinx Woolson, and Connie Wright.

Gigantic EASTER EGGS

PEEK-A-BOO EGG
(plastic-foam trays, plastic grass,
permanent markers, felt, fabric trim)

Follow the steps below, then
cut a hole in one side of the
egg. Draw and cut out two
rabbits and an Easter basket
with pointed bottoms from
plastic-foam trays. Decorate
them with felt and permanent
markers. Place some plastic
grass inside the egg with the
rabbits and their basket. Glue
some fabric trim around the
hole and hang up the egg.

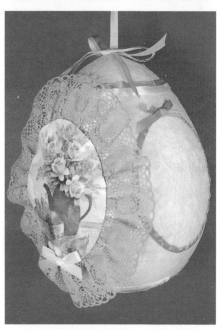

VICTORIAN EGG
(old greeting card, lace, ribbon)

Follow the steps below, then
cut a scene from an old
greeting card in the shape of
an oval. Glue it to one side of
the egg. Cut three oval shapes
from lace, and glue them to
the other sides of the egg.
Decorate the egg with more
ribbon.

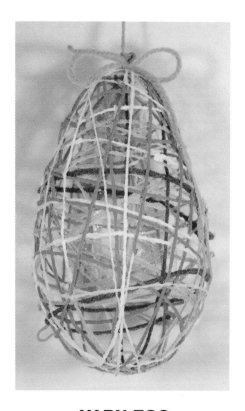

YARN EGG
(different-colored yarn)

Follow the steps below, except
instead of using white tissue
paper, dip different-colored
lengths of yarn into the
mixture. Wrap the yarn
around an inflated balloon
and let dry. Pop the balloon
and pull it out from between
the yarn. Attach a yarn
hanger.

BASIC STEPS FOR MAKING A GIANT EASTER EGG
(egg-shaped balloons, a large plastic food container, glue, water, white tissue paper, string)

1. Make a mixture of equal amounts of white glue
and water in a large plastic food container. Blow
up an egg-shaped, light-colored balloon and knot
the end. Tie a piece of string around the knot.

2. Tear strips of white tissue paper, and dip them
into the mixture. Cover the balloon with the
strips.

3. Hang the balloon to dry. Add more layers,
letting each one dry before adding another.

4. Pop the balloon and pull it out of the egg shape
by pulling gently on the string. Cover the hole
where the balloon knot was with paper and glue
if needed. Place a piece of yarn or ribbon at the
same spot for a hanger. Add layers of tissue
paper, letting each dry as before, to cover the hole
and to hold the ribbon in place.

**NOTE: Always cover your work surface, and
be sure to clean up your mess.**

BOX BUNNY SURPRISE
(quart-size milk carton, construction paper, tissue paper)

1. Measure 2 1/2 inches from the bottom of a quart-size milk carton, and draw a line around the carton.

2. On one side, draw a rabbit's head above the line. Cut around the rabbit's head and then on the line around the three other sides. Cut and glue a strip of construction paper around the carton.

3. Lay the rabbit side down on a piece of paper, and trace around it twice. Cut out the rabbit shapes. Glue one to the outside, covering the carton, and glue the other one to the inside.

4. Cut out eyes, a mouth, a nose, whiskers, and ears from paper, and glue them on the bunny. Line the "bunny box" with tissue paper, and fill with nuts, cookies, or candy for a holiday surprise.

EASTER EGG CARD
(poster board, yarn)

1. Fold a piece of poster board in half to make a card.

2. Draw and cut out an egg shape from another piece of poster board. Spread several lines of white glue on the egg shape, dividing it into sections. Press black yarn into the glue.

3. Fill the sections with glue, and press pieces of yarn into the glue, starting at the outline of each section and moving toward the middle.

4. Glue the yarn egg to the front of the card. Write a holiday message.

EASTER MOBILE
(yarn, two wooden sticks, poster board)

1. Place two wooden sticks together to form an X. Wrap yarn around the center, adding glue. Add a yarn loop for hanging.

2. Cut four eggs, four chicks, and a rabbit from white poster board. Decorate them with markers or crayons. Punch a hole in the top of each shape.

3. Using short pieces of yarn, tie the eggs to the ends of the sticks. Using longer pieces of yarn, tie the chicks halfway between the ends and the center. Using an even longer piece of yarn, tie the rabbit to the center of the X.

4. Slide the shapes along the sticks until the mobile hangs evenly.

GIFT BAG

(brown paper bag, yarn, old greeting card)

1. Cut a picture from an old greeting card, and glue it onto a brown paper bag. Write a message. Place a gift inside.

2. Fold about 1 inch of the bag's top inside. Close the bag and punch four holes across the top. String a piece of yarn through the holes and tie a bow.

SPOON-FLOWER PLACE CARD

(plastic spoon, 1-inch plastic-foam ball, poster board, toothpicks)

1. Paint the bowl part of a plastic spoon to look like a flower and let it dry. Paint the handle to look like the stem of the flower.

2. Press a 1-inch plastic-foam ball against a hard surface to flatten one side. Glue it to a piece of poster board. Push the stem of the flower into the top of the ball.

3. Cut leaves from poster board, and glue each leaf onto a toothpick, leaving the pointed end of the toothpick showing on the bottom. Push the leaves into the ball next to the stem.

4. Write a name on a piece of poster board. Glue it to a small piece of toothpick, and push it into the ball in front of the flower.

A GIFT THAT GROWS

(yarn, plastic food container)

1. Spread an inch of glue around the outside bottom of a plastic food container.

2. Working from the bottom, press the end of a piece of yarn into the glue, and start winding it around the container. Use different colors of yarn. Glue a decoration on the front and let it dry.

3. Place small stones in the bottom of the container for drainage. Add some dirt and clippings from a growing plant, or place a potted plant in the container.

FELT EASTER EGGS
(felt, lace, ribbon, cotton balls)

1. For each egg, cut two ovals from felt. Glue lace or ribbon on the ovals for decoration.

2. Turn the ovals to the undecorated side. Spread glue on the edges of the ovals, and place a few cotton balls in the center of one oval.

3. Place the second oval on top of the first, pressing the ovals together at the edges.

COTTON-BALL RABBIT
(cardboard, felt, buttons, black yarn, string, cotton balls)

1. Draw and cut out a rabbit shape from cardboard. Cover the ears with pieces of pink felt. Outline them with glue and cotton balls.

2. Spread glue over the rest of the rabbit, and completely cover it with cotton balls.

3. From felt, cut out and glue on eyes, a nose, and a bow tie. Glue buttons onto the body. Glue on black yarn for the mouth.

4. Attach a piece of short string to the top of the rabbit for a hanger.

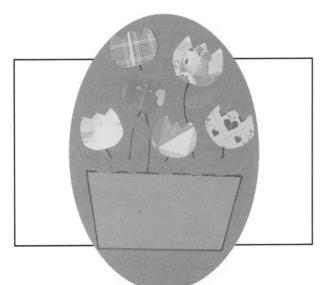

GIFT WRAP EASTER CARD
(construction paper, gift wrap)

1. On a piece of folded construction paper, draw and cut out an egg shape, with the left side on the fold.

2. Cut out flower shapes from bits of gift wrap paper, and glue them to the front of the egg. Cut a vase and leaves from construction paper, and glue them in place. Use a marker to draw stems.

3. Write an Easter message inside the card.

EASTER WREATH
(cardboard, yarn, plastic-foam trays, glitter)

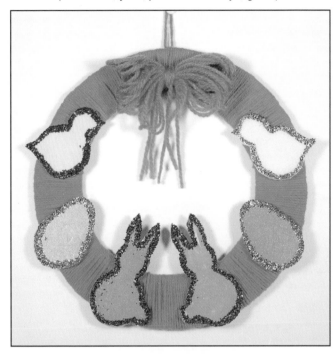

1. Cut a doughnut shape from cardboard to make a wreath. Wrap yarn completely around it.

2. Draw and cut out chicks, rabbits, and eggs from plastic-foam trays. Spread glue around the edges of each shape, sprinkle them with glitter, and let dry. Glue the shapes to the wreath.

3. Add a yarn bow for decoration. Attach a loop of yarn to the back of the wreath for a hanger.

BUTTON RINGS
(pipe cleaners, buttons with two large holes)

1. Using a button with two large holes, push a pipe cleaner through one hole and back down through the other.

2. Twist the ends of the pipe cleaner together, adjusting the ring to the size of your finger.

JELLY-BEAN POLE
(paper towel tube, cardboard, poster paint, construction paper, toothpicks, jelly beans)

1. Cut a paper towel tube to measure 7 inches in length. To make a base, cut a small cardboard circle and glue it to one end of the tube. Cover with poster paint and let dry.

2. Use the tip of a ball-point pen to poke holes around the tube. Put a jelly bean on one end of a toothpick, and stick the other end of the toothpick into a hole.

3. Draw and cut out a small bunny and glue it to the inside of the tube, so the bunny appears to be peeking over the top.

EGG-TO-CHICK EASTER CARD

(poster board, construction paper, gift wrap)

1. Draw three large egg shapes, touching each other, on white poster board. Cut around them to make the shape shown.

2. Color one side of the eggs yellow. Make a bill and eyes for the chick from construction paper, and glue them to the center yellow egg.

3. Fold the outer eggs over the center one. Draw a zigzag line down the center of the egg on top, and cut along the line with scissors. Fold over the cut egg, trace along the zigzag edge on the white egg underneath, and then cut along the edge. Unfold the eggs.

4. Glue a piece of gift wrap to the outside of each egg half and let dry. Trim around the edges with scissors. Write a message inside the card.

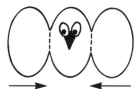

Fold over on dotted line

STAINED-GLASS WINDOW

(plastic-foam tray, colored tissue paper, glitter, newspaper)

1. Draw an outline of a stained-glass window design on a plastic-foam tray. Press out the sections of the window with a dull table knife.

2. Cut pieces of colored tissue paper slightly larger than the cutout sections of the window. Tape these pieces to the back of the tray, covering the cutout section.

3. On a work area covered with newspaper, spread glue on the outline of the window, and sprinkle with glitter. Add a yarn loop to hang in a window.

MINI EASTER BASKET

(plastic food container, two pipe cleaners, fabric, ribbon, plastic grass)

1. Punch a hole on both sides of a plastic food container near the top with a paper punch.

2. Wrap two pipe cleaners around each other, insert each end into a hole, and twist the ends together for the handle.

3. Glue fabric and ribbon to the outside of the container.

4. Decorate the handle with ribbon and a bow. Fill the basket with plastic grass and treats.

BABY BUNNY
(washcloth, rubber band, ribbon, moveable plastic eyes,
string, yarn, cotton ball)

1. Place a washcloth on the table in front of you. Tightly roll one corner to the center. Hold the rolled section in place while you turn the washcloth around and roll the opposite corner toward the center. (See Diagram 1.)

2. With the rolled side down, fold the washcloth in half. (See Diagram 2.) Then fold back about 2 inches from one end. Place a rubber band around this section to form the bunny's head. (See Diagram 3.) Tie a ribbon over the rubber band.

3. Add moveable plastic eyes, a yarn nose, and string whiskers to the head. Glue on a cotton ball for a tail.

Diagram 1　　**Diagram 2**　　**Diagram 3**

EGG-CARTON NUT CUP
(cardboard egg carton, construction paper)

1. Cut one cup section from a cardboard egg carton. Scallop the edge with a pair of scissors.

2. For a base, draw and cut out the green leafy part of a flower from construction paper. Then cut a flower with long petals. Glue the leaf section and the flower together.

3. Glue the scalloped cup section to the middle of the base. Put peanuts in the cup.

EASTER RABBIT HAT
(poster board, paper doily, construction paper)

1. Cut a rabbit head from poster board. Add pink ears from construction paper.

2. Glue a small paper doily over the rabbit's head. Add paper eyes, nose, mouth, and whiskers to the face.

3. Cut a long strip of poster board, and glue the rabbit to the center of the strip. Staple the ends of the strip together so that it fits on your head.

BUNNY PARTY CUP
(plastic-foam cup, construction paper, yarn)

1. Draw bunny ears on the middle of a plastic-foam cup. Cut the cup in half, cutting around the bunny ears.

2. Paper-punch two black eyes from construction paper, and glue them to the cup below the ears.

3. Cut pieces of yarn, and glue them on as whiskers. Add other features with a marker, and glue on a cotton-ball tail.

STAND-UP EASTER CARD
(poster board)

1. Fold a long piece of poster board in half. Open the card, and draw an egg on the bottom half just below the fold. On the top half, just above the fold, draw a chick coming out of the egg.

2. Write a message on the egg, and color the drawing with crayons or markers. Cut around the outline of the chick with scissors just to the fold of the paper. Fold back the card so it will stand up.

CHICK IN A NEST
(cardboard egg carton, yarn, an eggshell half, construction paper, paint)

1. Cut a cup section from a cardboard egg carton. Spread glue around the outside of the cup. Press the end of a piece of yarn into the glue, and wind the yarn around the cup.

2. Glue pieces of yellow yarn inside the nest for straw. Paint half of an eggshell.

3. Add features cut from paper, and glue the chick inside the nest.

EASTER PLACE MAT
(construction paper)

1. Place a sheet of construction paper 12 inches by 18 inches lengthwise in front of you. Cut vertical slits 8 inches long and 2 1/2 inches apart.

2. Using paper of another color, cut three strips 2 1/2 inches by 18 inches. Weave them in and out of the slits on the large sheet of paper to form a checkerboard pattern. Glue down the ends of the strips.

3. Decorate some of the squares with decorated paper eggs.

FAN FLOWERS
(fabric, pipe cleaners)

1. Cut a piece of fabric 2 1/2 inches wide and 8 inches long. Starting at the narrow end, fold over 1/3 of an inch and continue to fold into accordion pleats until the entire piece is pleated.

2. Bend one end of a long pipe cleaner around the center of the folded fabric, and twist it to make the flower and stem. Pull the folded flower open into a circle.

3. For the leaves, loop and twist short pieces of pipe cleaner onto the stem. Make several flowers, and place them in a vase.

HOLIDAY BELT
(plastic lids, permanent marker, pipe cleaners, yarn)

1. Cut egg and tulip shapes from plastic lids, such as those used on coffee, margarine, peanut, or cereal containers. Color the edges of the eggs and tulips with a permanent marker.

2. Punch a hole at the edge of each shape, and join them with pieces of pipe cleaners or yarn. Continue to make as many shapes as you need to go around your waist.

3. At each end of the belt, tie on a longer piece of yarn to fasten the belt around your waist.

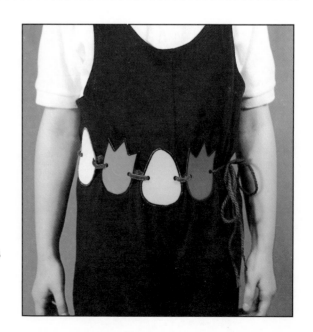

STAND-UP DECORATION
(construction paper)

1. Fold a 6-inch-by-8-inch piece of construction paper in half the long way, then across. Measure 1/2 inch up from the longer unfolded side and draw a line for the base.

2. At the folded side, draw half an egg on the base as shown. Beside the egg, draw a chick with the head touching the top fold and the bottom touching the base. Cut through all four layers and unfold.

3. Add details to the chicks with markers. Draw a decorative border, and write a name on the egg. Stand the decoration up by opening the bottom slightly.

EGG HEADBAND
(poster board, poster paint)

1. Cut a strip of poster board about 3 inches wide and long enough to go around your head, overlapping the ends a little. Tape or glue the ends together.

2. Cut out egg-shaped pieces from poster board. Decorate them with poster paint. When the eggs are dry, glue them evenly around the band.

BUNNY EASTER BASKET
(two plastic-foam egg cartons of the same color, one cardboard egg carton, cotton balls, construction paper, fabric)

1. Cut off the tops of both plastic-foam cartons and cut one of the bottoms in half the long way, making a row of six cups. Glue this row, upside down, over half of the other foam carton, leaving the other half open for the basket.

2. Decorate the row of egg shapes with cotton noses and paper whiskers, eyes, and heart shapes for feet. Make ears from paper, and glue one pair to the back of each bunny head.

3. On every other bunny, glue on a bow of fabric to the top of the head.

4. Cut little hats from the cardboard carton's peaked dividers. Paint them black, and glue each to a circle of black paper. Glue the hats to the remaining bunny heads.

FLOWER PIN
(seeds from fruit or sunflowers, lightweight cardboard,
popcorn kernels, felt, safety pin)

1. Wash and dry seeds from apples, melons, lemons, or sunflowers.

2. Cut a circle from lightweight cardboard.

3. Glue a row of seeds, with their points toward the center, around the outer edge of the circle. Glue on another row of seeds, overlapping the first row. Continue with three or four rows.

4. Glue popcorn kernels in the center.

5. Glue on green felt leaves and a safety pin to the back of the cardboard.

COFFEE-FILTER FLOWERS
(coffee filters, food coloring, pipe cleaners)

1. For each flower, fold a coffee filter into quarters. Dampen the filter with water. Add drops of food coloring onto the filter in any pattern.

2. Press the filter between pieces of waxed paper to spread the color. Open the filter, and let it dry on paper towels.

3. Fold the filter in quarters again, forming a point at the bottom. Twist a pipe cleaner around the point for a stem.

WOOLLY LAMB
(poster board, yarn, moveable plastic eyes)

1. For the body of the lamb, cut a rectangle from white poster board. Cut three strips of black poster board and fold in half for the legs and the head of the lamb.

2. Cut one more black strip, smaller in size, and fold it in half for the tail of the lamb. Glue the legs, tail, and head to the white poster board. Add moveable plastic eyes and a piece of yarn for the mouth.

3. Spread glue on the white poster board and sprinkle on cut pieces of white yarn, covering the entire lamb. Glue a loop of yarn to the back for a hanger.

RUB-A-PICTURE
(crayon, cardboard, construction paper)

1. Cut shapes such as rabbits, eggs, chicks, or flowers from cardboard. Glue them on a sheet of construction paper.

2. Place a sheet of construction paper over the cardboard picture. Rub over the paper with the side of a crayon. Watch the picture appear.

3. The rabbit pictured here shows how the different parts are cut and glued. The overlapping parts are brought out in detail in the rubbed picture.

EASTER BASKET
(cereal box, construction paper, plastic grass)

1. Cut a large corner section from the bottom of a cereal box to make the top of the basket. Cut a smaller corner section from the bottom to make the bottom of the basket. Cover both pieces with glue and construction paper.

2. Cut the point off the bottom corner section of the basket as shown.

3. Turn the large corner section so the opening is up, and glue the bottom into the opening of the bottom section.

4. Decorate the basket with paper. Cut strips of construction paper, and glue them to the basket to make a handle.

BUNNY PUPPET
(construction paper, two spring-type clothespins, old sock)

1. From paper, cut out bunny ears long enough to cover spring-type clothespins. Glue the ears to the clothespins.

2. Lay an old sock on a table. Cut out eyes, nose, and whiskers from paper. Glue them to the bottom of the sock.

3. Place your hand inside the sock, and clip the bunny ears to the heel of the sock.

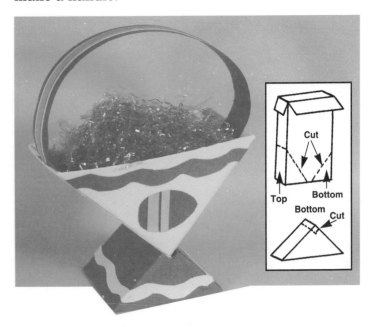

EASTER BRACELET
(plastic-foam cup, yarn, felt)

1. Draw a line about 1 inch from the top edge of a plastic-foam cup. Cut around the cup on the line, making the bracelet form.

2. Wrap yarn around the bracelet. Glue the ends to the inside. Glue on flowers cut from felt.

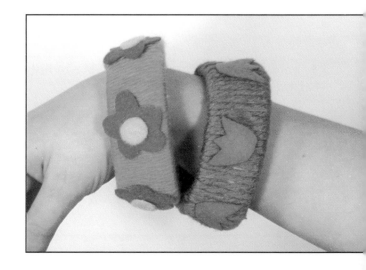

HYACINTH DECORATION
(pinecone, plastic top, colored aluminum foil, tissue paper, ribbon)

1. Glue a pinecone upright in a plastic top covered with colored aluminum foil.

2. Cut tissue paper into 1 1/2-inch squares. Put the point of a pencil in the center of the tissue. Gently twist the paper around the pencil point. Dip the tip into glue, and stick it between the petals of the pinecone.

3. Add a ribbon bow and leaves cut from green paper.

COTTON-BALL SHEEP FAMILY
(cardboard, cotton balls, felt, ribbon)

1. For each sheep, cut two matching sheep shapes from cardboard. Glue the shapes together except for the feet.

2. Glue cotton balls on both sides of the sheep. From felt, cut ears, eyes, cheeks, a nose, a mouth, and feet. Glue them on the sheep. Add a ribbon to each sheep.

3. Bend the feet out a little, until the sheep can stand.

LAMB CARD

(construction paper, self-adhesive reinforcement rings)

1. Fold a piece of construction paper in half to make a card. Draw a lamb on the front.

2. To make its wool look curly, cover the lamb's body with many self-adhesive reinforcement rings.

3. Add grass, flowers, and other scenery with crayons or markers. Write a message inside.

AN EASTER EGG TO HATCH

(poster board, brass fastener)

1. Draw and cut out an egg shape on a piece of poster board. Draw designs on the egg with markers. Cut the egg in half along a jagged line.

2. Draw and cut out a chick from poster board. Glue the chick to the back of the bottom half of the eggshell so that it seems to be sitting in the shell.

3. Attach the top half of the egg to the bottom half with a brass fastener. The egg can then be opened and closed.

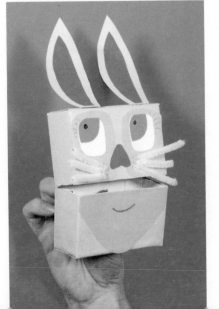

RABBIT BOX-PUPPET

(individual-sized cereal box, construction paper, pipe cleaner)

1. Tape the openings of an individual-sized cereal box closed, and cover the box with construction paper.

2. Cut through the box at the center, leaving the back uncut. Cut and glue paper features for the rabbit's face, using the cut at the center as its mouth.

3. Cut pieces from a pipe cleaner and glue them on for whiskers. Cut ears from paper and glue them to the rabbit's head.

4. Cut two small holes through the back, one at the top for your index finger and one at the bottom for your thumb to fit into. Work the puppet with your fingers inside the holes.

FORK-FLOWER CORSAGE
(thick yarn, four-pronged fork, cardboard, construction paper, safety pin)

1. For each flower, weave a piece of thick yarn, about 2 feet long, through a four-pronged fork to make the flowers. Start at the base of the prongs, and weave in a figure 8 pattern by placing the yarn in front of the first two prongs. Then slip the yarn between the second and third prongs; wrap it behind the third and fourth prongs, then in front of them, back between the second and third prongs, behind the first and second prongs, in front of them, and so on. Continue until the fork is full of yarn.

2. Insert an 8-inch piece of green yarn below the wrapped yarn between the second and third prongs. Wrap the green yarn one time around all the yarn on the fork, and tie it loosely.

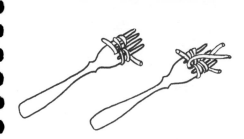

3. Slip all the yarn off the fork, and tighten the knot. Trim the excess yarn with scissors. Make flowers in a variety of colors, and glue them to a small piece of cardboard.

4. Glue leaves made from construction paper around the flowers. Glue a safety pin to the back of the corsage.

PATCHWORK FLOWERPOT
(fabric, flowerpot)

1. Cut an assortment of colorful scraps of fabric into 1-inch pieces.

2. Spread glue on a small area of the flowerpot and press the pieces of fabric into the glue. Continue until the entire flowerpot is covered.

3. When the fabric is dry, place a flower into the patchwork flowerpot.

CHICK FINGER-PUPPET
(bathroom tissue tube, poster paint, construction paper)

1. Cut points at one end of a bathroom tissue tube. Paint the outside of the tube with poster paint and let dry.

2. Cut a diamond-shaped bill, eyes, and feathers from construction paper. Glue them to the tube.

3. Place a couple of fingers in the bottom of the tube to work the chick puppet.

MY LOVE GROWS
(construction paper, package of flower seeds)

1. For the card, fold a piece of construction paper in half. Fold up a strip about 2 inches from the bottom to make a pocket inside.

2. Decorate the front of the card with markers.

3. Place a package of flower seeds in the pocket inside the card and write a message.

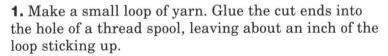

BUNNY NECKLACE
(thread spool, cotton balls, felt, yarn, plastic lid)

1. Make a small loop of yarn. Glue the cut ends into the hole of a thread spool, leaving about an inch of the loop sticking up.

2. Cut two ears from a plastic lid. Glue the ears to the spool. Cover the spool with cotton balls.

3. Cut features from felt and attach them with glue.

4. Thread yarn through the loop for the necklace.

HANGING CHICK-BASKET
(two paper plates, two cupcake liners, cardboard, tissue paper, construction paper, plastic grass, ribbon)

1. For the body, staple two paper plates together about two-thirds of the way around with the bottoms of the two plates facing out. Fold down the unstapled part of each plate to form wings and staple in place.

2. For the head, flatten two cupcake liners and glue them together with a circle of cardboard in the middle to stiffen them. Staple it to one end of the body.

3. Cut tissue paper into 1-inch squares. Wrap each square around your finger. Dip the tip in glue and stick it onto the chick's body.

4. Cut a beak and eyes from construction paper, and glue them to the head. Stuff the basket with plastic grass. Punch a hole on each side, and tie a ribbon for a hanger.

EASTER TOP HAT
(poster board, ribbon)

1. To make the top of the hat, cut out a piece of poster board 8 inches long and wide enough to fit around your head. Staple and tape the two ends together. Place the top on another piece of poster board, and draw around the circle.

2. Measure about 2 inches out from the circle, and draw another circle. Cut out on both lines as shown, making the brim. Use 1-inch pieces of tape to fasten the brim to the top.

3. At the other end of the top hat, brush glue around the poster board edge. Place it on another piece of poster board. Add more glue to the inside of the hat and let dry. Trim off the extra board with scissors.

4. Glue a ribbon around the brim of the hat.

EGG-CARTON TULIPS
(cardboard egg carton, poster paint, pipe cleaners, large frozen juice container, construction paper, yarn)

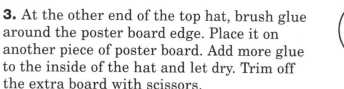

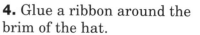

1. To make the flowers, cut out the cup sections from a cardboard egg carton. Trim the corners, making the shape of a tulip petal. Cover the cups with poster paint and let dry.

2. Poke a hole in the bottom of each cup. Push a pipe cleaner through the hole for a stem. Tie a knot about 1 inch away from the other end for the stamen. Add glue and let dry.

3. Cover a large frozen juice container with construction paper. Wrap yarn around the container and tie a bow. Cut long tulip leaves from paper, and place them in the container along with the tulips.

RABBIT STITCHERY
(plastic-foam tray, paper, pen, large-eyed needle, yarn)

1. Wash and dry a plastic-foam tray. On a piece of paper smaller than the tray, draw a rabbit.

2. Tape the picture on the inside of the tray. Poke holes along the lines of the rabbit with a pen. Remove the paper.

French Knot

3. With a needle and yarn, weave in and out of the holes using straight stitches or French knots as shown. Attach a piece of yarn for a hanger.

Straight Stitch

EASTER EGG MOBILE

(plastic-foam egg carton, colored tissue paper, string, wide plastic food container, yarn)

1. Cut cups from a plastic-foam egg carton. For each egg, glue two cups together.

2. Cut designs from colored tissue paper, and glue them to the eggs.

3. Attach a string to each egg for a hanger. Tie all the eggs to a ring cut from a plastic container.

4. Punch four evenly spaced holes in the ring, and tie a length of yarn into each hole. Tie the pieces of yarn together at the top to hang the mobile.

ENVELOPE CHICK

(small white envelope, paper)

1. Open the flap of a small white envelope. With the back of the envelope facing you, draw the eyes and beak of a chick on the flap.

2. Draw wings along the two inner edges of the side flaps.

3. Color your chick yellow and glue it to a piece of paper. Draw legs on the paper.

4. Write your greeting on a piece of paper, and tuck it in the envelope.

PAPER-PLATE RABBIT

(two paper plates, construction paper, cotton, pipe cleaners, yarn)

1. Use one paper plate for the rabbit's head. Cut another paper plate as shown to make the ears and a bow tie. Staple them to the head.

2. Cut a nose, ear centers, and eyes from construction paper. Glue them in place. Glue cotton around the features.

3. Add whiskers made from pipe cleaners. Color the bow tie.

4. Punch a hole at the top of the head, and tie a piece of yarn through the hole for a hanger.

Bow Tie   Ears

CURLY LITTLE LAMB
(bathroom tissue tube,
black and white paper)

1. Cut a bathroom tissue tube to measure about 2 1/2 inches long. Roll a 4-inch-wide piece of black paper and insert it into one end of the tube with about 1 1/2 inches sticking out.

2. Crease the paper and cut out the shape of a head. Glue the sides together. Cut a slit and glue on paper ears. Add eyes.

3. Roll four 1/2-inch-wide pieces of black paper very tightly for the legs. Poke four holes in the tube and insert the legs, adding glue.

4. Cut a piece of white paper the same length as the lamb's body. Make it long enough to go over the body and hang down. Cut two more sheets of paper, each one a little shorter than the last. Cut slits at the ends as shown.

5. Curl the slits by rolling them over a pencil. Glue the curled sheets of paper so the curls are turned under. Glue on the longest sheet first and the shortest sheet last.

Slits   Slit   Ears

HOLIDAY EGG BASKET
(eight ice-cream sticks,
glitter, paint, plastic-foam trays,
permanent markers, plastic grass,
plastic berry basket)

1. Paint eight ice-cream sticks with paint.

2. Cut out eight eggs from plastic-foam trays. Decorate them with glue and glitter. Glue the eggs to the ends of the sticks.

3. Weave the sticks through the sides of a plastic berry basket. Add plastic grass.

FABRIC EASTER BAG
(fabric, tape, pins, embroidery floss,
embroidery needle, felt, shoelace)

1. Cut a piece of fabric about 22 inches long and 14 inches wide. Fold a 3/4-inch hem at each short end. Use pieces of tape or pins to hold in place. Sew together with embroidery floss using straight stitches as shown on page 19.

2. Cut flowers, stems, and leaves from felt. Sew them to the top half of the fabric. Leave a 2-inch border around the edges. Turn the flower side over. Fold a 3/4-inch hem on each long side and hold with tape or pins.

3. With the right side out, fold the fabric in half. Stitch the sides together. Turn the bag inside out, and remove the tape or pins.

4. To make the handle, cut two pieces from a long shoelace. Sew one piece to each side of the bag.

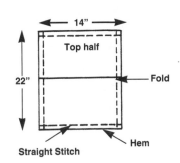
14"
Top half
22"   Fold
Straight Stitch   Hem

POT OF LILIES

(plastic-foam cup, aluminum foil, ribbon, construction paper,
clay, pipe cleaners, tissue paper)

1. For each lily, draw and cut a circle from construction paper. Cut a slit to the center of each circle. Glue the ends together, making a cone shape. Cut six small points around the edge of each lily. Curl the points back by rolling them around a pencil.

2. Cut a tiny hole in the pointed end of each lily. Curl one end of a pipe cleaner, and push the other end through the hole, making the stamen and stem of each lily.

3. Draw and cut two identical paper stem-and-leaf sections for each lily. Make the stem wide enough for the pipe cleaner to fit onto. Place the pipe cleaner of each lily between the two leaf sections and glue together.

4. Place a small amount of clay in the bottom of a plastic-foam cup. Press the stems of the lilies into the clay. Add some tissue paper on top. Wrap the cup with aluminum foil, and add a bow.

ROCKY CHICK

(small paper plate, construction paper, markers)

1. Fold a small paper plate in half.

2. Draw and cut out two chicks the same size from construction paper. Glue the chicks together from their heads to the middle of their bodies.

3. Place the chicks on the fold of the paper plate so that half the chick is on each side. Glue in place.

4. Add features with markers. Stand the rocky chick toy on a table and make it rock.

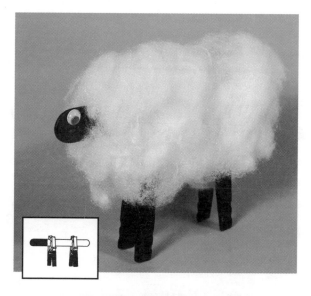

CLOTHESPIN LAMB

(two spring-type clothespins, ice-cream stick,
cotton balls, moveable plastic eyes, poster paint)

1. Attach two spring-type clothespins to an ice-cream stick as shown. Paint the head and legs with black poster paint and let dry.

2. Glue cotton all over the lamb's body, leaving just the legs and head peeking out.

3. Glue moveable plastic eyes to each side of the lamb's head.

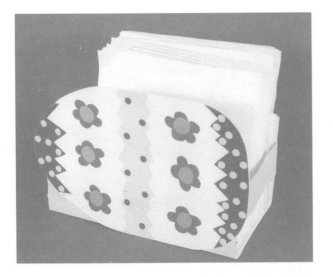

EGG NAPKIN HOLDER
(half-gallon milk carton, construction paper)

1. To make the holder, cut off the top, bottom, and one side of a half-gallon milk carton. Glue construction paper to the outside of the carton. Staple a strip of paper to each opened end of the carton.

2. Draw an egg shape on paper and decorate it. Cut it out, and glue it on one side of the carton. Place napkins inside the holder.

CONE BASKET
(ice-cream cone, plastic food wrap, ribbon)

1. Fill an empty ice-cream cone with assorted candies.

2. Cut a circle from plastic food wrap, and lay it over the top of the cone. Tie two ribbons around the top rim of the cone, and knot at opposite sides.

3. Bring the four ends of the ribbons up, and tie them together in a bow to make the handle. Hang the cone basket on someone's doorknob.

BUNNY IN A BASKET
(construction paper, yarn)

1. Fold a piece of construction paper in half. Cut out a basket about the size of your hand, using the fold as the bottom of the basket. Glue only the sides together.

2. Cut a paper handle for the basket, and glue the ends inside the basket. Decorate the front of the basket.

3. Make a bunny from two circles of paper. Add ears, eyes, and a nose from paper. Glue on yarn whiskers. Write an Easter message on the bunny's body, and slip the bunny inside the basket.

4. Cut a small gift tag from paper. On it write the name of the person the card is for and "Please pull out the bunny." Attach it to the handle of the basket with a piece of yarn.

NEST OF CHICKS

(plastic-foam trays, plastic grass, ribbon)

1. Cut chicks from plastic-foam trays. Add a ribbon bow around the neck of each chick and glue on paper-dot eyes.

2. Turn a plastic-foam tray over so the bottom is facing up. Make a slit where you want each chick to sit, using the point of a pencil or pen.

3. Place each chick in a slit with some glue. Brush glue around the chicks on the tray bottom. Press plastic grass into the glue and around the chicks. Let your decoration dry.

BUNNY BOOKHOLDER

(wire clothes hanger, one 2-inch and one 3-inch plastic-foam ball, construction paper, yarn)

1. Hold the top and bottom of a wire clothes hanger and pull. Bend up about 7 inches for the top and 5 inches for the bottom to form the shape for the base.

2. Decorate a 3-inch plastic-foam ball for the bunny head. Cut ears, eyes, and a nose from construction paper. Add a yarn mouth. Put the head on the 7-inch hanger section.

3. Use the 2-inch plastic-foam ball for the tail. Place it on the 5-inch hanger section. Place books between the head and the tail.

FOAM-TRAY NECKLACE

(plastic drinking straws, plastic-foam trays, string)

1. Cut shapes from different-colored plastic-foam trays.

2. Cut small pieces of plastic drinking straws.

3. Cut a piece of string long enough to go around your neck. Thread it onto a needle.

4. String a piece of plastic foam and then a section of straw onto the string. Continue with foam and straw until you have reached the end of the string.

5. Sew the end of the string through the first piece of plastic foam and knot the end, finishing the necklace.

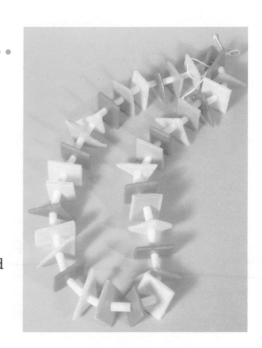

LITTLE LAMB EASTER CARD
(construction paper, cotton balls, yarn)

1. Draw around your hand on a piece of black construction paper, and cut the shape out. The thumb is for the lamb's head, and the four fingers are for its legs.

2. Cover the rest of the body with cotton balls to look like wool. Add a paper dot for an eye. Cut and tie a piece of yarn around its neck.

3. Cut a small card from paper. Write a greeting on the card. Punch a hole in the card and one where the lamb's tail might be. Slip a piece of yarn through both holes and tie the ends.

STUFFED CHICKEN
(paper, felt, cotton balls, needle, thread)

1. Draw the outline of a chicken about 10 inches tall on paper. Place the pattern on a piece of felt and draw around it with a pencil. Do this again and cut out both chickens.

2. Place the two chickens together with the pencil lines on the inside. Sew them together around the edge, leaving a small section open.

3. Stuff cotton balls or pieces of scrap fabric inside the chicken through the small opening. Finish sewing, stuffing as you go.

4. Glue felt eyes and wings to the chicken.

DANCING BUNNIES
(construction paper)

1. Cut a piece of white paper 6 inches by 12 inches. Fold in half three times to 6 inches by 3 inches.

2. Draw and cut out half a bunny shape on the fold, but don't cut the ends of the arms.

3. Cut dresses, hair bows, slacks, suspenders, and bow ties from paper, and glue them to the bunnies. Add features with colored pens.

CUTOUT PAPER FAN
(paper, ribbon)

1. Use a sheet of paper about 8 1/2 inches by 11 inches. Fold it in accordion pleats, making the pleats 1/2 inch wide.

2. Holding the pleats together, turn one end over 1/2 inch and staple it together. Cut designs along the edges of the pleats about halfway down the pleats.

3. Tie a ribbon at the stapled end, and open the fan to see the design.

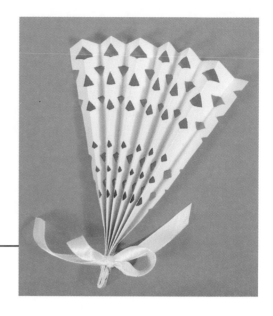

CHICKIE-IN-AN-EGG
(construction paper, plastic-foam cup, cotton balls, plastic drinking straw, plastic grass)

1. Glue or tape a piece of construction paper around a plastic-foam cup. Cut a jagged edge around the top of the cup to look like a broken eggshell.

2. Glue two cotton balls, one on top of the other, to the top of a drinking straw. Cut two eyes and a tiny beak from paper, and glue them to the chickie's head.

3. Glue plastic grass inside the cup. Use a pencil to poke a hole in the bottom of the cup. Push the end of the straw down through the hole, with the chickie in the cup.

4. Move the chickie in and out of its egg.

RABBIT-HEAD PUPPET
(cardboard egg carton, poster board, poster paint,
construction paper, toothpicks, ribbon)

1. Cut one cup section from a cardboard egg carton. Cover it with white poster paint and let it dry.

2. To make the rabbit head, cut eyes, a nose, and a mouth from construction paper. Glue them to the bottom of the cup.

3. Paint six toothpicks for whiskers. Poke three holes on each side of the cup. Place the whiskers in the holes with glue.

4. Cut a small strip of poster board, and glue it to the back of the rabbit's head. Leave enough room so two fingers will fit inside. Glue a bow under his chin.

BOUQUET CARD
(construction paper, yarn, ribbon)

1. Fold a piece of white construction paper in half.

2. To make the flower buds, cut several 3 1/2-inch pieces of yarn. Spread circles of glue on the front of the card. Press a coil of yarn into each circle of glue. Glue a smaller coil of yarn on top of some of the flower buds.

3. Draw a stem and leaves for each flower bud. Add a ribbon bow to the bottom of the bouquet. Write a message inside the card.

BUNNY JUG BASKET
(one-gallon plastic jug, construction paper, ribbon, plastic grass)

1. Soak a one-gallon plastic jug in warm water to help soften it for cutting. Dry the jug. Draw the rabbit design at one end of the jug as shown in the picture. Cut along the lines.

2. To make the border, glue different-colored ribbon around the edge. Add features to the bunny's face with construction paper.

3. Fill the basket with plastic grass.

SHIMMERING JEWELRY
(large coffee can, coffee cup, poster board, paper, yarn)

1. Trace around a large coffee can on a piece of poster board. Do the same with a coffee cup.

2. Measure approximately 1/4 inch inside each line, and draw another line. Cut these circles along the lines, making two circular strips. One will be the necklace, the other, the bracelet.

3. Glue a piece of yarn to the back of each strip, leaving extra yarn at the ends.

4. Cut squares and circles from shiny, bright paper. Fold these shapes over the circular strips, and glue them in place.

5. Wear the jewelry by tying the ends of the yarn into bows.

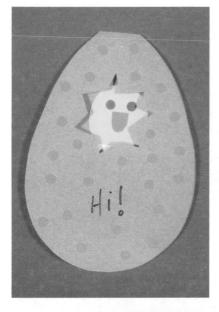 

PEEKING-DUCK EASTER CARD
(construction paper)

1. Fold a piece of construction paper in half. Cut out an egg, keeping the top on the fold.

2. Open the egg and cut a jagged window out of the front. Close the egg and write "Hi!" under the window. Punch out paper dots and glue them around the window.

3. Cut out a circle of paper just large enough to fill the window. Glue on a paper beak and eyes, and glue the duck's head inside the card.

4. Write "Happy Easter" on a piece of paper and sign your name. Glue it to the front of the duck. Add paper wings and feet.

MILK CARTON EASTER BASKET
(half-gallon milk carton, construction paper)

1. To make the basket, cut a half-gallon milk carton in half.

2. For the handle, cut a 1-inch-wide section from the part that is leftover. Cut away one side of this section.

3. Cover the basket and handle with construction paper. Glue the handle to the basket. Decorate with cut-paper designs.

SMALL PUFFY PURSE
(felt, toothpick, shoestring)

1. Cut out a circle of felt 9 inches in diameter.

2. About 1 inch from the edge of the felt, draw twelve dots in the same positions as numbers on a clock.

3. Push a toothpick through each dot, and then thread a shoestring in and out of the holes.

4. Draw the ends of the shoestring together, and tie them in a tight bow.

FUZZY-WUZZY RABBIT PIN
(cardboard, cotton ball, moveable plastic eyes, construction paper, yarn, safety pin)

1. Cut a small circle from a piece of cardboard. Glue a cotton ball on top of the circle.

2. To make the rabbit's face, glue on two moveable plastic eyes and ears and whiskers made from construction paper.

3. Glue a small safety pin to the back of the cardboard. Attach the fuzzy-wuzzy rabbit to your shirt.

RABBIT MASK
(platter, poster board, construction paper, yarn)

1. Place a platter on a piece of poster board, and trace around the edge. Cut out the shape. Cut a slit from the edge to the center as shown. Pull one edge of the slit over the top of the other to form a small cone. Glue to hold it in place.

2. From construction paper, cut two large white circles and two smaller black circles for eyes and two triangle shapes for eyebrows. Glue them in place on the front of the mask.

3. Cut holes to see through in the center of each paper eye. Add ears, whiskers, and a mouth made from paper.

4. Poke a hole in each side of the mask and add yarn ties.

slits

THREE-D CHICK
(cardboard, bathroom tissue tube, poster paint)

1. Cut two identical chicks from cardboard. Cover them with poster paint and let them dry. Add eyes, beaks, and wings cut from painted cardboard.

2. Cut a 1-inch section from a bathroom tissue tube. Glue it between the two chicks.

LAMB PUPPET
(small brown paper bag, paper)

1. Draw and cut the lamb's head and ears from paper. Add eyes, a nose, and a mouth.

2. To make the lamb's curls, cut strips of paper and curl them by wrapping them around a pencil. Glue them between the lamb's ears. Glue the head to the bottom of the bag.

3. Cut the body from paper and glue it to the front of the bag. Add two paper feet.

4. Place your hand inside the bag, and curve your fingers over the fold to move the puppet's head.

FLUFFY RABBIT
(bathroom tissue tube, cotton, lightweight cardboard, construction paper)

1. To make the body, cut legs and feet from lightweight cardboard, and glue them to a bathroom tissue tube. Cover body, legs, and feet with glue and cotton.

2. Cut ears, eyes, whiskers, nose, and mouth from construction paper. Glue them to the bunny body. Add a large cotton ball for the tail.

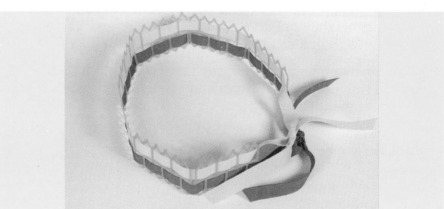

BERRY-BASKET RIBBON BELT
(two plastic berry baskets, ribbon)

1. Cut the bottoms from two plastic berry baskets and throw them away. Then cut through the corner of each side section, making a total of eight sections. (Because there are different basket designs, you may have a different pattern than shown.)

2. Weave two pieces of ribbon, each a yard long, in and out through the holes, adding new sections of the baskets as you need them.

3. When the belt fits your waist, tie the ends of the ribbons, and your belt will be finished.

EASTER BASKET SURPRISE

(two plastic-foam cups, paper doily, pipe cleaner, ribbon, construction paper, plastic grass)

1. Place a saucer on a piece of construction paper and draw around it. Cut out the circle and glue a paper doily on top.

2. Cut about 1 1/2 inches from the bottom of one plastic-foam cup. Turn another plastic-foam cup upside down and glue the first cup on top. Tie a ribbon around the center where the cups join.

3. Punch a hole in each side of the top cup. Insert a pipe cleaner for the handle, twisting the ends to hold it in place. Add a ribbon. Fill the top with plastic grass and a treat.

4. Place the basket on the paper doily at each table setting. Place a small candy rabbit or candy egg in the center of the doily, and put the basket over it.

5. When the guests pick up their baskets, they will find the surprise underneath.

EASTER MOBILE

(construction paper, toothpicks, four buttons, string)

1. Following the photo, cut two of each shape from construction paper.

2. Glue two ear pieces back to back. Then glue the other two ear pieces together. Insert the ears between the two top-of-head sections, and glue the head pieces together.

3. Glue the eye pieces together in pairs. Do the same with the chin sections. For whiskers, color six toothpicks and insert them between the nose pieces, and glue the nose in place.

4. Punch small holes and insert strings to assemble the pieces of the mobile as shown. Glue a small button to each side of both eye pieces. Add a string hanger.

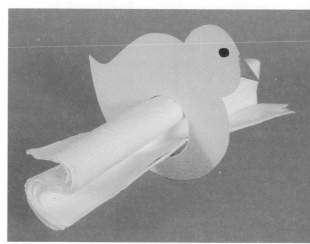

CHICK NAPKIN RING

(poster board, poster paint, paper napkin)

1. Draw and cut a chick from a piece of poster board. Add an eye and beak using poster paint.

2. Draw and cut out a circle from the middle of the chick.

3. Insert a paper napkin through the hole. Place one chick with a napkin for each guest at the dinner table.

Eggs, Eggs, and More Eggs...

EGG HEAD
(hard-boiled egg, permanent markers, yarn)

1. Sketch features on a hard-boiled egg. Color them with permanent markers.

2. Add glue and yarn for hair.

HOW TO MAKE A HARD-BOILED EGG
(whole raw egg, saucepan, water, stove)

1. Have an adult help you use the stove. Fill a saucepan halfway with cool water. Place the egg in the pan and bring the water to a slow boil, using low heat.

2. Cook the egg for seven minutes from the boiling point. Remove the pan from the heat and let the egg cool.

HOW TO BLOW OUT THE INSIDE OF A RAW EGG
(whole raw egg, large sewing needle)

1. Stick a large sewing needle into the pointed end of a raw egg, making sure to poke through the membrane under the shell. Turn the egg over, and stick the needle through the other end, making a larger hole than the first.

2. Over a large bowl, blow through the small hole, allowing the inside of the egg to flow into the bowl. Carefully rinse the shell in cold water.

HOW TO DYE EGGS WITH FOOD COLORING
(blown or hard-boiled eggs, food coloring, coffee mug, a teaspoon, white vinegar)

1. Add one teaspoon of white vinegar to one cup of hot water from the kitchen tap. Place several drops of food coloring into the hot water.

2. Place an egg in the mixture. Hold the egg down gently in the mixture with a spoon.

3. When the egg reaches the color you want, remove it and let it dry on a paper towel.

COLOR CHART	
To make:	**Combine:**
LIME GREEN	1 drop green + 3 drops yellow
ORANGE	2 drops red + 3 drops yellow
TURQUOISE	1 drop green + 4 drops blue
VIOLET	2 drops red + 2 drops blue
Experiment on your own to find other colors.	

33

POLKA-DOT EGG

(hard-boiled egg, construction paper)

Using a paper punch, punch many different-colored dots from construction paper. Glue them to a hard-boiled egg.

EGG ANIMAL

(blown egg, pipe cleaner, cardboard egg carton, construction paper)

1. To make a piglet, cut and glue construction-paper features on a brown egg. Glue on a small piece of pipe cleaner for the tail.

2. Cut a cup section from a cardboard egg carton, and paint it with poster paints for the pig's feet. Glue the egg to the feet.

YARN GIFT EGG

(blown egg, yarn)

1. Draw a design on an egg lightly with a pencil. Trace over a small section of the design with glue.

2. Place yarn in the glue. Continue until you have covered the design with yarn.

WHITE-CRAYON SURPRISE EGG

(hard-boiled egg, white crayon)

1. Before you dye some eggs, draw designs on white eggs with a white crayon. Any areas of the egg covered with the white crayon will not take the color of the dye.

2. After you have dyed the egg, you will see your design appear.

KALEIDOSCOPE EGG

(blown egg, old magazine, clear nail polish)

1. Cut small squares of several colors from old magazine pages. Glue the squares on the eggshell, overlapping each square until the egg is covered.

2. After the squares are dry, paint the egg with one or two coats of clear nail polish.

RABBIT PLACE CARD
(poster board, cotton ball, construction paper, yarn, paper doily)

1. Fold a small piece of poster board in half. Glue on a cotton ball for the rabbit's head.

2. Add pieces cut from a paper doily, construction paper, and yarn to create the rabbit's features.

3. Write a dinner guest's name on the card.

HATCH A CHICK
(hard-boiled egg, poster board)

1. Use a hard-boiled egg for the body of the chick.

2. On a folded piece of poster board, draw and cut out a tail and a head and neck as shown. The part that touches the fold should not be cut.

3. Glue the neck to the egg, leaving the feather ends free. Glue the tail in place.

4. Cut small teardrop-shaped feathers from poster board. Glue only the pointed end of each feather to the egg, inserting each one under the neck feathers and so on down the body. No feathers are needed on the bottom.

5. After the glue has dried, carefully bend out each feather, and you'll find the chick can stand without tipping over.

GIFT WRAP HAT
(gift wrap, yarn, tissue paper)

1. Cut two 20-inch circles from gift wrap. Glue them back to back so the pattern shows on both sides.

2. While the circle is still damp from the glue, put it on your head. Look in the mirror as you mold the center of the circle to fit the shape of your head (or have someone help you).

3. Leave the edges of the circle sticking out all around as a brim. Tie a piece of yarn around the hat where the brim begins.

4. Remove the yarn when the hat is dry. Make a tissue paper bow, and glue it to the hat.

MAGNETIC BUNNY

(plastic-foam egg carton, paper, felt,
magnetic strip, broom straw)

1. Cut two egg cups from a plastic-foam egg carton.

2. To make the rabbit shape, draw circles that are larger than an egg cup on a piece of heavy paper. Add ears and feet. Cut out the paper rabbit pattern.

3. Place the pattern on a piece of felt, and trace around it with a pencil. Cut out the felt rabbit.

4. Glue the two egg cups on the rabbit. Add features from felt and whiskers from broom straw. Glue a magnetic strip to the back of the rabbit.

5. Place your rabbit on the refrigerator door for the holiday.

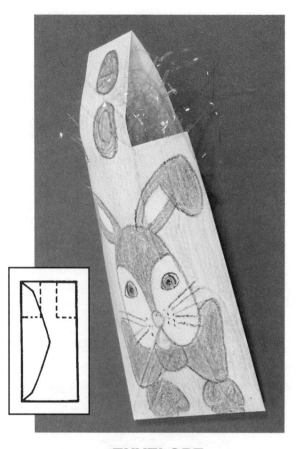

ENVELOPE
EASTER BASKET

(unused envelope, crayons, plastic grass)

1. Moisten the flap of an unused long white envelope and seal it shut. Cut out two sections of the envelope as shown.

2. Decorate the basket with drawings made with crayons. Fill the basket with plastic grass.

BUTTON PIN

(buttons, felt, embroidery needle,
embroidery floss, cardboard, safety pin)

1. Cut a small strip of felt. Using embroidery floss and a needle, sew some buttons on the felt.

2. Glue the piece of felt with the buttons on a piece of cardboard and let dry.

3. Trim the edges with scissors to look like leaves. Glue a safety pin to the back.

EGG-CARTON PLACE CARD
(cardboard egg carton, construction paper)

1. Cut two cups from a cardboard egg carton for each place card. Glue the two cups with their bottoms together.

2. Cut a chick from construction paper. Add features with paper, and glue the chick inside the cup.

3. Print a guest's name on a piece of paper, and glue it to the front of the cup. Put a few jelly beans inside.

BUNNY CARD
(construction paper, cotton ball)

1. Draw a bunny on white construction paper and cut it out.

2. Glue the bunny to the inside of a piece of folded paper so that half is on one side of the fold and half is on the other side. Add paper ears and write a message.

3. Make the spring by cutting two strips of paper and folding as shown. Glue the spring between the two halves of the card.

4. Write a greeting on the front of the card.

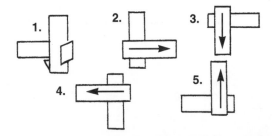

EASTER EGGCUP
(cardboard egg carton, poster paint, construction paper)

1. To make a special cup for Easter eggs, cut two cup sections from a cardboard egg carton.

2. Trim one top evenly for the base. Trim the other one to look like flower petals. Glue the two cups with their bottoms together.

3. Cover the cups with poster paint. When dry decorate with paper-punch dots.

RABBIT'S RING-TOSS GAME
(paper towel tube, cardboard, poster paint, rubber bands, poster board)

1. Cut a head, front feet, and back feet for the rabbit from a piece of cardboard. Paint them white and let dry. Add details with paint and markers.

2. For the body of the rabbit, paint a paper towel tube white and let dry. Cut two vertical slits almost in the middle of the tube. Insert the front feet through the slits.

3. Glue the head and the back feet to the body. Hold in place with rubber bands until dry. Glue the rabbit to a square cardboard base.

4. Cut strips of poster board, and tape them together to form rings. Make up a point system for the game. For example, a ring on an ear might be worth 10 points and one on a paw, 15 points.

JELLY-BEAN BASKET
(small margarine container, construction paper, poster board, brass fasteners, plastic grass)

1. Use a small margarine container for the basket.

2. For the handle, cut a strip of poster board, and punch a hole at each end. Punch a hole at opposite sides of the basket. Fasten the handle to the basket with brass fasteners.

3. Decorate the basket with cut-paper flowers. Add some plastic grass and jelly beans.

FLOWER HAT
(6-inch paper plate, poster paint, construction paper, ribbon)

1. For the center of the flower, paint the back of a 6-inch paper plate with poster paint and let dry.

2. From construction paper, cut six flower-shaped petals about 6 inches long. Glue these around the edge of the plate.

3. Cut and glue two leaves between two of the petals on opposite sides of the plate.

4. Punch a hole on opposite sides of the plate, going through a leaf on each side. Thread a piece of long ribbon through the holes with the ribbon on top of the flower center. Tie the ribbon in a bow under your chin.

CHICK EASTER CARD

(construction paper)

1. On a piece of folded white paper, draw a chick with its back on the fold. Cut it out. Color the chick's front yellow, its eye black, and its beak orange.

2. Fold a piece of construction paper for a card. Glue the chick to the front of the card.

3. Cut out and glue on tail feathers of various colors. Cut one wing on a fold of yellow paper, and glue it to the chick. Add legs and feet with a marker.

4. Outline the edge of the inside of the chick with yellow marker. Write "Easter Greetings" on the inside of the chick. Write a message inside the card.

TULIP WREATH

(sixteen ice-cream sticks, poster paint, construction paper)

1. Paint sixteen ice-cream sticks with poster paint, and let them dry thoroughly.

2. Glue two of the sticks together at the center so they form a skinny X. Continue to form X's with the remaining sticks.

3. Make the wreath by arranging the X's in a circle and gluing them together, end to end.

4. Cut and glue construction-paper tulips and leaves. Make a bow from tissue paper, and glue it to the wreath.

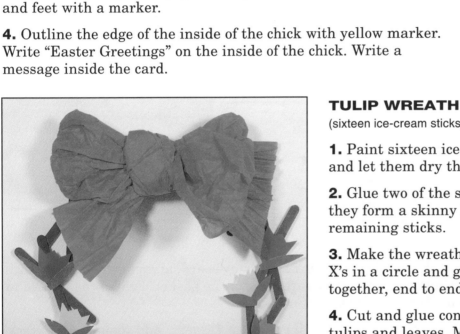

BUNNY BASKET

(milk carton, poster board, cotton, felt, construction paper)

1. For the basket, cut away the top portion of the milk carton.

2. Cut two ears from poster board, and glue them to the basket.

3. Cover the base and ears with glue and cotton.

4. Add eyes, a nose, and a mouth cut from felt. Cut paper features for the ears.

5. Cut a strip of construction paper for the handle, and glue it to the basket.

GIFT WRAP TIE

(gift wrap, poster board, shoestring)

1. Glue gift wrap to both sides of a strip of poster board. Cut the poster board in the shape of a man's necktie.

2. Glue the knot end of the tie to the middle of a shoestring. Cover the string with some of the gift wrap.

3. Cut out a white paper bunny, and glue it to the front of the tie.

4. To wear the tie, place the shoestring under your shirt collar. Tie the ends together in a bow.

MISTER RABBIT

(washcloth, safety pin, needle, heavy thread, cotton)

1. Roll in two sides of a washcloth tightly to the center. Pin in the middle with a safety pin.

2. To make the ears, hold the rolled sides down and push the cloth down between the rolls halfway to the pin. Tie each ear at the base with heavy thread.

3. Tie the cloth in the middle to form the head, and remove the pin. Open out the head, stuff with cotton, and sew shut.

4. For the legs, open the rolled ends slightly, tuck a thin layer of cotton up into each side, and roll tightly again. With the rolled side down, push up the cloth between the rolls to the "tummy" and sew it to the legs.

5. Open the body and stuff with cotton. Sew up the back. Add features to the rabbit's face with felt. Use thread for the whiskers. Add a felt bow under his chin.

6. Cut a coat from felt and sew up the sides. Stuff cotton-ball hands in the sleeves, and sew in place. Dress the rabbit in his coat. Sew on a cotton ball for the tail. Add a felt scarf.

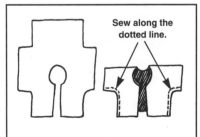

Sew along the dotted line.

EGG-SHELL CUP

(white egg shells, rolling pin, wooden board, poster paint, construction paper, small cardboard container)

1. Wash white egg shells and remove the thin skin from the inside. Let them dry for several days. Place the shells on a wooden board. With a rolling pin, crush them into fine pieces, but not powder.

2. Mix white poster paint with glue until the mixture is like yogurt and has a nice white color.

3. Glue a construction paper handle to the outer sides of a small cardboard container. Cover the handle ends and the container with construction paper.

4. Using the glue-paint mixture, paint a design on the container. Sprinkle the crushed eggshells over the design. The eggshells will stick to the mixture, giving the design a delicate, lacy look.

EGG-CARTON BASKET

(plastic-foam egg cartons, pipe cleaner, paper, plastic grass)

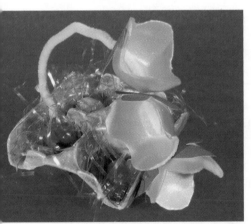

1. For the base of the basket, cut out the center section of a plastic-foam egg carton containing four cups.

2. For the flowers, cut out egg cups from another carton of a different color and poke two holes, opposite each other, in the cup bottom.

3. For the handle, poke a hole at opposite sides of the carton. Push a long pipe cleaner into one hole and twist the end. Thread the flowers onto the pipe cleaner, and push the end into the other hole on the carton and twist the end. Add paper leaves.

BOX BUNNY

(cardboard cookie box, heavy white paper, 6-inch paper plates, white tissue paper)

1. Secure the ends of a cardboard cookie box with tape. Wrap the box with heavy white paper.

2. Cut strips of 2-inch-wide white tissue paper. Fold the strips and fringe them by cutting 1-inch slits about 1/4 inch apart. Glue the strips to the sides of the box, beginning at the bottom and overlapping each new strip.

3. For the bunny head, glue short strips of fringe around the edge of a 6-inch paper plate. Cut the ears from another paper plate, and glue them to the back of the first paper plate.

4. Cut a 4-inch-round circle from heavy white paper for the bunny face. Add features with markers. Glue the face in the center of the head. Glue the head to the body of the bunny.

SEE-THROUGH EASTER CARD
(construction paper, plastic food wrap, permanent markers)

1. For each card, place two sheets of 9-by-12-inch construction paper on top of each other. On the 12-inch side of each sheet, draw a vertical line at 4 inches and at 8 inches, dividing the sheets into three panels.

2. Cut a tulip design from the center of another piece of paper measuring 4-by-9 inches. Using this as a stencil, trace the design on each panel and cut out the tulip.

3. Spread glue around the edges of the paper and the tulip design. Place a piece of plastic food wrap on top. Spread glue around the edges of the food wrap. Place the other piece of paper on top of this. Press together.

4. Using a marker, color one area of the plastic-wrap tulip design on one panel only. Use another marker and color another area of the design on another panel of plastic wrap. Then color the last panel with a third marker. Fold the outside panels over the center panel so the designs overlap.

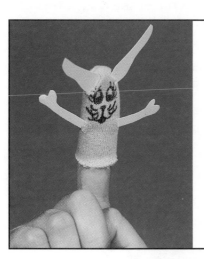

GLOVE FINGER PUPPET
(old cotton glove, fine-line permanent marker, heavy white paper)

1. Cut off the finger of an old glove. Draw a face on the tip of the finger with a fine-line permanent marker.

2. From heavy white paper, cut out rabbit ears and paws. Cut tiny slits in the glove finger, and glue the ears and paws in place.

EASTER RABBIT HAT
(construction paper, moveable plastic eyes)

1. Draw and cut out a pattern of two bunny heads and a headband as shown. Fold an 18-by-12-inch sheet of construction paper in half.

2. Place the pattern with the heads on the fold, and trace around the pattern.

3. Cut out the bunnies and the headband up to the fold, which should be left uncut.

4. Unfold and decorate the bunnies with markers, and add moveable plastic eyes. Cut the headband strip to fit around your head, and glue the ends together.

RICKRACK NOTE CARD
(construction paper, rickrack)

1. Fold a piece of construction paper in half to form a card.

2. Cut small pieces of rickrack and glue them to the front of the card. With a marker decorate them to look like chicks.

3. Add other details to the card with more rickrack, paper, and markers. Write a message inside.

FLOWER-BOX MOBILE
(four small gelatin boxes, one large box, construction paper, yarn)

1. Cover a large box with glue and construction paper. Poke two holes, one opposite the other, in the middle of the narrow sides of the box. Glue the ends of a piece of yarn into each hole to form a hanger. Glue a strip of paper around the top of the box, covering the yarn on each side, to help hold the yarn hanger in place.

2. Cover four small gelatin boxes with glue and paper. Create paper flowers and glue them to the boxes. With a pencil, poke a hole in the top of each box and glue a piece of yarn into each hole.

3. Poke four holes in the bottom of the large box. Insert the yarn ends from the four small boxes and glue them in place. After the glue has dried, hang the mobile.

CROSS FOR EASTER
(poster board, white tissue paper, old newspaper, plastic spray bottle, water, food coloring, string)

1. Draw and cut out a cross from a piece of poster board. Cut out small shapes using scissors and a paper punch.

2. Place sheets of old newspaper on your work surface. Lay white tissue, larger than the cross, on top of the newspaper.

3. Fill a spray bottle with water and moisten the tissue paper with a fine mist, making it damp, not wet. Sprinkle drops of food coloring on the tissue paper and let dry.

4. Put a thin layer of glue on one side of the cross and lay it on the tissue paper. Trim the edges. Punch a hole at the top and attach a string hanger.

5. Hang the cross in a window.

WOVEN BASKET
(9-inch paper plate, 18-by-12-inch construction paper)

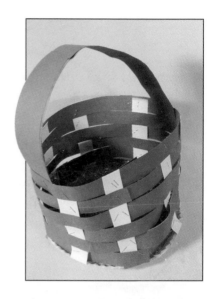

1. Cut eight strips of white construction paper, each 9 inches long and 1 inch wide. Staple the ends of the strips to the bottom edge of a 9-inch paper plate at equal distances apart. Bend the strips upward at the edge of the plate.

2. Cut strips of brown construction paper, each 18 inches long and 1 inch wide. Staple two strips together and weave in and out through the white strips. Cut off the excess. Staple where each vertical strip crosses a horizontal strip.

3. Continue weaving until you reach the top of the white strips or stop and cut off the excess. Cut two 2-inch-wide strips for the handle and glue together. Staple the ends to the basket.

FELT BOARD EGG HUNT
(corrugated cardboard, felt)

1. Cut a piece of cardboard to measure 18 inches by 12 inches. Spread glue on one side, and cover it with a piece of felt. Trim the edges with scissors, or tape them to the back.

2. To make the picture, cut pieces of felt in the shape of a rabbit, a basket, a chick, a tree, clouds, a stone wall—or other items—and place them on the felt board.

3. Cut out small felt eggs. Hide them behind the felt objects in your picture.

4. Let your friends take turns searching behind the felt objects for the eggs. Change the picture over and over.

TUBE RABBIT
(bathroom tissue tube, poster paint, heavy white paper, construction paper, cotton ball)

1. Paint a bathroom tissue tube with poster paint and let dry. Cut front and back legs, ears, and a circle from heavy white paper. Paint them and let dry.

2. Place the tube end on the circle and draw around the outside. Cut out the circle. This will be the head.

3. Glue the head, with the ears in between, at one end of the tube. Glue the legs on each side of the tube. Add a cotton-ball tail.

4. Cut out paper features, and glue them to the rabbit head.

GIFT BOX

(old calendar picture, toothpick box)

1. Carefully take a toothpick box apart at the places where it is glued. Flatten the piece of cardboard.

2. Lay the cardboard on the back of an old calendar picture, so an interesting part of the picture will appear on the top of the box.

3. Trace around the cardboard edge with a pencil, and cut out the shape with scissors.

4. Glue the calendar picture to the cardboard. Fold the box and glue it together. Place a small gift inside.

GLITTER EGG MOBILE

(white poster board, glitter, string)

1. Cut a basket from an 8-inch-square piece of white poster board. Cut four eggs from poster board.

2. Squeeze glue on the basket and the eggs, creating designs. Sprinkle on glitter and let dry. Do the same on the other side.

3. Punch one hole at the top of the basket and a hole at the bottom for each egg. Punch a hole at the top of each egg.

4. Attach the eggs with pieces of string. Make a loop hanger at the top of the basket.

SEED-FLOWER BOUQUET

(poster board, pipe cleaner, pumpkin seeds, round food container, clay, fabric)

1. For each flower, cut a 1-inch circle from a piece of poster board. With a pen, poke two small holes in the center of each circle.

2. Insert one end of a pipe cleaner through the holes and wrap it around the stem underneath the circle. Glue pumpkin seeds on the top of the circle to create flower petals.

3. Loop short pieces of pipe cleaner and twist them onto the stems for leaves.

4. Press clay into a round food container to hold the stems in place.

5. Cover the outside of the container with glue and fabric.

PAPER BASKET
(construction paper)

1. With a ruler and a pencil, mark a 9-by-12-inch piece of construction paper as shown.

2. Cut on the solid lines. Cut little holes in the larger sections. Fold on all the dotted lines as shown.

3. Glue the bottom flaps in place and join the sides of the basket at the fold. Cut out a long narrow strip of paper, and glue it to the basket for the handle.

4. Decorate the sides with cutout pieces of paper.

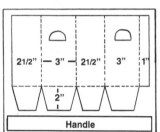

BUNNY BOX
(bathroom tissue tube, half-gallon milk carton, construction paper, plastic grass, cotton ball)

1. To make the basket, cut a half-gallon milk carton so that a 2-inch-high box is left. Cover the basket with construction paper.

2. To make the head, cover a bathroom tissue tube with construction paper. Decorate with cut-paper features for the bunny's face.

3. Cut out bunny ears. Glue the ears between the basket and the bunny's head. Hold together with paper clips until the glue is dry. Add plastic grass and a cotton-ball tail.

COTTON-BALL CHICK
(poster board, cotton balls, paper)

1. From poster board, cut the body base and feet as shown.

2. Glue the feet to the body base. Cover them with cotton balls glued together to form the body of a chick.

3. From paper, cut and glue a beak and eyes to the chick.

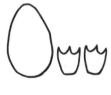

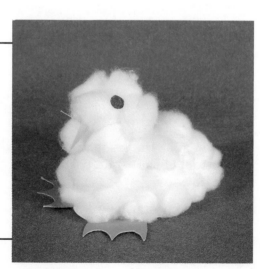

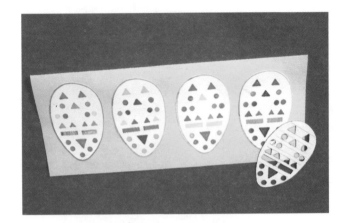

STENCIL EGG CARD

(heavy white paper, construction paper, permanent markers,
paper punch)

1. Fold a piece of construction paper in half to make a card.

2. Cut an egg shape from heavy white paper. Cut small shapes from the egg with a paper punch and scissors to make a stencil.

3. Place the egg stencil on white paper. Color around the egg and in the holes with permanent markers. Cut out the eggs and glue them to the outside of the card. Write a message inside the card.

CANDLE CENTERPIECE

(bathroom tissue tube, 6-inch paper plate, glitter, construction paper)

1. Spread glue around the rim of a 6-inch paper plate. Sprinkle some glitter on the glue. Let dry and shake off the loose glitter.

2. Cover a bathroom tissue tube with paper. Dip one end of the tube in glue, and place it in the center of the paper plate. Let dry. Add a paper flame.

3. Cut leaves and colorful flower petals from paper. Glue them around the candle. Wad up a piece of paper, and glue it in the center of the flower.

FLOWER BASKET

(half-gallon milk carton, construction paper, white poster board,
margarine tub)

1. Measure 3 1/2 inches from the bottom of a half-gallon milk carton. Cut off the top and cover the bottom with construction paper to make a flower pot.

2. From white poster board, cut two 5-by-11-inch pieces. Cut a slot for a handle about 3/4 of an inch from the top of each piece.

3. Glue paper the same color as the bottom half of the carton to the bottom of the white poster board pieces. Cut and glue on a paper flower.

4. Glue the poster board pieces on opposite sides of the carton, joining the handle at the top. Hold in place with spring-type clothespins until dry. Place a small flower plant in a margarine tub and put it inside the basket.

BOBBIN' HEAD BUNNY

(gelatin box, small stones, construction paper, heavy paper, pipe cleaner, cotton ball)

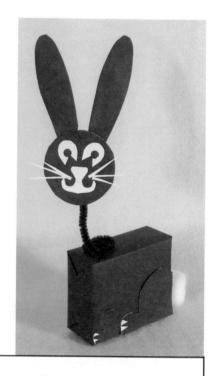

1. To make the bunny body, place small stones inside a gelatin box and tape the flaps shut. Cover the box with construction paper.

2. To make the bunny head, cut two circles and four ears from construction paper. Cut one circle and two ears from heavier paper. These must all be the same size.

3. To assemble, glue the construction-paper ears to each side of the heavier-paper ears. Glue the construction-paper circles to each side of the heavier-paper circle, inserting the ears and the end of a 5-inch pipe cleaner in between. Hold all in place with paper clips until dry. Add paper features.

4. Coil up the other end of the pipe cleaner and glue it to the body. Cut out four legs and glue them to the sides. Add a cotton ball for the tail.

5. Tap the bunny head and watch it bob back and forth.

SPOOL NECKLACE

(empty thread spools, gift wrap paper, paper punch, yarn)

1. Cut and glue strips of gift wrap paper around empty thread spools of various sizes.

2. Place the spool ends on the gift wrap paper and trace around them with a pencil. Cut out the circles of paper and glue them on the spool ends. Push a pencil point through the center hole.

3. Thread the spools on a piece of yarn long enough to go loosely around your neck. Tie a bow at the ends.

EASTER BONNET CUP

(paper doily, construction paper, ribbon, plastic grass)

1. Cut a 2 1/2-inch circle from the center of an 8-inch-round paper doily. Cut the doily as shown, creating tabs around the circle. Bend the tabs upward.

2. Cut a 6-inch circle of construction paper, and glue the paper doily in the center with the tabs bent upward.

3. Cut a strip of construction paper 2 inches by 9 inches long. Wrap the strip around the tabs in the doily. Glue the tabs to the inside of the strip. Glue the ends of the strip together.

4. Decorate with pieces of cut paper doily and ribbon. Fill the cup with plastic grass and treats.

BUNNY CARD
(construction paper, two tongue depressors, poster paint, gift wrap)

1. Fold a 10-by-12-inch piece of construction paper in half.

2. Paint two tongue depressors with white poster paint. They will need two coats of paint to cover completely.

3. Glue the depressors on the front of the card for the bunny's ears. Cut a circle from construction paper for the bunny's head.

4. Cut a tie from gift wrap, and glue it in place. Draw a face with a marker. Write a message inside.

EGG CHAIN
(heavy white paper, markers, ribbon)

1. Cut out eggs from heavy white paper. The more eggs, the longer the chain will be.

2. In the middle of each egg, cut two vertical slits. Using markers, draw designs on the eggs.

3. Form the chain by weaving a long piece of ribbon through the slits in each egg.

RABBIT AND CHICK BOX
(aluminum foil box, construction paper, poster board, plastic grass)

1. With scissors, cut the metal edge from the front of an aluminum foil box. Cover the sides and the front of the box with construction paper. Tape to hold in place.

2. Trim off the top lid edge and cut seven tabs as shown.

3. Draw and cut out rabbits and chicks from poster board. Decorate with markers. Glue them to the front of the tabs.

4. Fill the box with plastic grass and wait for Peter Cottontail.

Box top →

Back of box →

FANCY PHOTO FRAME

(lightweight cardboard, gift wrap, white paper, poster paint)

1. Cut two identical rectangular pieces of lightweight cardboard, one for the back section and one for the front section. From the front section, cut out an area large enough to fit a photo.

2. Cover one side of each cardboard with gift wrap and tape the edges on the back. To help fit the paper around the cutout section, cut an X from corner to corner, fold the paper back, and secure with tape.

3. Place a photo in the opening, and tape it to the back of the front section. Glue the two sections together around the edges.

4. Cut a small piece of cardboard, and cover it with paper. Tape it to the middle of the back of the frame to help make it stand up.

5. Draw and cut out eggs, rabbits, and chicks from white paper and decorate. Glue them around the picture frame.

BUTTON FLOWERS

(white poster board, lightweight fabric, pipe cleaners, large flat two-hole buttons)

1. Insert a pipe cleaner through one hole in a large, flat button and back through the other hole. Twist the ends together under the button to make a stem.

2. Spread glue on a piece of white poster board and press a piece of lightweight fabric on top. Let dry.

3. Cut out several fabric petals, and glue them to the underside of the button.

4. Bend short pieces of pipe cleaner into leaf shapes, and twist them onto the stem.

FLOWER BLOSSOM PICTURE

(construction paper, poster board, plastic-foam egg cartons)

1. For the background of your picture, glue a piece of blue construction paper to a piece of poster board.

2. Cut out stems and leaves from green paper, and glue to the background.

3. Cut out plastic-foam egg carton cups. With scissors, trim the cups to look like flowers. Glue them to the stems.

4. Add a paper butterfly in the sky.

SHINY EASTER CARD

(heavy white paper, gift wrap)

1. Fold a piece of heavy white paper in half to make a card.

2. Cut a scalloped edge at the bottom of the front of the card. Glue a strip of shiny gift wrap, on the inside bottom of the back half of the card.

3. Cut flowers from the same shiny gift wrap and glue them to the front of the card. Add stems and leaves with a marker.

HANGING EASTER BASKET

(construction paper, ribbon, cardboard, silk or dried flowers)

1. Fold a square piece of construction paper as shown in A. At the top point, draw a circle the size of a doorknob and cut it out as shown in B.

2. Fold up the bottom point of the paper to meet the top edge as shown in C, and staple to hold the basket shape. Glue a ribbon bow on top of the staple.

3. To reinforce the hole, cut a hole in a square piece of cardboard to match the size of the hole in the paper. Glue the cardboard hole to the back of the paper directly behind the hole.

4. Fill the basket with silk or dried flowers and hang it on a doorknob as a gift.

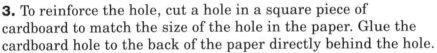

RABBIT WITH BUILT-IN EARS

(cardboard egg carton, bathroom tissue tube, poster paint, gift wrap, felt, paper, ribbon, cotton ball)

1. Cut a four-cup section from a cardboard egg carton for the base. Trim evenly around the cups with scissors. Cover the section with poster paint.

2. Paint an ice-cream stick and let dry. Push the ice-cream stick through the middle of the cone-shaped divider to create arms.

3. Look carefully at a bathroom tissue tube. You will see that at each end the cardboard ends in a point. Pry the points up and peel them back to form ears. Paint the tube inside and out.

4. Cut 1-inch-deep fringes around the tube ends. Bend the fringes out. Add pieces of felt and paper for the rabbit's face and gift wrap for the ears.

5. Make a neck hole about the size of a dime in the bottom of the tube. Spread glue around the cone top in the center of the four-cup section, and place the tube on top, above the arms. Let dry. Tie a ribbon around the rabbit's neck. Add a cotton ball for a tail.

EGG DOLL
(blown egg, bathroom tissue tube, paper baking cups, paper, ribbon, permanent marker)

1. Blow out an egg, following the directions on page 32, and set it aside.

2. Use a bathroom tissue tube for the body. Cut out the bottoms from paper baking cups, and slip them over the tube for the dress. Add tape if needed.

3. Glue the egg to the top of the tube and let dry. Draw a face with a permanent marker.

4. Tie a ribbon around the doll's neck. Fold a baking cup to look like a bonnet, and glue it to the doll's head. Add cut-paper flowers.

FRINGE FLOWERS
(poster board, burlap, string)

1. Cut simple shapes for grass and flowers from a loosely woven fabric like burlap.

2. Pull the threads carefully, one by one, from one or more edges of the shape to give a "fringed" look.

3. Glue the shapes on a piece of poster board. Add a string to the back for a hanger.

BUNNY CRAYON FUZZIES
(construction paper, heavy paper, crayons, string)

1. Draw rabbit shapes on heavy paper, and cut them out to use as patterns.

2. Place the rabbit pattern on a piece of construction paper. Starting in about a 1/2 inch on the pattern, stroke a crayon over the edge and onto the paper. Use zigzag, curly, or straight strokes for different effects.

3. Remove the pattern and add other features with crayons or markers.

4. Glue your picture to a large piece of heavy paper for a frame. Add a string hanger.

EASTER EGG-HUNT CARD

(construction paper, plastic grass)

1. For the card, cut a 6-by-9-inch piece of construction paper. Fold it in half. On the front write, "Look for the hidden Easter message inside."

2. Draw several eggs on white paper. Draw one egg with a 1-inch tab at the bottom.

3. Cut out the eggs, and color them with markers. Write your message on the back of the egg that has the tab.

4. On the bottom of the inside of the card, spread glue and press plastic grass for a nest. Glue the eggs in place, but leave an unglued space in which to slip the tabbed egg.

5. The receiver of the card will need to hunt for the message.

LACY BASKET

(paper cup, paper doily, pipe cleaner, ribbon)

1. Place a cup upside down in the center of a round paper doily and trace around it.

2. Poke a hole in the center of the doily and cut to the circle you have traced.

3. Make eight cuts as shown, going to different points on the circle.

4. Place the cup upright on the center of the doily and push the doily up to the rim of the cup. Add a little glue.

5. Poke a hole in each side of the cup, and push a pipe cleaner through the holes to make a handle. Add bows made from ribbon.

EASTER TREE

(construction paper, fabric, plastic-foam cup, clay, fallen tree branch, thread, yarn)

1. Place a fallen tree branch into a plastic-foam cup filled with clay. Cut out a circle of fabric about 12 inches in diameter. Place the cup in the center, and gather the fabric around the base of the branch. Tie a piece of yarn to hold the fabric in place.

2. Cut out lots of paper eggs. Decorate them with markers. Punch a hole through the top of each egg. String a short piece of thread through each hole, and tie the other end to a twig.

FLOATING WATER LILIES

(large glass or ceramic bowl, water, food coloring, plastic-foam egg cartons)

1. For each flower, scallop the edges of two cups cut from a plastic-foam egg carton. Glue one inside another.

2. Cut leaves from the flat part of the carton. Glue the flower on top.

3. Fill a bowl with water colored with blue food coloring in the kitchen sink. Float the lilies on the water.

4. Have an adult help you place the bowl in the center of the dining room table.

BUTTON-BUNNY PLACE CARD

(poster board, buttons, permanent marker)

1. Fold a 4-inch-square piece of poster board in half.

2. Glue a large smooth-top button on the left side of the card, near the bottom, for the bunny's body.

3. Glue a small two-hole button above the large button. With a marker, darken in the small button holes for eyes. Add other features. Cut pieces of thread, and glue them in place for whiskers.

4. Print the name of your guest on the place card.

DOUGH BEADS

(white bread, white glue, acrylic paint, plastic bags, waxed paper, rolling pin, toothpick, needle and heavy thread, button)

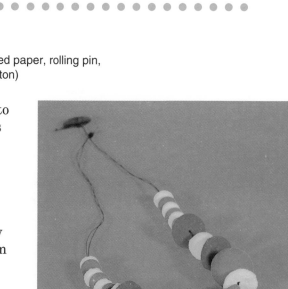

1. Remove the crust from a slice of bread, and tear the bread into small pieces in a bowl. Add a tablespoon of white glue and drops of acrylic paint, and mix it all together.

2. Knead by working the dough in your hands and on a flat surface until it's smooth and elastic.

3. Use a rolling pin to roll the dough out onto a sheet of waxed paper. Form the dough into small balls and circles. Let them dry for an hour. Then make a hole in each with a toothpick. Let them dry for a day.

4. With a needle, string the beads on a heavy piece of doubled thread. After you have finished, tie a knot at one end of the thread. Tie a button at the other end. Place the button in the loop to fasten the beads around your neck.

HAPPY EASTER FAN

(five ice-cream sticks, construction paper, ribbon)

1. Arrange five ice-cream sticks in a fan shape. Glue the sticks together at the bottom where they meet and let dry.

2. Lay the sticks on a piece of paper, and trace around the fan shape with a pencil. Cut out the fan shape and decorate it with cut-paper pieces.

3. Glue the paper fan on the ice-cream sticks. Make a ribbon bow, and glue it to the bottom of the fan.

LID CHICK MOBILE

(frozen-juice pull-top lids, poster board, construction paper, string, heavy paper plate)

1. For each small chick, trace around a frozen-juice pull-top lid twice on a piece of yellow poster board, and cut out the circles. Place the end of a long string on one side of each lid. Glue a circle to each side of the lids, keeping the string in the middle.

2. Fold a piece of orange paper in half. On the fold, cut out beaks and wings for each chick. With the folded ends pointing outward, glue the cut ends on each side of a chick. Add eyes with a marker.

3. Draw and cut out a large chick, and glue it to the back of a heavy paper plate. Add a beak and wings. Draw an eye.

4. Punch a hole at the top of the plate, and tie a loop of string for the hanger. Punch holes at the bottom of the plate and tie a chick to each hole.

WOVEN EGG BASKET

(construction paper)

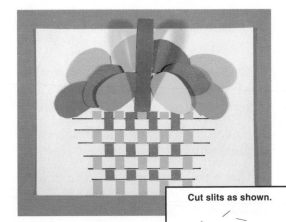

1. On a 9-by-12-inch sheet of construction paper, draw the lines as shown in the diagram to begin the basket. Cut along the lines with scissors.

2. Cut strips measuring 4 1/2 inches by 1/2 inch from two colors of paper. Weave these in and out of the slits to form a basket. Glue the ends in place.

3. Cut an 11-inch strip of paper for the handle. Bend in half and glue it to the basket.

4. Draw and cut out paper eggs, each with a tab as shown. Cut slits above the basket and slip the eggs in them. Turn over the sheet of paper, and glue the tabs of the eggs in place.

5. Bend the handle and eggs forward so they stand away from the background.

Cut slits as shown.

PETER COTTONTAIL

(plastic-foam cup, 2 1/2-inch plastic-foam ball, paper, broom straw, ribbon)

1. Glue a 2 1/2-inch plastic-foam ball to the bottom of a plastic-foam cup.

2. Cut paper eyes, a nose, and a mouth, and glue them to the ball to create the face. Make slits in the top of the head with a table knife and insert paper ears. Push in small pieces of broom straw for the whiskers.

3. Tie a ribbon bow around the neck. Add circles of ribbon for buttons. Glue a ring of ribbon to the bottom of the cup. Add a cotton-ball tail.

TUBE OF FLOWERS

(bathroom tissue tube, construction paper, cardboard, pipe cleaners)

1. Spread glue on a bathroom tissue tube, and cover it with paper. Cut a circle from a piece of cardboard for the base, and glue paper on top of it.

2. Glue the tube to the center of the base. Glue on a cut-paper flower.

3. Cut two flower shapes from paper for each flower. Place a pipe cleaner in between them and glue together.

4. Place the flowers in the tube.

TISSUE PAPER PLACE MATS

(white poster board, colored tissue paper, old newspaper, glue and water, plastic cup, paper towel, clear self-adhesive paper)

1. Cut a piece of white poster board to measure about 12 inches by 18 inches.

2. Cut colored tissue paper in the shapes of flower petals and leaves.

3. Cover your work surface with old newspaper. Mix white glue and some water in a plastic cup.

4. Place a tissue petal on a paper towel and brush it with the glue mixture. Place the petal on the poster board. Continue until your design is finished.

5. Cut a piece of clear self-adhesive paper larger than the poster board. Have someone help you remove the backing. Place the adhesive paper over your design. Fold the edges over to the back and trim if necessary.

EGG WITH CHICK MESSAGE
(construction paper)

1. Cut two eggs from orange construction paper. Print "Happy Easter" on one.

2. Place a small amount of glue around the side and bottom edges of the other egg. With "Happy Easter" on top, press the two eggs together, leaving an opening.

3. From yellow paper, cut out a chick to fit inside the opening. Write a message on the chick, and place it inside the egg with its head poking out.

RABBIT TABLE DECORATION
(construction paper)

1. Draw a rabbit in the center of a sheet of construction paper, making sure that it touches along the bottom.

2. Draw long strips on both sides of the bottom as shown.

3. Cut out the rabbit and the strips. Glue on paper ears, eyes, a nose, a mouth, whiskers, and front paws.

4. Pull the strips around to the back, overlap the ends, and staple or glue.

SPRING POUCH
(felt, paper towel, button)

Diagram 1

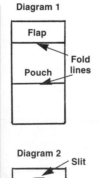

Flap

Fold lines

Pouch

1. Cut a strip of felt 9 inches by 4 1/2 inches. Fold the felt strip as shown in Diagram 1, leaving a 2-inch flap at the top.

2. Glue along the sides to form a pouch. Place a paper towel on top and then a heavy book to hold the pouch in place until the glue dries.

Diagram 2

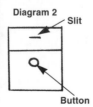

Slit

Button

3. Sew a button to the pouch and cut a small slit in the flap as shown in Diagram 2. Button the pouch closed. Decorate with pieces of cut felt.

LOLLIPOP FLOWER

(lollipop in cellophane, construction paper)

1. Use a medium-sized lollipop wrapped in cellophane for each flower.

2. Cut a strip of green construction paper 1/2 inch by 5 inches long for the stem. Glue one end of the strip at the bottom of the candy, and wind it around the stick. Glue it at the end. Add paper leaves. Hold the paper in place with paper clips if needed.

3. Cut out a 2-inch-round circle. Cut a small circle from the center. Trim around the edges to form a flower. Glue it on top of the candy. Round off the corners of the cellophane with scissors.

PLASTIC-FOAM CUP BUNNY

(two plastic-foam cups, poster board, paper, ribbon)

1. Turn one plastic-foam cup upside down and glue the side of another one to the top and let dry.

2. Cut two big ears and eyes from white poster board. Add pink paper to the ears and black paper to the eyes.

3. Cut a slit with a table knife along the rim of the cup and insert the ears. Cut a slit for each eye and push the paper eyes in place. Add glue to hold.

4. Cut a nose, mouth, and whiskers from paper. Attach them with glue. Tie a ribbon around the bunny's neck.

EASTER EGG BASKET

(facial tissue box, heavy white paper, poster paint, plastic grass)

1. Use a 3-by-9-by-5-inch facial tissue box for the base of the basket. Trim around the opening of the box so there is a 1-inch border.

2. Cut slits all the way around the border. Paint it to look like straw. Paint the rest of the box another color.

3. Cut two identical eggs from 8-by-10-inch pieces of heavy white paper. Cut a small opening at the top of the eggs for a handle. Decorate with markers. Glue the tops of the handles together.

4. Glue one egg to each side of the box. Hold in place with paper clips. Place plastic grass inside.

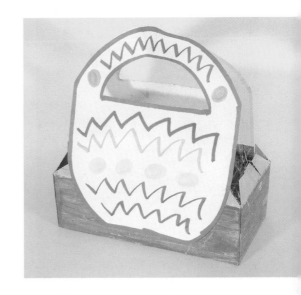

EASTER CHICK CARD
(construction paper)

1. Fold a piece of construction paper in the shape of a card. Write a message on the inside.

2. Cut a piece of paper to fit the width of the card, and make slits to look like grass. Glue it to the bottom of the card.

3. Draw and cut out a chick. Glue it standing in the grass.

COIN FLOWERS
(various coins, construction paper, markers)

1. Cut a vase shape from construction paper, and glue it to a large piece of construction paper.

2. Trace around the edges of quarters, dimes, nickels, and pennies to form flowers. Color the flowers with markers.

3. Draw stems and leaves to join the flowers to the vase.

BASKET BOX
(cereal box, construction paper, fabric, plastic grass)

1. Cut a cereal box as shown, removing the top flaps and a section of the front and the back of the box. Cover it with construction paper, taping it to hold in place.

2. Staple the side strips together to form a handle.

3. Cut small circles of fabric, and glue them on top of each other to form flowers. Glue them to the front of the box. Add a fabric bow and plastic grass.

HANDKERCHIEF BUNNY

(white handkerchief, buttons, thread, ribbon, juice glass)

1. Fold a large white handkerchief in half diagonally, as shown in the first diagram. Fold up the bottom of A and B about 2 inches.

2. Fold the points A and B over the middle of C as shown to form the bunny ears.

3. Turn the handkerchief over, and fold point C down to form the bunny head.

4. Gather the handkerchief together around the neck and tie a ribbon. Sew on two button eyes and thread for whiskers.

5. Place the bunny on a juice glass at Dad's place at the breakfast table for a surprise Easter gift.

Fold in half

Fold up bottom 2"

Cross two corners

Turn down point C on dotted line

CHICK NEST

(6-inch paper plate, poster board, plastic grass, hard-boiled egg)

1. Cut two chicks as shown in the diagram from two 5-by-6-inch pieces of yellow poster board. Outline the edges and create eyes, a bill, and wings with black marker.

2. Glue the two heads together. Fold up the feet and glue them to the bottom of a 6-inch paper plate. Glue plastic grass around the chick.

3. Hard-boil an egg following the directions on page 32. Place the egg in between the two chicks and serve for breakfast.

RABBIT NUT CUP

(bathroom tissue tube, paper, paper baking cups)

1. Cut a 1 1/2-inch section from a bathroom tissue tube. Cover it with white paper.

2. Cut out a circle for the base, larger than the end of the tube. Glue the tube in the center of the circle and let dry.

3. Make a bow tie from a paper baking cup by creasing it in three evenly spaced places in the middle. Staple to hold it in place. Glue it on the edge of the circle.

4. Cut a paper baking cup in half and form the halves into two cone shapes for the ears. Glue them inside the tube. Add a rabbit face with markers and fill the cup with nuts.

60

BABY CHICK EASTER EGG
(construction paper, rickrack)

1. Fold a piece of construction paper in half for the card. Draw and cut out an egg from paper and glue it to the front of the card.

2. Draw and cut out a chick's head from paper, and glue it to the center of the egg.

3. Cut a small piece of rickrack, and glue it to the bottom of the chick as if the chick is peeping through a crack in the eggshell. Write a message inside.

FLUTED FLOWERPOT
(plastic margarine tub, 9-inch paper plate, ribbon, pipe cleaner, plant)

1. Glue the bottom of a round plastic margarine tub to the center of a 9-inch paper plate and let dry. Cut flaps every 2 or 3 inches from the outer edge of the plate to the bottom of the tub.

2. Bend up the flaps, and glue them to the tub. Hold the paper plate in place with a rubber band until it has dried, and glue a ribbon in its place. Add small bows to the sides.

3. For a handle, insert two pipe cleaners, twisted together, into holes on opposite sides of the tub. Twist the ends tightly.

4. Fill the container with a small potted plant.

BRANCH WREATH
(branches, leftover non-paste wallpaper, rubber band)

1. Take several thin branches, and bend the ends together to form an egg-shaped wreath. You may need someone to help hold the ends together as you place a heavy rubber band around them.

2. Cut strips of non-paste wallpaper, and glue the ends together to make a long ribbon. Wrap the ribbon around the wreath and glue the ends.

3. Cut out wallpaper eggs and glue them to the wreath.

4. To make the bow, cut strips of wallpaper about 12 inches in length. Glue the ends of each strip together to form a circle. Staple the round strip in the middle, forming a figure 8. Do this with several strips.

5. Place the stapled strips on top of each other to form a bow, and staple all of them together in the middle. Glue or tie the bow to the wreath.

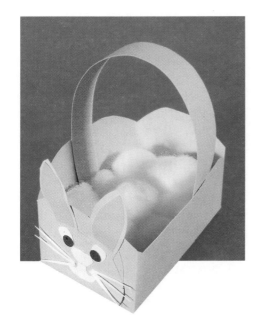

PAPER-RABBIT BASKET
(construction paper, cotton balls)

1. Draw the pattern shown on a 9-by-12-inch piece of construction paper. Cut along the solid lines.

2. Set aside the narrow strip at the edge to be used for the handle.

3. Fold up the sides and ends of the basket on the dotted lines. Glue together the ends marked A, then the ends marked B. This will make a little box.

4. Fold up the head and tail, and glue in place. Add a face with cut paper and a cotton-ball tail. Fill the basket with more cotton balls.

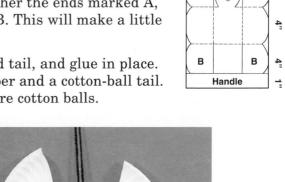

EGG RABBIT
(hard-boiled egg, cotton ball, heavy white paper)

1. Make a hard-boiled egg, following the directions given on page 32.

2. From heavy white paper, cut two ears, two small front legs, and two large back legs and glue them on the egg. Add a cotton-ball tail.

3. Draw a face with markers.

RABBIT CARD HOLDER
(two 9-inch paper plates, yarn, construction paper)

1. Cut away a small section of two 9-inch paper plates. These will be the rabbit's ears.

2. Place the larger sections of the plates together face to face. Staple around the edges, leaving the cut edges open.

3. For the face, cut out construction paper eyes, a nose, and a mouth and glue to one side of the plate. Add yarn whiskers. With a stapler, attach the ears to the plate in back of the face.

4. Tape a yarn loop to the back. Hang the holder, and place your Easter cards inside.

MATERIAL INDEX

175 Easy-to-Do

EVERYDAY CRAFTS

CREATIVE USES FOR RECYCLABLES

Edited by
Sharon Dunn Umnik

175 Easy-to-Do
EVERYDAY CRAFTS

Edited by Sharon Dunn Umnik

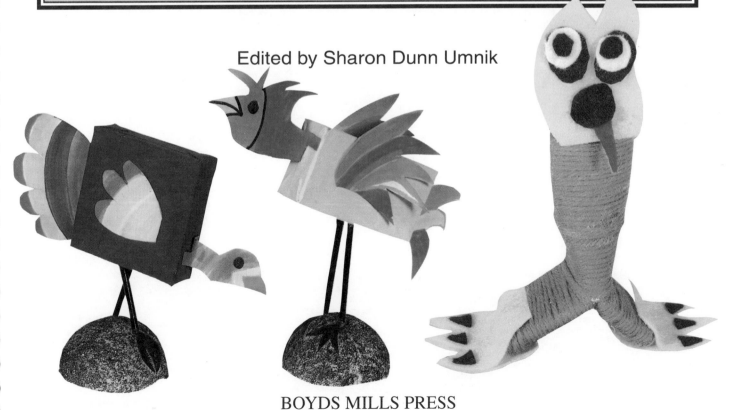

BOYDS MILLS PRESS

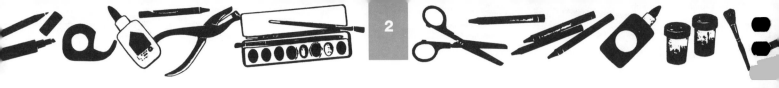

Inside this book...
you'll find a fabulous assortment of crafts made from
recyclable items and inexpensive things found in
or around your house. Have pencils, crayons,
scissors, tape, paintbrushes, and other supplies for craft
making close by. – *the Editor*

Published by Bell Books
Boyds Mills Press, Inc.
A Highlights Company
815 Church Street
Honesdale, Pennsylvania 18431
Printed in China

Publisher Cataloging-in-Publication Data
Main entry under title :
    175 easy-to-do everyday crafts : creative uses for recyclables /
edited by Sharon Dunn Umnik.—1st ed.
[64]p. : col. ill. ; cm.
Summàry : Includes step-by-step directions to make simple crafts from
household items.
ISBN 1-56397-441-X
1. Handicraft—Juvenile literature. [1. Handicraft.] I. Umnik, Sharon Dunn.
II. Title.
745.5—dc20   1995   CIP
Library of Congress Catalog Card Number: 94-72626

First edition, 1995
Book designed by Charlie Cary
The text of this book is set in 11-point New Century Schoolbook.

10 9 8 7 6 5 4 3

Craft Contributors: Helen Afana, Laura Arlon, Jennifer Arnold, Denwood Barksdale, Kathy Bayly, Laura G. Beer, Barbara Bell, Peg Biegler, Linda Bloomgren, Peggy Boozer, Doris Boutin, Phil A. Bowie, Eunice Bremer, Judy Chiss, Sandra E. Csippan, Peggy Welton De Shan, Ruth Dougherty, Linda Douglas, Marianne J. Dyson, Susan P. Easter, Laurie Edwards, Kathy Everett, Clara Flammang, JoAnn Fluegeman, Carole Forman, Nancy H. Giles, Sid Gilmer, Sandra Godfrey, Monica M. Graham, Mavis Grant, Mary Alma Harper, Edna Harrington, Nan Hathaway, Patricia O. Hester, Barbara Hill, Olive Howie, Helen Jeffries, Ruth Ann Johnson, Tama Kain, Garnett C. Kooker, Kathy Kranch, Virginia L. Kroll, K.S. Kubona, Twilla Lamm, Lila LeBaron, Janet Rose Lehmberg, Ann Lewandowski, Lee Lindeman, Marion Bonsteel Lyke, Lory MacRae, Agnes Maddy, Linda K. Marchi, H. Marcin, JoAnn Markway, Carol McCall, Mary Minerman, Clare Mishica, June Rose Mobly, Patricia Moseser, Bridget Pakenham Murphy, Mary Ellen Norlen, Helen M. Pedersen, Beatrice Bachrach Perri, James W. Perrin Jr., Judy Peterson, Louise Poe, Jane K. Priewe, Necia Sneed Ramsey, Kathy Ross, S.R. Shaphren, Mary Shea, Dorothea V. Shull, Andrew J. Smith, Barbara Smith, Romy Squeri, Darcy Mason Swope, Mary S. Toth, Sharon Dunn Umnik, Joy Warrell, Patricia Wilson, D.A. Woodliff, Norma Bennett Woolf, Jabeen Y. Yusufali, Peg Ziegler, and Patsy Zimmerman.

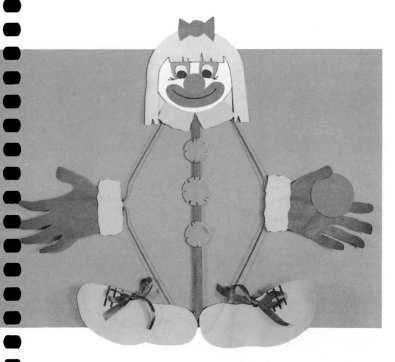

HANGER PEOPLE
(two wire clothes hangers, construction paper, ribbon)

1. Tape together the bottoms of two wire clothes hangers.

2. Cut two large identical construction paper circles for the head. Glue the circles together with one end of the hanger in between them. Glue on cut-paper features and hair.

3. On paper, trace around each of your hands and feet twice. Cut them out.

4. Place one of the cutout left hands on top of the hook of one hanger and one of the right hands underneath. Glue the hands together. Do the same to the other hook. Glue the feet on the other end of the hanger, opposite the head.

5. Decorate the shoes with ribbon.

BUTTON BAUBLE PINS
(lightweight cardboard, buttons, safety pin, felt)

1. Cut small shapes from lightweight cardboard. Glue buttons on the cardboard shapes and let them dry.

2. Hold a safety pin by the side that opens, and glue the other side to the back of the cardboard. Do this with each button pin.

3. Cut a small narrow strip of felt for each button pin. Glue the strip to the cardboard and across the back of each safety pin. When dry, wear the pin or give as a gift.

WATERMELON CHECKERBOARD
(heavy corrugated cardboard, poster paint, black permanent marker, twelve watermelon seeds, twelve squash seeds)

1. Cut a circle about 14 inches wide from heavy corrugated cardboard. Paint the outer inch of the circle with green poster paint. Paint the inside of the circle red. Paint a thin white line where the two colors meet.

2. With a pencil, draw an 8-inch square in the red area. Mark off every inch on each side of the square. Connect the marks on opposite sides of the square, dividing it into sixty-four small squares.

3. With a permanent black marker, outline the large square. Color in every other small square to form a checkerboard. Draw on watermelon seeds.

4. Use twelve black seeds from a watermelon and twelve white seeds from a squash as your game's playing pieces.

AUTOGRAPH POOCH
(brown paper bag, crayons or markers)

1. Cut a large brown paper bag into a rectangle 18 inches long and 6 inches wide. On the long edges of the paper, make pencil marks 6 inches in from each end.

2. Fold the ends of the paper toward the center at these marks. Fold the ends back to meet those folds.

3. Open up the paper. Draw a dog across the whole piece of paper, with its head on the far right panel and its tail end on the far left.

4. Draw a collar or bandanna on the dog, and put your name on it.

5. Have your friends sign your Autograph Pooch at the end of the school year. Or give a Pooch, signed by your whole class, to your teacher.

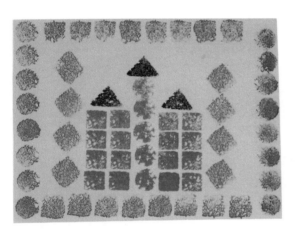

SPONGE PAINTING
(cellulose sponge, poster paint, poster board)

1. Cut several shapes from a cellulose sponge (the kind that has irregular holes).

2. Dip the sponge shapes in paint, and blot them on a piece of scrap paper to remove any extra paint.

3. Paint a picture by dabbing the sponge shapes onto a piece of poster board.

YARN AND BEAD BANGLE
(metal first-aid tape container, yarn, twelve beads)

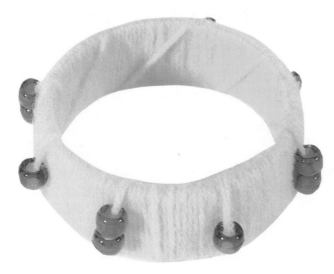

1. Tie one end of a strand of yarn, several yards long, around the cover of a metal first-aid tape container. Tape the knot to the inside.

2. Roll the strand of yarn into a small ball to make it easy to handle. Tightly wrap the yarn around the entire cover, keeping the strands close together.

3. Cut the yarn, leaving a 6-inch tail. Loop the tail under a few of the strands on the inside of the cover, knot it, and trim.

4. Tie one end of a 20-inch strand of yarn to the inside of the cover. String twelve or more beads on it.

5. Wrap the yarn and beads around the cover to form a design on the bracelet. On the inside, loop the tail under a few strands, knot it, and trim the end.

PAPIER-MÂCHÉ PETS
(newspaper, flour and water, aluminum foil, poster paint, string)

1. Cover your work area with lots of newspaper. Mix 1 cup of flour with 1 cup of water to make a paste.

2. Wad up pieces of newspaper to form a core for the animal you want to make. Tear small strips of newspaper and dip them into the paste. Place the strips on the core, forming the animal's body.

3. Add more newspaper wads for legs and the head. Mold paste-covered strips of paper around them with your hands.

4. Place the papier-mâché pets on aluminum foil and let them dry overnight, or until they are hard. Then paint the pets, adding details with string.

"BOOK" BOOKENDS
(two corrugated-cardboard packing boxes, small stones, plastic food-storage bags, construction paper, markers)

1. Fill two corrugated-cardboard packing boxes with unpopped popcorn, small stones, or sand in plastic bags. Tape the lids shut.

2. Decorate the boxes with strips of construction paper and markers, making them look like books lined up on a shelf.

3. Write your favorite book titles along the book "bindings."

4. Use the "book" bookends to hold your books upright on a shelf.

SOAP BASKET
(plastic food container, fabric, ribbon)

1. Place an empty round plastic food container in the center of a piece of fabric. With a ruler, measure the height of the container. Add 1 to 1 1/2 inches to that measurement.

2. With the ruler, measure the fabric starting from the bottom of the container until you reach the total measurement. Make small marks with a pencil, going all the way around the container. You should see a circle forming. Remove the container and cut out the circle.

3. Squeeze glue along the inside rim of the container. Place the container in the center of the fabric and pull the fabric up over the rim and into the glue. Work the fabric evenly around the rim and let dry. Tie a ribbon around the outside. Place soaps in the basket.

THE BANK BUILDING
(cocoa container with round metal lid, construction paper)

1. Wash and dry an empty cocoa container.

2. Cover the sides of the container with glue and a piece of construction paper. Turn the container so the round metal lid is on the bottom. Glue pieces of paper to the top to make it look like a roof.

3. Using cut paper, decorate the rest of the container to look like a bank building.

4. On the back of the bank, have an adult help you cut a slit just under the roof, large enough to slip money through.

5. After you have filled the bank building with coins and bills, pop open the round metal lid to remove the money and deposit it into a real bank.

MINIATURE BOOK BOOKMARK
(felt, paper, newspaper)

1. Cut a small rectangle of felt and fold it in half, making a book cover. Cut three pieces of paper the same size as the rectangle.

2. Fold the pieces of paper in half, place them in the book, and staple them from the outside in the center along the fold.

3. Cut two long felt strips and glue them inside the back of the book. Trim the ends by cutting an upside-down V shape into them.

4. Cut out a title from an old newspaper and glue it to the front of the book, or write one with a pen on a piece of paper.

FARMHAND PUPPETS
(felt, old cotton glove, thread)

1. Cut five felt circles just large enough to cover your fingertips.

2. Place an old cotton glove palm-side up. Glue a felt circle to each fingertip to make an animal head.

3. Cut and glue felt pieces on the circles to make facial features for each animal. Add pieces of thread for whiskers. Let dry.

4. Place your hand inside the glove, and make up your own puppet play.

STARLIGHT MOBILE
(lightweight cardboard, aluminum foil, tinsel, thread)

1. Cut a crescent moon and three star shapes from lightweight cardboard. Trace around each shape twice onto aluminum foil and cut out the shapes.

2. Glue the foil crescents to each side of the cardboard moon.

3. Glue tinsel to each of the cardboard stars. Glue the foil stars to each side of the cardboard stars.

4. Tape a dark-colored thread from each star to the moon. Glue a long piece of thread along the inside curve of the moon.

5. When the glue dries, hang the mobile in a window.

DANCIN' HUMPTY DUMPTY
(poster board, construction paper, chenille sticks, string, yarn)

1. Cut two large identically sized egg shapes from poster board.

2. For Humpty Dumpty's front, decorate one egg shape with facial features cut from construction paper and chenille sticks. Use the other egg shape for his back and decorate.

3. Place chenille-stick arms and legs between the two egg shapes. Use tape and glue to attach the shapes together.

4. Cut four hand shapes and four shoe shapes from paper. Glue two hands to the end of each arm, and glue two shoe shapes to the end of each leg.

5. Punch a hole in the top of the egg and tie a string through it. Add a large yarn pompon for hair. Bounce the string to see Humpty Dumpty dance.

RING TOSS
(corrugated cardboard, masking tape, poster paint, pushpins, plastic-ring beverage holder)

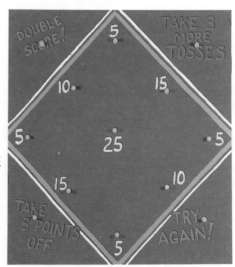

1. Glue two 18-by-20-inch pieces of corrugated cardboard back to back to make a game board. Cover the edges with masking tape.

2. Paint the game board and let it dry. Then paint numbers and scoring directions on the board, as shown.

3. Put glue on the bottom of a pushpin. Push the pin into the board at one of the painted numbers. Repeat with more pushpins—one for each of the numbers. (If the pins come through the back of the game board, cover them with cotton and masking tape.)

4. Cut plastic rings from a six-pack beverage holder. To play the game, toss the rings at the game board and add up your score.

CEREAL BOX SCRAPBOOK
(cereal box, gift wrap, brown paper bags, shoelace)

1. Cut out the front, bottom, and back from a cereal box in one piece. Glue on gift wrap to cover it.

2. To make pages, cut pieces the same size as the book cover from brown paper bags.

3. Punch two holes in the front and back covers, then punch holes in the pages, making sure all holes line up.

4. Place the pages between the covers. Pull a shoelace through the holes in the back cover, through the pages, and to the front cover. Tie the shoelace into a bow.

RIBBON PICTURE HOLDER
(white poster board, old greeting cards, ribbon)

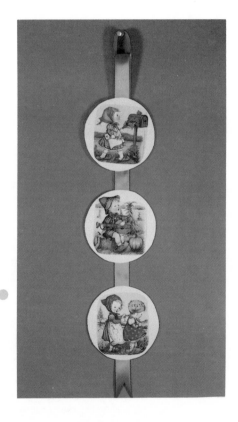

1. Cut three circles from white poster board. Cut pictures from old greeting cards and glue them on top of the circles.

2. Cut a long piece of ribbon. Make a loop in the ribbon at one end and staple it. Cut a small piece of ribbon. Place it through the first loop and staple the ends together for a hanger.

3. Glue the three circles with pictures to the long piece of ribbon. Let dry and then hang up.

PLASTIC-BOX FISH TANK
(greeting card box with clear acetate top, construction paper, yarn)

1. Cut and glue construction paper inside a greeting card box that has a clear acetate top.

2. Cut out fish and seaweed from paper. Glue them inside the box.

3. Place the clear acetate top on the box. Cut a piece of yarn and glue or tape it to the back of the box for a hanger.

TWINE PLANTER
(cardboard food container, clear plastic from a greeting card box, white cotton cord, poster paint)

1. Wash and dry a cardboard food container like one in which peanuts are packaged.

2. Start at the bottom of the container and spread a little glue around the outside. Press the end of a long piece of white cotton cord into the glue, and wind the cord around the container until it is covered.

3. To make a stencil, cut a small plastic square from a greeting card box. Draw a flower in the middle. Start in the middle of the flower and cut it out, leaving a border of plastic around it. Do the same for a stem and leaves.

4. Dip a dry brush in just a little poster paint. Wipe the brush on a towel to get rid of excess paint.

5. Hold the stencil for the stem and leaves near the base of the container. Rub the dry brush over the cutout stem and leaves. The paint will fill the cutout area. Do the same for the flower.

FOOT PICTURES
(construction paper, buttons, chenille sticks, yarn, fabric)

1. Trace around your shoe on a sheet of light-colored construction paper.

2. Create a character by decorating the shoe outline with buttons, chenille sticks, yarn, fabric, and markers.

HANDY-DANDY HANGER
(wire clothes hanger, lightweight cardboard, fabric, spring-type clothespins, lace or ribbon)

1. Lay a wire clothes hanger on a piece of cardboard and trace around the outside with a pencil. Do this again and cut out the two pieces.

2. Place the hanger between the two cardboard pieces and tape them tightly together. Cover with glue and fabric.

3. Glue spring-type clothespins to the fabric. Decorate with lace or ribbon.

4. Hang scarves, ribbons, or hair clips from the clothespins.

WALLPAPER PLACE MATS
(wallpaper, poster board, yarn)

1. Cut a piece of wallpaper to measure 9 inches by 13 inches. Cut a piece of poster board the same size.

2. If you use prepasted wallpaper, wet the back with a little warm water. If you use a piece of plain wallpaper, spread glue on the back. Press the paper onto the poster board.

3. Make the border by punching holes around the edges with a paper punch. Weave a piece of yarn in and out of the holes.

4. Join the ends together and tie a bow.

CEREAL-BOX CAR
(cereal box, felt or construction paper, cardboard)

1. Tape the flaps of a cereal box closed. Follow the diagrams to create a car shape by cutting and folding.

2. Cover the car with felt or paper. Cut tires and a steering wheel from cardboard. Add felt or paper and glue them to the car.

3. Finish the car with a license plate, lights, and door handles. Add a couple of passengers.

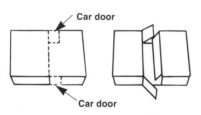

Car door

Car door

PAPER-PLATE MONKEY
(two paper plates, construction paper)

1. Place two paper plates on top of each other, right-side up. Staple them together halfway around the edges. Fold each unstapled plate-half over the stapled section.

2. Place your fingers inside the pocket created. Note where your thumb falls on the back, and tape on a paper loop for your thumb to slide into.

3. Decorate the plate with paper and markers to make the monkey.

PLASTIC CIRCLE BRACELET
(large plastic lid, yarn, tape)

1. Draw 1-inch circles on a large plastic lid. Cut them out with scissors.

2. With a paper punch, punch two holes, one opposite the other, in each plastic circle.

3. Cut an 18-inch piece of yarn. Make a point with a small piece of tape on one end of the yarn, like a needle.

4. Weave the yarn through the circles. When finished, cut the tape off and tie the ends of the yarn into a bow.

SHOPPER'S HELPERS
(envelopes, old magazines)

1. Cut out pictures of food or other household items from old magazines. Glue the pictures on one end of an envelope.

2. Below the pictures, make lines for items on a shopping list. Make a special column to check if there's a coupon.

3. Place any coupons inside the envelope. Take the envelope with you when you shop for groceries.

HORSESHOE PAPERWEIGHT
(corrugated cardboard, poster paint, small stones)

1. Cut a horseshoe shape from a piece of corrugated cardboard. Paint it a bright color.

2. Select an assortment of small stones that are all about the same size and thickness. Wash them and let dry.

3. Paint the stones a contrasting color to the horseshoe.

4. When the paint is dry, glue the stones around the horseshoe.

STRAW-BACKED PORCUPINE

(one 2- and one 3-inch plastic-foam ball, table knife, ice-cream stick, poster paint, sponge, felt, plastic drinking straws)

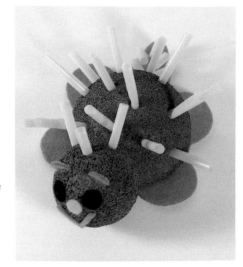

1. Cut a 3-inch plastic-foam ball in half with a table knife. Use one half for the body and save the other half for another craft.

2. Break an ice-cream stick in half. Put glue on one end of the stick, and push it into the body for the neck. Put glue on the other end of the stick, and push a 2-inch plastic-foam ball onto it for the head. Cover the body with poster paint, using a small piece of sponge, and let dry.

3. Place the body on a piece of felt, trace around it, and add four feet and a tail. Cut out the felt shape and glue it to the bottom of the body. Cut out facial features from felt, and glue in place. Make a small slit above each eye and push in pieces of felt for the ears.

4. Using a pencil, poke holes in the body, head, and tail. Put glue in each hole, and insert small pieces of plastic drinking straws for quills.

MILK CAP PENDANT

(plastic milk cap, ribbon)

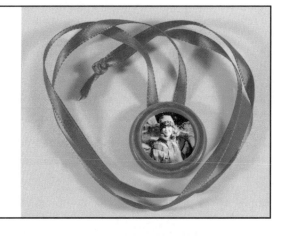

1. Cut a photo to fit inside a plastic milk cap. Glue the photo inside the cap.

2. Cut a ribbon long enough to go around your neck and tie it together at the ends.

3. Glue the back of the milk cap to the ribbon.

AIRPLANE

(two paper towel tubes, one bathroom tissue tube, poster paint, three ice-cream sticks)

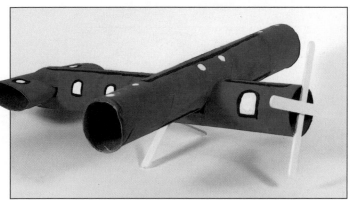

1. Measure 3 inches from one end of a paper towel tube and draw a line. Measure 2 inches from this point, draw another line, and cut the small 2-inch section from half of the tube. Insert another paper towel tube crosswise for the wing section, attaching the two tubes with glue.

2. For the tail, cut a slit on each side of the body at the other end of the tube. Glue a small bathroom tissue tube between the slits.

3. Paint three ice-cream sticks. Glue two together to form an X. Glue them to the front of the airplane for the propeller.

4. Break one ice-cream stick in half. Poke a hole through the bottom of the plane, and glue the sticks in place for the landing gear. Paint on windows and other details.

CLEVER GIFT BAGS
(brown paper bag, construction paper)

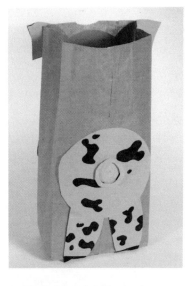

1. From construction paper, draw and cut out animal features.

2. Glue the features to one side of a paper bag for the front of the animal.

3. Cut out features for the back of the animal to decorate the back of the bag.

4. Create cats, dogs, and other animals.

TOUCH-ME NUMBER POSTER
(ten of some object such as buttons, nine of another object,
and so on down to one object, cardboard)

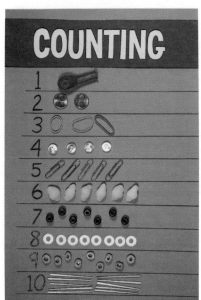

1. Collect interesting small objects that are alike. You'll need ten of some object, nine of another, and so on. Plan ahead so you have room for everything.

2. Draw ten evenly spaced lines across a piece of cardboard, leaving space at the top for a title.

3. Add the title using markers or paper.

4. Draw the number 1 on the first line and glue on one object (maybe a balloon). On the second line, draw the number 2 and glue on two objects that are alike. Continue writing numbers and adding objects until you complete the number 10.

FELT APPLE PINCUSHION
(felt, needle and thread, cotton balls)

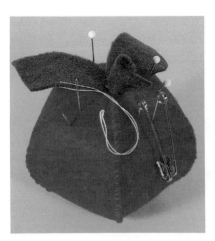

1. Cut five felt pieces using the pattern shown. Sew them together with seams facing out to form the apple shape.

2. Stuff the apple with cotton balls before sewing the last seam closed.

3. Cut a strip of felt and roll it into a stem. Stitch it to the apple. Cut felt leaves and stitch those to the apple. Place sewing pins in the apple.

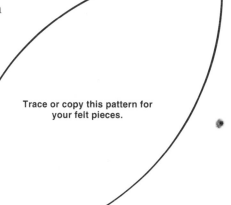

Trace or copy this pattern for
your felt pieces.

DECOUPAGE PENCIL HOLDER
(frozen-juice container, green construction paper, white glue and water, bowl,
old flower catalogs, clear nail polish)

1. Cover the outside of a frozen-juice container with green construction paper. Cut pictures of different kinds of flowers from an old flower catalog.

2. Mix white glue and a little water together in a bowl. Brush the glue mixture on the backs of the flower cutouts and place them around the container.

3. When the container is covered with flowers, brush a little of the glue mixture over the entire outside of the container and let dry.

4. Give the flowers a shiny finish with coats of clear nail polish.

STICK FRAME
(four ice-cream sticks, yarn)

1. Glue four ice-cream sticks together to form a square frame.

2. Attach a picture or photo with glue, and let dry.

3. Glue a piece of yarn to the back for a hanger.

A FUNNY STORYBOOK
(old magazines, construction paper,
white writing paper, yarn,
self-adhesive reinforcement rings)

1. Cut out ten pictures from old magazines.

2. Take five pieces of construction paper and glue one picture on each side. Leave room under each picture to glue a 4-by-6-inch piece of white writing paper.

3. Write a story from one picture to the next on the white paper.

4. Make a front and back cover for the book from construction paper. Write the title on the front with markers or crayons.

5. Holding the pages in order, punch holes on the left side. Place self-adhesive reinforcement rings over the holes, and tie pieces of yarn through the holes to keep the book together.

SPONGE HAND PUPPETS
(soft sponges, construction paper)

1. In the edge of a sponge, cut a slit large enough so your three middle fingers will fit inside.

2. From construction paper, cut out a mouth, eyes, ears, and a nose for each puppet. Glue them in place. The ears can be glued to the back side of the sponge.

3. Put your middle fingers inside and let your thumb and little finger represent the puppet's arms.

GET-WELL MESSAGE
(round oatmeal container, gift wrap, table knife, paper)

1. Measure 2 1/2 inches up from the bottom of a round oatmeal container. Cut off the top part, but save the lid for later.

2. Glue gift wrap around the sides and the lid. Draw a face on the bottom. Then, using a table knife, make a slit about 1 1/2 inches wide for a mouth.

3. Cut a long strip of plain paper, narrower than the mouth opening. Write a get-well message on the strip. Add jokes and riddles or write a story.

4. Roll the strip around a pencil and place the message inside the box. Thread the beginning of the message through the mouth. Pull the strip to read the message.

CARRYING CASE FOR GLASSES
(fabric, poster board, rickrack)

1. Cut two pieces of fabric 8 inches square. Cut a piece of poster board the same size and place it between the fabric squares. Glue all the layers together.

2. Fold in half. Glue the long side and one short side together. Leave the other short side unglued as an opening for the glasses.

3. Decorate the front by gluing on pieces of rickrack to make a design. Let dry overnight.

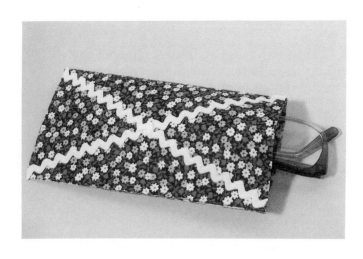

DOORKNOB HANGER
(poster board, old magazines)

1. Cut out a piece of poster board 4 inches wide and 8 inches long.

2. Measure down about an inch on the long side of the poster board and draw a circle in the middle, about 1 1/2 to 2 inches in diameter.

3. With scissors, cut a slit from the edge of the board to the middle of the circle. Cut out the circle so the hanger will fit over the doorknob.

4. Write your name with a marker and add paper cutouts from old magazines.

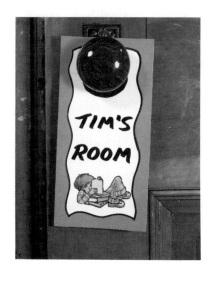

STRIPED CATERPILLAR
(round oatmeal container, felt, chenille stick, bathroom tissue tube, poster paint)

1. Cover a round oatmeal container with glue and strips of colored felt. For the face, glue eyes, a mouth, and a nose cut from felt onto the bottom of the container.

2. With a pencil, poke two holes (2 inches apart, 1 inch back from the face) on top of the head. Insert a chenille stick into one hole. Then reach inside the container and push the other end of the stick through the other hole. Curl the ends with a pencil.

3. Cut three 1-inch rings from the bathroom tissue tube. Cut the rings in half and paint them black. Once they dry, glue three halves to each side of the caterpillar for feet.

4. With the cover as the caterpillar's tail, you can use the caterpillar as a storage container.

DINOSAUR
(large and small toothpaste boxes, gray construction paper)

1. Using large and small toothpaste boxes, cut sections to form the dinosaur. Use one box for the main body.

2. Cut the box sections for the neck and tail on an angle, as shown. Cut smaller box sections for the head and legs.

3. Cover each section with gray construction paper. Glue the sections together and let dry.

4. Draw eyes and a mouth with a marker.

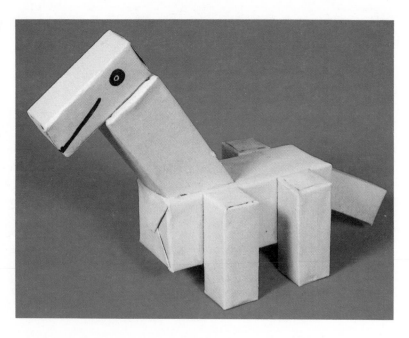

PARTY HAT
(paper, yarn)

1. Fold a 9-by-12-inch sheet of paper in half. Place it in front of you with the fold at the top.

2. Fold each top corner down.

3. Take hold of the upper sheet at the bottom and fold it over the turned-down corners. Turn the hat over and do the same to the other side.

4. Turn down the little tabs that are sticking out and staple them in place.

5. Punch a hole at each side of the hat. Tie a piece of yarn in each hole to tie the hat on your head.

(You can make bigger hats by using sheets of newspaper or gift wrap, or make tiny ones for your dolls from half sheets of paper.)

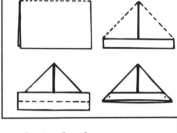

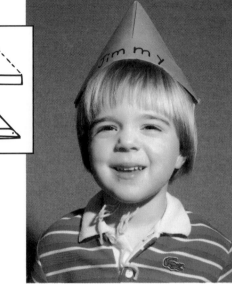

ONE-SEASON BIRDHOUSE
(half-gallon milk carton, masking tape, brown shoe polish, cloth, cord)

1. Wash and dry a half-gallon milk carton. With the spout out, staple the top shut, as shown.

2. Tear off small pieces of masking tape and cover the entire milk carton. Using a soft cloth, rub brown shoe polish over the masking tape, giving it a rough, barklike look.

3. Cut an entrance hole about 4 1/2 inches above the floor. The hole should be a little less than 1 1/2 inches across.

4. Poke some small drainage holes in the floor and two ventilation holes near the top of the carton below the spout.

5. Use a paper punch to punch a hole in the top of the house. Thread a piece of cord through the hole and tie the birdhouse to a tree limb.

INITIAL PENDANT
(paper, plastic food wrap, yarn, glue)

1. Draw the outline of an initial of your name on a piece of paper. Cover the paper with plastic food wrap. Tape at the corners to hold in place.

2. Squeeze glue over the initial. Cut and press pieces of yarn onto the glue. Paint the yarn with a coat of glue.

3. Glue a loop of yarn at the top. When dry, peel the yarn letter away from the plastic. Thread a long piece of yarn through the loop.

LACED BEAR PUPPET
(large brown paper bag, yarn)

1. Cut down the seam of a large brown paper bag. Then cut the bottom out of the bag so that you have a long flat sheet of brown paper.

2. Fold the paper in half and draw a bear shape on it. Holding the paper together, cut out two bear shapes the same size.

3. Draw on features with crayons or markers. Holding the bears together, punch holes around the outside edges, leaving the bottom unpunched.

4. Lace the bears together with a piece of long yarn, weaving in and out of the holes. Tie a knot at the ends. Place your hand inside the bear to work the puppet.

TWIST-TIE PICTURE
(paper- and plastic-coated twist-ties, construction paper)

1. Collect paper- and plastic-coated twist-ties that are left over from all types of food packages. Gather a variety of colors.

2. Select a piece of construction paper for the background.

3. The twists can be left in blocks of color, separated, or cut into shapes, using scissors. Wrap the twists around a pencil to make curls.

4. Using glue, attach the twists to the paper to create a picture.

KEEPSAKE BOX
(shoe box, brown wrapping paper, old magazines)

1. Cover a shoe box and lid with brown wrapping paper. Think of a theme that you would like the keepsake box to represent. If you like horses, for example, cut out horse pictures from old magazines or an old calendar. If you like baseball, cut out baseball pictures.

2. Decorate the outside of the box with these theme pictures. Store mementoes in the box.

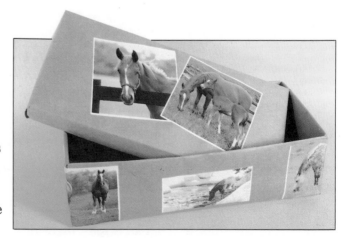

OCTOPUS
(cardboard egg carton, heavy yarn, paper, poster paint)

1. Glue together two cup sections from the bottom of a cardboard egg carton. Cover them with paint and let dry.

2. Glue eight heavy yarn tentacles to the bottom.

3. Cut eyes and a mouth from paper, and glue them in place.

OVER THE MOON
(poster board, paper plate, two brass fasteners)

1. Make a cow from poster board. Add features with markers.

2. Draw a face on a paper plate to make it look like the moon.

3. With a brass fastener, attach the cow to one end of a strip of poster board. Use a second brass fastener to attach the other end of the strip to the center of the plate.

4. By moving the cow around the plate, you can make the cow jump over the moon.

BOTTLE HOOPLA
(plastic food bottle, pebbles, one 1 1/2-inch plastic-foam ball, construction paper, moveable plastic eyes, push-pull detergent cap, three plastic lids)

1. Wash the plastic food bottle and scrub off the label. Put some pebbles in the bottle so it will not tip over easily.

2. For the head, firmly push and twist a 1 1/2-inch plastic-foam ball over the neck of the bottle. For the hat, push and twist a push-pull detergent cap onto the head.

3. Decorate with construction paper cutouts. Glue on moveable plastic eyes.

4. Cut the centers from three plastic lids, leaving the rims, to use as hoops. (Be sure they are the right size to "ring" the bottle figure.)

5. Score one point for each ringer.

BOX MOBILE
(three small cardboard boxes, construction paper, yarn)

1. Cover three small cardboard boxes with glue and construction paper. Cut out a shape from each box. Decorate the boxes with markers or crayons.

2. Make a small hole in the top and bottom of two boxes. Make one hole in the third box.

3. Glue pieces of yarn in the holes to connect the boxes. Tie a loop at the top to hang the mobile.

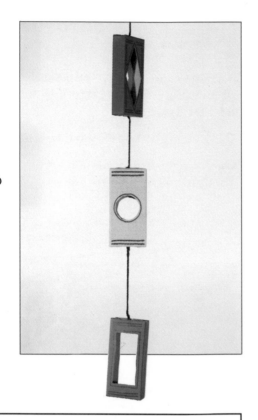

PENNY PAPERWEIGHT
(plastic jar lid, pennies, felt)

1. Glue pennies to the top of a plastic jar lid.

2. Cut a strip of felt and glue it around the edge of the lid.

BUTTON NAME PLAQUE
(heavy cardboard, fabric, rickrack, buttons, ribbon)

1. Cover a rectangular piece of heavy cardboard with glue and fabric. Add rickrack around the edges.

2. Print a name on the fabric. Squeeze glue on each letter and press buttons into the glue.

3. When dry, glue a piece of ribbon on the back for a hanger.

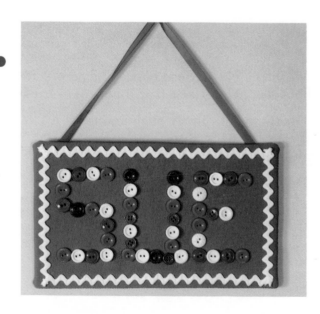

TRIANGLE PUPPY NOTE
(construction paper, marker)

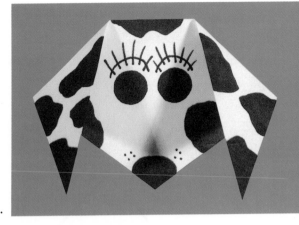

1. Cut a piece of construction paper in half the long way.

2. Mark the center of the long side of one piece and draw lines from the center to each end of the other long side. Cut away the side pieces, leaving a long, thin triangle.

3. Turn the triangle so the tip is the puppy's nose. Fold two sides of the triangle down for its ears. Draw eyes and nose with a marker. Add spots.

4. Write a message on the back and send as a note to a friend.

SCENTED KEEPSAKE
(lightweight cotton fabric, lace, rubber band, ribbon, potpourri of herbs, flowers, and spices)

1. Cut out two identical round circles, one from a piece of lightweight cotton fabric and the other from a piece of lace.

2. Place the cotton fabric right-side down on top of the lace. Pour a potpourri of herbs, flowers, and spices in the center of the circle.

3. Gather the cotton and lace around the potpourri and hold together tightly with a rubber band.

4. Tie a ribbon over the rubber band. Place the scented bag in a clothing drawer.

PAPIER-MÂCHÉ PHOTO FRAME
(corrugated cardboard, old newspaper or paper towels, flour and water, bowl, poster paint, lightweight cardboard, yarn)

1. Have an adult help you cut a picture frame shape from corrugated cardboard.

2. Cut small shapes from scrap cardboard and glue them on top of the frame to make a design.

3. To make papier-mâché, mix flour and water together in a bowl until it is the consistency of ketchup.

4. Tear small strips of newspaper or paper towels and dip them into the flour mixture. Place the strips on the frame, covering the edges and the back. Let dry for at least one day.

5. Paint the frame with several coats of poster paint. Let each coat dry before adding another one.

6. When finished, tape a photo in the frame. Place a sheet of lightweight cardboard over the back of the photo to protect it. Add a yarn hanger.

PAPER-PUNCH NOTE CARD
(paper)

1. Fold a sheet of 5-by-7-inch paper in half.

2. Punch out dots from colorful paper. Glue the dots to the front of the card.

3. Complete your designs with markers, colored pencils, or crayons.

FOUR SEASONS CLIPBOARD
(heavy cardboard, construction paper, two spring-type clothespins, string)

1. Cover a piece of heavy cardboard with light-colored construction paper.

2. Glue two spring-type clothespins at the top center of the board.

3. To decorate, cut and glue on four trees from brown paper. Add a few leaves to the first tree for spring, a green treetop to the second for summer, an orange treetop to the third for fall, and leave the last tree bare for winter.

4. Tape a piece of string to the back of the clipboard for a hanger.

CUBE PICTURE STORY
(poster board, crayons or markers)

1. Cut six pieces of poster board, each 6 inches square.

2. Think of a very short story. Number four squares of poster board 1 through 4. Draw a picture and write a sentence on each one for the story.

3. Lay the four squares side by side and tape them together, as shown. Pick up the taped squares and fold them to form a cube. Tape square 1 to square 4.

4. Put your story title on the fifth square, and tape it to the top. Tape the blank square to the bottom.

5. Share your story with friends and family.

DESK ORGANIZER
(large cereal box, construction paper, several small boxes)

1. Cut away the front of a large cereal box. Cover the sides, inside and out, and the inside bottom of the box with glue and construction paper.

2. Arrange several small boxes inside the large box. Cover the small boxes with paper, and glue them into position. Let dry.

3. Place rubber bands, pencils, pens, and other supplies in the boxes.

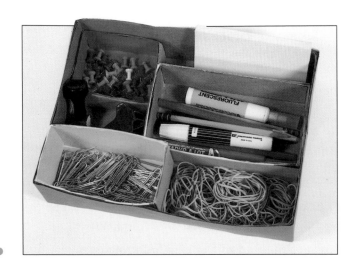

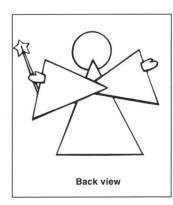

GOURD ANIMAL
(small gourd, scrap cloth, acrylic paint, construction paper, metal washer)

1. Wash a small gourd, and polish the outer skin with a cloth.

2. With a pencil, draw the pattern of a penguin, goose, kangaroo, or other animal onto the gourd.

3. Paint the gourd with acrylic paint and let dry. Add features from construction paper.

4. Glue a metal washer about the size of a quarter to the bottom of the gourd so it will stand up.

TRIANGLE TOOTH FAIRY
(white paper, toothpick, large plastic cap, markers, cotton)

1. To make the Tooth Fairy's body, cut one large and two smaller triangles from white paper. Cut out a head and two hands. Glue the pieces together, as shown. Add a face and hair with markers.

2. To make a wand, attach a cut-paper or sticker star to the end of a toothpick. Glue it in the fairy's hand.

3. Decorate the outside of a large plastic cap. Place some cotton inside the cap so it will be a safe place to leave a tooth.

4. Glue the Tooth Fairy body behind the cap.

Back view

DOG RIBBON CADDY

(paper towel tube, corrugated cardboard, fabric,
chenille stick, paper clips)

1. For the body, spread glue on a paper towel tube and cover it with fabric.

2. For the head and feet, cut front and back pieces from corrugated cardboard. Cover them with fabric and attach to the ends of the tube.

3. For the tail, poke a hole in the back piece and insert a chenille stick with some glue.

4. For the head of the dog, add features cut from fabric or paper. Wrap ribbons around the dog's body. Hold with paper clips.

HALF-GALLON BUS

(half-gallon milk carton, construction paper,
stickers, cardboard, bottle tops)

1. Press down to flatten the top of a half-gallon milk carton. Tape to hold in place. Cover the carton with glue and construction paper.

2. Decorate the bus with paper and markers to make a sign and windows. Add stickers or draw on faces.

3. Draw and cut out wheels from cardboard. Paint them black. When they are dry, glue them to the bus. Glue on bottle tops for headlights.

BOX SCULPTURE

(corrugated cardboard, small cardboard boxes, poster paint,
construction paper, yarn)

1. Use a piece of heavy corrugated cardboard for the base of the sculpture. Glue small cardboard boxes in a design on top and let dry.

2. Paint the boxes and the cardboard base. Decorate the boxes with paint or pieces of construction paper.

3. Glue a yarn loop hanger to the back.

BOOKWORM BOOKENDS
(two half-gallon juice or milk cartons, construction paper, rocks)

1. Cut two half-gallon juice or milk cartons in half and discard the tops.

2. Cover the carton halves with glue and paper. Draw a worm shape on paper. Add features with markers and cut out the worm.

3. Cut the worm in half. Glue the front part of the worm onto one bookend and print the word "BOOK" below it. Glue the back part of the worm onto the other bookend and print the word "WORM" below it.

4. Place rocks inside each bookend so they will be heavy enough to hold books in place.

SEWING KIT
(poster board, fabric, rickrack, felt)

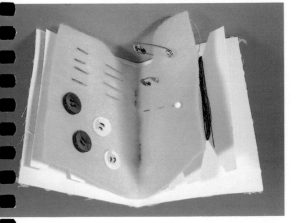

1. Cut a piece of poster board for the cover of the sewing kit. Cover it with glue and fabric. Trim the edges and add rickrack. Fold in half and open.

2. Cut another piece of poster board and a piece of felt a little smaller than the cover. Cut parallel notches on each side of the poster board and wind thread through the notches.

3. Place the poster board of thread inside the cover. Place the felt on top. Turn all layers over so the outside of the cover is facing right-side up. Staple through all three layers at the fold.

4. Add needles, buttons, straight pins, and safety pins to the felt section of the sewing kit.

NEWSPAPER NELSON
(old newspaper, paper, yarn)

1. Use four sheets of newspaper for the front and four sheets of newspaper for the back of Newspaper Nelson. Fold other sheets of newspaper into long strips for his arms and legs.

2. Place the sheets of newspaper together and start stapling Nelson's body together at the edge. As you come to the places where arms and legs belong, insert them before stapling. Leave the whole top open for stuffing later.

3. Cut feet, hands, and facial features from paper. Staple or glue them in place.

4. Crumple sheets of newspaper and carefully stuff the body. Staple the top together, adding yarn for hair as you staple.

PATCHWORK TRIVET
(corrugated cardboard, fabric, cord)

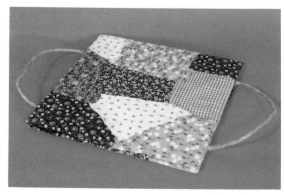

1. Cut two identical squares of corrugated cardboard.

2. Glue different shapes of fabric scraps to one side of each square, starting in a corner and wrapping the outside pieces of fabric over the edges of the cardboard to the back.

3. For the handles, cut two pieces of cord. Glue the handles to the back of one square.

4. Spread glue on the backs of both squares and press them together.

SLEEPY BEAR MITTEN HANGER
(plastic lid, two paper plates, construction paper, cotton, two plastic spring-type clothespins with holes, yarn)

1. Glue a plastic lid to the bottom of a paper plate for the bear's snout. Roll a strip of black construction paper and glue it to the snout.

2. To make the eyes, cut two rectangles of black paper. Then cut slits and curl them with a pencil for lashes. Glue them to the paper plate.

3. Make a hat from construction paper. Attach the hat with glue, adding some cotton for trim. Cut sections from another paper plate for the bear's ears and glue these on at the sides of the hat.

4. Punch two holes under the bear's chin. Cut two pieces of yarn, each about 20 inches long. Thread a clothespin onto each piece of yarn. Tie the yarn into a bow through the two holes.

5. Punch two holes behind the hat and thread a piece of yarn through them. Tie the ends in a bow for a hanger.

BOX FISH
(cereal box, construction paper, yarn)

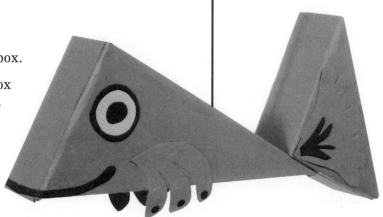

1. Cut a long and a short corner from a cereal box.

2. Glue pieces of construction paper over the box corners and glue them together in a fish shape. Add features cut from paper.

3. Lightly tape a piece of yarn to the top of the fish so it will hang straight. Once you find the right spot, poke a hole through the top of the fish.

4. Glue the piece of yarn in the hole. Tie a loop at the other end of the yarn and hang the fish.

TOOTHBRUSH HOLDER
(white plastic dishwashing detergent bottle, cellulose sponge, permanent marker)

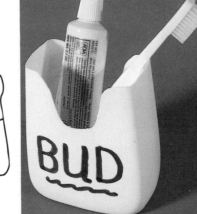

1. Have an adult help you cut off the top half of a plastic dishwashing detergent bottle. Wash and dry the bottom half. Discard the top.

2. Cut rounded sections from the front and the back of the bottle half to look like a big tooth, as shown. Poke small holes in the bottom for drainage.

3. Cut a piece of cellulose sponge to fit in the bottom of the holder to absorb moisture.

4. Write your name (or the name of the person you are making this for) with a permanent marker on the front of the holder.

SILHOUETTE, OR SHADOW PICTURE
(flashlight or slide projector, white and black construction paper, poster board, yarn)

1. In a dark room, place a lit flashlight or slide projector on a table. Lightly tape a piece of white construction paper to the wall right where the light is shining. Sit between the light and the paper, so that your profile falls on the paper. Move closer to or farther from the paper until the silhouette, or shadow, is the size you want.

2. Have a partner draw around your silhouette on the paper. Remove the paper from the wall and go over the outline, correcting any shaky lines.

3. Cut out the silhouette. Place it on a piece of black construction paper, trace around it, and cut it out.

4. Glue the black silhouette onto a piece of white paper. Mount the picture on a piece of poster board. Sign your name and the date. Add a piece of yarn to the back for a hanger.

PET PLACE MAT
(white poster board, construction paper, clear self-adhesive paper)

1. Cut a piece of white poster board large enough for your pet's food dishes.

2. Design a picture of your pet with markers and cutouts from construction paper. You could print your pet's name on part of the picture.

3. Cut two pieces of clear self-adhesive paper a little larger than the mat itself. (You may need an adult to help you separate the paper.) Cover the front and the back of the place mat. Trim the edges with scissors.

4. Keep the mat clean with a damp cloth.

PERKY PENGUIN
(uncooked egg, large sewing needle, bowl, cardboard, construction paper, 1-inch plastic foam ball)

1. Wash and dry an uncooked egg. Stick a large sewing needle into the pointed end of the egg, making sure to poke through the membrane under the shell. Turn the egg over, and stick the needle through the other end, making a larger hole than the first.

2. Over a bowl, blow through the small hole, allowing the inside of the egg to flow into the bowl. Carefully rinse the shell in cold water. (Use the egg for baking or scramble it for breakfast.)

3. Cut two large feet from cardboard in the shape shown, and cover them with construction paper. Glue the eggshell to the feet and let dry.

4. Paint the eggshell, making a penguin body. Glue a 1-inch plastic-foam ball to the top of the body for the head. Decorate with markers and paper.

SPRING BIRD'S HOME
(grass, leaves, twigs, flour, water, large plastic lid, miniature marshmallows, construction paper)

1. In a small bowl, mix together three tablespoons of water and three tablespoons of flour.

2. Place nesting material such as grass, leaves, and twigs on a large plastic lid. Pour half of the flour mixture over it and shape it into a nest.

3. Dip miniature marshmallows into some of the mixture, and place them inside the nest for eggs.

4. Decorate the nest with birds and flowers made from construction paper.

WOODEN PLAQUE
(twelve ice-cream sticks, old magazine or greeting card, yarn)

1. Spread a thin layer of glue on two ice-cream sticks. Place them, glue-side up, several inches apart. Position the remaining ice-cream sticks on top, as shown.

2. Cut a picture from an old magazine or greeting card, and glue it onto the sticks.

3. For a hanger, glue a piece of yarn to the back.

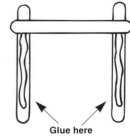

Glue here

DECORATED NOTE PAPER
(white or colored paper, rickrack, ribbon)

1. With a pencil, lightly sketch a design on a piece of white or colored paper.

2. Cut pieces of rickrack and ribbon to make the shapes you want. Arrange them on the sketch to make a design.

3. Use a little glue to attach them to the paper. Blot up any extra glue with a tissue.

4. When dry, use a marker to add such details as eyes, legs, stems, or leaves.

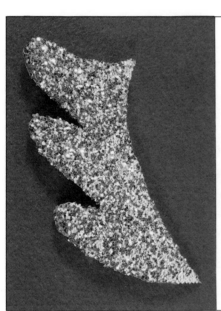

GLITTER PIN
(heavy cardboard, safety pin, glitter)

1. Cut a design from a piece of heavy cardboard.

2. Cover one side of the design with glue and sprinkle it with glitter. Let it dry thoroughly. Then shake off any excess glitter.

3. Tape or glue a safety pin to the back of the glittery design.

SCULPTURE FROM SCRAPS
(scraps of wood, nuts, bolts, washers, poster paint)

1. Stack various pieces of wood in interesting shapes.

2. Glue the wood pieces together. It may be necessary to let some sections dry before adding others to the sculpture.

3. Paint the wood sculpture, and glue on bolts and washers to add details.

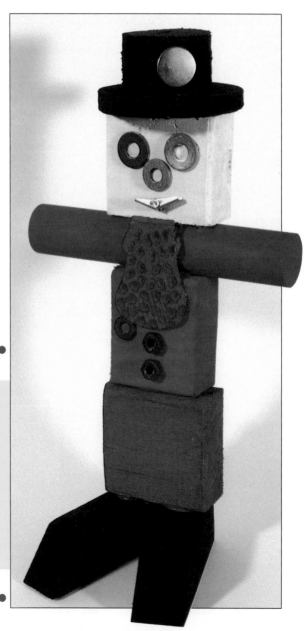

PUPPY PAPERWEIGHT
(small gelatin box, dried beans or stones, fabric, felt, ribbon)

1. Fill a gelatin box with stones or beans. Secure both ends of the box with tape.

2. Cover the box with fabric. Cut ears from felt and glue one on each side, attaching them only at the top so the ears can flop away from the head.

3. Add other features from felt. Add a ribbon collar.

TRAILER TRUCK
(cracker box, two pudding boxes, poster paint, construction paper, cardboard, bottle caps)

1. To make the trailer, tape the flaps on a cracker box shut. Tape two pudding boxes together for the cab. Cover the cab and the trailer with glue and construction paper.

2. Glue the trailer and the cab together. Draw and cut out wheels from cardboard. Paint them, then glue them to the truck.

3. Decorate with construction paper and markers. Roll a piece of paper into a tube and glue it to the side of the cab for an exhaust pipe.

4. Add bottle caps for headlights.

THE LOOK-AROUND CLOWN
(plastic drinking cup, plastic-foam ball, ice-cream stick, felt, rickrack, chenille stick)

1. Dip an ice-cream stick in glue and push it into the center of a plastic-foam ball.

2. Turn a plastic drinking cup upside down. Poke a hole in the center of the bottom of the cup, large enough so the stick can turn around.

3. Decorate the head and body with pieces of felt, rickrack, and chenille stick.

4. Put the ice-cream stick into the cup through the hole. By holding the stick with your hand inside the cup, you can move the clown's head up, down, and around.

JACK AND THE BEANSTALK

(one paper towel tube, four bathroom tissue tubes, construction paper, poster paint, yarn, paper clips, plastic drinking straw, cotton, ice-cream stick)

1. Paint a paper towel tube green and let it dry. Cut leaf shapes from construction paper and glue them to the tube. For the stem, glue a long piece of yarn around the leaves.

2. Glue together four bathroom tissue tubes to make a castle. Hold them together with paper clips until the glue dries. Cut sections from the castle towers. Paint the castle. Add a door and windows cut from paper.

3. Print "Giant" on a pennant made from paper. Glue it to a drinking straw. Place the pennant on top of the castle with glue.

4. Glue the beanstalk and castle together, holding with paper clips until the glue dries.

5. Place glue around the bottom of the castle and the beanstalk. Glue cotton in place to look like clouds.

6. Draw Jack on paper and staple him to a long piece of yarn twice the length of the beanstalk. Tie the other end of the yarn to an ice-cream stick.

7. Drop the stick down the beanstalk. When the stick comes out at the bottom, pull on the yarn and see Jack go up the beanstalk.

RAIN GAUGE

(clear plastic 35mm film canister, ice-cream stick, rubber band, permanent marker, clear nail polish)

1. Carefully measure from the bottom of a clear plastic 35mm film canister, drawing short lines every 1/4 inch with a permanent marker. Apply a coat of clear nail polish over the lines, making them waterproof.

2. Glue the canister to an ice-cream stick. Also attach a rubber band to help hold the canister in place.

3. Push the stick into the ground in an open space where there are no bushes or trees.

HANDY KEEPER

(food container with plastic lid, scrap wallpaper, old magazines)

1. Cover a food container with a scrap piece of wallpaper.

2. Paste on cartoons cut from old magazines.

3. Label the front of the container "Tiny Toys" or the name of whatever it will store.

YARN AND PLASTIC NECKLACE
(large plastic lid, yarn)

1. Cut around the edge of a large plastic lid, making a design.

2. With a paper punch, punch holes evenly around the edge of the lid. Gently fold the lid in half and punch a hole on the fold. Unfold. There should be one hole in the center of the lid.

3. Cut a long piece of yarn. Wrap one end with tape, making a point. Thread the yarn through the holes around the edges and through the center, making a design.

4. Glue the yarn ends on the back of the necklace. Glue one punched plastic dot in the center. Thread a long piece of yarn through one of the holes so you can wear it around your neck.

NIFTY PAGE MARKER
(old envelope)

1. Cut the bottom corner from an envelope, giving the edge a decorative shape.

2. Use crayons, markers, or paper cutouts to decorate the bookmark.

3. Slip the bookmark over the top corner of a page in your book to mark your place.

CATERPILLAR NAMEPLATE
(6-inch paper plates, paper punch, ribbon)

1. Use one paper plate for each letter of a first name plus one paper plate for the caterpillar's head.

2. Color the edges of the paper plates with markers. Draw one letter of the name in the center of each plate.

3. Decorate one paper plate as the caterpillar's head. Add paper antennae.

4. Place the paper plates in order. Punch a hole at the edge of each paper plate and join them with bows tied from ribbon.

5. To hang, punch a hole in the plate at each end and attach a ribbon loop.

BROOM FRIEND

(large brown paper bag, paint, paper, an old hat,
newspaper, broom, string, handkerchief)

1. Turn a large brown paper bag upside down, and paint a face on one side.

2. Cut strips of paper and glue them to the bag for hair. Glue on an old hat.

3. Fill the bag with crumpled newspaper. Place a broomstick into the center of the bag. Tie a piece of string tightly around the bottom of the bag. Tie a handkerchief over the string.

BEAN BOXES

(small cardboard jewelry box; dried beans, peas,
and pumpkin seeds; clear nail polish)

1. Use a small cardboard jewelry box with a removable cover. Plan an interesting design that you can make from assorted dried beans, peas, or pumpkin seeds.

2. Arrange the dried beans, peas, or pumpkin seeds on the box and its cover and attach with glue. You may need to let one area dry before moving on to another.

3. Coat the box with clear nail polish to give it a shiny finish.

RACING CARS

(wooden clothespins, poster paint, poster board, paper)

1. Cover clothespins with poster paint for the car bodies. Cut wheels from poster board and glue them to the clothespins.

2. Draw drivers on paper, cut them out, and glue them in the slots of the clothespins.

FREE-FORM ART
(water and white glue, plastic bowl, construction paper, watercolors, felt-tipped pen)

1. Mix a solution of one part white glue and one part water in a small plastic bowl. Brush the solution onto a piece of construction paper.

2. While the paper is still wet, press the tip of a paintbrush filled with watercolor onto your paper to create each flower.

3. When the paint is dry, outline the flowers with ink or a felt-tipped pen.

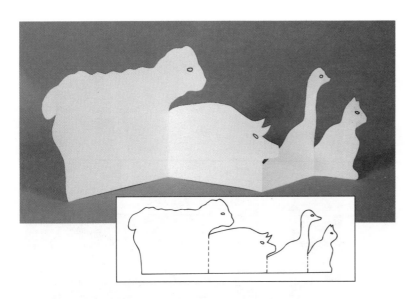

ANIMAL NOTE CARD
(paper)

1. On paper, draw side views, or profiles, of animals all in a row.

2. At each place where a new animal begins, draw a dotted line to the bottom of the paper.

3. Fold back and forth along the dotted lines. Unfold and cut around the solid lines of the animals, as shown. When unfolded, the card will stand up.

4. Write a message on the back of the card.

PARKING GARAGE
(cardboard box with flap, white paper, crayons, paints or markers)

1. Find a cardboard box with one big flap that can be used as the opening of the building.

2. Glue a piece of white paper to the front of the flap. Use crayons, paints, or markers to draw designs, such as bricks or siding, on the flap, making it look like the front of a parking garage.

3. Continue the design around the rest of the box.

4. Store toy cars, trucks, and other playthings in the storage-box building.

BIRDHOUSE WALL DECORATION
(plastic-foam tray, fabric, ribbon, rickrack, construction paper, yarn)

1. Draw a house shape on a large plastic-foam tray. Draw a separate roof shape for the house, as shown. Cut out the two shapes.

2. Wrap fabric over the house, taping the fabric to the back. Do the same with the roof. Then glue the roof to the house.

3. Add ribbon and rickrack to trim the roof. Cut and glue pieces of construction paper for the bird, door, and flowers.

4. To hang the decoration, glue a piece of yarn on the back. Glue paper on the back to cover the taped fabric.

Roof

House

POMPON PET
(yarn, cardboard, felt)

Wrap yarn

1. Wrap yarn around a 3-inch square of cardboard. (The more yarn you wind, the fluffier the pet will be.)

Tie around center

2. Carefully slip the yarn from the cardboard and tie a small piece of yarn tightly around the center, as shown.

Cut loops

3. Cut through all the loops, and fluff up the yarn. Cut features from felt, and attach them with glue.

BIG BEAR BANK
(cardboard container with plastic lid, felt, yarn)

1. Place a plastic lid from a cardboard container on a piece of felt. Trace around the lid twice, making two circles. Cut out the felt circles and glue one to the lid and one to the bottom of the container.

2. Cut out felt ears and glue them just under the edge of the felt circle on the lid. Cut other facial features from felt and glue them in place. Add a small tail to the other end.

3. Have an adult help you cut a slit in the side of the container, large enough to slip money through.

4. Brush a 1/2-inch strip of glue on one edge of the container. Press yarn pulled from a ball or skein into the glue, and wind the yarn around

the container until it is covered. Glue the end in place. When dry, cut away the yarn to uncover the slit.

5. Cut out cardboard feet and cover them with felt. Trim around the edges with scissors. Add felt claws. Glue the feet to the container to keep it from rolling.

MAKEUP HOLDER
(three quart-size milk cartons, white glue and water, paintbrush, bowl, fabric, spring-type clothespins, rubber bands, ribbon)

1. Measure 3 inches from the bottom of three quart-size milk cartons. Cut off the tops of the cartons and discard.

2. Cut three strips of fabric, each 4 inches wide and 12 inches long. Mix white glue and a little water together in a bowl.

3. Brush the glue mixture on one side of a carton. Press one strip of fabric into the glue with the top edges even. Continue around the other three sides. Glue the excess fabric to the bottom. Repeat with the other two cartons.

4. Place the cartons side by side and glue them together. Hold the centers together with spring-type clothespins. Place a rubber band around the bottoms.

5. When dry, remove the rubber band and clothespins. Add a piece of ribbon and a bow. Place makeup and hair care items in the holder.

TABLE TURTLE
(smooth round rock, poster board, poster paint)

1. Find a smooth round rock. Wash it and let dry.

2. Draw a turtle shape, larger than the rock, on a piece of poster board. Cut out the turtle shape, cover it with green paint, and let dry.

3. Glue the rock to the turtle shape. Then paint the rock green. Using black paint, add details to the shell and head of the turtle.

4. Use as a paperweight or table decoration.

DOORKNOB SIGNS
(graph paper, thin yarn, plastic drinking straw, markers)

1. On a piece of graph paper about 6 inches wide and 9 inches long, form letters by coloring in the squares with markers. Spell out a message.

2. Cut a piece of thin yarn approximately 20 inches long.

3. Tightly wrap a small piece of tape around one end of the yarn, and thread the yarn through a straw. Then cut the tape off the yarn and tie the ends together.

4. Fold the top of the graph paper over the straw, and tape it to the back. Hang the sign on a doorknob.

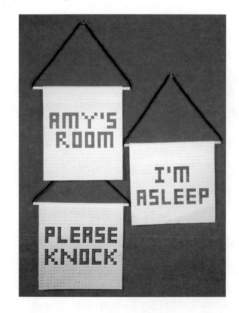

STAND-UP PICTURE FRAMES
(small box with lid, fabric, pictures or photos, poster board)

1. Cover a small box and lid with spots of glue. Press fabric into the glue, covering the entire box and overlapping the fabric to the inside.

2. Cut two pieces of poster board that will fit snugly into the boxes. Glue a picture to each one. Cut strips of fabric and glue them around the pictures as trim. Glue pictures to the inside.

3. To join the box and lid, cut two small pieces of fabric and glue them to each box, making hinges. When the glue is dry, stand the boxes up.

STACKING CONE FAMILY
(white poster board, markers, string)

1. Cut out a small, a medium, and a large circle from white poster board. Cut a slit to the center of each circle and pull one edge of the poster board over the other edge to form a cone shape. Tape along the seam edges.

2. Create faces with markers.

3. Tie a knot near the bottom of a long piece of string and thread the string through the smallest cone.

4. With the smallest cone resting on top of the first knot, tie another knot a few inches higher, and thread the medium cone. Repeat for the large cone.

5. Tape the string inside each cone to keep it from slipping. Knot a loop at the very top of the string.

6. Stack the cones with the biggest on top. As you lift the string, each smaller cone will appear. Hang it as a decoration, or play with it as a stacking toy.

"ME, MYSELF, AND I" BODY COLLAGE
(two large brown paper bags, old magazines, yarn)

1. Cut open two large brown paper bags. Tape the ends together to make one long piece of paper, a little longer and a little wider than yourself.

2. Carefully lie down on the paper, making sure all of you is inside the edges. Ask a partner to trace around you with a pencil. Cut out the body shape.

3. Cut out pictures of things you like from old magazines. Glue them to the body shape.

4. Attach a loop of yarn to the top to hang the collage on a door.

ROBOT
(plastic-foam cup, 1 1/2-inch plastic-foam ball, table knife, toothpicks, chenille stick, thread spool, paper)

1. Use a plastic-foam cup for the robot's body.

2. For the head, cut a 1 1/2-inch plastic-foam ball in half with a table knife and glue one half to the bottom of the cup. Cut the remaining piece of ball into quarters, and press two of the pieces on ends of toothpicks. Insert them into the head for antenae.

3. To make the wheel, thread a chenille stick through the sides of the cup and through a thread spool so that the spool extends just a little above the rim of the cup, as shown. Bend the ends of the chenille stick to form arms. Press two of the quartered foam pieces onto the ends of the arms.

4. Add cut-paper features to decorate the robot. A gentle push from the back moves the robot along a smooth surface.

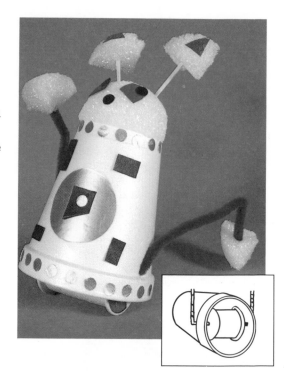

VAN
(elbow-macaroni cardboard box, construction paper, cardboard)

1. Cut a small section from an elbow-macaroni box, as shown. Cover the box with construction paper.

2. Draw and cut out wheels from cardboard. Glue the wheels on each side of the van.

3. Decorate the van with paper and markers.

BOOKWORM
(ice-cream stick, poster paint, pompon, marker, chenille stick, moveable plastic eyes)

1. Paint an ice-cream stick with poster paint and let dry.

2. Glue a pompon at one end for the head. Add other details to the ice-cream stick with a marker.

3. Cut a small piece of chenille stick. Bend it in the shape of antenae and glue it to the head. Glue on moveable plastic eyes.

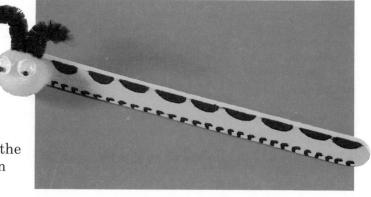

PLASTIC BOTTLE PENCIL HOLDER
(plastic detergent bottle, yarn, ribbon, construction paper)

1. Soak the detergent bottle in warm water to help soften the plastic and to remove the label. Then cut off the top half, leaving an oval-shaped piece attached to the back for the head.

2. Decorate the holder with paper and markers.

3. Make braided hair from yarn. To braid, cut three pieces of yarn the same length. Line up the pieces, and tie them together into a knot about 1 inch from one end. Braid by folding A over B and then C over A. Continue until the yarn is braided. Tie the ends into a knot again about 1 inch from the end. Glue the braid in place and tie a ribbon on each end.

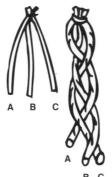

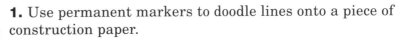

FRAMED DOODLE DESIGN
(construction paper, poster board, yarn, permanent markers, paints, or crayons)

1. Use permanent markers to doodle lines onto a piece of construction paper.

2. Fill in the spaces with colors, using permanent markers, paints, or crayons.

3. To make a frame, cut four strips of poster board, each about 1 inch wide. Cut two for the length and two for the width, making each 1 inch longer than the picture.

4. Glue the long pair of strips in place over the front of the picture's edge. Then glue the shorter pair of strips in place. Make all four corners even.

5. Glue a piece of yarn to the back of the frame for a hanger.

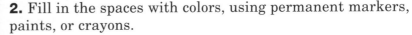

PIE PAN TAMBOURINE
(two 8-inch aluminum pie pans, plastic- or paper-coated twist-ties)

1. Poke eight holes, 1 to 2 inches apart, just inside the rim of an 8-inch aluminum pie pan.

2. Cut small circles from the other aluminum pie pan for jangles. Punch a small hole in each one.

3. Using twist-ties, attach the jangles by twisting the ties at the very ends, so the jangles will hang loosely. Leave a space where there are no holes so you can hold the tambourine.

SEASHELL PLANTER
(small plastic bottle, sand, seashells)

1. Soak a small plastic bottle in warm water to make it easier to cut and to remove the label. Using scissors, cut away the top section.

2. Glue seashells onto the bottle in a pattern and let them dry.

3. Spread glue over the rest of the bottle, and sprinkle it with sand. Gently press the sand into the glue to help it stick.

CARDBOARD CAMERA
(tape, cereal box, construction paper,
gift-wrap tube, paper)

1. Secure the ends of a cereal box with tape. Cover the box with construction paper.

2. Cut a gift-wrap tube in half and cover it with paper. Cut a hole in each narrow side of the box, near the top, large enough to slide the tube through.

3. Decorate the camera with paper and draw meters, dials, and switches.

NEWSPAPER PUPPET
(newspaper, white paper)

1. You will need six pieces of newspaper, each 11 by 14 inches.

2. Roll five pieces together lengthwise, then wrap the sixth piece around them and tape together.

3. Make 3-inch cuts at one end, about 1/2 inch apart, for the hair. On white paper, draw features with markers and glue them in place.

PENNANTS
(felt or cloth)

1. Cut a pennant shape from felt or cloth.

2. Make letters that spell a short word or form initials. Glue these to the pennant along with other designs you cut out.

3. Hang the pennant in your room.

TORTOISE AND HARE RACERS
(walnut-shell halves, marbles, felt)

1. Use half of a walnut shell for each body. Remove the meat inside the shell.

2. Cut out heads and legs from felt. Glue them to the bodies.

3. Place a marble under each shell. The animals will race down a smooth slope, such as a board or box lid.

PRINT ART
(plastic-foam tray, pencil, tempera paint, construction paper)

1. Wash and dry a plastic-foam tray. Using a pencil, draw a picture on the inside of the tray. Make sure you press hard enough so that the lines are indented.

2. Brush a thin coat of tempera paint across the whole picture. Place a piece of construction paper on the painted surface, and rub your finger over the paper.

3. Carefully lift the paper from the tray, and let the painting dry.

4. Wash any remaining paint from the tray, and let dry. You can repeat this process with other colors of paint and paper.

WALLPAPER-COVERED WASTEBASKET

(large, round cardboard ice-cream container, scrap wallpaper, gift wrap, or fabric)

1. Glue scrap wallpaper, fancy gift wrap, or fabric to the outside of a cardboard container.

2. Decorate the outside with paper cutouts.

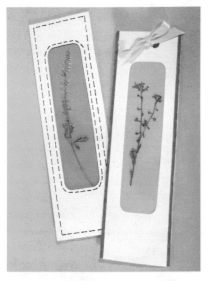

NATURE BOOKMARKS

(flowers, weeds, leaves, paper towels, large book, construction paper, old window envelope, ribbon)

1. Place cuttings of flowers, weeds, or leaves between paper towels. Press them between the pages of a large book. Keep them in the book three to seven days to dry.

2. Following the diagram, cut a section from an old window envelope. Cut a piece of construction paper a little smaller than the cut section.

3. Glue the pressed plants on the paper, and place them in the envelope section so they will show through the window.

4. Seal the edges with glue. Decorate with markers, or punch two holes in the top and tie a ribbon through the holes.

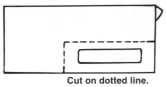

Cut on dotted line.

THINGS-I-WANT-TO-SAVE BOOK

(eight plastic sandwich bags, scrap wallpaper, yarn)

1. Stack about eight plastic sandwich bags together with the openings all at one end. Cut two pieces of scrap wallpaper slightly larger than the size of the sandwich bags.

2. Place the bags between the two pieces of wallpaper. Hold these together, and punch two holes at the closed ends of the bags.

3. Thread a piece of yarn through each hole, and tie the ends together in a bow.

4. Make a label from a piece of paper, and print "Things I Want to Save" on it. Glue the label to the cover.

5. Save postcards or other items in your book. During the year, you can look over what you have collected.

HAIR-CLIP HOLDER
(corrugated cardboard, 10-inch dinner plate,
poster paint, yarn, fabric)

1. Place a 10-inch dinner plate on a piece of corrugated cardboard and trace around it. Cut out the circle.

2. Cut out a section, as shown. This will be the top of the head where the hair clips are attached.

3. Paint part of the cardboard to look like a face. Paint around the cutout area, using a color to match the yarn you plan to use for hair.

4. Cut pieces of yarn for hair. Fold them in half and glue them as loops around the face. Add paper features. Add a fabric bow below the chin.

5. Punch a hole in the center at the top. Tie a piece of yarn for a hanger. Attach hair clips to the holder.

KITTY PLAYHOUSE
(large corrugated cardboard box, construction paper, string, fabric, thread spools)

1. Find a large, 2-foot-deep corrugated cardboard box.

2. Turn the box over so the bottom faces up. Cut a door on one side of the box. Glue or staple a fabric flap over the door.

3. Cut out circles, squares, and triangles from the sides of the box.

4. Tie string to thread spools or other toys and hang them from the inside of the playhouse roof.

BUTTON-NOSE CLOWN
(felt, yarn)

1. Cut out a circle from felt. In the center of the circle, cut a slit that is large enough for a shirt button to go through.

2. Glue on pieces of yarn and felt to make a clown face, hair, and hat. Do not give the clown a nose.

3. Button the clown to your shirt through the slit in its face. The button will be the clown's nose.

MINIATURE CASTLE
(construction paper, cardboard box)

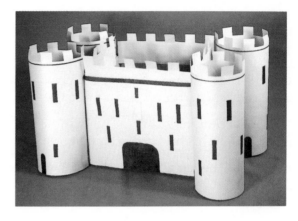

1. Remove the lid from a small cardboard box. Glue construction paper to the outside of the box and let dry.

2. Use crayons or markers to sketch in a drawbridge and windows.

3. Cut teeth, or castle turrets, along one side of four strips of construction paper. Glue the strips around the top edge of the inside of the box.

4. Cut turrets along one side of four sheets of 8 1/2-by-11-inch paper. Add windows and doors with crayons or markers.

5. Roll each sheet into a tube, and glue or tape it closed. Glue the four rolls to the corners of the castle.

MAGNET MAZE
(8-inch paper plate, lightweight cardboard, magnetic strip, ice-cream stick)

1. On a paper plate, use markers or crayons to draw a circular maze. Draw a moon in the center. The starting point, or "Launch Pad," should be at the edge of the plate, and the finish should be in the center at the "Moon."

2. From lightweight cardboard, cut out the shape of a rocket, about the size of a quarter, and decorate it. Glue the rocket to a small magnet cut from a magnetic strip. Glue another small magnet to the end of an ice-cream stick. (Make sure you glue the right side of the magnet up—that is, the side that will attract, rather than repel, the other magnet when the two are placed back to back.)

3. Hold the magnetic stick under the plate, and guide your rocket from the launch pad to the moon.

PEN AND PENCIL HOLDER
(old magazines, pencil, paper clips, round cardboard container, construction paper)

1. Remove colorful pages from an old magazine. Lay a pencil at one edge of a page. Brush a thin line of glue at the other edge of the page. Roll the page around the pencil and press the glued edge into place.

2. Pull the pencil out of the tube. If the glue is not quite dry, slip paper clips onto the ends of the tube to hold the paper in place.

3. Use a round cardboard container, like the kind peanuts come in, for the holder. Cut the tubes the same height as the container. Brush glue on the seam of each tube, and glue the tubes onto the container. Have enough tubes handy to cover the entire container.

4. Cut and glue strips of construction paper to decorate the top and the bottom of the holder.

LION PUPPET
(small brown paper bag, construction paper)

1. To make the lion's head, draw and cut out from construction paper a head and ears about the same width as the bottom of the paper bag. Add eyes, a nose, a mouth, and whiskers.

2. Glue the lion's head to the center of a sheet of paper. Cut 2 to 3 inches away from the lion's head to make the mane. Then cut slits around the edges, and use a pencil to curl the fringe a little. Glue the lion's head to the bottom of the paper bag.

3. To make the body, draw and cut out a piece of paper and glue it to the front of the bag just under the lion's head. Add two paper feet.

4. Place your hand inside the bag and curve your fingers over the fold to move the lion's head.

MIXED-UP CHARACTER MOBILE
(lightweight cardboard, crayons or markers, string)

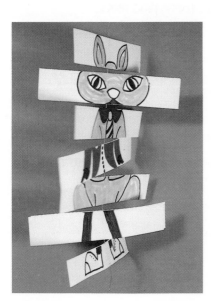

1. On two pieces of lightweight cardboard, draw six or seven horizontal lines about an inch apart.

2. On each piece of cardboard, draw a picture of a different character. Start with the head within the first two lines. Cut the pictures apart along the horizontal lines.

3. Lay the strips of one picture facedown, leaving small spaces between the strips. Apply glue to the backs of these strips and lay a piece of string in the center, leaving extra string at the top for a hanger.

4. Glue each piece of the second picture faceup on top of the pieces of the first picture. Be sure to keep the pieces in the correct order.

EGG-CARTON CATERPILLAR
(cardboard egg carton, poster paint, construction paper)

1. Cut through the center section of a cardboard egg carton, making the long six-cup section the body of the caterpillar. Make the legs by cutting a small section from both sides of the cups.

2. Paint the outside with green paint. Glue the body to a piece of black paper. Trim around the edge when dry.

3. Cut the head from green paper and draw on features with a marker. Make the antennae from black paper and glue them to the head.

A HAPPY FAMILY
(old stockings, cotton balls, yarn, cardboard, felt)

1. Wash and dry a pair of old stockings. Cut out three sections, each a different length.

2. Tie a knot at one end of each section. Turn the sections inside out, and stuff them with cotton. When they are full, tie knots to close them.

3. Glue on scraps of felt, yarn, and cotton to create the faces.

4. Cut three squares of cardboard for bases, and cover them with felt cut the same size.

5. Glue a happy family member on top of each base.

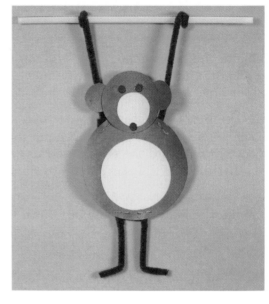

TWIRLING MONKEY
(construction paper, chenille sticks, plastic drinking straw)

1. Draw and cut out circles from construction paper. Glue these together to make the monkey.

2. Staple pieces of chenille sticks to the monkey for the arms and the legs.

3. Wrap the ends of the arms around a plastic drinking straw.

4. Hold the straw in your hand, and swing the monkey around the straw.

BOX BIRDS
(small cardboard box, construction paper, poster board, 3-inch plastic-foam ball, table knife, wooden or plastic stir sticks)

1. Cover a small cardboard box with construction paper. Cut out a head, wings, and a tail from poster board. Decorate with markers or crayons and glue the body parts in place.

2. Cut a 3-inch plastic-foam ball in half with a table knife. Color one half with a marker. Save the other half for another bird.

3. Poke stir sticks into the bottom of the box for legs and add glue. Let dry. Push the legs into the plastic-foam ball half and add glue.

4. Cut feet from paper and glue them to the ball.

BINOCULARS
(two 5-inch cardboard tubes, construction paper,
wood or heavy cardboard, yarn)

1. Cover two 5-inch cardboard tubes with construction paper. Glue a piece of wood or heavy cardboard between the tubes to separate them enough to fit your eyes.

2. Cut a strip of paper about 1 1/2 inches wide and long enough to go around both tubes. Glue this strip around the tubes at the viewing end.

3. To attach a strap, paper punch a hole in each side of the binoculars, thread a piece of yarn through, and tie a knot at each end.

TONGUE DEPRESSOR BRACELET
(wooden tongue depressor, warm water, frozen-juice container, rubber bands, poster paint, sequins, clear nail polish)

1. Soak a wooden tongue depressor in warm water about an hour or until you can gently bend it around a frozen-juice container.

2. Once it is around the container, place rubber bands on top of the tongue depressor to hold it in place. Let dry for one day.

3. Remove the tongue depressor, cover it with poster paint, and let dry. Glue sequins around the outside. When dry, cover with clear nail polish.

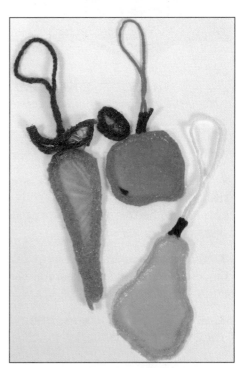

WINDOW VEGETABLE GARDEN
(cardboard, plastic wrap, white glue, yarn, food coloring, paper plate)

1. Draw the outlines of vegetables on a piece of cardboard. Cover with plastic wrap. Squeeze white glue on the outline of each vegetable. Press two strands of yarn into the glue.

2. On a paper plate, mix a few drops of food coloring with white glue. Pour the colored glue inside the vegetable outline. Make a loop of yarn for a hanger. Dry for several days.

3. Peel the vegetables from the plastic wrap and hang them in the window.

DOG BISCUIT CARD
(poster board, dog bone-shaped biscuit)

1. Fold a piece of 5-by-10-inch poster board in half to form a card.

2. Open the card. Place a dog bone-shaped biscuit on the front and trace around it. Cut out the bone shape and fold the card.

3. On the panel directly behind the cutout, glue the dog biscuit in place. Close the card. The dog biscuit should pop through the opening.

4. On the front of the card write "A Wish...", and inside the card write "of happiness with your new puppy."

CAR CARRIER
(half-gallon milk carton, old magazines, yarn)

1. Wash a half-gallon milk carton. Cut off the top and discard it.

2. Cut out lots of pictures of cars, trucks, planes, and boats from old magazines and glue them all over the outside of the milk carton.

3. Use a paper punch to punch a hole on opposite sides of the carton near the top edge. Tie yarn through the holes for a handle.

RUBBER-BAND BULLETIN BOARD
(corrugated cardboard, shelf paper or wrapping paper, rubber bands, yarn)

1. Cover a 10-by-12-inch piece of corrugated cardboard with brightly colored self-adhesive shelf paper or gift wrap.

2. Use scissors to cut several small slits along each side of the cardboard. Stretch different-colored rubber bands across the board, inserting them in the slits, to make a criss-cross design.

3. To hang your bulletin board, make a loop by threading a piece of yarn through two holes at the top and tying the ends together.

4. Slide phone messages, reminders, and photographs under the rubber bands.

THE MOUSE AND THE CHEESE
(cellulose sponge, Brazil nut, construction paper, felt, ribbon)

1. Cut a small triangle from a cellulose sponge. Glue a Brazil nut on top.

2. From black felt, cut two large teardrop shapes for the ears and a small strip for the tail. Glue these to the nut.

3. To make the eyes, paper-punch two white dots and draw a black dot in the center of each. Glue these in place.

4. Tie a small ribbon into a bow, and glue it between the nut and the sponge.

TISSUE SNOWMAN
(construction paper, white facial tissues)

1. On a sheet of construction paper, draw an outline of a snowman.

2. Tear narrow strips from the long edge of white facial tissues, and then tear each strip apart in the middle.

3. Crumple the tissue strips into small wads. Spread glue on the snowman, and place the wads on the snowman until his entire body is covered.

4. Cut out a hat, eyes, and other details from paper and glue them on the snowman.

5. Add snow around the base of the snowman by gluing down more tissue wads.

COOKIE TRAY
(7-inch paper plate, 10-inch lace-paper doily, poster board)

1. Glue a 10-inch lace-paper doily in the center of a 7-inch paper plate.

2. Cut a 1-inch strip of poster board. Staple the ends to the paper plate, making a handle. Decorate with pieces cut from another doily.

3. Place cookies on the tray and serve them to your family or friends.

SPOOL DOLLS

(thread spools, paint, fabric, felt, 1-inch plastic-foam balls, buttons, sequins, rickrack, ribbon, pompons)

1. Decorate a spool with paint or scraps of fabric. Glue a small 1-inch plastic-foam ball to one end for the head.

2. Use colored yarn for hair and scraps of felt or fabric for the nose, mouth, and eyes.

3. Buttons, sequins, rickrack, yarn, and pompons can be glued on the spool to make many different kinds of spool dolls.

STAMP-AND-STICKER SAVER

(cardboard food container with plastic lid, stamps or stickers)

1. Use a clean, empty cardboard container that has a plastic lid.

2. Attach stamps or stickers to the outside of the container. Overlap some so that all the spaces are covered.

3. Save other stamps or stickers that you collect and place them inside the container.

PINCUSHION AND SCISSOR HOLDER

(frozen-juice container, toothpaste box, fabric, ribbon, cotton balls)

1. For the pincushion, cut a frozen-juice container in half. For the scissor holder, cut a large toothpaste box in half. Discard the top halves.

2. Cover the box and the container with glue and press fabric all the way around them, overlapping the fabric onto the inside edges. Add some ribbon for decoration.

3. Fill the pincushion with cotton balls. Cover the cotton with a piece of fabric, and glue it into the box.

4. Glue the pincushion and scissor holder together.

EASY STRING ART
(lightweight cardboard, yarn of different colors)

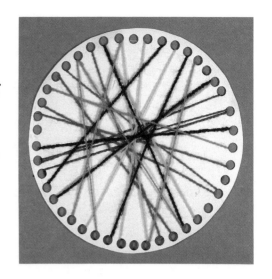

1. Cut out a simple shape, like a circle, from lightweight cardboard. Carefully paper-punch holes all around the edges of the shape.

2. Cut a long piece of yarn, and tape one end to the back of the cardboard. Thread the other end of the yarn up through a hole, across the front of the cardboard, and down into another hole.

3. Pull the yarn across the back of the cardboard, thread it up through another hole, and stretch it again across the front of the cardboard.

4. Continue to do this until you use up all the yarn. Tape the end to the back of the cardboard.

5. Pick another piece of yarn, of a different color, and repeat steps 2, 3, and 4. Attach a yarn loop at the top, and hang your piece of art.

TERRYCLOTH DOG
(terrycloth washcloth, felt, buttons, thread, string, ribbon)

1. Roll opposite sides of a terrycloth facecloth toward the center until they meet. Keeping the rolled sides together, fold down the ends evenly, forming two corners to make the legs.

2. Tie string snugly around each corner to form the head and the rear of the dog.

3. Cut and sew felt ears, a tail, and a tongue to the dog. Sew on button eyes and a nose. Sew on thread for whiskers.

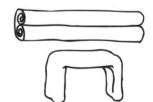

4. Tie a ribbon around the dog's neck.

BILLY BUG
(12-inch paper towel tube, poster paint, paper, yarn, felt)

1. Cover a 12-inch paper towel tube with poster paint and let dry.

2. Cut six 2-inch lengths from the paper towel tube. Using a paper punch, punch holes opposite each other and on each end in four tubes. Tie them together loosely with yarn to form the middle of the bug's body.

3. Punch holes at one end only in the remaining two tubes. Attach one to the body for the head and attach the other for the tail.

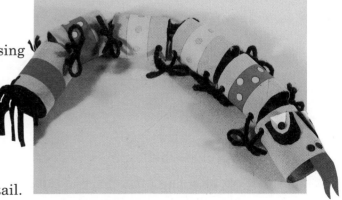

4. Decorate with cutout paper and felt. Attach a yarn tail.

CRAWL-ALONG ALLIGATOR
(rectangular tissue box, green construction paper,
two 1-inch plastic-foam balls, chenille stick, thread spool)

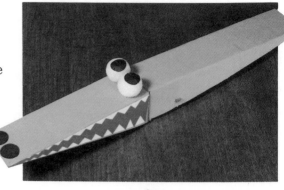

1. Cut wedge shapes from two sides of a rectangular tissue box. Make one wedge shape longer than the other, as shown.

2. Cover the shapes with green construction paper. Glue the square ends of the wedges together.

3. To make the alligator's eyes, glue construction paper and 1-inch plastic-foam balls on the shorter wedge shape.

4. Cut and glue construction paper for the mouth, teeth, and nose. Thread a piece of chenille stick through a thread spool to use as a wheel and axle.

5. Poke a hole on each side of the larger wedge so that the wheel is positioned to allow the alligator to roll along.

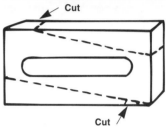

Cut

Cut

CLOWN STICK PUPPET
(plastic detergent bottle, yarn, construction paper,
cotton, wooden dowel)

1. Soak the label off a plastic detergent bottle and dry. Turn the bottle upside down and glue pieces of yarn to the bottle for hair.

2. To make the handle, soak a wad of cotton in a mixture of white glue and water. Wrap enough of the cotton around the end of a wooden stick so that the stick will fit tightly into the spout of the bottle. The soaked cotton will dry and hold the stick in place.

3. Glue on pieces of construction paper for the facial features. Add a paper bow tie.

SHELL AND STONE WREATH
(heavy cardboard, seashells, stones, yarn or string)

1. Cut a doughnut shape from a piece of heavy cardboard for the base of the wreath.

2. Glue colorful seashells and stones onto the cardboard.

3. Glue yarn or string to the back of the wreath for a hanger.

KITTEN BANK
(cardboard pudding box, felt, paper, cardboard)

1. Trim the side flaps at the open end of a cardboard pudding box so they are shaped like kitten ears. Glue pink felt to the inside of the ears.

2. Tape the other flaps shut. Cover the rest of the box with felt. Cut a coin slit in the top.

3. Cut eyes, a nose, and a mouth from felt and glue in place. Add whiskers made from strips of paper.

4. Cut a cardboard tail and cover it with felt. Glue the tail to the bottom of the kitten's body.

JUICE-LID WIND CHIMES
(two ice-cream sticks, yarn, sixteen frozen-juice lids)

1. Glue two ice-cream sticks together at their centers to form an X. Tie a piece of yarn at the X to help hold the sticks together and to make a loop for hanging.

2. Wash and dry sixteen frozen-juice lids. Cut four 1-foot pieces of yarn and a fifth piece 1 1/2 feet long.

3. Using three lids, glue one of the lids to the end of a piece of yarn, another one almost at the center, and the last one near the top, leaving about 3 inches of yarn. Repeat this three more times. Tie each piece of yarn to an end of one of the sticks.

4. Glue the remaining four lids onto the 1 1/2-foot length of yarn, leaving about 2 1/2 inches to be tied to the center of the sticks.

HALF AND HALF
(construction paper, markers)

1. Fold a piece of construction paper in half. Draw part of a head on one half of the paper, using a dark-colored marker. (Be sure to draw your lines to the edge of the fold.)

2. Turn the folded paper over and place it against a windowpane so the blank half is facing you.

3. If you look closely, you can see the lines you drew underneath. Trace over the lines, completing the head.

4. Finish the picture with colored markers.

54

PLASTIC-BOTTLE CAR
(two plastic detergent bottles, poster board,
construction paper)

1. Soak the labels from two plastic detergent bottles and dry the bottles. Use one for the body of the car.

2. To make the cab of the car, cut the other bottle about 2 inches from the bottom and discard the top. Glue the bottom piece onto the body of the car.

3. Cut wheels from poster board and glue them onto the body. Add other features with construction paper.

ROLLERO GAME
(two bathroom tissue tubes, construction paper,
plastic drinking straw)

1. Cover two bathroom tissue tubes with glue and construction paper. Let dry.

2. With a pencil, mark off 1 1/2 inches along each tube. Cut the tubes at the 1 1/2-inch marks. Decorate the tubes with stripes of different-colored paper for each player.

3. Set a starting point and a finish line on the table or floor. Race to the finish line by blowing through a plastic drinking straw to move your Rollero along.

BEAN BUG
(fabric, needle and thread, felt, dried beans or macaroni)

1. From fabric, cut two bug shapes about 6 inches long. From a contrasting fabric, cut a head shape to fit over the end of one bug piece and sew it in place.

2. With right sides together, sew almost all the way around the bug shapes. Turn the piece inside out and stuff it loosely with dried beans or small macaroni. Finish sewing.

3. Cut eyes and other details from felt or fabric. Sew them on.

4. Use the bug for a beanbag or a paperweight.

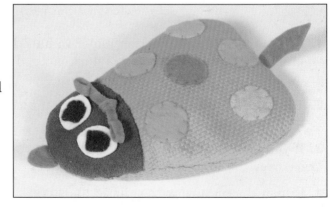

STICK MASK

(8-inch heavy paper plate, construction paper, markers or paint,
lightweight cardboard, masking tape, ruler)

1. Have an adult help you cut two eyeholes in an
8-inch heavy paper plate. Then draw, paint, or cut
out features. Glue the cutouts in place.

2. To make the holder, cut a rectangle of lightweight
cardboard. Place it on the back of the mask and tape the
top and the sides of the rectangle, leaving the bottom open.

3. Put the end of a ruler into this "pocket," and you can
hold the mask in front of your face.

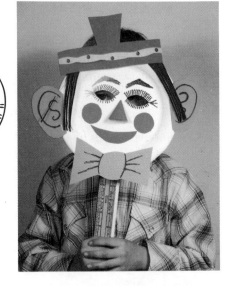

JEWELRY BOX

(candy box with cardboard lid, lightweight fabric, white glue and water,
plastic bowl, lace, string of craft pearls, ribbon)

1. In a small plastic bowl, mix white glue with a little
water. Set aside, along with a paintbrush.

2. To cover the box lid, place the fabric right-side down
on a flat surface. Place the lid right-side down in the
middle of the fabric.

3. Measure a few inches out from the edge of the box
lid so the fabric will wrap around the edges to the
inside of the lid. Mark the fabric and cut it out.

4. With a paintbrush, spread the glue mixture on the
outside of the lid. Press the outside of the lid on top of
the fabric. Cut a diagonal line in the fabric to each
corner of the lid. Spread glue on the outside and inside
edges of the lid. Wrap the fabric up and inside the box
lid. Add more glue if necessary. Let dry.

5. If there are sections inside the candy box, cut pieces
of fabric and glue them inside the bottom of the box.

6. Decorate the outside lid with lace, pearls, and
ribbon.

NEWSPAPER-YARN CREATURE

(newspaper, yarn, felt, paper)

1. Roll newspaper loosely. Bend, twist,
and tape the roll into a creature shape.

2. Squeeze glue onto the roll and wrap
it with yarn. Fill in small areas with
pieces of yarn and glue.

3. Cut features from felt and glue them
in place.

PLASTIC-FOAM PUZZLE
(plastic-foam tray, pencil, permanent markers or crayons)

1. Draw a picture on the back of a plastic-foam tray. Use a sharpened pencil to punch tiny holes close together along the lines you have drawn. Push the pieces out.

2. Color both sides of the puzzle pieces, using different colors. You can use either side of the puzzle pieces to make colorful pictures.

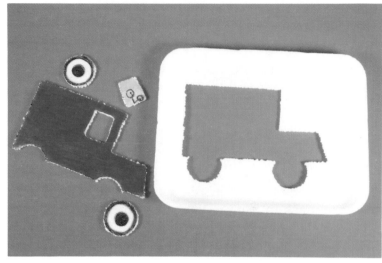

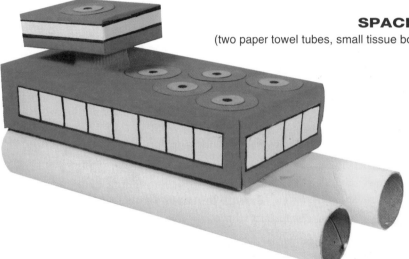

SPACE VEHICLE
(two paper towel tubes, small tissue box, gelatin box, construction paper, plastic lid)

1. Cover two paper towel tubes, a small tissue box, and a gelatin box with construction paper.

2. Glue the tubes to the bottom of the tissue box. Glue a small plastic lid between the tissue box and the gelatin box.

3. Add windows and other decorations made from paper.

WIGGLY CATERPILLAR
(cardboard egg carton, yarn, paper)

1. Cut twelve cups from a cardboard egg carton. Make a small hole in the bottom of each cup.

2. Tie a knot at one end of a long piece of yarn, and string the other end through the holes in the cups. String the cups on the yarn in the same direction.

3. When the twelve cups are strung together, knot the other end.

4. The knot at the first egg cup will be the nose of the caterpillar. Add paper eyes.

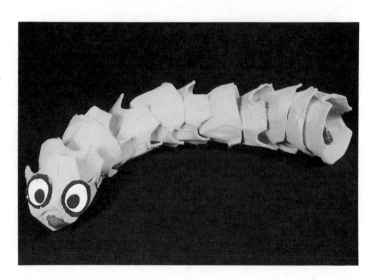

57

CIRCLES BEAR

(plate, bowl, cup, juice glass, construction paper or poster board)

1. Trace around a plate on construction paper or poster board to make one big circle for the body of the bear. Trace around a bowl to make the head.

2. Trace around a cup for the legs and ears of the bear. Trace around a juice glass for the eyes and a nose.

3. Cut out all the circles and glue them together to make the bear. Draw on a mouth.

NATURE BRACELET

(poster board; dried beans, peas, or barley; yarn)

1. Cut a strip of poster board to fit around your wrist.

2. Glue on dried beans, peas, or barley for decoration.

3. Punch a hole in each end and string a piece of yarn through the holes. Tie the bracelet around your wrist.

RACCOON PUPPET

(cardboard food container, felt, fabric)

1. Wash and dry a cardboard food container like one in which peanuts are packaged.

2. Place the bottom of the container on a piece of felt and trace around the edge with a pencil or marker. Cut out the circle and glue it to the bottom of the container for the top of the puppet.

3. Cut felt ears and glue them to opposite sides of the container. Measure the container and cut a piece of felt to fit all the way around it. Glue the felt in place.

4. Make eyes, a nose, and a mouth from felt. Attach them with glue.

5. Cut a piece of fabric to fit around the inside edge of the container and to cover part of your arm. Spread some glue around the inside edge and wait until glue is tacky.

6. Press the fabric into the glue and let dry. Place your arm and hand inside the container to move your puppet.

MOON ROCKET GAME

(quart-size cardboard milk carton, construction paper, five wooden clothespins, poster board)

1. Wash and dry a quart-size milk carton. Cut off the top. Cover the carton with construction paper.

2. Create a moon scene with stars and a rugged landscape made from cut paper or markers.

3. Use five wooden clothespins for the rockets. For the rocket fins, cut V shapes from poster board and glue them to the inside of the clothespins.

4. Place the "moon" milk carton on the floor in front of you. Hold each rocket by its fin, at waist level. Then drop it, trying to land it in the moon.

5. Take turns with a friend. The first player to score ten landings is the winner.

NATURE PAPERWEIGHT

(clear plastic bottle, heavy cardboard, poster paint, stones, dried flowers, leaves)

1. Wash and dry a clear plastic bottle. Cut about a third of it from the bottom and discard the top.

2. Place the cut end on a piece of heavy cardboard, trace around it, and cut it out, making it slightly larger. Paint it green.

3. Glue small stones, flowers, and leaves on the green cardboard.

4. Glue the bottom half of the plastic bottle on top.

PHOTO HOLDER

(photos, two plastic-foam trays, table knife, plastic wrap, sandpaper, a large needle, yarn)

1. Choose five favorite photos. Cut a circle around each person or animal face in each photo.

2. Cut the sides from two identical plastic-foam trays, creating two pieces the same size.

3. On one piece, draw circles a little smaller than the photos. Press along each circle with a table knife until the circle can be pulled out. Smooth the edges with sandpaper if necessary.

4. Cut and glue a piece of plastic wrap to cover one side of the tray. Spread glue around each circle and place a picture, face down on top of the plastic wrap, covering the circle.

5. Glue the second plastic-foam tray to cover the wrap and the back of the pictures. Place something heavy on top until the glue dries.

6. With a large needle and yarn, sew around the edges, as shown. To make a hanger, thread a piece of yarn through the center of the back and tie a bow.

SCRATCH-A-PICTURE

(white plastic jug, nail, poster paint, rag, poster board)

1. Soak a white plastic jug in warm water to soften it for cutting. Cut a square section from the side of the jug.

2. With a pencil, sketch a picture on the plastic. Go over the sketch with a nail, scratching the picture into the plastic. (The more scratches, the more your design will show.)

3. Spread black poster paint over the picture. Then wipe over it with a dry rag to remove the paint that is not in the nail grooves.

4. Glue the picture to a piece of poster board. Attach a yarn hanger to the back.

BOX-AND-BAG HORSE

(two small boxes, one medium-sized box, two small brown paper bags, construction paper, old newspaper)

1. To make the body of the horse, use one medium-sized box. Use two small boxes for the legs and hooves.

2. Cover the boxes with construction paper. Glue the boxes together.

3. Stuff one small brown paper bag with rolled-up newspaper. Tape it to the body for the neck and head of the horse.

4. Cut a tail and mane from another small brown paper bag. Attach them with glue. Cut circles from the bag for spots and glue them on the horse. Add features with paper and markers.

HAPPY BIRTHDAY POP-UP CARD

(construction paper)

1. Fold an 8 1/2-by-11-inch piece of construction paper in half the long way. Then fold it in half the narrow way.

2. Open the card. At the point where the folds meet, cut and glue balloons, working from the center out and up. Trim with scissors around the balloons.

3. Write "Happy Birthday to you, (add name)" on the balloons. Make a drawing of a clown holding the balloons with his dog. Write another message in the card.

4. Fold the card with the balloon section inside. On the front of the card, glue another piece of paper and write "It's your special day!"

5. When the card is opened, the balloons should pop up.

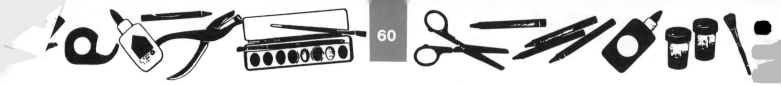

MAKE-IT-YOURSELF PUZZLE
(large cereal box, masking tape, permanent markers)

1. Cut the front from an empty box of cereal. Put masking tape on all four sides, folding it over the edge.

2. Working on a newspaper, color the tape with permanent markers.

3. Cut the picture into several pieces, like a puzzle. Scramble the pieces and try to put the picture back together again.

LEAFY PAPERWEIGHT
(smooth rock, small leaves, poster paint, clear nail polish)

1. Paint one side of a small leaf with poster paint.

2. While the paint is still wet, press the leaf wet-side down on the rock. Carefully lift up the leaf. Repeat several times to complete the pattern.

3. After the prints have dried, coat the rock with clear nail polish to preserve the design.

MUSIC-PAGE NOTES
(paper, felt, spring-type clothespins)

1. Draw a musical note on a piece of paper to use as a pattern. Cut out the pattern and pin it on a piece of felt.

2. Cut out the felt note. Make another one the same size.

3. Glue one felt note to each of two spring-type clothespins. Use them to hold your page of music in place.

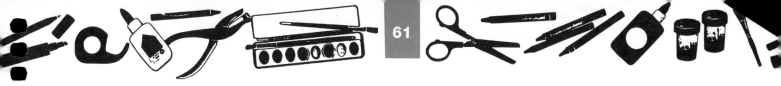

GIRAFFE
(paper towel tube, construction paper)

1. Cover a paper towel tube with glue and yellow construction paper.

2. Cut up from the bottom for the legs and down from the top for the neck and head.

3. Make small cuts down on either side of the horns, and fold forward for the head.

4. Cut spots from brown paper. Cut out eyes, a nose, and hooves from black paper. Glue them in place.

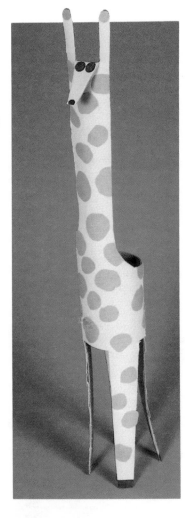

THREAD-SPOOL LIGHTHOUSE
(thread spools, construction paper)

1. Cover spools of different sizes with glue and construction paper. Glue the spools together with the smaller spools on top.

2. Add windows and the door.

MAGAZINE HOLDER
(heavy cardboard box, old magazines)

1. Find a heavy cardboard box the right size to hold your magazines.

2. Cut it down, making a fancy edge if you wish.

3. Cut pictures from old magazines and glue them all over the outside of the box.

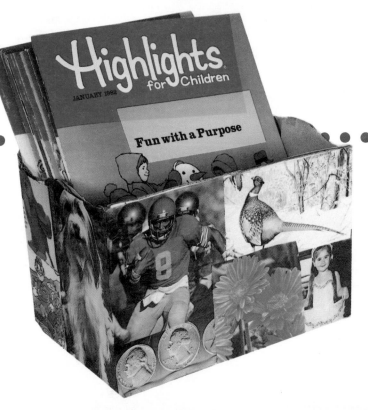

MATERIAL INDEX